T0367052

THE

PUBLICATIONS

OF THE

SURTEES SOCIETY

VOL. CLXXXVI

*Made and Printed in Great Britain
by Northumberland Press Limited,
Gateshead*

THE

PUBLICATIONS

OF THE

SURTEES SOCIETY

ESTABLISHED IN THE YEAR

M.DCCC.XXXIV

VOL. CLXXXVI

FOR THE YEAR M.CM.LXIX

At a COUNCIL MEETING of the SURTEES SOCIETY held in Durham Castle on 13th December, 1971, the Dean of Durham in the chair, it was ORDERED—

"That Mrs. J. W. Percy's edition of the York Memorandum Book should be printed as a volume of the Society's publications."

W. A. L. SEAMAN
Secretary.

YORK
MEMORANDUM BOOK

BY

VOLUME CLXXXVI

EDITED BY

JOYCE W. PERCY

PRINTED FOR THE SOCIETY BY
NORTHUMBERLAND PRESS LIMITED
GATESHEAD
1973

INTRODUCTION

This York Memorandum Book is one of the earliest volumes preserved among the York City Archives in the City Library.[1] Its
general condition is quite good, despite unsuitable storage for several
centuries. The city records were originally kept in locked wooden
boxes, in the Council Chamber on the old Ouse Bridge. By the
eighteenth century, however, Darcy Preston, one of the more per-
ceptive Town Clerks, was concerned about their preservation.
Surprisingly, when they were moved in 1738 to the Evidence Room
(or Record Chamber) above the Micklegate Ward Room at the
Guildhall, the reason given was not damp from the river but
because the Guildhall was 'much safer from fire and more convenient than the present record room on Ouse Bridge'.[2] Yet it was
at the Guildhall that the worst calamity befell the Memorandum
Book. It was seriously damaged, along with many other records, by
heavy floods in 1892. A flood mark still shows across the lower half
of many of the folios, some of which are illegible except under ultra-
violet light.

The Memorandum Book was restored by the Public Record Office
and now has a vellum binding, 12½" × 9". An entry in the York
Corporation House Books, dated 25 November 1561, reveals that it
was originally bound in elaborately tooled leather. The minute
ordered that the ordinances of the minstrels should be observed as
enrolled in 'the old registr of parchement with the bosses'.[3] The
volume consists of 250 folios, including one or two later insertions.
Many of the folios have one, two or occasionally three older numera-
tions, none of them complete and consecutive. The foliation used
in this edition is the modern one entered at the foot of each folio.

The Memorandum Book was commenced in 1371 and entries continued until 1596. Some items of earlier date were registered in
retrospect without regard to chronological order. Their position
is not to be explained by the re-binding. Although entries are in

---

[1] It was originally known as B/Y and is now classified as E 20A.
[2] House Book 42, f.231v.
[3] House Book 23, f.40. The minstrels' ordinances appear on ff.222-223v below.

several different hands, Roger Burton, the meticulous Common (Town) Clerk, 1415-1436, is the most prolific contributor, as is evident from his signed entries.

The contents of the volume are very similar to those of the contemporary York Memorandum Book A/Y, edited by Dr. Maud Sellers for the Surtees Society (vols. 120 and 125). Both contain ordinances of the city's craft guilds, descriptions of the boundaries of the city, amounts collected from the parishes towards the Fifteenth and Tenth, deeds, leases of city property and many other items relating to civic administration and the trade and life of York from the fourteenth to the sixteenth centuries. It is difficult to understand why the two volumes were in use at the same time for such similar entries. A possible explanation is that B/Y was intended originally as a register of deeds, since the first third of the volume, for the period 1371-c.1430 is devoted entirely to records of this kind. Later, although deeds continued to be registered, a wider variety of entries occurs. In contrast, there are relatively few deeds in the Memorandum Book A/Y.

Most, although by no means all, of the deeds relate to property in the City of York and give us some of our earliest information, however scanty, about the inhabitants of the medieval city and the land and property they owned. The original deeds were brought before the Mayor in the Council Chamber by one of the parties, in order to be registered as a safeguard against loss by fire, theft or forgery. Frequently, a deed was witnessed in the presence of the Mayor and the official mayoral seal was appended to the original deed as an additional safeguard. The city itself owned a very considerable amount of property as is apparent from the number of leases granted in the name of the Mayor and Commonalty.

The many guild ordinances complement the generally earlier ordinances in the Memorandum Book A/Y and those recorded in the House Books from 1476. In addition to the usual administrative clauses relating to the appointment of searchers, attendance at meetings and employment of apprentices, several regulate hours and wages and the type of work to be undertaken by guild members. A list of prices to be charged by the skinners for various tasks is exceptionally detailed.[4]

Among items of special interest are a description of the city's three swords of state, arbitration concerning responsibility for the

[4] f.171.

deterioration of the fishpond of the Foss and the death of fish, expenses incurred for a new charter and an explanation of the use of both Roman and Arabic numerals. Unfortunately, the latter is not dated. It is very lucid but it is interesting that Arabic numerals do not occur elsewhere in the volume.

Several charters and letters patent are copied in the Memorandum Book, also a grant by the Mayor and Commonalty to the Corpus Christi guild. This conferred a place in St. William's chapel for keeping the Corpus Christi shrine. In addition there are copies of the foundation deeds of the hospital of Jesus Christ and the Blessed Virgin Mary in Fossgate, which became the Merchant Adventurers' Hall, and of the deeds of several chantries and a number of obits. The originals of some of these are among the City Archives.

There are two cases of forgery. In one both the vicar and clerk of Nafferton confessed that the vicar had forged a deed in order to extort money from the Abbot of St. Mary's, York. The seal was taken from another deed.[5] In the other case, Warmebold Harlam, a goldsmith, vigorously denied that he had been a party to two deeds bearing his name and declared that the seal was not his. He used an armorial seal bearing a lion rampant, and engraved with the letters of his name, a fact which was agreed by many of those present. He threw down his glove in challenge to anyone who asserted the contrary, saying that he was wrong in his head.[6]

Historians have used some of the more interesting items in the Memorandum Book, but no systematic translation or calendar of the whole volume has previously been published. Footnote references are made to relevant translations and articles.

Note. Dr. Maud Sellers, in her introduction to the Memorandum Book A/Y, included an explanation of the civic government of York and of the craft gilds. It is recommended to the reader of this companion volume.

Editor's Notes

In preparing this volume for publication, the editor has attempted to present the various entries in the form most likely to be helpful to all historians and students of the mediaeval City of York. Deeds are accordingly calendared rather than transcribed, whether the originals are in Latin or English. Although common formulae are omitted, all persons and places are named as in the original and all

[5] ff.38-38v.　　　　　　　　　　[6] ff.36v-37.

interesting or unusual clauses included. The only omissions are in a person's full title, occupation and place of origin where these are repeated word for word in a group of deeds, clauses of warranty which occur almost invariably throughout the volume, and the fact that rents were payable twice yearly on the feast of St. Martin in Winter and Whit Sunday. Any variations are noted. The language of all calendared entries is given in square brackets at the end.

Entries other than deeds are translated from the Latin. Those in English are transcribed literally as many are of interest to students of dialect and Middle English. Surnames and place names are invariably spelt as in the original, although Christian names are modernised in the calendared entries. Latinised surnames, however, have been given their English equivalent. Ranulph de Albo Monasterio, for instance, appears as Ranulph de Whitchurch, the surname de Cestria as de Chester and Tinctor as Dyer. Modern spellings of place names, where these differ markedly from the original, have been ascertained from the volumes of the English Place Names Society and are added in square brackets. Similarly, the meanings of words now obsolete are supplied in footnotes, based on the Oxford English Dictionary or Wright's Dialect Dictionary, unless some other source is mentioned. The title *dominus* occurs very frequently in the Latin deeds. Where it is a purely courtesy title given to a chaplain or other cleric it has been omitted. In other cases it is translated by Lord or Sir as appropriate. Roman numerals have been transcribed throughout by Arabic, in accordance with modern practice. The dating of entries is invariably given as in the original, the year being added in new style dating, within square brackets, where necessary.

Parts of the text are badly faded, as is explained in the introduction. Wherever a passage has proved particularly difficult to read and errors may have occurred a footnote to this effect has been added.

Headings which have been inserted by the editor are printed in capitals, those which occur in the text itself in italics. Marginal notes, which are few and very brief, have only been transcribed where they add to the information in the text.

For the terms used to describe the deeds I am indebted to the introduction by R. B. Pugh, to his 'Calendar of Antrobus Deeds before 1625' (Wiltshire Archaeological and Natural History Society, Records Branch, Vol. III), the only difference being my use of the later term *feoffment* instead of *gift* for the conveyance of real property. *Gift* is reserved more specifically for the *gift of goods and chattels*. The Memorandum Book contains a number of such gifts, which were generally liable to the suspicion of being fictitious and intended to deceive creditors. Some, however, may have been intended to serve as wills, as the first entry of this type is headed *The last will of Richard de Lydyate of York, draper*. A gift might also be used to satisfy a debt or, instead of a bond, as a pledge for payment. The goods and chattels probably remained in the donor's possession in most cases. There are several instances of family settlements being affected by a feoffment and re-enfeoffment, and of feoffments followed by quitclaims made by the feoffor to the feoffee, which were no doubt intended to further secure the title. In addition to the various deeds, accounts of several Inquisitions post Mortem and Assizes of Fresh Force, held before the Mayor in the Guildhall, are also included. The latter was the remedy available to anyone wrongfully dispossessed of lands or tenements within a city or borough, one of the conditions being that the action must be brought within forty days. It provided a more rapid remedy than the Assize of Novel Disseisin instituted by Henry II as it did not require a royal writ. The action was tried by a jury of twelve men.

BIBLIOGRAPHY

PRIMARY SOURCES

York Corporation House (Minute) Books. (York City Library)

Registers of Wills, Vols. I, II. (Borthwick Institute of Historical Research, York)

Register of Archbishop Henry Bowet (Borthwick Institute of Historical Research, York)

R. H. Scaife, *Civic Officials of York and Parliamentary Representatives* 3 mss. volumes (York City Library)

PRINTED MATERIAL

Surtees Society series

M. Sellers, *York Memorandum Book* (Vols. 120, 125)

M. Sellers, *York Mercers and Merchant Adventures, 1356-1917* (Vol. 129)

J. Raine, *English Miscellanies* (Vol. 85)

R. H. Scaife, *The Guild of Corpus Christi, York* (Vol. 57)

Testamenta Eboracensia or *Wills Registered at York* (Vols. 4, 30, 45, 53, 79, 106)

J. C. Atkinson, *The Whitby Cartulary* (Vols. 69, 72)

Yorkshire Archaeological Society Record Series:

A. Raine, *York Civic Records* (Vols. 98, 103, 106, 108, 110, 112, 115, 119)

Index of Wills in the York Registry (Vols. 6, 11, 14, 19, 22, 24)

Calendars of Charter Rolls preserved in the Public Record Office (C.Ch.R.)

Calendars of Patent Rolls preserved in the Public Record Office (C.P.R.)

Calendars of Close Rolls preserved in the Public Record Office (C.Cl.R.)

Calendars of Inquisitions Post Mortem preserved in the Public Record Office, 2nd Series, Vols. II, III

Statutes of the Realm, 22 Hen. VIII, c.4.

               5 Eliz.   c.4.

T. Widdrington, *Analecta Eboracensia*, ed. Caesar Caine, 1897.

F. Drake, *Eboracum*, 1736.

P. M. Tillott (ed.), *The Victoria County History: The City of York*, 1961.

A. Raine, *Mediaeval York*, 1955.

R. Davies, *A Memoir of the York Press*, 1868.

R. Davies, *The State Swords of the York Corporation* (Yorks. Philosophical Society Annual Report, 1868).

L. Toulmin Smith, *York Plays*, 1885.

A. H. Smith (ed.), *The Place Names of the West Riding*, 1961; *The Place Names of the North Riding*, 1928; *The Place Names of the East Riding and York*, 1937.

E. M. Veale, *The English Fur Trade in the Later Middle Ages,* 1966.

Ll. Jewitt and W. H. St. John Hope, *Corporation Plate and Insignia of Office*, Vol. II, 1895.

C. R. Cheney, *Handbook of Dates for Students of English History*, 1945.

F. M. Powicke and E. B. Fryde, *Handbook of British Chronology*, 1961.

R. B. Pugh, *Calendar of Antrobus Deeds before 1625* (Wiltshire Archaeological and Natural History Society, Records Branch, Vol. III).

R. E. Latham, *Revised Mediaeval Latin Word-List*, 1965.

Dictionary of National Biography.

ACKNOWLEDGMENTS

My sincere thanks are due to Mrs. N. K. M. Gurney, Archivist of the Borthwick Institute of Historical Research, York, who suggested I should publish this volume. Her advice on interpretation and that of her assistant, Mr. A. N. Webb, have been invaluable.

I am also grateful to the York Library Committee for permission to edit and publish this volume of the City Archives, to Mr. O. S. Tomlinson, City Librarian, and Mr. M. Smith, Reference Librarian, for their constant interest and assistance, and to Miss V. Suter who so competently typed the text.

Joyce W. Percy.

YORK MEMORANDUM BOOK

B/Y.

1371-1596.

(f.1) *The book or register of memoranda relating to the city, beginning in the time of John de Gisburn, Mayor, 45 Edward III* [*1371*]. [Latin]

On Saturday in Easter week, 45 Edward III [12 April 1371], Robert G[unnays] of Hayton came before John de Gyseburn, Mayor, in the Mayor's chamber on Ouse Bridge, acknowledged that the following deed was his own and sought its enrolment in the common register of the city. [Latin].

QUITCLAIM

Robert Gunnays of Hayton,

to Henry de Hugate and John de Staveley, chaplains,

lands and tenements, rents, services and mills which they held at Holtby near Warthill [in] Bulmerschire.

Witnesses. Richard Bernard, Robert de Bollton, Thomas de—— [illegible], Thomas de Swynton, Robert B—— [illegible]

Given at Newesom [Newsam] in Rydale, on the Monday after Easter, 45 Edward III [7 April 1371] in the [presence?] of William de Nessefeld, Richard Bernard, John de Beverley.

[Latin]

[The following passage is so faint as to be illegible without the use of ultra-violet light, and is therefore transcribed in full].

Memorandum quod die lune proximo post festum —— virginis anno regni regis Edwardi tercii post conquestum quadragesimo venit Radulphus de Horneby de Ebor. draper, coram Rogero de Hovyngham tunc maire civitatis Ebor. et cognovit quandam cartam quam dedit Domino Roberto de ——, capellano —— esse cartam suam et factum suum que —— carta irrotulatur in libro et registro dicte civitatis. Et die veneris, viz. ultimo die mensis Marcii anno regni dicti regis Edwardi quadragesimo secundo [1368], venerunt prefati Dominus Robertus et Johannes coram Roberto de Howom tunc maiore dicte civitatis —— cartam esse suam et factum suum per quam dederunt omnia et singula —— in civitate predicte Ricardo de Esshewra, parsone ——, Johanne Yole de Ebor., draper, et Ricardo de Esyngwald —— que quedam carta irrotulatur——.

(f.iv) And also on 12 October 43 Edward III [1369], Richard de Esshwra, John Yole and Richard de Esyngwald came before Roger de Seleby, Mayor, and acknowledged that another deed had been made by them, conveying to Robert de Bretby, chaplain, John de Rypon, John de Wyllton, John de Bedale, litster, and William de Levesham, the aforesaid lands and tenements in the city and sought that the deed be enrolled in the same register of the city. And so the three deeds were entered in the same register. And now on Friday, the feast of St. Gregory the Pope, 46 Edward III [12 March 1372], Robert de Bretby, John de Rypon and others came before John de Gyseburn, Mayor, acknowledged the following deed to be their own and sought that it be enrolled as follows. [Latin].

FEOFFMENT.

Robert de Bretby, chaplain, John de Rypon, John de Wyllton, John de Bedale, litster, and William de Levesham,
    to Ralph de Horneby, citizen and merchant of York, and William Aky, chaplain,
lands and tenements in the city and suburbs of York, which they had by the gift of Richard de Esshwra, parson of St. Helen's Church, Stayngate, John Yole of York, draper, and Richard de Esyngwald.

Witnesses. John de Gyseburn, Mayor, William de Hovyngham, William Tondew and John Swerd, Bailiffs, Roger de Seleby, Richard de Thoresby, John de Santon, John Yole, John de Rypon, Robert del Gare, George de Coupmanthorp, Alan de Alnewyk.

Given at York, the Saturday before the Purification of the Blessed Virgin Mary, 46 Edward III [30 Jan. 1372] [Latin]

FEOFFMENT.

Matilda, daughter of John de St. Oswald of York,
    to William de Neuton, of York, chaplain,
a messuage with appurtenances situated in Overousegate, between the land of John de Qwixlay, draper, and that of John de Santon,

and extending in length from the high street of Overousegate in front to the oven of Annabel de Holme behind.

Witnesses. Robert de Howom, Mayor, Roger de Moreton, junior, John de Clayton, John de Essheton, Bailiffs, William de Beverley, John de Santon, Richard de Thoresby, Nicholas de Touthorp, John Hode, Robert de Brigg, William de Chester of York, clerk.

Given at York on Wednesday, the vigil of the Ascension [17 May] 1368, 42 Edward III. [Latin]

(f. 2) FEOFFMENT.

William de Newton, chaplain,
to Robert Cristendome, bower,
the messuage and appurtenances in Overousegate [as above], which he had by the feoffment of Matilda, daughter of John de St. Oswald of York, spinster.

Witnesses. John de Gyseburn, Mayor, William Tundeu, John Swerde, William de Hovyngham, Bailiffs, William Gra, John de Acastre, John de Santon, Robert de Ampillford, John de Brathwayte, Robert de Brigg, William de Chester of York, clerk.

Given at York, 19 March 1371/2, 46 Edward III. [Latin]

GIFT.

The last will of Richard de Lydyate of York, draper

Richard de Lydyate of York, draper,
to John de Dernyngton, chaplain, Richard, his son and Joan, his [the testator's] wife,
all his goods and chattels, to be disposed of by them free from all claims of his heirs or executors.

Witnesses. John de Gyseburn, Mayor, William Tundew, John Swerd, William de Hovyngham, Bailiffs, Richard de Hoton, William de Chester of York, clerk, public notary, John de Craven.

Given at York, 5 September 46 Edward III [1372]. [Latin]

FEOFFMENT.

Isabel, daughter and co-heiress of Richard Sampsone, late citizen of York,
to Robert Lacerer, John de Lutton and Alan Cob, chaplains,
her share in a messuage and appurtenances in Mikellgate, which lately belonged to her father, and lay in width between the land of John de Acastre on the one side and the other part of the messuage which lately belonged to Agnes, wife of Master William

de Otryngton, clerk, her sister, and co-heiress of Richard Sampsone on the other side; and extending in length from the high street of Mikellgate to the garden of Thomas de Nessefeld.

(f. 2v) Witnesses. John de Gyseburn, Mayor, William Tundew, John Swerd and William de Hovyngham, Bailiffs, Thomas de Nessefeld, John Weland, Robert Sauvage, William son of Ralph Sauvage, John de Eysshton, William Giry, Robert Barry, John de Poynton, Ellis Lyttester, Adam Candeler, Thomas de Strensall, Richard de Taunton, Henry de Collton, Henry Couper, Richard de Raysebek, John de Bampton, Robert de Cleburn of York, clerk. Given at York, the Tuesday before the feast of the Nativity of the Blessed Virgin Mary, 46 Edward III [7 September 1372]. [Latin]

RE-ENFEOFFMENT.

Robert Lacerer, John de Lutton and Alan Cob, chaplains,
to Isabel, daughter and co-heiress of Richard Sampsone, and the heirs of her body, in default thereof to Robert, son of the said Master William de Otryngton and the heirs of his body, in default thereof to Margaret, daughter of Master William de Otryngton, and the heirs of her body, in default thereof to William, son of Ralph Sauvage of York and his heirs.
the moiety of a messuage in Mikellgate [as above] which they lately received by the feoffment of the said Isabel.

Witnesses. John de Gyseburn, Mayor, William Tundew, John Swerd and William de Hovyngham, Bailiffs, Thomas de Nessefeld, John Weland, Robert Sauvage, Walter de Askham, John de Esshton, William Giry, Robert Barry, John de Poynton, Thomas de Collton, Ellis Lyttester, Adam Candeler, Thomas de Strensall, Richard de Taunton, Henry de Collton, John de Bedale, Richard de Raysebek, Robert Lyttester, William Bell, Richard de Alne, Henry Couper, John de Bampton, Robert de Cleburn of York, clerk.

Given at York, the Friday after the feast of the Nativity of the Blessed Virgin Mary, 46 Edward III [10 September 1372].

[Latin]

(f. 3) APPRENTICESHIP INDENTURE.[1]
of Nicholas, son of John de Kyghlay,
to John de Bradlay of York, bower.

[1] Transcribed in *York Memorandum Book* I, pp. 54-55.

The apprentice was to live with his master from the feast of St. Peter ad Vincula [1 August] 1371 for seven years, willingly perform his master's orders and keep his secrets and counsel; not to cause him any loss worth 6d per year or more and knowing of any threat was to prevent it or immediately warn his master. He was not to waste his master's goods not lend them to anyone without his special consent. He was not to play at dice nor frequent taverns, the chess-board or brothels, nor commit adultery or fornication with his master's wife or daughter, under penalty of doubling the length of his apprenticeship. He was not to contract matrimony with any woman during his term of seven years, except with his master's consent. He was not to withdraw from his master's service unlawfully nor absent himself by day or night. John de Bradlay was to instruct and inform Nicholas, his apprentice, as well as he knew how in the *bowercrafte*, in buying and selling, without concealing anything, and was to provide him with food and drink, linen and woollen clothing, a bed, shoes and all necessities for all the said term. Thomas de Kyghlay, chaplain, was to give John de Bradlay 6s 8d each year for three years for him to teach Nicholas as aforesaid. William del Clogh of York, bower, was to act as surety for John de Bradlay's fulfilment of the premises, and the said Thomas as surety for the apprentice. Sealed by the parties and their sureties.

Witnesses. John Swerd, Robert Cristendome, Roger Bower, Robert Garnet, Philip Bower.

Given at York, on the feast and year aforesaid. [Latin]

APPRENTICESHIP INDENTURE.

of Robert de Hotoft of Gaytburton in Lyndesey,

to Robert Christendome of York, bower, for seven years from the Monday after the feast of St. Michael the Archangel [4 October] 1372.

[Conditions as in the indenture above].

(f. 3v) Robert Dart, messenger of the Archbishop of York and warden of his gaol, was to stand surety for Robert de Hotoft.

Witnesses. Philip Carpentar, William de Chester of York, clerk.

Given at York, the day and year aforesaid. [Latin]

On the Tuesday after the feast of St. Hillary in the same year, [18 January 1372/3], Margaret Wyvell came before the Mayor and

Bailiffs and sought the enrolment of the following deed in the
register. [Latin]

ACQUITTANCE.
  Margaret Wyvell
  to Sir Ralph de Hastynges, knight,
from all manner of actions, real and personal.
  Given at York, the Monday after the feast of St. Hillary, 46
Edward III [17 January 1373] [French]

On 3 July 49 Edward III [1375], John Brett came before the
Mayor and Bailiffs and sought enrolment of the following deed in
the register. [Latin]

GIFT.
  John Brette of York,
  to Richard de Ottelay, parson in St. Peter's Church,
  York, and Roger de Ake, vicar of the church at Calveton
  [Calton], and Thomas Potter, citizen of York,
  all his goods and chattels both within the liberties of York and
beyond.
  Witnesses. Thomas Gra, Mayor, Robert Sauvage, John de
Howden, John de Brathwayt, Bailiffs, Thomas de Howme, John de
Acastre.
  Given at York, on the feast of the Purification of the Blessed
Virgin Mary, 49 Edward III [2 February 1375]. [Latin]

(f. 4) On 6 September 49 Edward III [1375], William de Cawod
and Cecily, his wife, came before Thomas Gra, Mayor, Robert
Savage, Ellis de Everyngham and Richard de Brikenall, in the
Mayor's chamber on Ouse Bridge and sought the enrolment of the
following deed in the register.
  [The entry is crossed through with a marginal note to the effect
that on 29 January [1378] the said William came before John de
Santon, Mayor, John de Acastre, Robert de Howom, Roger de
Moreton, junior, Thomas Gra and William de Tykehill, and asked
that it be cancelled].

FEOFFMENT.
  William de Cawode, citizen and merchant of York,
  and Cecily his wife,
  to John de Rufford, citizen of York, and John Clement, chaplain,

lands and tenements in the city and suburbs of York which they had by the feoffment of William de Horton, chaplain, and John de Manfeld, chaplain.

Witnesses. Thomas Gra, Mayor, Robert Sauvage, John de Howeden and John de Brathwayte, Bailiffs, William Gra, John de Gisburn, Robert de Howom, George de Coupmanthorp, Simon de Quixlay, William Fissher, Ellis de Everyngham, litster.

Given at York, 6 September 49 Edward III [1375].   [Latin]

Item, another deed relating to the goods and chattels of the said William is enrolled on the next page [f. 4v].   [Latin]

On 8 September 49 Edward III [1375], Mariot, wife of the late Henry de Hesyll, citizen of York, came before Thomas Gra, Mayor, in the Mayor's chamber on Ouse Bridge and sought the enrolment of a deed as follows.

GIFT.
   Mariot, wife of the late Henry de Hesyll, citizen of York,
   to William Giry, citizen and merchant of York,
all her goods and chattels and rents from various tenements bequeathed to her for twelve years by the will of the said Henry.

Given at York, 3 September 49 Edward III [1375].   [Latin]

(f. 4v) GIFT [crossed through—see above, f.4]
   William de Cawode,
   to John de Rufford and John Clement,
all his ships with their rigging and equipment, his goods and chattels, woods, underwoods and timber in the woods of Byrkyn [Birkin], at Byrkynbothe and within the park of Nonneappilton [Nun Appleton].

Witnesses. Thomas Gra, Mayor, John de Howden, Robert Sauvage, John de Brathwayte, Bailiffs, William Gra, John de Gysburn, John de Acastre, Roger de Moreton, junior, Robert de Howom, Thomas de Howom, George de Coupemanthorp, Simon de Quixlay.

Given at York, 6 September 49 Edward III [1375].   [Latin]

FEOFFMENT.
   Inoria, wife of the late Robert Lette of Clifton,

to her daughter Alice and the heirs of her body begotten,
the moiety of a wood with appurtenances in Bouthom, lying in
length from the high street of Bouthom to the *Kenyngdyk*, and
in width between the land of the Abbot of St. Mary's, York, and
the land and toft which the said Alice had by the feoffment of her
mother;

also two acres of land with appurtenances, of which one lay in the
field of Cliffton in length from the high street leading from Bouthom to Clifton and the *Kenyngdyk*, and in width between the land
of Richard atte Strete and the land which the said Alice had by the
feoffment of her mother; and the other acre lay in the field of
Roucliff, one half at *Stifurlang* between the land of the said Alice
and that of John Brok, and the other half at *Colcrossyk*, in length
from the high street to *Hurtbuk*.

Witnesses. Robert de Bouthom, John son of Gilbert, Thomas son
of John Clerk, John de Rome, Thomas de [Dueston?], Thomas
Londrais, John de Roucliff, John, son of William Bell.

Given at Clifton on Wednesday, the vigil of the Ascension [19
May] 1322.   [Latin]

On 10 September 49 Edward III [1375], John son of William de
Skelton, citizen of York, came before Thomas Gra, Mayor, John
de Howden, and the other Bailiffs, Roger de Moreton, junior, and
Richard Brikenall in the Mayor's chamber on Ouse Bridge and
sought the enrolment of a deed in the common register as follows.

(f. 5) FEOFFMENT.

John, son of William de Skelton, citizen of York,
    to John de Lutton and William de Thorne, chaplains,

[1] a messuage with buildings and appurtenances in Walmegate,
lying in width between the land formerly of William de Gremmesby and Sir Henry de Percy, knight, on the one side and the land
formerly of William de Moreby, which he recently gave to his
sister Joan for life, on the other side, and extending in length from
the high street of Walmegate to the River Foss.

[2] a messuage with buildings and appurtenances in Fisshergate,
lying in width between the king's ditch and the land of the Prior
and Convent of Wartre, and in length from Fisshergate to the
Benehill.

[3] a messuage with buildings and appurtenances in Northstrete,
lying in width between the land formerly of William de Broune,

late citizen of York, and a lane called the Lymelendyng, and extending in length from Northstrete to the River Ouse.

[4] a messuage with buildings and appurtenances on Bisshopeshill, lying in width between the land formerly of William de Shirburn, which once belonged to Alan le White, and the land formerly of Sir Ranulph de Whitchurch, and extending in length from the high street to the land of the said Sir Ranulph.

[5] a messuage with buildings and appurtenances in Walmegate, lying in width between the land formerly of Robert Solace and the land which Robert de Waterton lately held, and extending in length from Walmegate in front to the River Foss and the land formerly of John de Benyngburgh and John de Fosse behind.

[6] a messuage with buildings and appurtenances in Clementhorp in the suburbs of York, lying in width between the land formerly of Adam Berlot and that formerly of John le Coke and extending in length from the high street of Clementhorp to the meadow called the *Lytteleng* belonging to the Prioress and Convent of the nuns of Clementhorp.

[7] a messuage with buildings and appurtenances in Northstrete, lying in width between the land formerly of Richard le Ferrour and that formerly of William de Portyngton, and extending in length from Northstrete to the land of the said Richard le Ferrour.

(f. 5v) All his other lands and tenements, rents and services in the City of York, and its suburbs.

Witnesses. Thomas Gra, Mayor, John de Howeden, Robert Sauvage, John de Brathwayte, Bailiffs, William Gra, John de Gisburn, John de Acastre, Roger de Moreton, junior, Robert de Howom, Ralph de Hornby, John de Berden, William de Beverleye, Simon de Quixlay, Richard de Taunton, George de Coupemanthorp, William Fissher, Walter Ferrour, Nicholas de Skelton, cook, William de Duresme.

Given at York, 29 August 49 Edward III [1375].   [Latin]

(ff. 5v-6v) QUITCLAIM.
John son of William de Skelton, citizen of York,
to John de Lutton and William de Thorne, chaplains,
messuages, lands and tenements [as above, ff. 5-5v.]
Witnesses [as above].
Given at York, 1 September 49 Edward III [1375].   [Latin]

On the Tuesday after the feast of St. Andrew the Apostle, 49 Edward III [4 December 1375], John son and heir of John de Denton of Newcastle upon Tyne came into the court held in the *Tolboth* before Thomas Gra, Mayor of the City of York, Simon de Qwixlay, Robert de Duffeld and William de Helmeselay, Bailiffs, John de Acastre, Roger de Moreton, junior, and many others, and sought the enrolment of the following deed in the common register.

QUITCLAIM.

John, son and heir of John de Denton of Newcastle upon Tyne, to Adam de Fenrother, William de Meryngton, chaplain, Hugh de Brandon, William de Chevyngton and William de Seton, tenants of the manor of Denton, of which John de Whitewelle was also a feoffee on the day he died,
the manor of Denton with appurtenances near Neuburn.

Acknowledging and confirming a previous deed whereby the said John de Denton had quitclaimed to John de Emeldon, burgess of Newcastle, and Margaret, his wife, then tenants of the manor of Denton, the said manor and appurtenances. He had afterwards impleaded the said Margaret and others named in the writ, in an assize of Novel Disseisin, contrary to the deed hitherto denied by him, which still remained to be tried before the king's justices at Newcastle.

(f. 7) Because his seal would be unknown to many, he affirmed the deed in the full court of the king held at York before the Mayor and Bailiffs and caused it to be written in the register of the city called *Domeseday*.

Witnesses. The Mayor and Bailiffs [named as above], John de Gyseburn, William Gra, Ralph de Horneby, William de Beverlay and Robert Sauvage, fellow citizens of the Mayor and Bailiffs, also William de la Vale, Bertram Monboucher, Thomas de Hildirton, Henry de la Vale, knights, William de Hesilrig, John de Mitford, Nicholas Raymes, William de Acton, John del Chaumbre, John de Reefham and John de Bulkham, of the County of Northumberland.

Given at York, the year and day abovesaid, [4 December 1375].

Further, the said John, son and heir of John de Denton, promised the Mayor, Bailiffs and other witnesses to make sufficient security for the said manor before the king's justices at London when the parties should require it. Also he should return to them all evidences of title which he might have.   [Latin]

On the Tuesday before the feast of the Apostles Philip and
James, 50 Edward III [29 April 1376], Juliana, wife of the late
Henry son of Conan, knight, came into the Mayor's chamber on
Ouse Bridge before Ralph de Horneby, Mayor, William de Ireby,
and Thomas de Midellton, Chamberlains, and sought the enrol-
ment of a deed in the common register as follows.

QUITCLAIM.

Juliana, wife of the late Henry son of Conan, knight,
to John, son of John de Wodehall,

all her claim to dower in lands and tenements which her husband
had in Great Halton or Little Halton near Derfeld [Great and
Little Houghton near Darfield].

Witnesses. Ralph de Horneby, Mayor, William Gra, John de
Gysburn, John de Acastre, Thomas Gra, citizens of York, Thomas
Bosevyll of Ardeslaye, Thomas de Wodehall, Robert de Roklay,
Hugh de Wombewell.

Given at York, (f. 7v) the Monday before the feast of the apostles
Philip and James, 50 Edward III [28 April 1376].   [Latin]

On 7 February 2 Richard II [1379], John de Moriceby, senior, and
John, son and heir of John de Moriceby, came before John de
Acastre, Mayor, William de Tykehill and the other Bailiffs,
Thomas Graa, the Chamberlains and other citizens, and sought the
enrolment of two deeds, in the common register.

QUITCLAIM.

John de Moriceby, senior,
to William Marmyon, William Bussy, knights, Andrew Brun
and William Davy,

the manor of Brentbroughton [Brant Broughton] in the County of
Lincoln and the advowson of the church of the same and all his
other lands and tenements with the rents and services both of the
free tenants and of the villeins, and the woods, marshes, turbaries
and all other appurtenances; reciting that William Marmyon and
William Bussy, knights, John de Welby, Andrew Brun and William Davy held the said manor and advowson of the church for
the life of John de Moriceby, senior, by the gift and feoffment of
Ralph Daubeney, knight, Lord of Ingleby, who in turn had them
by the feoffment of the said John de Moriceby, senior.

Witnesses. James de Pykeryng, John de Hothom, knights, John de Acastre, Mayor of the City of York, William de Tykehill, Ellis Lyster, and John de Sheffeld, Bailiffs, Thomas Graa, Robert Holme, Thomas Holme, citizens of York.

Given at York, 7 February 2 Richard II [1379].　　　[Latin]

QUITCLAIM.

John, son and heir of John de Moriceby,
　to William Marmyon, William Bussy, knights, Andrew Brun and William Davy,
(f. 8) the manor of Brentbroughton and advowson of the church [as above].

Witnesses [as above].

Given at York, 8 February 2 Richard II [1379].　　　[Latin]

FEOFFMENT.

William de Meryngton, son of Alan de Meryngton,
　to Thomas son of William Gra, John son of John de Langton, Laurence Gra, William son of Walter de Meryngton, and Robert de Meryngton, chaplain,
a messuage in Skeldergate with all buildings, gardens and dovecots, lying in width between the lane which leads from Skeldergate next to the churchyard of St. Mary the Elder to Bisshophill, on the one side, and the lands and tenements of Hugh de Myton and Margaret his wife, of the Prioress and Convent of Nunappilton and the *Aldbayle* on the other side, and extending in length from Skeldergate in front to a lane leading from Bisshophill to the *Aldbayle* behind; also lands and tenements in Lombelyth and the advowson of a moiety of the said church.

Witnesses. Simon de Quixlay, Mayor, John de Quixlay, William Fisshe, William de Briddessall, Bailiffs, John de Berden, William de Selby, Robert Sauvage, William de Agland, William de Chester of York, clerk.

Given at York, 20 February 1382/3, 6 Richard II.　　　[Latin]

(f. 8v) QUITCLAIM.

Richard de Berewyk of Jarum [Yarm],
　to Sir Robert de Manfeld, Mayor of Beverlee, and Simon de Elvyngton of York,
messuages, tenements, shops, gardens, rents and services in the City

of York of which the said Robert and Simon were seised.

Given at York, on the feast of St. Peter Ad Vincula 7 Richard
II [1 August 1383].   [French]

QUITCLAIM.

Henry Littester, schoolmaster, of Jarum,

to Sir Robert de Manfeld and Simon de Elvynton,

messuages, tenements, shops, gardens, rents and services in the
City of York of which they were seised.

Witnesses. Robert Sauvage, Mayor of York, Richard de Santon,
Constantine del Dam, Thomas de Kelfeld, Bailiffs, John de Berden,
Robert del Gare, John de Appilton, John de Stillyngton, William
Seler, Roger de Burton, John de Wilton, cutler, John de Berghby.

Given at York, 2 August 7 Richard II [1383].   [French]

QUITCLAIM.

John de Crayke, son and heir of Robert de Crayke, late citizen
of York,

to Sir Robert de Manfeld and Simon de Elvyngton,

messuages, tenements, shops, gardens, rents and services in York
of which they were seised.

Witnesses. Robert Sauvage, Mayor, Richard de Santon, Constantine del Dam, Thomas de Kelfeld, Bailiffs, John de Berdne, Robert
del Gare, John de Appilton, John de Stillyngton, William Seler,
Roger de Burton, John de Wilton, cutler.

Given at York, 2 August 7 Richard II [1383].   [French]

(f. 9) FEOFFMENT.

George de Lillyng, son of Thomas de Lillyng,

to William Moubray, son of John Moubray, knight,

Ed[mund] Moubray and John Upsall,

lands and tenements at Nunwyk near Rypon which he had by the
gift and feoffment of Richard Brynnand, son of William Brynnand
of Knaresburgh and husband of Margaret, mother of the said
George.

Witnesses. Thomas Gra, John de Gysburn, Richard de Norton,
William de Ireby, Roger Wele.

Given at Nunwyk, 5 June 10 Richard II [1387].   [Latin]

LETTERS OF ATTORNEY.

William Moubray, son of John Moubray, knight, Ed[mund] Moubray and John de Upsall,

to John Clynt senior, chaplain, and Nicholas de Dall of Rypon, to deliver seisin to Katherine de Meryngton, widow of William de Meryngton, of lands and tenements at Nunwyk near Rypon, as described in a deed to the said Katherine [see below ff. 9-9v.] Given at York on Saturday, the feast of the apostles Peter and Paul [29 June] 1387, 11 Richard II.   [Latin]

LETTERS OF ATTORNEY.

William Moubray, Ed[mund] Moubray and John de Upsall, to Robert de Meryngton, chaplain, and John Riche, senior, of Nunwyk,

to receive seisin of lands and tenements in Nunwyk as in the feoffment made to them by George de Lillyng [see above].

Given at York, 5 June 10 Richard II [1387].   [Latin]

LETTERS OF ATTORNEY.

George de Lyllyng, son of Thomas de Lyllyng,

to John Tebbe and John Riche, junior, of Nunwyk, to deliver seisin to William Moubray, Ed[mund] Moubray and John de Upsall, of lands and tenements at Nunwyk, as in his deed of feoffment [see above].

Given at York, 5 June 10 Richard II [1387].   [Latin]

QUITCLAIM.

George de Lillyng,

to William Moubray, Edmund Moubray and John Upsall, lands and tenements at Nunwyk, which they had by the feoffment of the said George de Lillyng [see above].

Given at York, on Tuesday, the day after the Nativity of St. John the Baptist, 11 Richard II [25 June 1387].   [French]

FEOFFMENT.

William Moubray, Ed[mund] Moubray, and John de Upsall,

to Katherine de Meryngton, widow of William de Meryngton, land and tenements at Nunwyk near Ripon, which the feoffors had by the gift and feoffment of George de Lillyng, son of Thomas de Lillyng [see above].

(f. 9v) Rent. 60s. p.a. payable on the feasts of St. Martin in Winter and Whit Sunday, during the life of Margaret, wife of Richard Brynnand, son of William Brynnand of Knaresburgh, and the mother of the said George de Lillyng; or, should the said Richard die before her, 5 marks p.a. for the remainder of the life of Margaret.

If the rent should be in arrears during the life of the said Margaret, the feoffors were to have the right of distraint. If it was overdue by a quarter of a year, they were to re-enter and retain the premises until her death, the reversion of the lands and tenements thereafter being reserved to the said Katherine, her heirs and assigns.

Witnesses. William de Selby, Mayor, Thomas Gra, John de Gysburn, Robert Sauvage, Simon Quixlay, citizens of York, Richard de Norton, John de Haukeswyk of Ripon.

Given at York, on Saturday, the feast of the apostles Peter and Paul [29 June] 1387, 11 Richard II. [Latin]

QUITCLAIM.
Robert, son of Robert de Ros of Ingmanthorp, knight,
to Brian de Stapelton, knight, John Seel, parson of the church at Dighton [Deighton], John de Tyndale and Robert Rede, parson of the church of Broghton Hastelay [Broughton Astley, Lincs.]
the manors of Southdighton and Ingmanthorp and lands, tenements, rents and services in Northdighton and Styveton [Steeton] and elsewhere in the County of York and also the advowson of the church of Southdighton which they had by the feoffment of Robert de Ros, his father.

(f. 10) Witnesses. William de Aldeburgh, senior, William de Aldeburgh, junior, Robert de Plumpton, Richard de Goldesburgh, John Mauleverer and Nicholas de Middelton, knights, John Dayvill, William Moubray, John de Ingelby, Thomas Fayrefax, Robert de Arthyngton and Thomas de Thwayt.

Given at Ingmanthorp, 6 September 8 Richard II [1384]. [Latin]

QUITCLAIM.
Robert, son of Robert de Ros of Ingmanthorp, knight,
to Robert de Ros of Ingmanthorp, his father, for life,

remainder to Thomas de Ros, his brother, and Joan his wife, and the male heirs of their bodies begotten, remainder to the right heirs of the said Thomas,

manors, lands and tenements, rents and services and the advowson of the church [as above f. 9v]; reciting the recent feoffment by Brian de Stapelton, John Seel, John de Tyndale and Robert Rede to Robert de Ros for life, remainder to Thomas de Ros, Joan, his wife, and the male heirs of their bodies, remainder to the right heirs of Thomas.

Witnesses [as above].

Given at Ingmanthorp, 15 March 8 Richard II [1385]. [Latin]

(f. 10v) QUITCLAIM.

Margaret, daughter of Nicholas de Coleyne, late citizen of York, to Constantine del Dame, citizen and apothecary of York, and Joan his wife,

lands and tenements with buildings and appurtenances in York, which formerly belonged to her father, the said Nicholas.

Witnesses. Simon de Quixlay, Mayor, John de Quixlay, William Fisshe, William de Bridsall, Bailiffs, Thomas Smyth, Robert de Talkan, Roger de Moreton, Henry de Jarum, Adam de Burton.

Given at York, 10 March 1382/3, 6 Richard II.   [Latin]

WILL.

of Joan, wife of Constantine del Dame, citizen and apothecary,[2] desiring burial in the Church of St. Martin in Conyngstrete; and bequeathing and devising to Constantine, her husband, all her goods and chattels, to dispose of as he thought best for her, and two messuages in York. One was situated in Stayngate, in width between the lane called Swynegale and the land formerly of Roger Rabuk, and extended in length from the high street in front to the king's gutter behind; the other messuage was in Usegate, in width between the land of John de Brathwayt and that of William de Sallay and in length between the high street in front and the land of the Prioress and Convent of the nuns of Thykheved [Thicket] behind.

---

[2] The will of Constantine del Dame, dated 1 July 1398 and proved 7 August 1398, is printed in *Testamenta Eboracensia* I, p. 245. In it he bequeathed the contents of his shop—mortars, pestles, balances, weights, drugs and unguents, spices, plates of pewter and jars for green ginger.

Appointment of Constantine, her husband, and Robert de Clifford, chaplain, as her executors.

Given at York on Easter Sunday, 2 April 1385.

Probate was granted, 17 May 1387, before the Official and Commissary General of the Court of York and administration of the
goods of the deceased awarded to Constantine, named as an executor, the said Robert having refused to accept the same.   [Latin]

(f. 11) WILL.

of John de Bristoll, citizen of York,
desiring burial in the Cathedral of St. Peter, should he die in York,
and making the following bequests:— for his funeral expenses,
20s; 12 pounds of wax made into 8 candles for burning around his
body; 20s. for distributing bread to the poor on the day of his
burial; 13s 4d for a stone to cover his grave; to two chaplains to
say the *Placebo, Dirige* and *Commendation* daily for his soul and
the souls of those to whom he was beholden in St. Michael le Belfrey during the first year after his death, 12 marks; to the chaplain
of St. Michael le Belfrey at the time of his death, 2s; to the parish
clerk, 12d; and to the under-clerk 6d; to Joan, his wife, for life, all
the houses in Lop Lane, Petergate and Joubertgate, which he had by
the gift and feoffment of John Tall of Taunton and on which the
said John Tall and Juliana, his wife, had levied a fine in the king's
court. On the death of Joan, his wife, the houses were to be sold
within four months by the Official of the Court at York, with the
advice of the two senior advocates of the Court. Of the money thus
realised, the Official was to receive 40s. and the two advocates 20s.
each, provided all the persons mentioned below agreed. If the Official
and advocates did not wish to perform this task, then the Dean of
Christianity of York and the senior penitentiary of the Church
of St. Peter should sell the tenements and each should receive 2
marks of the money realised. The remainder was to be divided into
two parts, half to be given to secular non-beneficed chaplains to
celebrate divine service for his soul and the souls of those to whom
he was beholden in the church or chapel of St. Michael le Belfrey
(f. 11v) and other churches in York, no later than 7 months after the
sale, and each was to have a salary of 6 marks p.a. They were to
say the *Placebo, Dirige* and *Commendation* pertaining to the office
of the dead daily. The other half was to be distributed to the needy
poor of the City of York, 40d, 3s, 2s, and 12d. to each as required,

the distribution to be completed within forty days after the receipt of the money.

Also, to the hospital of St. Mary near the Horsfayre, his missal so that the chaplains of the hospital might pray for his soul. To Joan, his wife, the silver cup used on his pilgrimage to St. James. To Tephanie his niece and servant, 40s. To John and Ellen the children of his daughter Matilda, £4 to be divided equally between them. To John de Scoreby, son of Mariot, his daughter, a silver cup worth 10s. To the fabric of the Cathedral Church of St. Peter of York 13s 4d., that his body might be buried there.

Appointment of Joan his wife, Master Robert de Hakthorp, public notary, John de Thornton of Davygate and John de Difford, chaplain, as executors. To the said Master Robert 26s 8d, to the said John de Thornton 20s. and to the said John, chaplain, 20s. provided they undertook the said duty.

Of the remainder of his goods, he bequeathed half to his wife, and the other half to be distributed by his executors to the needy and the poor in York. If his goods were insufficient for all his bequests, each was to be reduced. All his silver vessels and other goods such as cauldrons, books, and chests were to be sold to implement the terms of the will.

To a chaplain to celebrate the *Placebo, Dirige, Commendation* and office of the dead daily for a year for the souls of Sir Roger de Lamley, and of John and Alice, for his dead boys, and for the souls of Margaret and himself, 6 marks.

Given at York on the Saturday before the feast of St. Nicholas the Bishop [5 December] 1349.

Sealed by the testator and the Dean of Christianity of York.

Probate was granted before the Official and Commissary General of the Court of York and administration of the goods of the deceased awarded to Joan, his widow, and John de Difford chaplain, executors named in the will.

Given at York, 15 December 1349.   [Latin]

(f. 12) FEOFFMENT.

Richard de Thorne, Official of the Court at York, with the advice of Masters John de Kyllom and John de Suthwell, senior advocates,

to John de Feriby, Thomas de Garton and John de Brodesworth, clerks,

houses in Lop Lane, Petergate and Jubretgate, according to the
terms of the will of John de Bristoll [as above].

Witnesses. William de Selby, Mayor, Robert de Louthe, John de
Askham, John de Lyndesay, Bailiffs, John de Rypon, John de
Beverlay, William de Hovyngham, William de Levesham, Thomas
del Garth, John Bouche, Richard Storour.

Given at York, 12 December 1388, 12 Richard II.   [Latin]

QUITCLAIM.

Leonard Hedon, clerk,
  to Nicholas Lyllyng, knight, William Wenlok, Martin Elys,
  Thomas Aldebury, clerks, and Roger Groton,
lands and tenements and the houses built thereon in Sarmoneres-
lane [Sermon Lane] in the parish of St. Gregory within St. Paul's
churchyard, London, which formerly belonged to John Bryd, citizen
and draper of London and Agnes his wife, daughter and one of
the heirs and executors of the will of William de Newenham, late
citizen of London.

Witnesses. Sir Nicholas Twyfford, knight, Mayor of London,
Thomas Austyn and Adam Karlill, Sheriffs, John More, vintner,
Alderman of that ward, John Vatoft, John Page, William Turk,
Robert Alom.

Given at London, the Saturday after the feast of the Ascension,
12 Richard II [29 May 1389].   [Latin]

(f. 12v) FEOFFMENT.

Robert de Clifford and Roger de Malton, chaplains,
  to John de Raghton,
a tenement in Walmegate, lying in length from Walmegate in
front to Fisshergate behind, and in width towards Walmegate
between the tenement of John de Cawod and the tenement lately
of Roger de Moreton; also another messuage in Walmegate lying
between the tenement lately of the said Roger de Moreton and the
tenement lately of Thomas Daunay, and which the feoffors had as
a garden by the gift and feoffment of William de Aldeburgh,
knight, son and heir of William de Aldeburgh, late Lord of
Harwod, knight.

Witnesses. Thomas Smyth, Mayor, Robert de Louthe, John de
Askham, John de Lyndesay, Bailiffs, John de Berden, William de

Pountfrayt, John de Thornton, John de Brathwayt, Henry Laken-snyder, James de Saltmersh, Peter de Appilton, clerk.

Given at York, on Saturday the vigil of Whit Sunday [5 June] 1389, 12 Richard II. [Latin]

QUITCLAIM.
Robert de Clifford and Roger de Malton,
to John de Raghton,
the tenement and messuage in Walmegate [as above].

Witnesses. Thomas Smyth, Mayor, Robert de Louthe, John de Askham, John de Lyndesay, Bailiffs, John de Berden, William de Pountfrayt, John de Thornton, John de Brathwayt, Henry Lakensnyder, James Saltmarsch, William de Dalton.

Given at York, on Monday in Whit week [7 June] 1389, 12 Richard II. [Latin]

(f. 13) FEOFFMENT.
John de Raghton,
to Thomas de Stanlay,
a tenement and a messuage in Walmegate [as above].

Witnesses. Thomas Smyth, Mayor, Robert de Louthe, John de Askham, John de Lyndesay, Bailiffs, John de Berden, John de Brathwayt, Constantine del Dam, Henry de Jarum, Henry Lakensnyder, John de Wilton, William de Bubwyth, Peter de Appilton, clerk.

Given at York, on Wednesday in Whit week [9 June] 1389, 12 Richard II. [Latin]

FEOFFMENT.
Thomas de Stanlay,
to Laurence de Laukeland,
a tenement and a messuage in Walmegate [as above]

Witnesses. Thomas Smyth, Mayor, Robert de Louthe, John de Askham, John de Lyndesay, Bailiffs, John de Berden, John de Brathwayt, Constantine del Dam, Henry de Jarum, Henry Lakensnyder, John de Wilton, James Saltmersh.

Given at York, the Sunday before the feast of St. Laurence [8 August] 1389, 13 Richard II. [Latin]

(f. 13v) FEOFFMENT.

Laurence de Laukeland,
to John de Parys,
a tenement and a messuage in Walmegate [as above].

Witnesses. Thomas Smyth, Mayor, Robert de Louth, John de Askham, John de Lyndesay, Bailiffs, John de Berden, John de Brathwayt, John de Thornton, William de Pountfrayt, James de Saltmersh.

Given at York on Saturday, the vigil of the Assumption of the Blessed Virgin Mary [14 August] 1389, 13 Richard II.   [Latin]

FEOFFMENT.

John de Parys,
to Adam Fournyvall, chaplain,
the tenement and messuage in Walmegate [as above].

Witnesses. Thomas Smyth, Mayor, Robert de Louthe, John de Askham, John de Lyndesay, Bailiffs, John de Berden, John de Brathwayt, Constantine de Dam, Henry de Jarum, John de Cauthorn.

Given at York, 11 September 1389, 13 Richard II.   [Latin]

FEOFFMENT.

Isabel, daughter and heir of William de Hadyngton and Juliana his wife, daughter of the late Thomas Verdenell, citizen of York,
to John de Horslay and John de Askham, chaplains,
lands and tenements in the City and suburbs of York, Heslyngton, Fulford, Middlethorp and elsewhere in the County of York, which descended to her by hereditary right on the death of Juliana, her mother, together with the reversion of all lands and tenements which Matilda, wife of the late John, son of Adam Verdenell her kinsman held as her dower.

(f. 14) Rent. 40s. p.a., payable on Whit Sunday and the feast of St. Martin in Winter during the life of the said Isabel. The feoffor was to have the right of re-entry if the rent was forty days in arrears.

Witnesses. Thomas Smyth, Mayor, Henry Lakensnyder, John de Topclyff, John Touche, Bailiffs, Thomas Gra, William de Selby, John de Berden, Thomas Thurkyll, Nicholas de Warthill, John de Cawode, Peter de Appilton, clerk.

Given at York, the Wednesday after the feast of St. Mark the

Evangelist [27 April] 1390, 13 Richard II.   [Latin]

FEOFFMENT.

Adam Fournyvall, chaplain,
to Roger de Moreton, of York, mercer, and Robert Pay, chaplain,
the tenement and messuage in Walmegate which he had by the gift
and feoffment of John de Parys [as above, f. 13v].

Witnesses. Thomas Smyth, Mayor, Henry (f. 14v) Lakensnyder,
John de Topcliff, John Tutthe, Bailiffs, John de Berden, John
de Brathwayt, William de Pountfrayt, John de Thornton, James
de Saltmershe, Peter de Appilton of York, clerk.

Given at York, 14 February 13 Richard II [1390].   [Latin]

FEOFFMENT.

Roger de Moreton, of York, mercer, and Robert Pay, chaplain,
to Robert Talkan, citizen and merchant of York,
the tenement and messuage in Walmegate [as above].

Witnesses. Thomas Smyth, Mayor, Henry Lakensnyder, John de
Topcliff, John Tutche, Bailiffs, John de Berden, John de Brathwayt,
William de Pountfrayt, John de Thornton, Henry de Jarum, Constantine del Dam, James de Saltmersh, Peter de Appilton of York,
clerk.

Given at York on Tuesday, the vigil of St. Bartholomew the
Apostle [23 August] 1390, 14 Richard II.   [Latin]

(ff. 14v-15) WILL.

of Andrew de Bolingbroke, of York,
desiring burial in All Saints' Church in Usegate, before the altar
of the Blessed Mary, bequeathing his best robe with a tabard as a
mortuary gift, and devising his houses in Brettegat in the parish of
St. Peter the Little to Roger his son, and Elizabeth, his daughter,
and the heirs of their bodies, or in default thereof, to his nearest
heirs.

Appointment of Agnes, his wife, and John de Munketon, chaplain, as executors.

Given on Friday, the feast of the Beheading of St. John the
Baptist [29 August] 1315.   [Latin]

WILL.

of Roger de Bolyngbrok, citizen of York, desiring burial at [the

church of] the Friars Minor of York next to his mother and
devising his property as follows:
his tenement in Northstret, lately in the tenure of Alan de Thorlethorp of York, barker, and still in the tenure of his assigns, to be
sold by his executors, and the money used for the good of his soul
at the discretion of Emma, his wife; all other lands and tenements
in the City and suburbs of York, to Emma his wife, for life,
remainder to Marion his daughter and the heirs of her body,
remainder to Thomas de Kyghlay, chaplain, and his heirs.

Appointment of Emma, his wife, and the said Sir Thomas as
executors.

Given, 24 November 1361. [Latin]

QUITCLAIM.

Thomas de Kyghlay, chaplain,
to Emma, wife of the late Roger de Bolyngbrok, citizen of York,
lands and tenements in the City and suburbs of York which were
in the possession of the said Roger on the day he died.

Witnesses. William Graa, Richard de Wadeby, William de
Meryngton, John Darell, Marmaduke Darell and George Darell,
his brother.

Given at York, 27 February 1365/6, 39 Edward III. [Latin]

(f. 15v) QUITCLAIM.

Richard de Staxton, son of William de Staxton and Alice his
wife, daughter of the late Nicholas del Hale of Ryghton,
to Henry Wolleman, citizen and merchant of York, and Joan his
wife, daughter of the said William and Alice, and sister of
Richard,
lands and tenements in Righton [Reighton] and Flixton, which
formerly belonged to Nicholas, grandfather of the said Richard.

Witnesses. Robert de Elvyngton, William de Dalton, Peter
Cokke, Walter Ferour, Richard Marshall, Richard de Wartre,
Robert de Northwell, clerk.

Given at York on Tuesday in the second week of Lent [5 March]
1387, 10 Richard II. [Latin]

QUITCLAIM.

Margaret, wife of the late Robert de Werkesworth,
to William de Irland, Rector of the Church of St. Dennis in

Walmegate, John de Thorp, chaplain, Robert de Popilton, carpenter, and Richard Hayne,

two tenements in Aldwark, lying between the tenement of the Prior and Convent of Wilberfosse on the south and a common lane called the Kirkelane on the north, and abutting on the church yard of St. Helen's on the east and the high street on the west.

Witnesses. Robert Sauvage, Mayor, John de Craven, John de Penreth and William Vescy, Bailiffs, Robert de Howom, John de Berden, Thomas Thurkyll.

Given at York, 24 September 1392, 16 Richard II.   [Latin]

(f. 16) FEOFFMENT.

John de Mansfeld, parson of a moiety of the church of St. Mary the Elder in York,

to Joan, wife of the late Roger de Normanvill, for life, remainder to John, son of the said Roger and the heirs of his body, remainder to William, son of Geoffrey de Wandesford of York and the heirs of his body, remainder to Walter, son of the said Geoffrey de Wandesford and the heirs of his body, remainder to Thomas, son of the said Geoffrey and the heirs of his body, remainder to John, son of the said Geoffrey and the heirs of his body, remainder to Richard, son of the said Geoffrey and the heirs of his body, remainder to Margaret, daughter of the said Geoffrey and the heirs of her body, remainder to the right heirs of the said Roger de Normanvill,

lands and tenements in the City of York which the said John de Mansfeld had by the gift and feoffment of Roger de Normanvill.

Witnesses. John de Langeton, Mayor, William Frankys, Robert Ampilford, Ralph de Horneby, Bailiffs, Henry de Scorby, William de Meryngton, Hugh de Myton, citizens and merchants of York. Tripartite indenture.

Given at York on the Friday after the feast of St. Katherine the Virgin [29 November] 1359, 33 Edward III.   [Latin]

(f. 16v) FEOFFMENT.

William de Strynsall, son and heir of Thomas de Strynsall, late citizen and goldsmith of York,

to Richard de Thorneton, and John Helmeslay, chaplains,

a tenement in Mikelgate, situated on the corner of Mikelgate and Northstrete, in which Henry de Sutton, spicer, and John Sherman now dwell, between the land of the late William de Cawod, butcher, on the one side and Northstrete on the other, and extending in length from Mikelgate in front to the tenement of the late William de Cawod behind; also a tenement in Stanegate in which John Chaundeller, John Augo, Alice Alkebarowe, John Pynchebek and Richard de Middelton now dwell, situated in width between the tenement of the prebend of Barneby on the east and that of the prebend of Bilton on the west, and extending in length from the high street in front to the tenement of the prebend of Masham behind.

Witnesses. Robert Sauvage, Mayor, William Vescy, John de Craven, John de Penreth, Bailiffs, Thomas Gra, William de Selby, Thomas de Staynlay, William de Hovyngham, Richard de Taunton.

Given at York, 4 July 1392, 16 Richard II. [Latin]

GRANT.

William de Strynsall,
    to Richard de Thorneton and John de Helmeslay,
the reversion of a tenement in Stayngate together with a shop and the upper storeys lately in the tenure of William Aynderby, which he leased to John de Croxton, chandler, the present tenant, for twenty years from the feast of St. Martin in Winter [11 November] 1392.

Witnesses. Robert Sauvage, Mayor, Roger de Ruseton, John Bouche, Thomas Horneby, Bailiffs, John de Rypon, William de Levesham, William de Hovyngham.

Given at York, 4 October 16 Richard II [1392]. [Latin]

(f. 17) RE-ENFEOFFMENT.

Richard de Thorneton, and John de Helmeslay,
    to William de Strynsall, Matilda his wife, and the heirs of their bodies, remainder to the right heirs of William,
a tenement on the corner of Mikelgate and Northstrete and a tenement in Staynegate [as above].

Witnesses. Robert Sauvage, Mayor, Roger de Roseton, John Bouche, Thomas Horneby, Bailiffs, John de Askham, John del Hale, William del Bothe, clerk.

Given at York, 27 October 16 Richard II [1392]. [Latin]

GRANT.

Richard de Thorneton and John de Helmeslay,

to William de Strynsall and Matilda, his wife, and the heirs of
their bodies begotten, remainder to the right heirs of William,
the reversion of a messuage and a shop and upper storeys in Stanegate, which they had by the grant of the said William de Strynsall
[as above].
Given at York, 28 October 16 Richard II [1392]. [Latin]

(f. 17v) LEASE.
Roger Dautry, Lord of Full Sutton,
to Thomas de Wartre of Stanfordbryg,
a water mill called Colbrand near Skirpenbek, together with appurtenances and free entry and exit to the mill.
Term. 6 years from the feast of St. Martin in Winter [11 Novem-
ber] 1394.
Rent. 27 marks of which 20 marks was to be paid in advance
and also 9 marks in the last two years of the said term.
The said Roger was to maintain all timber and the mill-pond,
do all other repairs at his own cost on fifteen days' notice, and not
to impede the water-course to the mill. The lessee was to provide
mill stones and to be allowed to remove them at the end of the lease.
Witnesses. William de Lund, Parson of the church of Full Sutton,
William Middelton of Wilberfosse, Robert Orwell of York, clerk.
Given at York, 20 September 1394, 18 Richard II. [Latin]

BOND.
Roger Dautry of Full Sutton and William Dautry, his son, in £20,
to be paid to Thomas de Wartre of Stanfordbrigg on the next
feast of the Nativity of Our Lord.
Given, 22 September 18 Richard II [1394]. [Latin]

DEFEASANCE.
Thomas de Wartre,
to Roger Dautry and William Dautry, his son,
of their bond in £20, provided he, his executors and assigns might
have peaceful possession of a water mill called Colbrand near
Skirpenbek, leased to him [as above].
Given at York, 24 September 18 Richard II [1394]. [Latin]

(ff. 18-18v) LEASE.
John, Abbot of the Monastery of St. Mary of Coverham and the

Convent of the same, with the consent of the whole Chapter,
to John de Appilton, citizen and merchant of York,
a tenement with buildings and appurtenances, lying in length from
the market place of Thoresdaymarket in front to Swynegale behind,
and in width between the land of Robert Sauvage, citizen of York,
on the one side and the land of Margaret Bird and that of Thomas
Gower on the other; also a tenement lying between the land
belonging to the chantry of the Blessed Mary, which Robert de
Folketon, chaplain, held in St. Sampson's church, on the one side
and Swynegale on the other, and extending in length from Swynegale in front to the land of the Vicars Choral of St. Peter's behind.

Term. 80 years from Whit Sunday, 1395.

Rent. 7 marks p.a. payable on the feast of St. Martin in Winter
and Whit Sunday, beginning on the feast of St. Martin in Winter
1395, also *housegabul*[3] due to the king and all other duties levied
on the tenements, except 5s p.a. due to the Prior of Kirkeham.

John de Appilton, his heirs and assigns were to undertake all
necessary repairs at their own cost and allow the said Abbot and
Convent free entry two or three times a year to inspect the property.
The latter were to have the right of distraint or re-entry should any
building remain unrepaired for a year or if the rent was forty days
in arrears.

Given in the Chapter House of the Abbot and Convent, 1 May
1387, 10 Richard II.   [Latin]

(ff. 18v-19) GRANT AND GIFT.

John de Appilton, citizen and merchant of York,
to William de Tunstall, chaplain, of York,
the rent of 8 marks p.a. from all lands, tenements, buildings and
appurtenances in Thoresdaymarket and Swynegale which he had by
the lease of the Abbot and Convent of Coverham.

Term. 72 years if the said William should live so long. He was to
have the right of distraint should the rent be forty days in arrears.

Also two sets of vestments, a missal, breviary, chalice and other
ornaments in Holy Trinity Church, King's Court, already in his
care, for the term of his life. He was to celebrate divine service for
the said John and Alice, his wife, so long as he was able.

Witnesses. William de Helmeslay, Mayor, Thomas del Gare,

---

[3]*housegabul*: house rent or tax.

Robert Tothe, John de Raghton, Bailiffs, John de Bolton, Robert de Louthe, William de Ruston.

Given at York, 10 January 1394/5, 18 Richard II.   [Latin]

(ff. 19-19v) QUITCLAIM.

Denise, wife of the late John de Castell,

to John de Doncastre, citizen and merchant of York,

a messuage with shops and all other buildings and appurtenances in which John Blakhorneby lately dwelt in Fesegale, lying in width between the messuage formerly of John, son of Simon Kyngesson of York, and the tenement of the Master and Chaplains of the Horsfayre, and in length from the high street in front to the land which John de Kirkham once held behind; a shop and the upper storeys in Fesegale, lying between the land formerly of Adam del Dyk and the land formerly of William de Nonyngton; and the rent of 8s p.a. received from the tenement of the said John, son of Simon Kyngesson in Fesegale.

Witnesses. William de Helmeslay, Mayor, Robert Tothe, Thomas del Gare, John de Raghton, Bailiffs, Thomas Gra, John de Houeden, William Palmer, John Wrawby, John Brynne, John Sythre, John Elleswyk.

Given at York, 25 January 1394/5, 18 Richard II.   [Latin]

QUITCLAIM.

Thomas de Acastre of York,

to John de Doncastre, citizen and merchant of York,

the messuage with shops and all other buildings and appurtenances in which John Blakhorneby lately dwelt in Fesegale [as above].

Witnesses. William de Helmeslay, Mayor, Robert Tothe, Thomas del Gare, John de Raghton, Bailiffs, Thomas Gra, John de Houeden, William Palmer, John Wrawby, John Brynne, John Sithre, John Elleswyk.

Given at York, 28 January 1394/5, 18 Richard II.   [Latin]

(ff. 19v-20) QUITCLAIM.

John de Horselay and Robert de Yukflete, chaplains,

to William de Saundeby,

the manor of Saundeby [Saundby] in the County of Nottingham, which the said John and Robert together with the late John Pikeryng, then Parson of St. Mary's Church in Castelgate, had by

the gift and feoffment of Meliora, wife of the late Adam de Rother-
feld, knight.

Witnesses. Thomas Hersy, John de Leek, Thomas de Rymeston,
knights, John de Markham of Markham, John de Gaytforth,
Gregory de Dunham and Robert Cressee of Markham.

Given, 29 August 1395, 19 Richard II.   [Latin]

FEOFFMENT.

John Daunay, son of Thomas Daunay of Escryk,
    to John de Stillyngton of York, mercer, and Richard de Fourneys,
    chaplain,
lands and tenements, rents and services in Huntyngton near York
which the said Thomas, his father, had by the gift and feoffment of
William de Ulveston, late citizen of York.

Witnesses. William Darell, John de Kenlay, William Halgate,
Robert de Huntyngton, John de Snaweshill.

Given at Huntyngton, 18 September 1395, 19 Richard II.
                                                        [Latin]

(ff. 20-20v) QUITCLAIM.

John Daunay,
    to John de Stillyngton and Richard de Fourneys,
lands and tenements, rents and services at Huntyngton [as above].

Witnesses. Robert Warde, Robert de Louthe, John de Craven,
John del More, Richard de Soureby.

Given at York, 20 September 1395, 19 Richard II.   [Latin]

GRANT.

John Daunay,
    to John de Stillyngton,
the rent of 100s. p.a. from all his lands and tenements in York and
the county of the same. If it was not paid on the feasts of St. Martin
in Winter and Whit Sunday each year, he was to have the right
of distraint. For better assurance John Daunay had given John de
Stillyngton one silver penny of the rent in the name of seisin.

Witnesses. Robert Warde, Robert de Louthe, John de Bolton,
John de Craven, John del More, William de Ruston.

Given at York, 22 September 1395, 19 Richard II.   [Latin]

(ff. 20v-21) DEFEASANCE.

John de Stillyngton,
    to John Daunay,

of the latter's grant of an annual rent of 100s. from his lands and tenements in York and the county of the same, provided he, John de Stillyngton, and Richard de Fourneys, chaplain, should have peaceful possession of the lands and tenements at Huntyngton which they had by the gift and feoffment of John Daunay, free from all claims except the dower of Ellen, wife of John Daunay.

Given at York, 22 September 1395, 19 Richard II.   [Latin]

(ff. 21-21v) QUITCLAIM.

Thomas de Laycestre, son of William de Laycestre, kinsman and heir of John de Rypon, late citizen of York,

to John de Thornton and William de Pountfrayt, citizens and drapers of York,

a messuage on the Pavement, lying in width between the land of the hospital of St. Leonard and the land of Thomas de Neuport, son and heir of William de Neuport, and in length from the high street in front to the land of the said hospital behind. John de Thornton and William de Pountfrayt had the messuage by the gift and feoffment of Alice, wife of the late John de Rypon and grandmother of the said Thomas, and of William de Laycestre, his father.

Witnesses. William Frost, Mayor, John del More and Thomas de Houeden, Sheriffs, John de Brathwayt, John de Quixlay, John de Penreth, Thomas de Santon, Peter de Appilton, clerk.

Given at York, 19 February 1396/7, 20 Richard II.   [Latin]

FEOFFMENT.

John de Kilburn and John de Carmell, chaplains, and John de Essheton,

to William de Thresk of York, walker, Ellen, his wife, and the heirs of their bodies, with the remainder to the heirs and assigns of William,

a messuage which the feoffors had by the gift and feoffment of Peter Kok of York, trumpeter, lying in Walmegate in the parish of St. Mary the Virgin and St. Margaret, in width between the tenement lately of John de Pathorn and that lately of William de Skelton, and in length from Walmegate in front to the Foss behind.

Witnesses. Robert Sauvage, Mayor, John de Craven, William Vescy, John de Penreth, Bailiffs, Robert de Elvyngton, John de Welton, Thomas del Wolde, John de Wyllerdby, John Bruys.

Given at York, 5 December 15 Richard II [1391]   [Latin]

LETTERS OF ATTORNEY.

John de Kilburn, John Carmell, and John de Essheton,
 to John de Ryvaux, barker, and Peter de Appilton, clerk,
to deliver seisin to William de Thresk and Ellen, his wife, of a
messuage in Walmegate.
 (f. 22) Given at York, 5 December 15 Richard II [1391].

[Latin]

QUITCLAIM.

Margaret Barbour of York, daughter and co-heiress of John Ayer
 of Wolleston,
 to Thomas de Weston, clerk, Peter del Hay, *scutifer*,[4] Thomas
 Gretham and Reginald Port, clerks,
lands and tenements, rents and services in Wolleston [? Wolviston,
Co. Durham] which the said Thomas, Peter, Thomas and Reginald
had by the gift and grant of Robert de Bisshopton of Eryom [Ery-
holme] on Tees, and John, his son, clerk.
 Witnesses. William de Fulthorp, Marmaduke de Lumley, knights,
Alan Lambard, William de Blakyston, William, son of Alan de
Wolleston and John de Pothowe.
 Given, 8 September 1398. [Latin]

QUITCLAIM.

Hugh Dunnok, John de Cotyngham and Nicholas del Withe,
 chaplain,
 to Isolda, wife of the late John de Acastre,
lands and tenements in the City and suburbs of York which the said
Hugh, John and Nicholas had by the gift and legacy of John de
Acastre.
 Witnesses. John de Gyseburn, Mayor, Robert Warde, Robert de
Talkan, Richard de Alghne, Bailiffs, Thomas Gra, Thomas de
Holme, John Berden.
 Given at York, 20 April 3 Richard II [1380]. [Latin]

(f. 22v.) WILL.

of William de Ledes, son and heir of Roger de Ledes, knight,
devising the manor of Okewell [Oakwell], to Joan, his mother, for
life, at 6os. rent p.a. payable to William Burgoigne, and after her
death it was to remain to the testator's heirs. His lands and tene-

---

[4] *scutifer*: esquire, literally shield-bearer.

ments in Morlay and Burlay were to be sold by the feoffees and the money used to satisfy his debts and those of Roger his father, and the residue employed for the good of their souls. All his other lands and tenements in the County of York he left to his right heirs.

Joan, his mother, was to have the manor of Ledes [Leeds] for life, to enable her to pay to Elizabeth and Katherine, his sisters, £20 each as a marriage portion. If either should die, the survivor was to receive the whole of the money.

Rents from the said manor of Ledes were to be paid as follows: to John Marsshall, his kinsman, for life, 20s.; to William Forester, his servant, for life, 13s. 4d.; to John Coke, his servant, for life, 13s. 4d.; to Dakyn Birche, his servant, for life, 13s. 4d.; to Robert de Brompton, chaplain, 20s. or a boy called Jak; to John de Morlay, chaplain, 6s. 8d. The residue of his goods was to be disposed of by Joan his mother as seemed best for the good of his soul.

Appointment of Joan, his mother, Thomas Gra, and William Burgoigne as executors.

Given at York, 22 July 1400.　　　　　　　　　　　　　[Latin]

(f. 23) QUITCLAIM

William Palmer, executor of the will of Richard de Wadeby, late citizen and merchant of York,

to William de Neusome, esquire, Joan, his wife, and the heirs and assigns of the said Joan,

lands and tenements in the City and suburbs of York which he had by the will of the said Richard.

Witnesses. William Frost, Mayor, Thomas de Doncastre, John de Bernardcastell, Sheriffs, Thomas Thurkill, Recorder, Thomas Gra, William de Selby.

Given at York, 12 July 1400, 1 Henry IV.　　　　　　　[Latin]

QUITCLAIM.

Robert, son of William de Burghbrigg, late of York, fishmonger,

to Thomas del Gare, citizen and merchant of York,

tenements with buildings and appurtenances which belonged to Adam Berlot, late citizen of York, lying in Netherousegate, in width between the land now of John de Kilburn, but formerly of Robert de Wystowe, on one side towards the east, and the lane called Fishelendyng below and the land formerly of William Fairefax above, on the other side towards the west, and extending in length from Netherousegate in front to the land lately of John de Lyndesay which Thomas Clyff once held, behind. Alice, wife of the said Robert son of William de Burghbrigg, and daughter of Adam Berlot, had the tenements by her father's will.

Witnesses. William Frost, Mayor, John de Wraueby, Edmund Cottesbroke, Sheriffs, John de Bolton, John de Appilton, John de Thorneton, John de Penreth, William del Bothe, clerk.

Given at York, 26 March 1401, 2 Henry IV.   [Latin]

(f. 23v.) FEOFFMENT.

Robert Sauvage, citizen and merchant of York,
to Thomas Smyth, citizen and merchant of York, and William de Rillyngton, chaplain,
a tenement in Northstrete in which the feoffor lived, lying between the tenement of the late William Burn, citizen and merchant, on the south and the lane called Develynstanes on the north, and in length from Northstrete in front to the River Ouse behind.

Witnesses. William Frost, Mayor, Thomas Houeden, John del More, Sheriffs, Richard Alne, William Alne, Henry Couper, Henry Burton, John Wraueby.

Given at York, on the [feast] of the——⁶ of the Holy Cross, 21 Richard II [1397].   [Latin]

QUITCLAIM.

William Sauvage, son and heir of Robert Sauvage, late citizen and merchant of York,
to William de Rillyngton, chaplain,
the tenement in Northstrete [as above] which William de Rillyngton and Thomas Smyth, citizen and merchant, deceased, had by the feoffment of Robert Sauvage, his father.

Witnesses. William Frost, Mayor, William Bowes, William del Lee, Sheriffs, Robert de Talkan, John Braythwayt, John de Raghton, Edmund Cottesbroke.

Given at York, 6 January 3 Henry IV [1402].   [Latin]

(f. 24) QUITCLAIM.

John son of Thomas Rabuk, late of York, skinner,
to Thomas Gra, son of William Gra,

⁶ Word illegible.

the tenement in Castelgate, which William Gra had by the gift and feoffment of the said John, situated in width between the land of the said Thomas on the one side, and the land formerly of William de Wirkesworth and the land of the Mayor and Commonalty of York on the other side, and in length from the churchyard of St. Mary, Castlegate, in front to the land of John de Kenlay behind.

Witnesses. William Frost, Mayor, William Bowes, William del Lee, Sheriffs, William Selby, John Braythwayte, William Pountfrayte, John de Quixlay, John Kenlay, William del Bothe of York, clerk.

Given at York, 3 February 1401/2, 3 Henry IV.   [Latin]

QUITCLAIM.
John Sauvage, son of Robert Sauvage, citizen and merchant, of York, deceased,
to William de Ryllyngton, chaplain,
the tenement in Northstrete [as above], of which William de Ryllyngton and Thomas Smyth, merchant, deceased, were enfeoffed by Robert, his father.

Witnesses. William Frost, Mayor, William Bowes, William del Lee, Sheriffs, Robert de Talkan, John Braythwayte, John Raghton, Edmund Cottesbroke, Robert de Rypon, Geoffrey Sauvage.

Given at York, 4 February 3 Henry IV [1402].   [Latin]

(f. 24v) QUITCLAIM.
Robert de Laton, son of John de Laton of Mersk,
to Thomas de Doncastre of York, mercer, and Alice, his wife,
lands and tenements in Mersk [Marske] which the said Robert had by the gift and feoffment of Richard Mersk, his maternal uncle, late Rector of the Church of Great Langton on Swale.

Witnesses. William Frost, Mayor, Adam del Brigg, Thomas de Santon, Sheriffs, Robert Louthe, Richard de Soureby, Thomas Bracebrigg.

Given at York, 9 June 1403, 4 Henry IV.   [Latin]

(f. 24v-25) QUITCLAIM.
Geoffrey de Crauncewyk, mason, son of John de Crauncewyk, to William Frost, son of Thomas Frost of Beverley, and William his son,

lands and tenements which belonged to William Crauncewyk of Huton Crauncewyk, senior, in Huton Crauncewyk [Hutton Cranswick], Driffeld, Wetewang [Wetwang], and Fymmer [Fimber] and elsewhere in the County of York.

Witnesses. Sir John de Hothom, Sir John Godard, Sir Edmund de Kyllyngwyk, knights, Hugh de Ardern, Philip de Lound, Ed. de Hothom, John Arnald.

Given 21 November 14 Richard II [1390].   [Latin]

(ff. 25-25v) FEOFFMENT.

John de Norton, Parson of the church of Folketon [Folkton] and John de Hogate, chaplain,

to Agnes, wife of the late William Fyssh of York, for life, remainder to Adam de Wellom and Mary his wife, their heirs and assigns,

lands and tenements in the City and suburbs of York which the said Agnes had by the wills of Agnes her daughter, wife of William son of Arnold de Rypon, and of the said William Fyssh, and which the feoffors had by her gift and feoffment. The said Agnes was to have one copy of the deed, and Adam de Wellom and Mary, his wife, the other.

Witnesses. John de Langton, Mayor, John de Twyselton, Richard de Thoresby, Robert de Pottowe, Bailiffs, Robert de Howom, Ralph de Romondby, John de Middelton, John de Boulton, mercer, Robert de Harom.

Given at York, 2 February 38 Edward III [1364].   [Latin]

(ff. 25v-26) RESIGNATION.

of Henry de Clytherowe, chaplain,

from the perpetual chantry at the altar of St. John the Baptist and St. Katherine in the Church of St. Martin in Mikelgate, founded by Richard Toller, late citizen of York; acknowledging that the disposition of the said chantry belonged to the Mayor and Commonalty.

The resignation was made publicly in the Church of St. Saviour before William Frost, Mayor, John de Stanton, public notary, Master John Harwodd, advocate of the Court of York, and Adam Wygan, public notary, Thomas Cundall, priest, John Howeden and John Eston, citizens of York, and a deed was drawn up by John de Stanton, public notary.

Given, 19 April 1404, the 12th year of the Indiction,[7] and the 15th year of the pontificate of Pope Boniface IX.   [Latin]

GIFT.

John Jerrard, citizen and merchant of York,
   to John Holbek, merchant, William Roundell, Thomas Bracebrigg, mercer, and Thomas de Neuton, coverlet weaver,
all his goods and chattels and all debts owed to him.

Witnesses. Robert de Talkan, Mayor, Thomas de Doncastre, John Bernardcastell, Sheriffs, Robert Crosby, John de Craven, baker.

Given at York, on the feast of St. Hillary, 1 Henry IV [13 January 1400].   [Latin]

(ff. 26-26v) QUITCLAIM.

Roger Crome, citizen of York,
   to Agnes, wife of the late John Fissheburn,
lands and tenements in Lownelyth in York, which the said Roger and Peter de Routhe had by the gift and feoffment of John Fissheburn and Agnes his wife, lying in width between the land of John de Langton on the east and the city walls on the west, and in length from Lownelyth in front to the Old Baile behind.

Witnesses. William Frost, Mayor, Henry de Preston and Richard del Howe, Sheriffs, Adam del Banke, William Vessy, John Kenlay, Robert Londesdale.

Given at York, on the vigil of St. Laurence [9 August] 1404, 5 Henry IV.

[Marginal note:] Memorandum, made on the acknowledgment of Roger Crome, 22 December 6 Henry IV [1404].   [Latin]

ACQUITTANCE.

John de Houeden,
   to Thomas Doncastre, merchant of York,
of £160 and all other debts due from the said Thomas; reciting a deed sealed at Caleys [Calais] whereby the late William de Sutton, as attorney of Thomas Doncastre, merchant, had bound himself and the said Thomas, in £160, to John de Houeden and William Agland, merchants of York.

Given at York, 10 February 6 Henry IV [1405].   [French]

---

[7] By the end of the thirteenth century the use of the indiction year in dating was rare except in documents drawn up by public notaries (see C. R. Cheney, *Handbook of Dates*, p. 2).

(ff. 26v-27v) FEOFFMENT AND GRANT.[8]

John de Grafton and John de Parisius of York, chaplains,
to Richard to Brignall, citizen and merchant of York, for life,
remainder to John Brignall, his son, and Juliana his wife, and the
heirs of their bodies begotten, remainder to the right heirs of the
said Richard,

three messuages in York and the rent of two others, all of which the
said John de Grafton and John de Parisius had by the gift and
feoffment and the grant of Richard de Brignall: —

[1] a messuage in Petergate, in width between the land formerly
of William de Capella, chaplain, and the land formerly of Margery
de Wyghton, and in length from Petergate to the land of the
Master and Brethren of St. Leonard's Hospital.

[2] a messuage in Northstrete, in width between the land formerly
of Richard Tunnock and the land formerly of Henry le Ku, and
in length from Northstrete to the River Ouse.

[3] a messuage in Felterlane, in width between the land of
William de Clapham and the land formerly of John Ithon, and
in length from Felterlane to the land of the said William de
Clapham.

[4] 10s. p.a. rent from the messuage formerly of John de Whitwell in Litelgate on Bysshophill, lying in width between the land
formerly of the said John and that formerly of Sir John de Walkyng-
ham, and in length from Litelgate to the land formerly of the said
Sir John.

[5] 5s. p.a. rent from the tenement of John le Sporier in Nessegate and Kergate, lying in width in Nessegate between the land
formerly of William de Quixelay and that formerly of Richard
Toller, and in length from Nessegate in front to the land of John
de Skauceby behind, and in Kergate between the land formerly of
the said Richard Toller and the land of the said John de Skauceby.

The feoffee was to have the right of distraint if the rents were in
arrears.

Witnesses. John de Shirburn, Mayor, John Tuk, John de Coupmanthorp, Bailiffs, Richard de Allerton, John de Woume, Nicholas
de Scorby, Stephen de Seteryngton, John Duraunt, William de

---

[8] This deed would appear from the context to have been made after the one
following. It seems likely, therefore, that the latter was dated the Friday after the
feast of the *translation* of St. Thomas the Martyr, 9 July 1344, not 31 December
1344.

Acastre, John Raudman, John de Soureby, Andrew Bogher, Henry le Scrop of Manfeld, Thomas son of Nigel de Menythorp, Richard de Heselyngton of York, clerk.

Given at York, the Wednesday after the feast of St. James the Apostle [28 July] 1344, 18 (France 5) Edward [III].   [Latin]

(ff. 27v-28) FEOFFMENT AND GRANT.
The deed of Richard Brignall registered at the instance of Thomas Houeden.

Richard de Brignall, of York,
to John de Grafton and John de Parisius of York, chaplains,
three messuages and the rents from two others [as above].

[1] the messuage in Petergate which he had by the gift and feoffment of John de Bristoll.

[2] the messuage in Northstrete which he had by the gift of Matill. de Seteryngton of York, litster.

[3] the messuage in Felterlane which he had by the gift of Elizabeth, wife of Robert Hardy.

[4] 10s. p.a. rent from the messuage in Litelgate on Bisshophill, which he had by grant of Agnes, wife of the late William de Moubray of Eseby in Clyveland [Easby in Cleveland].

[5] 5s. p.a. rent from a tenement in Nessegate and Kergate, which he had by the grant of the said Agnes.

The feoffees were to have the right of distraint if the rents were in arrears.

Witnesses. John de Shirburn, Mayor, John Tuck, John de Coupmanthorp, Bailiffs, John de Woume, Stephen de Seteryngton, John Duraunt, John de Bristoll, Hamon de Hessay, Henry le Goldbeter, John de Soureby, John de Catton, William de Acastre, Henry Lescrop of Manfeld, Andrew Bogher, Richard de Heselyngton of York, clerk.

Given at York, the Friday after the feast of St. Thomas the Martyr, Archbishop of Canterbury [31 December] 1344, 18 (France 5) Edward [III][9]   [Latin]

(ff. 28-28v) GIFT.
John de Crofton, citizen and merchant of York,
to Robert de Middelton, citizen and mercer,
all his goods and chattels and all debts owed to him.

[9] See footnote on the preceding deed.

Witnesses. William Frost, Mayor, John de Bedall, John de Wyton, Sheriffs, Thomas de Middelham, William del Bothe, clerk.

Given at York, 5 November 6 Henry IV [1404].   [Latin]

GRANT.

Richard de Plesyngton of York, tailor, and Cicely his wife,
to John de Plesyngton of York, their son,
two messuages in Mekilgate, lying in length from Mekilgate in front to Northstrete behind, and in width between the land of Robert Barry on the one side and the land of the Rector of the Church of St. Gregory and the land of John de Ripon on the other.
Rent. 10s. p.a. to Sir John de Pert, knight, his heirs and assigns.
Witnesses. Robert Sauvage, Mayor, William Vescy, John de Craven and John de Penreth, Bailiffs, Richard de Taunton, John de Cessay, John de Kilvyngton, Robert de Thorlethorp, John de Drynghous, John de Wighton, Thomas de Rigton.
(f. 29) Given at York, 10 February 1391/2, 15 Richard II.
[Latin]

QUITCLAIM.

Marginal note:— The remission of Richard de Plesyngton signed in the presence of Adam del Bank, Mayor, and shown on oath that the said son received seisin as specified.

Richard de Plesyngton, citizen of York,
to John de Plesyngton, citizen of York, his son,
two messuages with three gardens and buildings and appurtenances in Mikelgate [as above].
Witnesses. Adam del Bank, Mayor, John Bedale, John Wyton, Sheriffs, John de Sutton, marshal, Thomas Buscy, William Neuland, Richard Neuland, John Wardell, saddler, John de Thwayt, weaver.
Given at York, 12 April 1405, 6 Henry IV.   [Latin]

(ff. 29-29v) FEOFFMENT.

Ranulph del See, son of Richard del See,
to William de Collom, chaplain, John Cosyn, citizen and merchant of London and John Whitwell, chaplain,
lands and tenements in the City and suburbs of York and the county of the same, which descended to the said Ranulph on the death of Richard, his father.

Witnesses. Robert Sauvage, Mayor, John de Craven, William Vescy, John de Penreth, Bailiffs, Hugh Straunge, William de Rumlay, Richard de Soureby.

Given at York, 26 January 14 Richard II [1391].   [Latin]

LETTERS OF ATTORNEY.

John Cosyn, citizen and merchant of London,

 to John Percehay, citizen and merchant of York, and Richard del See son of Ranulph del See, esquire,

to receive the rents from the lands and tenements which he had by the gift and feoffment of the said Ranulph del See.

 [Undated]   [Latin]

(ff. 29v-30) GRANT OF ANNUITY.

The Mayor, Sheriffs, Aldermen and Commonalty of the City of York,

 to John Gude, officer at mace, in recognition of good and faithful service,

40s. p.a. for life to be paid by the Chamberlains, at the Exchequer in the Council Chamber on Ouse Bridge, quarterly on the feasts of the Nativity of Our Lord, Easter, the Nativity of St. John the Baptist and the feast of St. Michael the Archangel.

It was also granted that he should carry the mace in the presence of the Mayor and his successors during his lifetime and also, if he wished, make attachments and summonses as was fitting for an officer at mace, receiving nothing from the citizens for so doing unless it was freely given.

Given at York, under the common seal of the city, the Monday after the feast of St. Michael the Archangel [3 October] 1412, 14 Henry IV.   [Latin]

Here follow and are compiled the tenors of various deeds made between foreign persons [*personas extraneas*], beginning in the time of Thomas Gare, Mayor of York, by Roger de Burton, public notary, Common Clerk of this honourable city.   [Latin]

(ff. 30-30v) DEMISE.

William Lion, citizen of York, and Agnes his wife,

 to John Stafford, senior, citizen of York,

a messuage with buildings and appurtenances in Fossegate, lying in width between the land formerly of William Palmer and the land of John Clerk, and in length from Fossegate in front to the River Foss behind.

Term. 24 years from Whit Sunday 1420, 8 Henry V.

Rent. A red rose annually on Whit Sunday.

John Stafford, his heirs and assigns were to repair all timber, walls and roofs.

If the said William and Agnes and the heirs of their bodies begotten should die during the said term, John Stafford and his heirs were to have the messuage, and pay 10s. to the church wardens of St. Crux in Fossegate to be used for the good of the souls of William and Agnes, as directed by the executors named in their will.

Witnesses. Thomas Gare, Mayor, John Bolton and Thomas Davy, Sheriffs, John Waghen, Thomas Warde, John Clerk.

Given, 16 May [1420].   [Latin]

BOND.

William Lion and Agnes, his wife,
 to John Stafford, senior,
in 100 marks to be paid on Whit Sunday next, to ensure the latter's peaceful possession of a messuage in Fossegate.

Given, 20 July 8 Henry V [1420].   [Latin]

FEOFFMENT.

William Lion, and Agnes his wife,
 to William Eston and John Aunwik, chaplains, and John Stafford, junior,
a messuage in Fossegate [as above].

Witnesses. Thomas Gare, Mayor, John Bolton, and Thomas Davy, Sheriffs, John Waghen, Thomas Warde, John Clerk.

Given, 18 May 8 Henry V [1420].   [Latin]

(ff. 30v-31) DEFEASANCE.

William Eston and John Aunwik, chaplains, and John Stafford, junior,
 to William Lion and Agnes his wife,
of their feoffment with livery of seisin of the messuage in Fossegate, provided John Stafford, senior, should have peaceful possession of the same messuage for twenty-four years according to the lease of the said William and Agnes.

Witnesses. Thomas Gare, Mayor, John Bolton, and Thomas

Davy, Sheriffs, John Waghen, Thomas Warde, John Clerk.
Given, 18 May [1420].   [Latin]

(ff. 31-32) INSPEXIMUS AND CONFIRMATION.[10]

John de Castell, Prior of the Monastery of Holy Trinity, York,
of the order of St. Benedict, and the Convent of the same, patrons
of St. Cuthbert's Church, of the following feoffment: —

Robert Lincoln, Rector of St. Cuthbert's Church in Peseholm,
York, William Craven, son of John Craven, Richard Ferrour,
wright, and John Muston, barker, parishioners and *kyrk-
maisters* of the said church, William Gyselay, clerk, Walter
Sparowe and William Jonson, fellow parishioners, with the
consent of all the parishioners,

to John Richemond and Henry Topclif, chaplains, and William
Bowes, citizen and merchant of York,

a piece of waste land formerly of John Langton, son of John Langton, in the said parish, lying in width in front towards the high
street of Peseholm between the land of the said John Langton son
of John Langton, then in the tenure of Richard Ferrour, and the
churchyard of St. Cuthbert's, and containing 5 ells, and extending
from the front alongside the land of John Langton son of John
Langton, as far as the land of Robert Lincoln, Rector of the church,
behind, in length 29 ells, and on the side of the churchyard from
the front to the land of Robert Lincoln behind, in length 24½ ells.
In building houses on the land they were to be allowed to build
a *gette*[11] of reasonable size within the churchyard, according to the
advice of carpenters and other craftsmen.

Rent. 8d. p.a. to the Rector of the said church and 8d. p.a. to the
parishioners for work on the fabric of the church. If the rents were
ever forty days in arrears the feoffors were to have the right of
distraint.

The burial of bodies in the churchyard would not be impeded,
but rather the convenience of the church and parishioners would
be increased in future.

For greater security the Mayor's seal was affixed to both parts
of the indenture.

Witnesses. John de Moreton, Mayor, Robert Midelton and John

---

[10] Badly damaged by damp.
[11] *gette*, jetty, projecting part of a building, especially an overhanging upper
storey.

Baynbrig, Sheriffs, Nicholas Blakburn, senior, Robert Howom, Thomas Santon, William Alne, Richard Russell, John Bedale.

Given at York, 11 November 1418, 6 Henry V.

Confirmed at York in the Chapter House of Holy Trinity, and sealed with the common seal of the Priory, on the feast of the Conversion of St. Paul, 6 Henry V [25 January 1419].

Subscribed. Burton. [Latin]

GRANT OF FACULTY.[12]

Henry [Bowet] Archbishop of York,
to John Richemond, and Henry Topclif, chaplains, and William Bowes, citizen and merchant of York,
permitting them to build on the piece of waste land adjoining St. Cuthbert's churchyard, [as above].

[Undated.]
Subscribed: Burton. [Latin]

(f. 32v) WILL.[13]

of Richard Alne, citizen and tanner of York,
desiring burial in his parish church of All Saints', Northstrete, in the choir of St. Nicholas, and bequeathing to that church a white vestment with a cope to be used on feast days of the Blessed Mary and at all other suitable occasions, except for mass in the churching of women; and 20s. to the fabric of the church and for his burial;
to Robert, his son, 40 marks and the best piece of silver with a cover, half a dozen cushions with the heads of leopards, a coloured back-cloth [*doser stenyd*], with a picture from the history of Guy de Warwyk,[14] the best bed with appurtenances, a basin and pitcher and one dozen vessels of *peutre garnysh*.[15]

A tenement in Northstrete, formerly of Roger Bolyngbroke, 10s. rent from a tenement formerly of John Sturgys in York and the reversion of another tenement in Northstrete which Emma, the widow of John de Walkyngton held for life, to Robert, his son for life—the latter to pay 10s. p.a. for the testator's obit in the said

[12] Badly damaged by damp.
[13] All except the first few lines are completely illegible except under ultra-violet light.
[14] According to the legend, Guy de Warwick slew both a savage dragon which was devastating Northumberland and the Danish giant Colbrand at Winchester. (*Dictionary of National Biography*.)
[15] garnish, a set of vessels for table use, especially of pewter.

parish church and for mass to be celebrated the same day for the
souls of his father and Alice, his late wife—remainder to William
his son and the heirs of his body begotten [? on the same condition
as to Robert his son] remainder to the Master for the time being of
St. Peter's College [Peterhouse], Cambridge, in mortmain.—— The
Master and Fellows in their robes —— at the church should celebrate—— the *Placebo and Dirige*—— and on the following day,
Requiem mass was to be celebrated by the sub-deacon, for his soul
and for Alice his wife, and 10s. was then to be distributed equally
among the Master and Fellows taking part in the services——.

Given the last day of September 1408, [9?] Henry IV.

(ff. 32v-33). CODICIL.

Master Robert de Alne, his son, should not have the fee simple
of a tenement, formerly of Thomas de Walmegate, son and heir of
John de Walmegate, late citizen of York, situated in Northstrete in
width between the land formerly of Thomas de Cheworth and that
formerly of Thomas de Ingilby. The tenement of Roger de Bolyngbroke in Northstrete, the rent of 10s. from the tenement formerly
of John Sturgys in Northstrete, and the reversion of the tenement
which Emma, wife of the late John Walkyngton held for life,
should not pass to St. Peter's College, Cambridge.

Witnesses. Brother William Helmesley, of the preaching order
[Dominican], doctor, Adam del Bank, formerly Mayor, William
del Both, clerk, John Helmesley, merchant of York.

Given, 19 March 1408/9.

Probate and the administration of the goods of the deceased were
granted to William son of the deceased and John de Burneby,
executors, on 11 May 1409, and to Master Robert Alne, co-executor,
on 18 May 1409.

[Registered] at the request of Master Robert Alne, 10 January
1420/1, 8 Henry V, and in the mayoralty of Thomas Gare.

[Latin]

LETTERS OF ATTORNEY.

Robert del Alne, clerk,
    to Thomas Roderham, citizen of York,
to seek and distrain for the rents of the tenements formerly of
Roger Bolyngbrok and John Walkyngton in Northstrete, and 10s.
rent from a tenement of John Sturgys in Northstrete.

(f. 33v) Given, 3 January 8 Henry V [1420/1].　　　[Latin]

(ff. 33v-34v) WILL.
　of William Sauvage, son of Ralph Sauvage, late citizen and
　merchant of York,
desiring burial in the church of St. Mary, Castelgate, next to the
body of Isabel de Petirfeld, his aunt, and making the following
bequests: —
to the Rector of that church, his best vestment as a mortuary gift;
15 pounds of wax to burn around his body at the funeral services
and at mass on the day of his burial; six torches of wax each
weighing 12 pounds to burn at his funeral services and at mass on
the day of his burial, at various altars in the church—two at the
high altar, one at the altar of St. Mary where the chantry of Thomas
Howme is founded, one at the altar of St. John the Baptist, one
at the altar of St. Thomas of Canterbury and another at the altar
in the chapel at the west end of the church where the tenth
mass is celebrated daily; all other funeral expenses to be made at
the discretion of his executors.

　On the day of his burial there was to be no general distribution
to the poor, but his executors were to go through the streets and
lanes of the city and distribute to the weak and bed-ridden according to their discretion; to every order of mendicant friars in the
city, 6s. 8d; to every man and woman in the houses called Maisen-
dieux within the city and suburbs and in the leper houses in the
suburbs, 1d.; provided that the distributions to the friars and the
poor were not made in his lifetime.

　On the day of his burial, there should be no communal feast
or other large meal except with the Rector, chaplains and clerks of
that church and other honest persons with whom he was accustomed to associate, according to the discretion of his executors.

　He bequeathed to every chaplain of the said parish church, 6d;
to the parish clerk, 6d; to the sub-clerk 4d; and to the parish chaplain of the same church, 2s.; to John Wharton, servant of John
Werkesworth, 20s.; to John West and Joan Hunter, servants of the
said John Werkesworth, 6s. 8d. each; to John Werkesworth and
Joan his wife, their heirs and assigns, his tenement without Mykel-
lith in which William, son of John Sauvage, late citizen of York,
dwelt, a tenement in Walmegate in the parish of St. Margaret, two
strips of land without Fysshergate in the suburbs of York, which

Katherine, wife of the late Thomas Hesill, citizen and merchant of
York, held of him, a garden in Stanebowe lane in the parish of St.
Crux in Fossegate, and another garden in the parish of St. John
the Baptist in Hundgate; to John Dodyngton and Joan his wife,
his kinswoman, their heirs and assigns, a tenement in Northstrete
in the parish of St. John the Evangelist at Ouse Bridge end; to
William, his kinsman, son of John Sauvage, forgiveness for his
debts; to John Werkesworth and Joan his wife, their heirs and
assigns, all his tenements in Petirgate and Patrikpole which he had
by the gift and feoffment of John, son of Matilda de Aldeburgh, for
which they were to pay 5 marks p.a. to Robert Cooke, chaplain,
and his successors for the daily celebration for the souls of John
Eryum and Juliana his wife, in the chantry founded in the chapel
on Ouse Bridge. When the office of chaplain should become vacant,
they were to present another and place the said rent in his possession; to John Werkesworth and Joan, his wife, their heirs and
assigns, an annual rent of 40s, another annual rent of 5s. from a
tenement in Hertergate and Thruslane, formerly of Thomas Hesill
and Agnes his wife, by the right of the said Agnes, an annual rent
of 5s. from a tenement in Conyngstrete in the parish of St. Michael
at Ouse Bridge end, which formerly belonged to William de
Everingham, late citizen and cordwainer of York, an annual rent
of 18s. from a tenement on the Pament in the parish of St. Crux
in Fossegate, formerly of John de Berden, sometime Mayor of
York, in which John Holgate now lives, an annual rent of 5s. from
a tenement in Thoresdaymarket at the end of Fesegale which
formerly belonged to Walter Baxster, late citizen of York, and an
annual rent of 2s. from three tenements in Mikel Saynt Andrewgate
belonging to the chantry of St. John the Baptist in the Cathedral
Church of St. Peter, which Thomas Northhouse vicar in that
Cathedral now holds. From the profits of the said tenements, the
annual rents and the residue of his goods not otherwise bequeathed,
John Werkesworth and Joan his wife were to provide a suitable
and honest chaplain to celebrate mass for four years after the
testator's death for the souls of himself and Matilda his wife, his
parents and benefactors, in the Church of St. Mary in Castelgate;
    to Master Edmund de Kyrketon, penitentiary of the Archbishop
in the Cathedral Church of St. Peter, 20s.; to the fabric of that
cathedral, 6s. 8d.; to the fabric of his parish church for his burial,
6s. 8d.; to the clerk for making his will and other services, 20s.; to

each of his executors for his work, 40s.; to Guy Rouclyff, 40s. Guy
Rouclyff was to supervise his will to ensure that his executors
fulfilled his last wishes.

Also reciting his quitclaim to Joan Dodyngton, his kinswoman,
of all those lands and tenements which belonged to John Kyngeson,
her late husband.

Appointment of John Werkesworth and Joan his wife, as
executors.

Given at York, 4 December 1421.

Probate was granted, 22 December 1421, before the Official and
Commissary General of the Court of York, and administration
of the goods of William Sauvage granted to the executors named in
the will.   [Latin]

(ff. 34v-35) FEOFFMENT.[16]

William Sauvage, son of Ralph Sauvage, late citizen and merchant
of York,
   to John Malton, clerk,
two tenements lying together in Northstrete, between the tenement
of William Gayteshevede, citizen and goldsmith, and the tenement
of William Warmouth, citizen and litster, and Emma, his wife, in
which John Byall, citizen and webster, lived, and extending from
Northstrete in front to the tenement of the said William Gayteshevede behind.

Rent. 40s. p.a. during the life of William Sauvage. If the rent was
forty days in arrears, William Sauvage was to have distraint; if it
was unpaid for three months during his lifetime, he was to have
re-entry to the premises.

Witnesses. Richard Russell, Mayor, John Lyllynge, John Gas-
coigne, Sheriffs, John Moreton, Henry Moreton, Robert Burton,
John Lofthouse, John W[arde], mercer, William Rodys, Roger
Selby, spicer, citizens.

Given at York, 28 July 9 Henry V [1421].   [Latin]

(ff. 35-35v) QUITCLAIM.

William Sauvage,
   to John Malton,
two tenements in Northstrete [as above].

Rent and witnesses [as above]

Given at York, 29 July 9 Henry V [1421].   [Latin]

[16] Badly faded in parts.

(ff. 35v-36) WILL.[17]

of Thomas del Abbay, clerk, of York,

bequeathing his best cloak with a hood as a mortuary gift; 4 lbs. of wax to be burned around his body; 12d. to the fabric of St. Olave's Church; 6d. to the parish chaplain and 4d. to the parish clerk. All his tenements in the City and suburbs of York he left to Alice, his wife, for life, with remainder according to the terms of several deeds; the remainder of his goods to Alice, his wife, whom he appointed, together with William Goldsmyth and Juliana his servant, as his executors, to each of whom he bequeathed 3s. 4d.

Given at York, on the vigil of the Assumption of the Blessed Virgin Mary [14 August] 1394.

Codicil.

To the chaplains in St. Mary's Hospital near the Horsfayre, a murrhine vase[18] and a large bronze vessel, after the death of Alice his wife; to Juliana, his servant, 6s. 8d; to each member of the order of mendicant friars in York, 12d; to his brethren of the craft of tailors in York, after the death of Alice, his wife, two messuages in Walmegate in the suburbs of York, saving always the term of forty years leased to William de Barneby of York, wright, for which 40d. p.a. rent was to be paid twice yearly to Thomas de Monkton, his godson, as a marriage portion during his life; to the said brethren, after the death of Alice, his wife, his garden in Fysshergate. The two messuages and garden were not to be sold under penalty of paying £10 to the fabric of the Church of St. Peter and £10 to the Mayor for the repairs of the city walls; to Isabel, his niece, 6s. 8d. and to Richard Rivaux, chaplain, 12d.

His brethren and their successors were to ensure that thirteen masses were sung for his soul and for the souls of all departed brethren in the Church of the Friars Minor in York, on the Friday in the first week of Lent each year.

Given on the vigil of the Purification of the Blessed Virgin Mary, [1 February] 1393/4 [sic].

Probate was granted on 2 January in the said year and administration granted to the executors named, with the right reserved to William Selar.   [Latin]

---

[17] Badly damaged by damp. The entry has been checked against the copy in the Register of Wills, Vol. I, ff. 78v-79.

[18] *Murra*: a substance of which precious vases and other vessels are made.

(f. 36v) FEOFFMENT.

William Selby, citizen of York, and Howisia, his wife,

to John Selby, son of William Selby, citizen of York, weaver, and the male heirs of his body, remainder to the right heirs of the said William Selby,

land with buildings and appurtenances in Walmegate, lying between the land of the Prioress of Wilberfosse, now of John Austanemore on the one side, and the land of Emma de Wyndhyll, now of John Dodyngton on the other, and extending in length from Walmegate in front to the land of Beatrice le Moigne, now of John Northfolk of Naburn, behind.

For greater security the official mayoral seal was affixed to both parts of the deed.

Witnesses. Henry Preston, Mayor, John Austanemore, Thomas Aton, Sheriffs, Thomas Santon, John Northeby, John Waughen, Thomas Lyverton, William Skelton, Thomas Ward.

Given at York, 22 June 1422, 10 Henry V.   [Latin]

(ff. 36v-37) FEOFFMENT.

William de Ottelay, chaplain,

to Warmebold Harlam, citizen and goldsmith of York, and Laurencia, his wife, daughter of William de Selby, citizen of York, and the heirs of their bodies, remainder to the right heirs of Warmebold,

a messuage with buildings and appurtenances in the lane called Petirlane the Littyll, lying between the tenement of William Pountfreyt and John de Thornton, citizens and drapers, on the one side, and the tenement of Robert Barry on the other, and abutting on the common way of the said lane in front and the tenement of Robert de Hovyngham, behind. William de Ottelay had the messuage by the gift and feoffment of the said Warmebold Harlam.

Witnesses. William Frost, Mayor, Robert de Kyrkeby, John de Usburn, Sheriffs, John Brathwayt, John de Thornton, Thomas de Staynley, Henry Wyman, Thomas Kelfeld, John Sharowe.

Given at York, 23 December 1406, 8 Henry IV.   [Latin]

The above deed was shown in the Council Chamber by William Selby, named therein, on 6 October, 1 Henry VI [1422], in the presence of Henry Preston, Mayor, John Moreton, Alderman, Roger de Burton, Common Clerk and public notary, Thomas Warde, John Stafford, senior, John Stafford, junior, John Wandesford. William

Ottelay, chaplain, named in the deed, and John Kylleburn. Warmebold Harlam, also named in the deed, immediately came to the
Council Chamber and affirmed on oath that the deed shown by
William Selby was fictitious, false and forged, because he had never
sealed a deed by which William Ottelay was enfeoffed of the said
messuage, nor delivered seisin to him as mentioned in the deed,
to the intent that he should enfeoff him and Laurencia his wife
of the messuage in fee tail, nor that they should be seised in fee
tail by the said William Ottelay. He, Warmebold, was alone seised
of the messuage by the gift and feoffment of William Ottelay and
John Munkegate and Robert Semer, chaplains, until he enfeoffed
John Stafford, senior, and others.

Similarly, the same day and place, John Wandesford, esquire,
showed before the Mayor and others aforesaid, another deed by
which the said Warmebold enfeoffed William Ottelay, chaplain,
alone in the messuage. At this Warmebold, with great spirit, swore
on oath that the deed was not his but altogether false, fictitious and
forged, and that William Ottelay was never the sole feoffee of the
messuage by his alleged gift and feoffment or by any other means.
And when John Wandesford and William Ottelay declared that the
seal appended to the deed was that of Warmebold, the latter replied
and swore on oath that the seal was not his, that he had not
ordered, intended or wished the deed to be sealed, nor had he
known or heard of the deed before that day. He affirmed that the
seal with which he was accustomed to seal deeds was an armorial
seal, as was agreed by many, bearing a lion rampant with the letters
of his name engraved on the circumference, and showed them the
said seal. Then in the presence of the Mayor and persons aforesaid,
Warmebold offered to wage judicial combat against anyone who
asserted the contrary, saying that anyone who did so was wrong in
his head, and with great spirit he threw down his glove on to the
exchequer table.   [Latin]

(f. 37v) On 11 March, 1 Henry VI [1423], Thomas Warde, clerk,
Sheriff of York, came into the Council Chamber on Ouse Bridge
before Thomas Esyngwald, Mayor, William Bowes, Alderman,
William Brandesby, Chamberlain, and Roger de Burton, Common
Clerk, and showed part of an indenture which was made with his
knowledge and sought its enrolment in the register of deeds, in the
names of John Fyttelyng and Joan, his wife, as follows:—

FEOFFMENT AND ASSIGNMENT OF LEASE.

John Fyttelyng of Hull, merchant, and Joan his wife, formerly
the wife of Richard Wandesford of Caleys [Calais], esquire,
to John Haliday of Heslyngton,
lands and tenements in Fossegate in York and in Queldryk
[Wheldrake] with Queldryk *waterhouses*, which formerly belonged to John Mergrave of Queldryk;
also lands and tenements in Sutton and Neuton which the said
Joan held for life and which formerly belonged to John Mergrave,
for the life of the said Joan.

Rent. 10 marks pa. to John Fittelyng and Joan his wife, for the
life of Joan, from the lands and tenements in Fossegate, Queldryk,
Sutton and Neuton. John Fittelyng and Joan, his wife, were to have
distraint if the rent was forty days in arrears, and re-entry if it was
six months in arrears.

Witnesses. Richard Russell, Mayor, John Aldstanmore and
Thomas Aton, Sheriffs, Thomas Liverton, John Skyrmer, Henry
Acclom, Thomas Palmes, John Kenlay.

Given at York, 23 November 9 Henry V [1421].

Subscribed. Burton. [Latin]

(ff. 37v-38) Memorandum that on 17 May, I Henry VI [1423],
John Spaldyng, walker, and Beatrice, his wife, came into the Council Chamber before Thomas Esyngwald, Mayor, and showed and
sealed one part of the indenture which they acknowledged to have
been made by them. The said Beatrice publicly acknowledged that
she was in no way compelled to make and seal the deed, but did so
of her own free will, and that if she should survive John Spaldyng,
her husband, she would not claim dower in the tenement or orchard
or any payment except the rent of 2s. p.a., mentioned in the deed
as follows:—

LEASE.

John Spaldyng of York, walker, and Beatrice, his wife,
to Emmotte, wife of the late William Thrisk of York, walker,
a tenement in which Emmotte then lived and an orchard in Litil-
britgate in the parish of St. Margaret.

Term. The life of the said Emmotte.

Rent. 2s. p.a. to the said John and Beatrice and the heirs of
Beatrice.

The lessors were to have the right of distraint if the rent was forty days in arrears.

Witnesses. Thomas Esyngwald, Mayor, William Craven, Thomas Kirkham, Sheriffs, Thomas Kar, Thomas Palmer, Richard Burlay, Robert Thrisk, John Gisburgh.

Given at York, 20 May 1 Henry VI [1423].

Subscribed. Burton.   [Latin]

On 23 February 2 Henry VI [1424], Richard Scamston,[19] priest, Vicar of Nafferton, came before Thomas Bracebryg Mayor, and showed him a deed of which the true tenor was as follows:—

GRANT.

William, Abbot of the monastery of St. Mary at York, and the Convent of the same,

to Thomas Woydestoyke, Duke of Gloucester and Lord of Holdyrnese,

an annual rent of £40 from their lands and tenements at Hornese [Hornsea] in Holdyrnese and the whole demesne of the same.

If the rent was ever in arrears, Thomas, Duke of Gloucester was to have the right of entry.

Witnesses. John Cunstapill, knight, Robert de Twyre, knight, Robert Hilton, knight, Stephen de Thorpe, knight, William Grymston, esquire.

Given in the said monastery, 4 May 7 Richard II [1384].

                                                                [Latin]

And immediately afterwards, the said Richard Scamston made the following acknowledgement before Thomas Bracebryg, Mayor, which he then wrote on the dorse of the deed and delivered to the Mayor, seeking its enrolment as follows:—

(ff. 38-38v) I, Richard Scamston, Vicar of Nafferton, publicly and of my own free will acknowledge that I forged the said deed without the consent or knowledge of the Abbot and Convent of St. Mary's, York, that I wrote it with my own hand and took the seal from another deed. In testimony of my confession of deceit I have written the above with my own hand in the presence of the Mayor, Thomas Bracebryg, on 23 February 2 Henry VI [1424] and at my special request it was enrolled in the common book of the city by Roger de Burton, public notary, Secretary of the city, in the

[19] Richard Scamston was collated to Nafferton, 13 April 1421 (Register of Archbishop Henry Bowet, R.I. 18. f. 195).

presence of Sir Henry Neuton, Rector of Kyrkeby Hundolfdale
[Kirby Underdale], Nicholas Elslak, John Fenrothere, Guy Roclyff and Roger de Burton, 23 February 1423/4, 2 Henry VI, the second year of the Indiction and the seventh year of Pope Martin V.

On the last day of February in the said year, Stephen Frankys
of Nafferton, clerk, made the following confession before the
Mayor and sought its enrolment, the tenor of which follows: —

I, Stephen Frankys of Nafferton, clerk, of my own free will
acknowledge by this confession, written by my own hand, that
Richard Mabson [sic], Vicar of Nafferton, forged a deed in which
an annual rent of £40 from the manor of Hornese was granted by
the Abbot and Convent of St. Mary's, York, to Thomas Woydes-
tok, his heirs and assigns, according to the confession of the said
Richard and that I delivered the deed to the Abbot on the order of
the said Richard, so that we might extort money from the Abbot,
knowing that the deed was forged.

Present. John Raghton, Thomas Roderham, William Holthorp,
citizens of York.   [Latin]

GIFT.

Peter Bukcy, citizen and merchant of York,
    to Thomas Esyngwald, citizen and merchant of York and John
    Bukcy, his son,
his goods and chattels, on this side of the sea and beyond it, and
all debts owed to him.

For greater security Peter Bukcy delivered to the said Thomas
and John 1d. in the name of seisin.

Witnesses. Thomas Bracebrig, Mayor, William Bedale and William Gaytesheved, Sheriffs, Thomas More, John Bolton, Thomas
Doncastre, William Craven, citizens of York.

Given at York, 31 March 2 Henry VI [1424].

Subscribed. Burton.   [Latin]

(f. 39) [Added at the head of the folio:]
In two quires are contained *cunriours* [curriers], *sausmakers,*
——[20] *tilmakers, stryngars, goldsmyths, plasterers, telers* [tilers],
parchenners, girderelers, and *barkars, bochers* [butchers], *cokis*
[cooks], *brogg*[ers], ——[20] *wrightz, marchallz, fullers,* shearers
and prostitutes.   [Latin]
Here begins the quire of rents and farms of the Commonalty,

[20] Word illegible.

leased by several Mayors in the time of Roger de Burton, Secretary
and Common Clerk of this City.[21]   [Latin]

(ff. 39-39v) LEASE.
> The Mayor and Commonalty of York,
> > to Thomas Skelton, Richard Broghton, Thomas Stirtavant,
> > John Lancastre, tailors, and John Mallom, litster, Masters of the
> > Guild or Fraternity of St. John the Baptist in York, and the
> > brethren and sisters of the same,[22]

part of a ditch commonly called the *mote*, containing in length
100 ells of land from the outer corner of the tenement which the
said fraternity held of the city, opposite the churchyard of *St. Elene
Attealdwalles* on the south, as far as the fence erected by Thomas
Crofton on the north; and containing in width, where it abutted
on the land and hall of the said fraternity, 6 ells, and where it
abutted on the land of the Prior and Convent of Gyseburn [Guis-
borough], 12 ells, and so as far as the said fence and the corner of
a house built contiguous to that fence.

Term. 100 years from the feast of St. Martin in Winter, 1415.
Rent. 20d. p.a. to be paid by the masters of the guild to the Wardens
of Ouse Bridge.

The fraternity might enclose that part of the ditch, so as not to
damage the ditch and wall, but were to allow the Mayor and
Commonalty free entry and exit at all times during war to repair
and defend the walls.

The Mayor and Commonalty were to have distraint if the rent
was forty days in arrears, or the right of re-entry if there was insufficient distraint.

Given at York, the Monday after the feast of St. Andrew the
Apostle [2 December] 1415, 3 Henry V.   [Latin]

LEASE.
> The Mayor and Commonalty of York,
> > to William Bempton of York, chaplain,

space on Ouse Bridge and licence to build one or more tenements
between the tenement of the Mayor and Commonalty in the tenure

---

[21] Several of the following leases have been very lightly crossed through, presumably when they expired.

[22] The guild of St. John the Baptist was connected with the tailors' guild. This
lease contains the earliest known reference to the hall. (A Raine, *Mediaeval York*,
pp. 53-4).

of John Besyngby, senior, citizen and merchant, on the one side, and the stone cross on the said bridge on the other; and to place his timber on the stone piers on either side of the arch, both on the pier on which the tenement in the tenure of John Besyngby was built and on the other pier on which the stone cross stood, constructing the tenements for his greatest convenience and comfort, but so that they should not project in front towards the street beyond the foundations of other tenements anciently built there, and reserving reasonable space around the stone cross.

Term. 98 years from Whit Sunday, 1418.

Rent. 6s 8d p.a. to be paid to the Wardens of Ouse Bridge. If the rent should be half a year in arrears and sufficient distraint could not be found, the Mayor and Commonalty were to have the right of re-entry.

The Mayor and Commonalty were to repair the stone piers at their cost during that term; and the said William was to construct the tenements of sufficient oak timbers, plaster and roofing at his own cost, maintain and repair them when built, and deliver them in good repair to the Mayor and Commonalty at the end of the said term. He was to be allowed to place stones called *corbilles* on the piers for the support of the timber and tenements without damage or detriment to the bridge.

Given at York, the Monday after the feast of St. Katherine the Virgin [29 November] 1417, 5 Henry V. [Latin]

(f. 40) LEASE.

The Mayor and Commonalty of York,
    to Robert de Burton, citizen and merchant of York,
all those lands and tenements opposite the west end of All Saints' Church in Northestrete, lying between the tenement of William de Alne, citizen and merchant, and the garden of Thomas de Ellerton on the one side, and the lands and tenements of John de Garston on the other, and extending in length from the churchyard of the said church in front as far as the land of Robert de Thorlthorp and Robert de Plumpton, knights, behind.

Term. 99 years from the feast of St. Martin in Winter next.

Rent. 13s 4d. p.a. payable to the Wardens of Ouse Bridge.

If the rent was half a year in arrears, and the lessors could not obtain sufficient distraint, they were to have the right of re-entry.

Robert de Burton was to build a new tenement at his own cost, maintain and repair it, and return it in good repair to the Mayor and Commonalty at the end of the said term.

Given at York, 26 January 1417/8, 5 Henry V.   [Latin]

(ff. 40-40v) LEASE.

The Mayor and Commonalty of York,

to Richard Rykall, Thomas atthe Esshe, Adam Baker, and Thomas Welburn, bakers, and other masters of the craft of bakers,

a piece of waste land on the Toftes against the wall of the Friars Preachers, containing in length from the side of the postern in that wall towards the south 6 ells, and in width from that wall towards the west 5½ ells.

Term. 80 years from Whit Sunday 1418.

Rent. 12d. p.a. payable to the Wardens of Ouse Bridge.

The Mayor and Commonalty were to have the right of re-entry if the rent was forty days in arrears.

Given at York, 6 May 1418, 6 Henry V.   [Latin]

(ff. 40v-41) LEASE.

The Mayor and Commonalty of York,

to John Aldestanemore, merchant, and citizen of York,

a tenement in Northstrete together with rooms and other houses built there, which Richard Cleseby, goldsmith, lately held.

Term. 15 years from the feast of St. Martin in Winter, 1418.

Rent. 46s. 8d. p.a. payable to the Wardens of Ouse Bridge.

If the rent was forty days in arrears and the lessors could not find sufficient distraint, they were to have the right of re-entry.

The Mayor and Commonalty were to maintain and repair the property for the said term.

Given at York, 21 June 1418, 6 Henry V.   [Latin]

(ff. 41-41v) FEOFFMENT.

The Mayor and Commonalty of York,

to George, son of Marmaduke de Thweng, and Robert de Lyncoln, Rector of St. Cuthbert's Church in Peseholm,

a piece of land and all the houses and buildings erected thereon, lying beneath the city walls near the great gate of St. Leonard's Hospital leading to the River Ouse on the west, containing from the stone wall of the said hospital 15¼ ells in length and 7¼ ells

in length [sic] and 7½ ells 1 inch in width; another piece of land
and the house built thereon adjoining and annexed to the said wall
of the hospital towards the east, lying beyond the houses and buildings aforesaid and containing in width 1⅞ ells and a *nayle*,[23] and
in length 1⅜ ells; and another piece of land beyond the said houses
and buildings towards the city walls, for the outlet of water from
those houses and buildings, extending in length from the land
and house last mentioned as far as the end of the said buildings towards the Ouse and containing in width ¾ ell.

Rent. 5s. p.a.

The Mayor and Commonalty were to have the right of distraint
if the rent was in arrears. If it was not paid for a whole year and
they were unable to find sufficient distraint they were to regain
possession.

Given at York, 4 May 1417, 5 Henry V.   [Latin]

LEASE.

The Mayor and Commonalty of York,
  to Roger Burton, clerk, and Robert Wescowe, citizen and
  mariner,
a piece of waste land near the River Ouse at the foot of the stone
steps commonly called *Salteholegrese*, lying beneath a tenement
of the Mayor and Commonalty and extending in front towards the
staith from the outer corner of the *landstathe* at the foot of the said
steps as far as the outer corner of the outer arch towards the River
Ouse and containing 5⅝ ells; and in width at one end, from the
said outer corner of the outer arch as far as the other inner corner
of the same arch towards the *fyshelendyng*, 5 ells and a *nayle large*
and at the other end, from the corner of the *landestathe* in front as
far as the stone wall behind, which extended from the *landstathe*
and the said arch, 4½ ells;
and licence to enclose and build on the said land so as not to cause
any damage to Ouse Bridge or the tenements thereon.

Term. 120 years from the feast of St. Martin in Winter, 1418.

Rent. 12d p.a. payable to the Wardens of Ouse Bridge.

If the rent was forty days in arrears and the lessors were unable
to find sufficient distraint, they were to regain possession.

Should the tenants of the houses above the said piece of land
throw any urine or other filth or dirt onto the land to the detriment

---

[23] A nail was 1/16 yard, 2¼″.

or annoyance of the said Roger and Robert, their heirs and assigns, they would be punished accordingly.

Given at York, 3 November 1418, 6 Henry V.   [Latin]

(f. 42) LEASE.

The Mayor and Commonalty of York,
   to Alan de Bedale, and Henry Forester, citizens and goldsmiths,
   and searchers of that craft,
a piece of land on the Toftes lying alongside the wall of the Friars Preachers, and containing in width 4 ells and in length 5¾ ells, for building a house there to store the goldsmiths' pageant.[24]

Term. 80 years from the feast of St. Martin in Winter, 1420.

Rent. 8d p.a. payable to the Wardens of Ouse Bridge.

If the rent was eight days in arrears, the lessors were to regain possession.

The said searchers and their successors were to maintain and repair the house at their own cost and return it in good repair at the end of the term.

Given at York, 3 November 1420, 8 Henry V.   [Latin]

(ff. 42-42v) LEASE.

The Mayor and Commonalty of York,
   to John Preston, citizen and ironmonger,
a piece of waste land called *Kalomhall* on the bank of the River Ouse.[25]

Term. 90 years from the feast of St. Martin, 1421.

Rent. 5s p.a. payable to the Wardens of Ouse Bridge.

The Mayor and Commonalty were to have distraint if the rent was forty days in arrears, or the right of re-entry if they were unable to find sufficient distraint.

The said John Preston was not to lease the land, under penalty of expulsion, to any butcher for the disposal of the entrails of animals but was to keep it free from entrails and other filth causing foul smells during the said term.

Given at York, 3 November 1421, 9 Henry V.   [Latin]

---

[24] The pageant wagon used in the performance of the Corpus Christi plays.

[25] Calome Hall was in Spurriergate, near Low Ousegate. (A. Raine, *Mediaeval York*, pp. 151, 156).

(ff. 42v-43). LEASE.

The Mayor and Commonalty of York,

to John Yoman, bower,

a garden situated between the tenements of Ratonrawe and the stone wall of the city, with an entry between the *Paigenthowse* of the skinners on the north and the tenement of the Mayor and Commonalty in the tenure of Joan Mason on the south, and extending from the tenements of the Mayor and Commonalty in the tenure of Christiana Heb, Joan Kyrkeby and Joan Mason behind, as far as the city walls, and from the garden of Richard Cuke on the north to the garden of Richard Brewester on the south.

Term. 40 years from Whit Sunday next.

Rent. 12d p.a. payable to the Wardens of Ouse Bridge.

The Mayor and Commonalty were to have distraint if the rent was twenty days in arrears, or re-entry if they were unable to find sufficient distraint.

John Yoman was not to sow or plant or do any other manual work on the moat adjoining the said garden, causing damage to the moat or city walls, under penalty of a heavy fine and explusion from the garden.

Given at York, 1 February 1420/1, 8 Henry V.   [Latin]

LEASE.

The Mayor and Commonalty of York,

to Thomas Buteler, citizen and spurrier,

a tenement in Conyngstrete in which he dwelt.

Term. 10 years from the feast of St. Martin in Winter, 1421.

Rent. 9s 6d. on Whit Sunday next, 14s 6d. on the following feast of St. Martin in Winter and then 29s p.a. for the remaining nine years.

If the rent was forty days in arrears, the Mayor and Commonalty were to have distraint. They were to maintain and repair the premises at their expense.

Given at York, 6 November 1421, 9 Henry V.   [Latin]

(ff. 43-43v). LEASE.

The Mayor and Commonalty of York,

to John Bell of Fysshergate in the suburbs of York,

a piece of waste land at the south end of Fysshergate, containing in front facing the high street 65 ells and behind facing the land of the Abbot and Convent of Whytby, 61 ells in length, and in width at either end 9 ells and in the middle from north to south, 10 ells; together with the houses to be built there.

Term. 70 years from the feast of St. Martin in Winter, 1421.

Rent. 12d p.a. payable to the Wardens of Ouse Bridge.

The Mayor and Commonalty were to have distraint if the rent was forty days in arrears. If they were unable to find sufficient distraint within one month after the said forty days, they were to regain possession.

Given at York, 6 November 1421, 9 Henry V.   [Latin]

(ff. 43v-44) LEASE.

(Marginal note: surrendered to the Commonalty)

The Mayor and Commonalty of York,

to William Bempton, chaplain,

a tenement on Ouse Bridge in which John Warden, cutler, once dwelt.

Term. 40 years from Whit Sunday, 1420.

Rent. 13s 4d. p.a. payable to the Wardens of Ouse Bridge.

The Mayor and Commonalty were to have distraint if the rent was forty days in arrears. They were to repair and maintain the tenement at their cost during the said term.

Given at York, 2 May 1420, 8 Henry V.   [Latin]

LEASE.

The Mayor and Commonalty of York,

to John Lyllyng, citizen and mercer of York,

a piece of waste land in the lane next to the Stanebowe, lying in width between the land of Robert Thorneton, citizen, on the east and the land of the late William Sauvage, citizen, [? omission] in front as far as the land of St. Leonard's Hospital, behind.

Term. 20 years from the feast of St. Martin in Winter, 1422.

Rent. 2s. p.a. payable to the Wardens of Ouse Bridge

The Mayor and Commonalty were to have distraint if the rent was forty days in arrears. If they were unable to find sufficient distraint they were to regain possession.

John Lyllyng was to maintain the land at his own cost during that term.

Given at York, 2 November 1422, 1 Henry VI.   [Latin]

(ff. 44-44v) LEASE.

The Mayor and Commonalty of York,

to John Matheuson, citizen and walker of York,

a garden lately in the tenure of Henry Lord Fitzhugh, in the parish of St. Margaret in Walmegate, lying in length between the land of William Skelton on the west and a way leading to the River Foss from the said parish church on the east, and in width between the land of St. Leonard's Hospital on the north and the lane called Kyrkelane on the south.

Term. 40 years from the feast of St. Martin in Winter, 1422.

Rent. 3s. 4d. p.a. payable to the Wardens of Ouse Bridge.

If the rent was forty days in arrears and sufficient distraint could not be found, the Mayor and Commonalty were to regain possession.

Should the lessee be evicted from the garden at the end of the said term, the Mayor and Commonalty were to repay the expense incurred by him in enclosing the garden, according to the assessment of good and law-worthy men.

Given at York, 2 November 1422, 1 Henry VI.   [Latin]

(ff. 44v-45) LEASE.

The Mayor and Commonalty of York,

to William Stokton, junior, citizen and mercer of York,

the shop and rooms on Ouse Bridge already in his tenure.

Term. 10 years from Whit Sunday, 1422.

Rent. 26s. 8d. p.a. payable to the Wardens of Ouse Bridge.

If the rent was one month in arrears, the Mayor and Commonalty were to have distraint.

During the ten years, William Stokton was to contribute with the parishioners of St. Michael's Church at Ouse Bridge to the royal taxes and all other parish dues. If he should sub-let the shop and rooms, the tenant should pay the said dues.

The Mayor and Commonalty were to maintain the premises as necessary.

Given at York, 20 January 1421/2, 9 Henry V.   [Latin]

LEASE.

The Mayor and Commonalty of York,

to Robert Cattall of York,

two shops and the rooms above them in Nessegate, lately in the tenure of Richard Pape, late of York, spurrier.

Term. 20 years from the feast of St. Martin in Winter, 1422.
Rent. 13s. 4d. p.a. payable to the Wardens of Ouse Bridge.

The Mayor and Commonalty were to maintain and repair the
roofs and walls and bear other necessary expenses during the said
term.

Given at York, on the feast and year abovesaid [11 November
1422], 10 Henry V.   [Latin]

(ff. 45-45v) LEASE.
(Marginal note: void).
    The Mayor and Commonalty of York,
    to John de Moreton, esquire and citizen of York,
the moat with pasture and fishing extending from the right-hand
gate of Fysshergate as far as the causeway on the bank of the River
Foss.

Term. 20 years from the feast of St. Martin in Winter, 1422.
Rent. 2s. p.a. payable to the Wardens of Ouse Bridge.

If the rent was forty days in arrears and the Mayor and Commonalty could not find sufficient distraint, they were to regain
possession. They were to have the right of free entry and exit for
supervising and repairing the moat and city walls in time of war
and other suitable occasions.

Given at York, 2 November 1422, 1 Henry VI.   [Latin]

(ff. 45v-46) LEASE.
(Marginal note:—*Appilby Lane*)
    The Mayor and Commonalty of York,
    to Thomas Appilby, clerk and citizen of York,
a piece of waste land in the suburbs of the city without Walmegatebarr, against the mill in the street beyond St. Katherine's chapel,
and extending in length from the ditch which encloses the wall and
garden of the said chapel as far as the excavated (*concavum*) ditch
called a *Holghdyke* on the east, and in width from the high-street
in front as far as the bank which enclosed the arable field of St.
Nicholas's Hospital behind.

Term. 100 years from Whit Sunday, 1423.
Rent. 12d p.a. payable to the Wardens of Ouse Bridge.

If the rent was forty days in arrears, and the Mayor and Commonalty could not find sufficient distraint they were to have re-possession.

Thomas Appilby was not to encroach on or impede the stream flowing from the corner of the field of the said hospital next to the said chapel as far as the ditch called *Holghdyke*, but was to maintain a reasonable channel for the water.

Given at York, 2 May 1423, 1 Henry VI.   [Latin]

(ff. 46-46v) CONFIRMATION.
(Marginal note: void)
The Mayor and Commonalty of York,
to John Mylner alias Tutbag, citizen of York, and Alice his wife, two houses on Ouse Bridge, with the two rooms above them and another room over the stallage of the said bridge called *Salmonhole*, which they had by the assignment of Margaret Skyres, widow of William Skyres, goldsmith, and in which William Skyres lately dwelt; reciting the lease by which William Skyres had the houses of the Mayor and Commonalty.

Term. The remainder of a term of 20 years from Whit Sunday 1414, and an additional 8 years thereafter.

Rent. 40s. p.a. payable to the Wardens of Ouse Bridge.

The Mayor and Commonalty were to have distraint if the rent was forty days in arrears, and repossession if they were unable to find sufficient distraint. They were to maintain and repair the houses during that term.

Given at York, 31 October 1424, 3 Henry VI.   [Latin]

(ff. 46v-47) LEASE.
The Mayor and Commonalty of York,
to John Skypton, citizen and skinner of York,
a stone tower at the corner of the wall of the Friars Minor of York, lately in the tenure of John Davy, skinner.

Term. 20 years from the feast of St. Martin in Winter, 1424.

Rent. 3s. 4d. p.a. payable to the Wardens of Ouse Bridge.

The Mayor and Commonalty were to have distraint if the rent was forty days in arrears, and repossession if they were unable to find sufficient distraint.

John Skypton was to maintain and repair the tower at his own expense during the said term.

Given at York, on the feast and year aforesaid, [11 November] 1424, 3 Henry VI.   [Latin]

(ff. 47-47v) LEASE.
(Marginal note: void)
    The Mayor and Commonalty of York,
    to John Basyngham of York, cordwainer,
a shop with the room above, in which John Basyngham, father of the said John lately dwelt, situated in Conyngstrete against the Church of St. Michael the Archangel.
    Term. 20 years from Whit Sunday, 1423.
    Rent. 12s. p.a. payable to the Wardens of Ouse Bridge.
    The Mayor and Commonalty were to have distraint if the rent was forty days in arrears, and repossession if they were unable to find sufficient distraint.
    They were to maintain and repair the property during the lease.
    Given at York on Whit Sunday 1423, 1 Henry VI.
    Subscribed. Burton.   [Latin]

LEASE.
(Marginal note: void)
    The Mayor and Commonalty of York,
    to Richard Fyssh, currier,
a tenement with buildings and appurtenances in Nesgate which Robert Bolton, combsmith [*kaymsmyth*], lately held and lived in.
    Term. 10 years from Whit Sunday, 1424.
    Rent. 26s. 8d. p.a. payable to the Wardens of Ouse Bridge.
    The Mayor and Commonalty were to have distraint if the rent was forty days in arrears, and repossession if they were unable to find sufficient distraint. They were to repair and maintain the tenement during the said term.
    Given at York on Whit Sunday, 1424.   [Latin]

(f. 48) LEASE.
(Marginal note: void)
    The Mayor and Commonalty of York,
    to Thomas Clynt of York, glover,
a small shop with a room above in the tenure of the said Thomas, situated next to the *Counture* hall[26] between the entrance of the

---

[26] *Counture* hall: chamber or exchequer.

same and the prison called the *woman kytcote*[27] on Ouse Bridge.

Term. 20 years from Whit Sunday, 1423.

Rent. 10s. p.a. payable to the Wardens of Ouse Bridge.

The Mayor and Commonalty were to have distraint if the rent was forty days in arrears, and repossession if they were unable to find sufficient distraint. They were to repair and maintain the property as necessary during that term.

Given at York on Whit Sunday, 1423, 1 Henry VI.   [Latin]

(ff. 48-48v) LEASE.

The Mayor and Commonalty of York,

to John Holgill, cooper, William Brandesby, butcher, Henry Esteby, hairester, John Fryth, cooper, John Ase, plasterer, and Robert Lincoln, currier, citizens of York,

a piece of land next to the Horsfayre in the suburbs of York, lying in width between the ditch of St. Mary's Hospital and the high street, and extending in length from the Kenyngdyke on the north as far as an old thorn tree growing near the great gates of the said hospital against the City of York, on the south, as built and enclosed on all sides.

Term. 99 years from the feast of St. Martin in Winter, 1424.

Rent. 6s. 8d. p.a. payable to the Wardens of Ouse Bridge.

The Mayor and Commonalty were to have distraint if the rent was forty days in arrears. If they were unable to find sufficient distraint within half a year they were to regain possession. The lessees agreed to maintain and repair, with their alms and those of strangers, the stone pavement in the middle of Giligate, from the south end of that street towards Bouthum as far as the Horsfayre at the northern end of the piece of land; and to return the land in as good a condition or better than they found it. Should they alienate the land or part of it to any person other than an honest citizen of York permanently resident in the city, the Mayor and Commonalty were to have the right of re-entry.

Moreover, the lessees leased to Thomas Gare, senior, citizen and merchant, a parcel of that land at the north end of the same, for the whole of the said term, according to an indenture made between the parties.

---

[27] *woman kytcote*: the women's prison.

Given at York, on the feast of St. Martin aforesaid
[11 November 1424], 3 Henry VI.   [Latin]

(f. 49) LEASE.
(Marginal note: void)
   The Mayor and Commonalty of York,
   to John Popilton, barber, and citizen of York,
a shop, lying beneath the wall of St. William's Chapel on Ouse
Bridge, between other shops of the Mayor and Commonalty, one
in the tenure of John Hovyngham, cutler, and the other in the
tenure of William Glover.
   Term. 12 years from Whit Sunday next.
   Rent. 5s. p.a. payable to the Wardens of Ouse Bridge.
   If the rent was forty days in arrears and the Mayor and Commonalty were unable to find sufficient distraint, they were to regain
possession.
   At the end of that term, John Popilton was to leave in the shop
certain necessities to be provided by him for his own convenience,
and not cause them to be removed.
   The Mayor and Commonalty were to repair the roof and walls
of the shop at their expense during the said term.
   Given at York, 20 January 1422/3, 1 Henry VI.   [Latin]

(ff. 49-49v) LEASE.
(Marginal note: void)
   The Mayor and Commonalty of York,
   to William Calthorne, citizen and armourer of York,
a tenement with a summer hall and a fire-place in the tenement,
which the Mayor and Commonalty had by the gift of William
Whixlay, former Rector of Swyllyngton, situated in Thruslane in
Fossegate.
   Term. 12 years from the feast of St. Martin in Winter, 1421.
   Rent. 17s. p.a. payable to the Wardens of Ouse Bridge.
   The Mayor and Commonalty were to have distraint if the rent was
forty days in arrears and re-entry if they were unable to find suffi-
cient distraint. They were to repair the tenement and summer hall
as necessary.
   Given at York, 6 November 1421, 9 Henry V.   [Latin]

LEASE.

(Marginal note: void)

The Mayor and Commonalty of York,

to Robert Mason of York, clerk,

two tenements on Ouse Bridge, situated between the tenement in the tenure of John Besyngby, senior, and the tenement lately in the tenure of Giles Towton, deceased.

Term. 20 years from the feast of St. Martin in Winter, 1422.

Rent. 40s. p.a. payable to the Wardens of Ouse Bridge.

If the rent was forty days in arrears and the Mayor and Commonalty could not find sufficient distraint, they were to regain possession.

Robert Mason was bound by the lease to contribute at all times with the parishioners of St. Michael's Church near Ouse Bridge in lot and scot, taxes and all other dues, whether he dwelt in those tenements or elsewhere. The Mayor and Commonalty were to maintain and repair the two tenements as necessary.

Witnesses. Henry Preston, Mayor, William Craven, Thomas Kyrkham, Sheriffs, Thomas Ward, William del Bothe.

Given at York on the said feast [11 November 1422], 1 Henry VI.

[Latin]

(ff. 49v-50) LEASE.

(Marginal note: void)

The Mayor and Commonalty of York,

to William Holthorp, citizen and merchant of York,

a water-filled ditch and the fishing rights, without the postern next to Barkertowre against the Tylehowse, lying in length and width beneath the city moat and walls towards the River Ouse at one end and extending as far as a nearby high *demming* flowing towards the Bysshoplathes at the other end.

Term. 20 years from the feast of St. Martin in Winter, 1421.

Rent. 20d. p.a. to the Wardens of Ouse Bridge.

If the rent was one month in arrears, the Mayor and Commonalty were to have distraint in the lessee's dwelling houses.

Given at York, 6 November 1421, 9 Henry V.   [Latin]

(ff. 50-51) AGREEMENT.

between John Hikelyng, Warden of the Vicars of the Cathedral Church of St. Peter of York,

and Nicholas Blakburn, junior, lately Mayor of York, and the
Commonalty of the City,

concerning the rent of 22s. p.a. from two tenements of the Mayor
and Commonalty in Conyngstrete, one of which now in the tenure
of John Farnelay, spurrier, was formerly in the tenure of John
Ellerker, sergeant at law, and the other now in the tenure of Adam
Warter, spurrier, formerly belonged to William Whixlay, Parson
of Swylyngton. John Hikelyng claimed that the rent was wrongfully withheld by the Mayor and Commonalty, and he and the
Vicars showed certain deeds, ancient rolls and other evidences
recording the payment of the rent until the mayoralty of Henry
Wyman. The rent rolls of the city were also shown which confirmed
the annual payment of the rent to the Warden and Vicars. After due
consideration it was agreed by the Mayor and Council that the
Warden and Vicars should have the 22s. p.a. rent claimed by them
and their predecessors and that the Mayor and Commonalty had
no right or title to prevent them from receiving the same. Further,
the Vicars freely acquitted the Mayor and Commonalty of all arrears
of rent, estimated to amount to £13 and more, and the Mayor and
Commonalty placed the Vicars in possession and rendered seisin to
them by the payment of 11s for the term of St. Martin in Winter, 8
Henry VI [1429].

Similarly, John Hikelyng, Warden, in the name of the Vicars,
claimed that 2s. p.a. rent from a tenement of the Mayor and Commonalty in Jubertgate, formerly of Matilda Mallom [and now] in
the tenure of Agnes Gayregrafe, had not been paid from the mayoralty of Thomas Esyngwald until the mayoralty of Nicholas Blakburn. The wardens and Vicars showed proof of the payment of the
rent until the mayoralty of Thomas Esyngwald and the Mayor
and Commonalty showed nothing to exclude them from receiving
the rent. It was decided by Nicholas Blakburn, Mayor, and the
Council that the Warden and Vicars had the right to the rent, and
the latter in turn acquitted them of the arrears which amounted to
14s. The Mayor and Commonalty placed the Warden and Vicars
in possession of the annual rent of 2s. by the payment of 2s. for the
terms of Whit Sunday, 7 Henry VI [1429] and St. Martin in
Winter, 8 Henry VI [1429].

The Mayor and Commonalty granted that they and their successors would henceforth pay the rent of 22s. p.a. from the two
tenements in Conyngstrete and of 2s. p.a. from the tenement in

Jubretgate, in equal portions on Whit Sunday and the feast of St. Martin in Winter, for ever. [Latin]

(f. 51v.) [Blank.]

(f. 52) FEOFFMENT AND GIFT.
John de Aymonderby,
to Robert de Tynton, Rector of the Church of Uffyngton, Agnes de Hothom, Master John de Perschay and Adam de Wygan, chaplain,
lands and tenements in the County of York, both in the City of York and in the borough of Beverley, with all rents, services and appurtenances within the county, together with lands and tenements in Aymonderby [Amotherby] and Crayk, which he had as a pledge, obligation and mortgage from Robert de Merton, son and heir of Thomas de Merton; also all his goods and chattels within the said county.
Witnesses. Thomas de Etton, William de Kyrkeby, Thomas de Locton, Robert de Flamburgh, Richard de Pikeryng.
Given at Holm on Monday, 7 October 38 Edward III [1364].
[Latin]

(ff. 52-52v) FEOFFMENT.
John Bryane, kinsman and heir of Thomas Maunsell, late of Swynton in the County of York,
to Richard Clynt, citizen and bower of York, and Joan, his wife, Sir Thomas Toweton, Lord of Stillyngton, John Vavasour, esquire, and George de Whitby of York, chaplain, and the heirs of the bodies of Richard Clynt and Joan his wife or, in default thereof, to their right heirs,
lands and tenements in Overousegate in the parish of St. Michael at the end of Ouse Bridge, lying in width between the tenement of Robert de Sallay on the one side and a piece of waste land on the corner of Nessegate on the other, and in length from Overousegate in front as far as a tenement of the Mayor and Commonalty, behind.
Rent. 4 marks p.a. for the life of John Bryane, the first payment to be made on the feast of St. Martin in Winter next. If the rent was forty days in arrears, the feoffor was to have distraint, and if it was at any time half a year overdue the feoffees were to pay £5 p.a. for the life of the feoffor. Should the said £5 p.a. be forty days in

arrears the feoffor was to have distraint.

Witnesses. Thomas Bracebrig, Mayor, William Bedall, William Gaytesheved, Sheriffs, Thomas Gare, John Lillyng, Robert Ebchestre, Richard Rykall, Thomas atte Esshe, citizens of York.

Given at York, 16 May 2 Henry VI [1424].   [Latin]

LETTERS OF ATTORNEY.
John Bryane,
to Robert Feriby and Thomas Benson, citizens of York,
to deliver seisin to Richard Clynt and Joan his wife, Sir Thomas Toweton, John Vavasour, and George de Whitby, of lands and tenements in Overousegate.

Given at York, 16 May 2 Henry VI [1424].   [Latin]

BOND.
Richard Clynt,
to John Bryane, in £40, to be paid the following Easter,
to ensure payment of an annual rent of 4 marks, by the said Richard Clynt and Joan, his wife, Sir Thomas Toweton, John Vavasour and George de Whitby.

Given, 16 May 2 Henry VI [1424].   [Latin]

These deeds were enrolled at the request of John Bryane and Richard Clynt on 20 May 1424, in the mayoralty of Thomas Bracebryg.

Subscribed. Burton.   [Latin]

(ff. 53-53v) WILL.
of Nicholas Warthill of York,
desiring burial within the Church of St. Edward the King and Martyr in Walmegate without the city walls, for which he bequeathed 6s. 8d. to the fabric of the church, his best robe as a mortuary gift to the Rector according to the custom of the city, and ten pounds of wax in two candles for burning around his body. The funeral services on the day of his burial were to be determined by his executors.

Bequeathing to the chaplain to celebrate a trental daily from the day of his death until the eighth day, for the souls of himself and Isabel his first wife, 40s.; to the Rector of his parish church 13s. 4d., and to the clerk 2s.; to the fabric of the Church of St. Peter the Great, 6s. 8d. and to the high altar of the same, 6s. 8d.; to every order of mendicant friars in the city, 6s. 8d.; to Helewyse, his wife, for life, and John, his son, if he survived her, his silver vessels, his bowls and silver spoons and all other goods, that they might find a suitable chaplain to celebrate divine service for the souls of himself, Isabel his first wife, Richard Basee and Thomas de Moreton, in the Church of St. Edward aforesaid for two years. After their death, the goods were to be sold and the money distributed to the poor.

To Helewyse, his wife, for life, with remainder to John, his son, his capital messuage in which he lived in Walmegate; to John, his son, and his heirs, two messuages next to the churchyard of St. Edward the King and Martyr in Walmegate on the east side, and another four messuages next to the same churchyard on the west side, recently built by the testator; another messuage in Nether Owsegate, bought from William Leds; the rent of one mark from the tenement in Conyngstrete which formerly belonged to William Percy; the reversion of the messuage in the same street in which Alice Lambe, widow of John Lambe, cordwainer, then lived; two shops with the upper storeys in Conyngstrete, formerly in the tenure of Thomas de Horneby, saddler; and another shop in Netherousegate, formerly in the tenure of Adam de Ragwhton, spurrier.

The remainder of his goods he bequeathed to his executors for them to dispose of for the good of his soul.

Appointment of Helewyse, his wife, and John, his son, as his executors.

Given, 20 September 1413.

Probate was granted before the Official and Commissary General of the Court of York, the Archbishop's see being vacant, and administration of the goods of the said Nicholas awarded to the executors named in the will. [Latin]

Given at York, 22 May 1424. Enrolled in the mayoralty of Thomas Bracebryg by Master Roger de Burton, Secretary and Common Clerk, 11 July 1424, 2 Henry VI, in the presence of John Raghton, Thomas Roderham, Chamberlains, William Revetour, Deputy Clerk of the Chamber.

Subscribed. Burton R. [Latin]

The enrolment of the deed of William Barker of Tadcastre at the request of William Thorp.

FEOFFMENT AND GRANT.

William Barker of Tadcastre,

to William, son of William de Thorp near Houedon,

lands and tenements and a windmill, which the feoffor had by the gift and feoffment of Thomas de Thorp son of John de Thorp, in Qweldryk [Wheldrake] and Skirpenbek; and the reversion of a messuage, two oxgangs of land and two acres of meadow in Skirpenbek, after the death of Joan, wife of the late Robert Thurkyll.

Witnesses. William Chauncy, knight, Roger Dautry, John Mergrave, William Wodrawe, William son of Henry son of William, Thomas Porter, John Ayme.

Given at Qweldryk, the Wednesday after the feast of St. Peter Ad Vincula [4 August] 1395, 19 Richard II.

Subscribed. Burton.   [Latin]

The enrolment of certain indentures and deeds before Thomas Bracebryg, Mayor, 19 August 2 Henry VI [1424] at the request of John Aldestanemore and Master George de Plumpton, priest.

[Latin]

(ff. 53v-54) AGREEMENT.

between Sir William de Plumpton, knight, and Alice his wife, one of the daughters and heirs of John de Gysburn, late citizen and merchant of York,

and William Frost and Isabel his wife, the other daughter and heir of the said John,

dividing the lands and tenements, rents and services of John de Gysburn, which descended to the said Alice and Isabel on his death. Sir William de Plumpton and Alice were to have for their part, a messuage in Skeldregate in which William del Freres dwelt, a messuage on Bysshophill in which Thomas son of Thomas de Nessefeld lately lived and all the strips which belonged to the said John in the fields of Bysshopthorp, called in English *the Enges*; the annual rent of 5 marks from the lands and tenements which lately belonged to John de Tanfeld in the town of Rypon and also all the tenements which belonged to the said John [de Gysburn] in Northstrete, lying in width between a tenement of the Mayor and Commonalty of York, on the one side, and a tenement in which Robert de Thorlethorp dwelt on the other, and in length from

Northstret in front as far as a new gateway enclosed with two leaves[30] and with a room above; and the moiety of a garden lying towards the north. William Frost and Isabel were to have for their part, the capital messuage which belonged to the said John in Mykelgate with the four shops built in front thereof, lying in width between the tenement of Thomas de Kyllom, fisher, and the messuage of John de Drynghouses, fletcher, and in length from Mikelgate in front as far as a room, assigned to Sir William and Alice, abutting on the new gate with the room above, together with the other half of the garden abutting on the same new gate, with free entry and exit for horses and carts through the gate to Northstrete.

Witnesses. Robert Sauvage, Mayor, William Vescy, John de Craven, and John de Penryth, Bailiffs, Thomas de Rigton, Thomas Dygill, William de Hornby, John de Drynghouses, Henry de Burton, William de Esedyk.

Given at York, 13 January 15 Richard II [1392].   [French]

(ff. 54-54v) FEOFFMENT.

Alice, wife of the late William de Plompton, knight,
to Master Richard de Kendale, Rector of the Church of Rypley,
Master Adam de Wygan, Rector of St. Saviour's Church, York,
George de Plompton, Robert de Skelton, Rector in the Cathedral
Church of St. Peter, York, and Nicholas de Thorneby, chaplain,
tenements, rents and services in Northstrete and Skeldergate in York, the annual rent of 3s. 4d. from lands and tenements, formerly of Alan Hamerton, late citizen of York in Skeldergate, a burgage in the *Merketstede* in Ripon, lying between the messuage of John Tanfeld and that of Robert de Halomshir, two burgages which formerly belonged to William de Hannelay, lying between the messuage of John Topcliff and Ripon *Cornemarkett*, a close in Staymergate between the messuage of John Topcliff and the close of Sir Adam de Thornton, a garden in Alhalowgate lying between the messuage of John de Cleynt and that of Thomas de Ingylby, two acres of land lying at the *Keldbank* next to the footpath leading to Bisshopton mill, on the one side, and the meadow called *Pyper Inges* on the other, half an acre of meadow lying between the meadow of Walter Gill and that of John de Shirwod, an acre of land and meadow next to *Swylmyre*, on one side, and the land of Richard de Richemond on the other, three roods of land in *Aller-*

---

[30] a two-leaved gate, double gate.

wyke[31] between the land of John de Hawkeswyk and the land formerly of John de Shirwod, and two acres of land on the *Benehill*.

Witnesses. John de Bolton, Mayor of York, John Northeby, Robert del Gare, Sheriffs, William Tempest, knight, Geoffrey Pigot, William Fencote, William de Thornton.

Given at York, the vigil of St. Matthew the Apostle and Evangelist [20 September] 1410, 11 Henry IV.   [Latin]

LETTERS OF ATTORNEY.

Alice, wife of the late William de Plompton, knight,

    to Ralph Whelewrigth, son of Thomas Whelewrigth of Burghbrigg [Boroughbridge],

to deliver seisin to Master Richard de Kendale, Master Adam de Wygan, George de Plompton, Robert de Skelton and Nicholas de Thorneby, of the messuages, burgages, lands and tenements, rents and services in York and Ripon which they had by her gift.

Given at York, the vigil of St. Matthew [20 September] 1410, 11 Henry IV.   [Latin]

(ff. 54v-55) QUITCLAIM.

Robert de Skelton,

    to Master Richard de Kendale, Master Adam de Wygan, George de Plompton and Nicholas de Thorneby,

messuages, burgages, lands, tenements, rents and services in York and Ripon [as above] of which he was enfeoffed jointly with the said Master Richard de Kendale, Master Adam de Wygan, George Plompton and Nicholas de Thorneby.

Witnesses. John Craven, Mayor, Robert Lokton, Thomas del More, Sheriffs, William Newesom, William Alne, John Northeby.

Given at York, 27 February 1410/11, 12 Henry IV.

Subscribed. Burton.   [Latin]

FEOFFMENT.

William Skelton of York,

    to Master Richard Wetwang, Rector of the parish church of St. Dennis in Walmegate and John Alnewyk, Rector of the parish church of St. Peter the Little,

---

[31] *Allerwyke*, a field name in Ripon or Littlethorpe (*Place Names of the West Riding*, Vol. V, p. 172).

lands and tenements, rents and services in the City and suburbs of York.

Witnesses. Thomas Bracebrig, Mayor, William Bedale and William Gaiteshede, Sheriffs, Adam Hesham, Thomas Liverton, Robert Holdernes, John Clerke, Robert Fereby.

Given at York, 26 May 2 Henry VI [1424]. [Latin]

LETTERS OF ATTORNEY.

William Skelton,

to Robert Fereby of York, merchant,

to deliver seisin to Master Richard Wetewang, and John Alnewyk of lands and tenements in the City and suburbs of York, which they had by the feoffment of the said William Skelton,

Given at York, 26 May 2 Henry VI [1424].

Subscribed. Burton. [Latin]

(ff. 55-55v) FEOFFMENT.

Henry Lakensnyder, citizen of York,

to Thomas Roderham, citizen and merchant of York,

his capital messuage with buildings and appurtenances in Conyngstrete, lying in length from Conyngstrete in front to Davigate and the land of the Mayor and Commonalty of York behind, and in width between the tenement formerly of William de Wandesford and the land formerly of Thomas Dawetre, clerk, on the one side, and the tenement of William de Bolton on the other.

Because his seal was unknown to many, Henry Lakensnyder had caused the official mayoral seal of the city to be affixed to the deed.

Witnesses. Nicholas Blakburn, John de Moreton, Thomas Esyngwald, William Neuland, Peter Uppestall.

Given at York, 13 September 8 Henry V [1420]. [Latin]

QUITCLAIM.

Henry Lakensnyder,

to Thomas Rotherham,

the capital messuage in Conyngstrete [as above].

Witnesses. Nicholas Blakburn, John Moreton, Thomas Esyngwald, William Neuland, Peter Uppestall.

Given at York, 15 September 8 Henry V [1420]. [Latin]

(ff. 55v-56) QUITCLAIM.

Robert Saltmersh, son of James Saltmersh, late of York,
to Thomas Roderham,
the capital messuage in Conyngstrete [as above].

Witnesses. Richard Russell, Mayor, John Lillyng, John Gascoign,
Sheriffs, Thomas Esyngwald, William Neuland, Richard Neuland,
John Laxton.

Given at York, 14 September 9 Henry V [1424].   [Latin]

ARBITRATION.

by John Moreton and Alfred Manston, arbitrators chosen for
William Bowes senior, citizen and merchant of York,
and John Aldestanemore and Robert Ruddestan, arbitrators
chosen for John Bolton, senior, citizen and merchant of York,
to determine the right and title to a certain piece of land, concerning
which an assize of fresh force was prosecuted by John Bolton against
William Bowes. William Bowes, his heirs and assigns, were to have
the tenement in Peseholm in which he dwelt, as at present built
and enclosed on each side by houses and walls, and extending in
length from the high street of Peseholm in front as far as the
vivarium of the Foss behind; and John Bolton was to quitclaim the
tenement to him with a clause of warranty. William Bowes was
likewise to quitclaim to John Bolton, his heirs and assigns, his right
and title to John Bolton's tenement in Peseholm, next to the aforesaid tenement and lately in the tenure of William Gyselay, clerk,
provided always that William Bowes and his heirs should have the
annual rent of 12s. from that tenement with a clause allowing entry
and distraint for default therein.

Whereupon John Bolton made, sealed and delivered a quitclaim
to William Bowes, senior, in the presence of Thomas Bracebrig,
Mayor, John Moreton, John Aldestanemore, Alfred Manston and
Robert Ruddestan, citizens, the tenor of which follows:—

(ff. 56-56v) QUITCLAIM.

John Bolton, senior, citizen and merchant of York,
to William Bowes, senior, citizen and merchant of York,
the capital messuage in Peseholm in which William Bowes dwelt,
[as above], containing in length from the high street in front to
the River Foss behind the west side of the messuage, 82½ ells.

Witnesses. Thomas Bracebrig, Mayor, John Ward, John Louth,

Sheriffs, John Moreton, Thomas Esyngwald, John Austanemore.

Given at York, the feast of St. Luke the Evangelist, 3 Henry VI [18 October 1424].

William Bowes offered to make, seal and deliver to John Bolton a similar deed of release according to the arbitration. The latter declared that he did not desire such a deed but was content with the settlement. [Latin]

GRANT.

Marmaduke de la Ryvere, Lord of Brandesby, Elizabeth, his wife, and Henry FitzHenry, Lord of Kelfeld,
to William Neuland, citizen and tailor of York,

an annual rent of £20 from their manor of Brafferton, with the lands, tenements, rents and services appertaining to the same. If the rent was forty days in arrears, William Neuland was to have distraint. For greater security, the grantors delivered to William Neuland 1d. in the name of seisin.

Witnesses. William Bowes, Mayor, John Waughen, Thomas Snawedon, Sheriffs, John Haukeswell, dukeling (*duketto*) of Thweng, Thomas Lyverton, Thomas Roderham.

Given at York, 25 February 4 Henry V [1417]. [Latin]

BOND.

Marmaduke de la Ryvere, Elizabeth, his wife, Henry FitzHenry, William Garton, household servant of the said Marmaduke, and William Lokton of Brandesby,
to William Neuland,

in £100, to be paid on Whit Sunday next.

Given, 25 February 4 Henry V [1417]. [Latin]

(ff. 56v-57) DEFEASANCE.

William Neuland,
to Marmaduke de la Ryvere, Elizabeth, his wife, Henry Fitz-Henry, William Garton and William Lokton,

of their grant of £20 p.a. rent and their bond in £100 provided they should pay to him at the house in which he lived in York, £60 as follows: —

£10 on each Whit Sunday and a further £10 on each feast of St. Martin in Winter or within forty days after each feast during the next three years.

Given, 27 February 4 Henry V [1417].   [Latin]

FEOFFMENT.

William Selby of York,
to Thomas Bolton and John Dunkan of York, chaplains,
lands and tenements which belonged to John son of Simon Kynges-son of York in the City and suburbs of York, excepting only a shop in Conyngstrete, then in the tenure of Thomas Farneley, spurrier, all of which the said John son of Simon gave and devised in his will to the said William Selby and also to Ralph de Hornby, William de Helmeslay, William son of Ralph Sauvage and Robert de Talkan, after the death of Joan, his wife, and John, their son, should the latter die without heirs of his body begotten.

Witnesses. William Ormesheved, Mayor, John Louth, John Warde, Sheriffs, John Moreton, John Aldestanemore, John Lofthouse, William Craven, Richard Russell, vintner, Thomas Benson, John Gysburgh, clerk.

Given at York, 20 April 3 Henry VI [1425].   [Latin]

(f. 57v) QUITCLAIM.

William Selby,
to Thomas Bolton and John Dunkan,
lands and tenements which formerly belonged to John son of Simon Kyngesson and which Thomas Bolton and John Dunkan recently had by the gift and feoffment of the said William Selby, [as above].

Witnesses, [as above].

Given at York, 22 April 3 Henry VI [1425].   [Latin]

LETTERS OF ATTORNEY.

William Selby,
to John Naire of York, chaplain,
to deliver seisin to Thomas Bolton and John Dunkan of the lands and tenements formerly of John son of Simon de Kyngesson.

Given at York, 20 April 3 Henry VI [1425].   [Latin]

LETTERS OF ATTORNEY.

Thomas Bolton,
to John Dunkan,
to receive seisin of the lands and tenements formerly of John son of Simon de Kyngesson.

Given at York, 20 April 3 Henry VI [1425].   [Latin]

(f. 58) FEOFFMENT.

John Warthyll, son of John Warthyll of York,
    to Adam Hustethwayt and Mariot, his wife, and the heirs of their
    bodies,
a tenement with a garden and croft without Walmegatebarr in the
suburbs of York, in the parish of St. Laurence, lying between the
lands and tenements of John Naburn on the east, and the lands and
tenements of John Bayse on the west, and in length from the high
street in front to the king's ditch behind.

Rent. 12d. p.a.

If the rent was ever half a year in arrears, John Warthyll was to
have repossession.

Witnesses. John de Askham, Mayor, John de Appylby, Walter
Gower, Walter le Flemyng, Bailiffs, Vincent Verdenell, Thomas le
Wayder, John le Seteryngton, Robert Werdnell of Hornyngton,
William de Hayton, Geoffrey of the same.

Given at York, the Friday after the feast of St. Peter Ad Vincula
[4 August] 1307.   [Latin]

The above deed was enrolled in the register of deeds and wills in
the Council Chamber of the city, in the quire which begins,
Sciant presentes et futuri quod ego Johannes de Aymonderby, etc.
[f. 52]. Seisin of the croft was delivered by the Mayor on the feast
of the translation of St. Thomas the Martyr [7 July] 1425, 3 Henry
VI, as follows: —

Livery of Seisin.

William Ormesheved, Mayor, in the name of the Commonalty of
    York,
    to Robert Selby, weaver, and Alice, his wife, the kinswoman and
    nearest heir of Joan Knapton,
the croft mentioned in the above deed, extending in length from
the garden therein named as far as the king's ditch towards the
land of St. Nicholas's hospital behind, and lying in width between
the land of the Mayor and Commonalty on the west, in the tenure
of William Hugate, mason, and two short strips of land of the
Mayor and Commonalty, in the tenure of the said William Hugate,
abutting on the king's ditch, on the east. The croft had been
occupied for some time by the tenants of the Mayor and Commonalty.

And after the livery of seisin, John Ampylford, mason, John Hexham and Thomas Best, wrights and searchers and John Bolron, carpenter of the Commonalty, placed boundaries to the croft in the presence of the Mayor, John Moreton, Thomas Bracebryg, Aldermen, John Hewyk, Thomas del More and William Ryllyngton.

The feast of the translation of St. Thomas the Martyr [7 July] 1425, 3 Henry VI.   [Latin]

(ff. 58-58v) QUITCLAIM.

Roger Gower, son and heir of Elizabeth, wife of the late John Rose and aunt of Thomas Gower of Faceby,

to Christopher Boynton and John Pacok, chaplain,

lands and tenements, rents and services which the said Christopher and John had by the gift and feoffment of Thomas Gower, in Faceby, Carleton Parva, Worsall, Standenrig,[32] Whitton and Stillyngton. Because his seal was unknown to many, Roger Gower had caused the official mayoral seal of the City of York to be affixed to the deed.

Witnesses. Thomas Snawdon, Peter Thoresby, Ed. Barneburgh, William Thoresby, citizens of York, William Paule of Yarm.

Given, 10 September 4 Henry VI [1425].   [Latin]

The same day, Roger Gower sealed the deed in the presence of William Ormesheved, Mayor, John Radclyff, Chamberlain, Roger de Burton, Common Clerk, and it was enrolled at his request.

Subscribed. Burton R.   [Latin]

GRANT.

John Werkesworth of York and Joan, his wife,

to William Gascoigne and Alfred Manston,

an annual rent of 18s. from a tenement on the Pament in the parish of St. Crux in Fossegate, which formerly belonged to John Barden sometime Mayor of York and in which Thomas Warde then lived. The grantors had received the rent by the will of William Savage, dated at York, 4 December 1421.

Witnesses. William Ormesheved, Mayor, Richard Louth, John Dodyngton, Sheriffs, John Moreton, William Bowes, Thomas Kyrkham, Thomas Warde, citizens of York.

Given at York, 6 October 4 Henry VI [1425].   [Latin]

---

[32] Not identified.

On 11 October 1425, John Werkesworth and Joan, his wife, came personally before William Ormesheved, Mayor, in the Council Chamber and sought the enrolment of the deed, and it was enrolled by Roger de Burton, Secretary and Common Clerk. Subscribed. Burton R. [Latin]

(f. 59-59v) On 12 November 4 Henry VI [1425], Henry Preston, citizen and merchant, came before William Ormesheved, Mayor, and in the presence of Guy Roclyff, Recorder, Roger de Burton, clerk, John Stertevant, and John Kyrkeby, esquires, sought the enrolment of the following deed and that it should be kept safely in the Chamber.

FEOFFMENT.
Henry Preston, citizen and merchant of York,
to Thomas Preston, his son, and Katherine Howme, daughter of Robert Howme of York, merchant, and the male heirs of their bodies begotten, remainder to the male heirs of the body of Thomas, remainder to Robert, son of Henry Preston and the male heirs of his body, remainder to the heirs of the bodies of the said Thomas and Katherine, remainder to the heirs of the body of Thomas, remainder to the right heirs of Henry Preston, lands and tenements in the City of York and in the towns of Pontefract and Preston in the County of York, excepting only certain tenements in Grapelane in York in a place called Benetplace.[33]
Witnesses. Thomas Esyngwald, Thomas Doncastre, Robert Yarom, citizens and merchants of York, Thomas de Fox of Preston, Richard Wylkynson of the same.
Given at York, 20 September 4 Henry VI [1425]. [Latin]

GRANT.
Thomas de Barneby, son of William de Barneby, late of York, mercer,
to William de Barneby, his brother,
the annual rent of 5s. from the tenement of Thomas, son of William Gra of York, in Conyngstrete, lying in width between the land formerly of William Flemmyng and the land of the Mayor and Commonalty, and in length from the high street in front as far as

[33] The site of the church of St. Benedict which was demolished, probably before 1300 (A. Raine, Mediaeval York, p. 126).

the River Ouse behind. Thomas de Barneby had the rent by hereditary right after the death of Mary de Barneby, his mother.

If the rent was ever in arrears, William de Barneby was to have
distraint. For greater security, Thomas de Barneby paid to William,
his brother, 1d. of the 5s. rent in the name of seisin.

Witnesses. Robert Sauvage, Mayor, Constantine del Dam, Richard
de Santon, Thomas de Kelfeld, Bailiffs, John de Askham, Hugh
Straunge, Thomas de Lofthous, Peter de Appilton, clerk.

Given at York, 23 March 1383/4, 7 Richard II.   [Latin]

The enrolment of an indenture of Nicholas Warwyk of Pontefract, in the mayoralty of Peter Bukcy, 27 September 5 Henry VI
[1426], at the request of John Cartewryght, the assignee of Thomas
Dene, mason, and John Bolron, carpenter, and with the consent
of Thomas Dale, tutor of Henry Warwyk, son and heir of the said
Nicholas Warwyk, during his minority.

(ff. 59v-60) LEASE.

Nicholas Warwyk of Pontefract,

to Thomas Dene, mason, and John Bolron, carpenter,

lands and tenements in Colyergate lying between the tenements of
Christopher Spenser on either side, and in length from Colyergate
in front to the king's gutter behind.

Term. 99 years from Whit Sunday 1420.

Rent. 100s. p.a., the first payment being due on the feast of St.
Martin in Winter next.

If the rent was forty days in arrears, the lessor was to have distraint; if it was a year and a day in arrears he was to have re-entry.

The lessees were to build anew at their own costs the front of the
lands and tenements facing Colyergate, to a height of two rooms,
by Whit Sunday 1421, and two lower tenements, suitable for the
brewers, by Whit Sunday 1430. They were to build the foundations of all the walls of stone to a height of two feet above the
ground, maintain and repair the lands and tenements at their own
costs during the said term, and indemnify the said Nicholas
Warwyk from all customs and dues pertaining to the property.

Witnesses. John Burneby, Bailiff of Pontefract, John Halydaye
of the same, William Scryven, John York and William Forster,
spicer.

Given at Pountfreit, 4 March 7 Henry V [1420].   [Latin]

(ff. 60-60v) GRANT.[34]

Adam Wygan, Rector of St. Saviour's Church, York, and Ellis Yong, chaplain,

to John Dunkan of York, chaplain, and John Lancaster, citizen and tailor,

the rent of 40s. p.a. from five tenements in the City and suburbs of York, of which one lay in Mikelgate, in width between the tenement of John de Moreton, citizen of York, and that of Thomas Holbek, citizen of York, and Matilda, his wife, which lately belonged to William Savage, and in length from Mikelgate in front to the land of John Garston behind; another tenement was situated without Mikellyth in the suburbs of York, between the tenement of William Craven, of York, and the tenement of Alice Warde, and in length from the high street in front to a ditch called *Fosse* behind; the other three tenements lay on the west side without Mikellyth, between the tenement of the said William Craven and the tenement of John Maunby of York, smith, and in length from the high street in front as far as the land of John Clervaux of Croft behind. Reciting the deed by which the grantors had the five tenements of the said Thomas Holbek and Matilda his wife, and on which a fine was levied in the king's court at Westminster, and the feoffment by which Adam Wygan and Ellis Yong granted the five tenements to the said Thomas Holbek and Matilda at an annual rent of 40s.

If the rent was forty days in arrears, John Dunkan and John Lancaster were to have distraint; if it was a year and a day in arrears and they were unable to find sufficient distraint they were to have seisin.

Witnesses. Henry de Preston, Mayor, John Aldstanemore, Thomas Aton, Sheriffs, John Loufthouse, John Petyclerk, John Dothyngton, Roger Selby, spicer, William Rodes, William Brandesby.

Given at York, 28 June 10 Henry V [1422]. [Latin]

(f. 61) FEOFFMENT.

Thomas Gare, citizen and merchant of York,

to Thomas Gare, junior, his son, citizen and merchant,

lands and tenements, rents and services in Conyngstrete, Overousegate, Nether Ousegate and Lytyll Flesshamelles.

[34] Crossed through.

Rent. 20 marks p.a. for the life of Thomas Gare, senior.

If the rent was forty days in arrears, Thomas Gare, senior, was to have distraint.

Witnesses. John Aldstanmore, Mayor, John Brounflete, William Gyrlyngton, Sheriffs, John Moreton, William Ormeshede, Thomas Bracebrygg, Thomas Aton.

Given at York, 7 April 5 Henry VI [1427].   [Latin]

(ff. 61-61v) FEOFFMENT.

John Garston of York, senior,

to William Emlay, Rector of the Church of St. Wilfrid in Aldeconyngstrete,[35] York, and Thomas Emlay, citizen and tailor, his brother.

tenements in Skeldergate in the parish of St. Mary the Elder in York, formerly in the tenure of Stephen de Parische, citizen of York, lying in length from the high street in front on the east, as far as the churchyard of St. Mary the Elder on the west, and in width between the lane which leads to the Church of St. Mary the Elder on the south side and [? omission] Sir William Gascoigne, knight, and Lady Joan his wife, and the garden of John Topclyf, *sergeand of mace*, and Alice, his wife, on the north;

also lands and tenements in Skeldergate in the parish of St. Mary the Elder, lying between the River Ouse on the east and Skeldergate on the west, and in width between the land of the Abbot and Convent of Jervaux on the north and the lane extending as far as the River Ouse on the south;

also gardens in the parish of St. Mary Bishop's lying in width between the lands and tenements formerly of Brian de Stapilton, knight, on the east and the garden of the vicars of the Beddreden of St. Peter's on the west, and between the high street on the north and the garden of Lord le Roos and Sir Brian de Stapilton, behind, on the south.

Witnesses. Henry Priston, Mayor, Thomas Aton, John Austanmor, Sheriffs, Stephen le Parisch, William Scareburgh, Richard Stowe, Hugh Gill, William del Howe.

Given, 24 July 10 Henry V [1422].   [Latin]

(f. 62) GRANT.

Ralph le Furbur, citizen of York,

to all the carpenters of York,

---

[35] *Aldeconyngstrete*, now Lendal.

the annual rent of 6s., from the nearer stall at the doorway of his
house in Petergate facing south [*versus solem*] for the maintenance
of the candle of St. William the Confessor. Whenever the rent was
not paid, the carpenters were to have distraint in the grantor's house.

Witnesses. John de Seleby, Mayor, Andrew de Seleby, Walter
de Hertergate, Robert de Spaldinton, Bailiffs, Henry Clutepot,
Richard Hornepot, Alexander le Gaunter, Richard de Haxeby,
Simon Surlaf, William de Beverley, John de Kaldroner, William
de Haukeswell, William de Durame, Robert de Craven, Roger de
Haxeby, John de Gloucester, clerk.

Indenture sealed by the grantor and with the common seal of
the carpenters.

[Undated].³⁶   [Latin]

Henry Preston, tenant of the said house, was questioned by the
Mayor, John Aldestanemor, in the presence of the Sheriffs and
Aldermen, about the payment of the annual rent of 6s., on the day
after the feast of the Nativity of the Blessed Virgin Mary, 6 Henry
VI [9 September 1427]. He admitted that he should pay the rent
for the stall to the carpenters, and said that he would henceforth
pay it willingly each year, because Master William Gray, then Dean
of York, now Bishop of London, and Master John Carleton, Canon
of York, had reconciled him and the carpenters. He would pay the
rent to the carpenters at the agreed terms in future and would pay
the 3s. which he owed from Whit Sunday last.

Subscribed. Burton R.   [Latin]

The enrolment of the two deeds below was made with the consent
of Thomas Wyntworth of Pontefract, son and heir of Adam de
Wyntworth, late of York, and of William Lyttester of Kyngeston
on Hull, in the time of John Aldestanemore, Mayor, 12 September
6 Henry VI [1427].

(ff. 62-62v) GRANT.
    John de Knottynglay, chaplain,
       to Adam de Wenteworth of York,
the reversion of two messuages in York which Elizabeth, widow
of Richard Basy held in dower, one of which lay in Mikelgate in
the parish of St. Martin, between the messuage formerly of Stephen
Lescrope, knight, and the messuage of John Craven, and in length

³⁶ John de Selby was Mayor in the years 1251-3, 1264-8 and 1271. It is not known
in which year the bailiffs named held office.

from Mikelgate in front as far as Felterlane behind; the other lay in Skeldergate in the parish of St. Mary the Virgin called the Elder, between the messuage of the Abbot and Convent of Selby and that formerly of Henry Wyman, and in length from Skeldergate in front to the Old Baile behind; and the reversion of 10s. rent which Joan de Taunton held in dower, arising from the houses formerly of Thomas Doraunt in Nedellergate.

Thomas de Wenteworth and John Knottynglay had the said tenements and rents by a fine levied in the king's court and granted before the justices to them and the heirs and assigns of Thomas by the said Adam de Wenteworth and Agnes his wife. Thomas de Wenteworth had then released to John Knottynglay and his heirs his claim to the said reversions.

The said Elizabeth and Joan each delivered 2d. to Adam de Wenteworth as seisin of the reversion of the two messuages and of the rent.

Witnesses. John de Craven, Mayor, Peter Bukcy, Thomas Esyng-wald, Sheriffs, William Skelton, Robert Lonesdale, William Wadman, Thomas Wenteworth.

Given at York, the Tuesday after the feast of St. Wilfrid the Bishop, 13 Henry IV [13 October 1411].   [Latin]

QUITCLAIM.
   Thomas de Wynteworth,
      to John de Knottynglay, chaplain,
the reversion of the two messuages and rent [as above].

Witnesses. John de Brun, Richard de Drax, John Marsshall, Robert de Grayngham, William del Wathe, William Thomson of Selby.

Given at Selby, 12 July 1407, 8 Henry IV.

The seal of the Keeper of the Spirituality of Selby was affixed in testimony.

Subscribed. Burton Roger.   [Latin]

(ff. 62v-63) QUITCLAIM.
   John Malteby, Rector of the church of Ryther,
      to Thomas Bekwyth, son of William Bekwyth, esquire, John Pulayn and John Dewe, Rectors of the church of Haunby [Hawnby],

the manor of Scaulton [Scawton] and lands and tenements in Haunby.

Witnesses. John Etton, Richard Pykeryng, knights, George Etton, esquire.

Given at Scaulton, 2 October 6 Henry VI [1427].   [Latin]

On 12 February 6 Henry VI [1428], William Kyllom of Bristowe, shearman, son and heir of Richard Kyllom, late of York, fishmonger, came into the Council Chamber before William Bowes, Mayor, and sought the enrolment of the following deed of Richard de Tichill, former citizen and mercer of York.

FEOFFMENT.

Richard de Tichill, citizen and mercer of York,

to Richard, son of Thomas de Askham of York and Mariot his wife, daughter of the said Richard de Tichill, and the heirs of their bodies begotten, remainder to the heirs and assigns of Richard son of Thomas,

a tenement with buildings and appurtenances in Mikelgate, which the feoffor had by the gift and feoffment of the said Richard son of Thomas de Askham, lying in width between the land of William Fox and that of William de Friston, and in length from Mikelgate in front as far as the land of Adam de [? Armin] behind.

Witnesses. Henry de Goldbeter, Mayor, William Gra, Thomas de York, Bailiffs, Nicholas Fouk, William Foux, Richard de Brigenhall, William de Acastre, Walter de Otryngton, William de Wetherby, William de Appilton, clerk.

Given at York, on Wednesday, the day after the feast of St. James the Apostle [26 July] 1346, 20 Edward III.   [Latin]

A Clause of the Will of Peter Frothyngham of York.

Devising to William Rillyngton and Katherine his wife, mother of the testator, the tenement inhabited by Richard Gunas, spicer, in Netherousgate, for the life of the said Katherine, remainder to the right heirs of the testator; and to Alice, his wife for life, remainder to his right heirs, the tenement in which Richard Rikall dwelt in Netherousgate.

Appointment of Alice, his wife, William Rillyngton, William Strensall and William Welwyk, chaplains, as executors.

Given, 26 March 1424/5.   [Latin]

(f. 63v) On 11 March 6 Henry VI [1428], John Rasskelf, citizen and merchant, came before William Bowes, Mayor, in the Council Chamber and agreed to the enrolment of the following. Memorandum that on the above date John Rasskelf came before William Bowes, Mayor, William Belford, John Rukeby, William Wrawby, Chamberlains, and Master Roger de Burton, Secretary and Common Clerk, in the Council Chamber on Ouse Bridge, and agreed to pay to John Darell and John Kelk, churchwardens of St. Maurice's Church in Munkgate in the suburbs of York, and their successors, the annual rent of 6d. from his tenement on the north corner of Munkgate, lying between St. Maurice's churchyard and the high street towards Munkbarr. His parents used to pay the 6d. p.a. rent to the churchwardens for the maintenance of a lamp burning in the said church. If the rent was not paid, the Churchwardens were to have distraint.   [Latin]

The removal of sedges and other nuisances in the Foss.

When the most excellent prince, Humphrey Duke of Gloucester, Regent (*custos*) of England,[37] and the reverend father in Christ Thomas Longle, Bishop of Durham, Chancellor of England, were in York in July 8 Henry V [1420], great and serious complaints were made to them that so many large roots of sedges (*seggys*) and filth of the *mudde*, grasses and other noxious things had accumulated and were growing in the *vivarium* of the Foss behind Peseholm, that they were annually the cause of murrain and death of the fish to such an extent that unless a remedy was to be had quickly, all the fish on that side of the *vivarium* would very likely soon be destroyed. Having heard the complaint, they sent in the king's name for Thomas Gare, Mayor, and the City Council, and discussed the matter with them, seeking by what ways and means those defaults and grievances could best and most quickly be remedied, the murrain and death of fish prevented and the increase of fish in that *vivarium* fostered in future. The Mayor and Council informed them that the roots of the *seggys* and other filth which were the cause of the murrain and death of the fish had accumulated in the *vivarium* behind the capital messuage and land of William Bowes, senior, lying in width between the tenement of St. Leonard's Hospital on the east and that of John de Bolton (f. 64) on the west

[37] He replaced his elder brother, John, Duke of Bedford, as regent from January 1420 to February 1421 (*D.N.B.*).

and extending in length from the high street of Peseholm as far as
the Foss, and also behind three other tenements of the said William
Bowes, built on the land formerly of John de Langton in Peseholm,
lying together in width between Thruslane on the west and a
tenement of John Bolton, formerly of Robert de Bylton, on the
east, and extending in length from the high street of Peseholm in
front as far as the Foss behind. If there was to be any remedy it
must of necessity be behind the said messuage and three tenements.
The honourable lords then ordered the Mayor to cause William
Bowes to come before them. When he did so they spoke to him of
the grievances and, having heard his reply and the evidence and
information of many credible persons, they decided that the remedy
could only be had behind the messuage and three tenements aforesaid. They therefore granted licence to William Bowes to enclose
his ground from the land called the *maynland* behind the messuage
and three tenements into the Foss and to place pales there in length
from the dry land across or *endelang* the Foss from the said lane
as far as the ground belonging to St. Leonard's Hospital, according
to the supervision and advice of the warden of the *vivarium*. William Bowes was to remove from the water the roots and filth which
caused, and could in future cause, murrain and to keep the water
outside the pales clear for the feeding and rearing of fish.

And so John Forest, warden of the king's *vivarium*, assigned the
ground to William Bowes and in the presence of Thomas Gare,
Mayor, and many others placed there wooden pales in width from
the dry land and in length from the land of St. Leonard's Hospital
as far as the said lane. William Bowes sought that these details
should be attested and recorded under the mayoral seal.

Given at York, the last day of August 8 Henry V [1420].

[Latin]

(f. 64v) FEOFFMENT.[39]

Henry Bowet, clerk,
to William Skirwyth, clerk,
three messuages in Conyngstrete, lying together between the lands
and tenements formerly of Richard Roderham and the guildhall
of the Mayor and Commonalty, and in length from Conyngstrete in
front to the River Ouse behind, and which the feoffor had by the

---

[39] See also f.66v and f.67 below.

gift and feoffment of Stephen Ruddestane, Rector of the church of Bittyll,[40] son and heir of Agnes de Askham, widow of John de Askham, late citizen and merchant of York.

Witnesses. William Ormeshede, Mayor, John Louth, John Warde, Sheriffs, Thomas Roderham, William Newland, Richard Neuland, John Laxton.

Given at York, 6 March 3 Henry VI [1425].   [Latin]

QUITCLAIM.

Henry Bowet,
to William Skirwyth,
three messuages in Conyngstrete [as above].
Witnesses [as above].
Given at York, 8 March 3 Henry VI [1425].   [Latin]

(ff. 64v-65) LETTERS OF ATTORNEY.

Henry Bowet, clerk,
to Thomas Wylton, clerk, and Thomas Roderham, citizen and merchant,
to deliver seisin to William Skirwyth, clerk, of three messuages in Conyngstrete [as above].
Given at York, 6 March 3 Henry VI [1425].   [Latin]

(ff. 65-65v) WILL.

Of Alice, widow of John de Rughford, late of York, clerk, desiring burial in the Church of the Friars Preachers in York, for which she bequeathed 6s. 8d. to the fabric of the church, etc.[41] Devising to Walter, her son, and the heirs of his body, remainder to Margaret her daughter, and the heirs of her body, remainder to Margaret de

---

[40] Also spelt *Buttyll*, probably Bothel in Cumberland.

[41] The following clauses, omitted from the present volume, appear in the copy in the Register of Wills Vol. II f. 10v at the Borthwick Institute of Historical Research.

and 6s 8d as a pious donation to the said friars; to the Rector of her parish church of St. John at Ouse Bridge as a mortuary gift, her best garment tailored for her. She desired 6 lbs of wax made into six candles to burn around her body on the day of burial, half of them in her parish church of St. John and the others at the Friars Preachers.

To Joan, her servant, her gown with the *kyrtill* [skirt or outer petticoat]; to the poor in the *Masyndew* on Ouse Bridge 3s 4d, to be divided equally between them; to the chaplains and clerks continually celebrating at St. Mary's mass in the chapel on Ouse Bridge 3s 4d, equally divided beween them; to the Friars Minor of York 12d.

Ottryngton for life, with the reversion to the right heirs of Walter de Ottryngton, a tenement in Mikelgate at Ouse Bridge, lying in width between the lane which leads to the River Ouse and the *meason dieu* on the one side, and the messuage of Stephen Littester on the other, and in length from the high street in front to the messuage in which Thomas de Wenslawdale now lives behind; also to Walter, her son, and the heirs of his body, on condition that he should pay her debts, all her lands and tenements in Thrysk. Should the said Walter die without heirs of his body or fail to fulfil that condition, the lands and tenements were to remain to Margaret de Rughford, her daughter, and the heirs of her body, remainder to William de Moreton of York, butcher, and the heirs of his body; to Margaret, her daughter, and the heirs of her body, remainder to Walter, her son, and the heirs of his body, remainder to William de Moreton and Joan, his wife, and the heirs of their bodies, the tenement which William de Moreton of York, butcher, now holds in Mikelgate at the foot of Ouse Bridge.[42]

Appointment of Margaret, her daughter, and William de Moreton as executors.

Given, 22 January 1397/8.

Probate was granted, 1 February 1397/8, before the Official and Commissary General of the Court of York, the Archbishop's see being vacant, and administration granted to the executors named in the will. [Latin]

LICENCE.

The Mayor and Commonalty of York,

to William Craven,

to occupy and enclose his ground and free holding in Walmegate, lying in length from the land of the Prior and Convent of St. Andrew in front as far as the Foss behind, and in width between the land formerly of Isolda Dyer [*Tinctor*] and the lane called *Sayntdinisselendyng*, excepting only a piece of land, four feet in width at each end, outside his earth wall, which he was to leave unenclosed for the passage of men.

---

[42] Further omission.

To the Friars Preachers an annual rent of 5s for the twenty years after her death from her lands and tenements in the City and County of York, in order that they should perform exequies for herself and her husband annually during those years; the remainder of her goods to Margaret, her daughter, to be disposed of for the good of her soul.

William Craven had previously complained to John Aldestane-more, Mayor, that the parishioners of St. Denys's parish were wrongfully preventing him from enclosing his land. They declared that it belonged to the Commonalty. The Mayor had ordered the searchers of the masons and carpenters to view the ground and they found that it belonged to the said William, not to the Mayor and Commonalty. William Craven had again complained that the parishioners hindered him in enclosing the ground, contrary to the tenor of his deeds and the finding of the searchers. Guy Rouclyff and Thomas Warde of the Council were therefore ordered to view the ground and inspect the deeds and they reported that it belonged to William Craven. [Latin]

Undated [1427]

(f. 66) FEOFFMENT.

John Werkesworth, citizen of York, and Joan, his wife,
to William Couper of York, pinner,
a garden in Hundegate in the parish of St. John the Baptist, lying in width between the land of John Langton, knight, and the land of Thomas Roderham, and in length from Hundegate in front as far as the Fossedyke behind. The feoffors had the garden by the will of William Sauvage.

Witnesses. John Aldestanemore, Mayor, John Brounflete, William Girlyngton, Sheriffs, Thomas del Gare, William Ormesheved, John Wawne, John Radcliff, John Skirmer, Richard Chaundeler, John Belle.

Given at York, on the feast of St. Bartholomew the Apostle, 5 Henry VI [24 August 1427]. [Latin]

GRANT.

Joan Werkesworth, widow of John Werkesworth,
to William Couper of York, pinner,
an annual rent of 2s. from three tenements in Mikel Saynt Andrew-gate belonging to the chantry of St. John the Baptist founded in the Cathedral Church of St. Peter, which Thomas Northhouse, vicar in the Cathedral, lately had, and which William Derham, vicar, now has. The three tenements lay together between the tenement formerly of Robert Hovyngham and the tenement of John Louth, merchant.

If the rent was forty days in arrears, William Couper was to have distraint.

Witnesses. William Bowes, Mayor, Thomas Gare, junior, and John Raghton, Sheriffs, William Ormesheved, Thomas Bracebryg, John Radclif, John Skyrmer, John Belle.

Given at York, 20 October 7 Henry VI [1428].   [Latin]

(f. 66v) CERTIFICATE OF TITLE.

granted by the Mayor, Sheriffs and Aldermen on hearing the following evidence of Thomas Doncaster, junior, Richard Newland, tailor, John Bown, and Thomas Every.

Given under the mayoral seal, 6 June 7 Henry VI [1429].

Feoffment.

> Stephen Ruddestan, son and heir of Agnes Askham, widow of John Askham of York,
>
> to Henry Bowet, Archdeacon of Richemond and Henry Soulby, esquire,

lands and tenements in Conyngstrete, lying in width between the tenement of Thomas Roderham and the guildhall of the Mayor and Commonalty, and in length from the high street in front to the River Ouse behind.

Letters of Attorney.

> Henry Bowet and Henry Soulby,
>
> to Richard Newland,
>
> to collect the profits from those tenements and deliver them to Henry Bowet and Henry Soulby to the use of Master Henry Bowet, late Archbishop of York.

Acquittance.

> Henry Bowet, Archdeacon, and Henry Soulby,
>
> to Richard Newland,

from the collection of the profits from the tenements, following the death of the Archbishop and the receipt of the profits due on that date by Henry Bowet, Archdeacon.

Given, 18 March 2 Henry VI [1424].

Quitclaim.

> Henry Soulby,
>
> to Henry Bowet,

of the said tenements. He delivered all the deeds thereof in his possession to Henry Bowet, in the presence of those aforesaid, 18 March [1424].

Letters of Attorney.
Henry Bowet, Archdeacon, alone at the instance of Henry Souleby,
to Thomas Every,
to collect the profits from the tenements and deliver them to Henry Bowet.
Feoffment.[43]
Henry Bowet, Archdeacon,
to William Skirwyth,
the said lands and tenements. Seisin was delivered by Thomas Wilton, clerk, attorney, 6 March 3 Henry VI [1425].   [Latin]

(f. 67) The following quitclaim was exhibited by Henry Bowet, Archdeacon of Richemond, in the Chamber before Nicholas Blakburn, Mayor, 20 August 7 Henry VI [1429], and is here enrolled, word for word, in the common register of the city.   [Latin]

QUITCLAIM.
Henry Soulby of Cawode,
to Henry Bowet, Archdeacon of Richemond,
three messuages in Conyngstrete which they had jointly by the gift and feoffment of Stephen Ruddestan, Rector of the church of Buttill [as above ff. 64v, 66v].
Given at York, 18 March 2 Henry VI [1424].   [Latin]

On 12 September 9 Henry VI [1430] John Skyrmer, citizen and merchant of York, came into the Chamber and showed to Richard Russell, Mayor, the following deed of feoffment. He swore on oath that he had not alienated the tenement mentioned therein, and that he alone was seised of it.

(ff. 67-67v) FEOFFMENT.
Alice, widow of Thomas Miton, son and heir of Hugh de Miton, of York,
to John Skyrmer, citizen and merchant of York,
a tenement on the Pavement, anciently called Merketskyre, lying in width between Hosyergate and the churchyard of the church called *Crucekyrk*, and in length from Merketskyre in front as far as the land of John de Langton, knight, behind. Alice Miton had the tenement by the legacy of Thomas de Miton, her husband.

[43] See above, f. 64v.

Witnesses. Richard Russell, Mayor, John Aldstanmore, Thomas
Aton, Sheriffs, Thomas Santon, John Waughen, Robert de Fereby,
John Radclyf.

Given at York, 2 October 9 Henry V [1421].   [Latin]

FEOFFMENT.

John, son and heir of Richard Gra of York,
to Joan, daughter of Thomas de St. Oswald of York,
a messuage with appurtenances in Usegate, lying in length from
Usegate in front as far as Coppergate behind, and in width between
the land of Richard Plaindamors and the land held by William
Burgoillon.

Rent. 4s. p.a. for customary services to the Abbot of St. Mary's,
York, and 20s. p.a. to the feoffor, for all secular dues. If the rent was
in arrears, the feoffor was to have distraint. If it was a year in
arrears or the feoffee committed waste, so that no rent could be
raised, he was to have re-entry.

Witnesses. Nicholas le Flemyng, Mayor, Adam Kyngesun, Jordan
Sauvage, Thomas son of David, Bailiffs, Nicholas le Sauser, Robert
de Wyxstowe, Alan de Quixley, Robert de Sallay, Roger de Piker-
ing of York, clerk.

Given at York, the Thursday before the feast of St. George the
Martyr [19 April] 1319, 12 Edward son of Edward.   [Latin]

(f. 68) FEOFFMENT.

Thomas Parker, [Rector] of the parish church of Bolton Percy,
and Richard Colhome, clerk,
to Richard Bowet and the heirs of his body, remainder to Thomas
Bowet, esquire, his brother, and the male heirs of his body, remainder to Nicholas Bowet, nephew of the said Richard and the
heirs of his body, remainder to William Bowet, knight, and the
heirs of his body, remainder to Robert Bowet, son of the said
Richard, and the heirs of his body, remainder to the right heirs
of Elizabeth, daughter of Richard Brune and mother of the said
Richard Bowet,
a third of the lordship of Bothill [Bothel] together with lands and
tenements, rents and services which the feoffor had by the gift and
feoffment of the said Richard Bowet, in Dereham [Dearham],
Bownes cum Cardirnok [Cardurnock], Bronskath[44] and Karlell

[44] *Bronskath*, either Brunstock, or Brunskaith (now lost) in the parish of Burgh
by Sands.

[Carlisle] in the county of *Karliolen*.

Witnesses. John Skelton, Robert Mulcastre, William Osmunder-
ley, knights, Richard Skelton, William Kirkeby.

Given at Bothill aforesaid. [Undated].[45]   [Latin]

(f. 68v) ARBITRATION.

John Ampilford and John Crawe, masons, John Haxeby, senior,
the assign of Thomas Hunte, carpenter, one of the searchers of the
carpenters, in his absence, William Lancastre for both crafts, and
John Bolron, carpenter of the commonalty, were assigned by
Nicholas Blakburn, Mayor, to search and certify to whom a wooden
hedge in the suburb of Mikelgate belonged. The Prior of Holy
Trinity claimed that it belonged to that monastery and was on his
ground. Richard Bryan claimed that it belonged to the ground
which he leased from the Commonalty, lying without Mikelgate
Bar, between the land of the Abbot and Convent of Kyrkestall on
the west and the land of the aforesaid Prior on the east.

The searchers made a diligent search on either side of the hedge
and found that the whole hedge with the trees growing in it, extending in length from the post of the tenement of the Commonalty,
in the tenure of Richard Bryan, towards the monks' meadow,
belonged to the said Prior and his successors. They were henceforth
to hold it without any hindrance from the Mayor and Commonalty.

12 December 8 Henry VI, 1429.   [Latin]

(ff. 68v-69) LEASE.

William Strensall, sergeant at the Chamber of the King's Great
Council and Parliament,

to Alan Bedale, citizen and goldsmith of York, and Joan, his
wife,

lands and tenements in the parish of St. Michael le Belfrey in
Stayngate, lying between the tenement of the prebendary of Barneby
and that of the prebendary of Ampulford, and in length from
Stayngate in front to the tenement of the prebendary of Masseham
behind.

Term. The lives of Alan Bedale and Joan his wife.

---

[45] Between 1411 and 1423. The induction mandate of Thomas Parker as Rector
is dated 26 June 1411 (Register of Archbishop Henry Bowet, R.I.18. f. 99v). John
Selowe was collated, 6 Oct. 1423, on the death of Thomas Parker (R.I.18. f. 148).

Rent. 20s. p.a. which was now paid to William Strensall for the first three years.

The lessor was to have distraint if the rent was in arrears. If it was half a year overdue and he could not obtain sufficient distraint, he was to have re-entry.

The lessees were to maintain and repair the lands and tenements and protect them from wind and rain at their own costs, and pay any other charges falling on the property during that term.

Given on the vigil of St. Martin the Bishop 7 Henry VI, [10 November 1428]. [Latin]

ARBITRATION.

by Guy Rouclyff and Thomas Warde,

between the citizens of York and William Fox,

arising from the citizens' claim in the mayoralty of Richard Russell, 8 [Henry VI] [1430], to free entry through the holding of William Fox in Bouthom as far as Bouthom Leys. Having seen the evidence of both parties, they adjudged that William Fox should have the holding free from any claim of entry and should pay to the Mayor and citizens, 4d. p.a. for ever. [Latin]

(f. 69v) LEASE.

Henry Bowet, Archdeacon of Richemond in the Church of St. Peter, York,

to Thomas Doncaster, esquire,

a tenement in Stayngate belonging to the office of Archdeacon, with all houses and other buildings pertaining to it, lying in width between the lane called Swyngale and the land belonging to the chantry of St. William's altar in the Cathedral Church of York, and extending in length from Stayngate in front as far as the land of the Abbot and Convent of Coverham behind.

Term. 99 years from the feast of St. Martin in Winter, 1423.

Rent. 6s. 8d. p.a.

The lessor was to have distraint if the rent was in arrears. If he was unable to find sufficient distraint within fifteen days, he was to have re-entry. The lessee was to maintain and repair the property at his own costs and to return it in as good condition or better, without waste or destruction, at the end of the term.

Given at York, 14 October 1423, 2 Henry VI. [Latin]

(f. 70) ACQUITTANCE.

Henry Bowet, Archdeacon of Richemond,

to Thomas Doncaster, esquire, for the life of Henry Bowet, from payment of 6s. 8d. p.a. rent from a tenement in Stayngate, leased to the said Thomas Doncaster [as above].

Given at York, 20 October 1423, 2 Henry VI.   [Latin]

GRANT.

Thomas Doncastre son of Thomas Doncastre, citizen and merchant of York,

to Thomas Doncastre, his father, and Robert Doncastre, his brother,

his interest in the houses, shops, lands and tenements in Stayngate which he had by the lease of Henry Bowet, Archdeacon of Richemond.

Given at York, 8 October 8 Henry VI [1429].   [Latin]

(ff. 70-70v.) *Examination concerning seisin* [of a messuage.]

On 6 January 9 Henry VI [1431], John Shirwod, formerly of York, butcher, came before Richard Russell, Mayor, and Roger de Burton, Common Clerk, and of his own free will affirmed on oath that John Loftehouse and Thomas Holbek, citizens of York, had by virtue of letters of attorney of Walter Rufford, delivered seisin to Richard Hastynges, knight, and others, about Whit Sunday, 8 Henry VI, of a messuage lying next to the lane leading to the River Ouse at the west end of Ouse Bridge, on the north side thereof; and that the said Walter had died before the delivery of seisin, namely about the feast of the Annunciation of the Blessed Virgin Mary, in Lent, 8 Henry VI. Further, he said, at the time of the delivery of seisin in the messuage, he, John Shirwod, was the tenant for twenty years, by the right of Alice his wife, executrix of the will of Thomas Braine, her late husband, to whom the said Walter had granted an indenture and delivered seisin. At the time of the delivery of seisin he had not appointed Richard Hastynges as his attorney, nor had the same Richard Hastynges caused him to remove from the messuage. Also, Alice, the wife of Thomas Rygecok, then being in distant parts, the tenant of the said messuage at the will of John Shirwod, had delivered 1d. to Richard Hastynges, which she was forbidden to do by the said John Shirwod.

Thomas Holbeck, on being examined, said that as attorney of Walter Rufford by virtue of his letters of attorney he, together with

John Loftehouse, had delivered seisin in the messuage to Richard Hastynges, as aforesaid, about Whit Sunday in the said year; that Alice, the wife of Thomas Rygecok, had delivered 1d. to Richard Hastyngs, contrary to the wish of John Shirwod, and that before seisin was delivered, he had heard tell that the said Walter had died about the feast of the Annunciation.

Thereupon, John Stafford, junior, personally made the following grant. [Latin]

CONFIRMATION.

John Stafford, junior,
to John Shirwod, former butcher and citizen of York,
the interest which John Shirwod had by the lease of John del Hall of London and Alice, his wife, daughter and heir of Margaret Rufford, the daughter and heir of John Rufford, late of York, clerk, in a tenement lying on the south side of Mikelgate in the parish of St. John at Ouse Bridge, between the tenement of John Moubray and the tenement in which Thomas Midelham dwelt.

Term. 8 years from the feast of the Nativity of St. John the Baptist next. [Latin]

(ff. 70-71) WILL.[46]

of Margaret, wife of Sir John Gra, knight,
desiring burial in the chancel of the Priory of Kyrkebellers [Kirby Bellars] next to her grandfather, and making the following bequests: —

For the celebration of two trentals for her soul, 20.; to Annora Perpunt, a *violet* gown with large sleeves, and fur pouches, a lined *sangwyn* gown, a pair of *templers*[47] *de perle de Treyfoillez* in the custody of William Smyth, and a pair of *trussyng coffers*;[48] to Agnes Crawen, a green gown with *stranelyn*[49] fur, a black gown furred with *meniver*,[50] a *ridyng gowne*, a *heyke*[51] and a pair of *trussing coffers*; to Agnes Perpunt, two garments of *lawne* and three of *umple*[52] and all other garments with the *nekkerchiefs* and

---

[46] Partially illegible except under ultra violet light.
[47] *templers*, temples, ornaments of jewellery worn on the forehead.
[48] *trussyng coffers*, packing chests, for travelling.
[49] *stranelyn*, strandling; ? fur of the squirrel taken at Michaelmas, (R. E. Latham, *Revised Mediaeval Latin Word-List*)
[50] *meniver*; miniver, kind of fur used for trimming; stoat or ermine.
[51] *heyke*: cloak.
[52] *umple*: fine linen.

three camises; to Joan, wife of John Crawen, a *scarlet* gown lined
with *fustian*; to Richard Reynacres, 40s; to Nicholas Croft, a murrey
gown with *grey* fur and large sleeves; to Thomas Lewenthorp, a
scarlet gown with fur pouches and *poket sleves*; to Annora Perpunt
and Agnes Craven, all other *capucia de attyre*;[53] all her other
kyrtells were to be distributed to the poor and other items (*capicia*)
sold and the money distributed to the poor; to Henry Wylly, 20s; to
the said Agnes, a saddle in which she used to ride with the *harnes*
of her saddle; a white horse called Lyard as a mortuary gift, to go
before her body to the Priory Church of Kyrkebellers; to Joan
Hothom, nun of Heenynges [Heynings], a gold ring with a
diamand.

Appointment of Sir John Gra, knight, her husband, John Haget,
clerk, Richard Reynacres and Nicholas Croft, as her executors to
pay her debts and afterwards to fulfil her will. To the said executors,
with the consent of John Gra, her husband, a tenement called
Neseldplace, which was to be sold by them and the money used for
the good of her soul and her ancestors' in alms and other good
works, according to their discretion; and a tenement in the town
of Notyngham in the tenure of Lady Joyce called *Dame Joyousplace,*
all messuages, lands and tenements, rents and services in the town
of Notyngham which she had by hereditary right, and a tenement in
Leycestre called *Sporour place*, to be sold and the money disposed
of as above. The lands and tenements, rents and services held in
fee simple in the town of Kyrkebybellers and elsewhere in the
County of Leycestre, of which Hugh de Wyllughby and others
were enfeoffed, and also all manors, lands and tenements, rents and
services in the Counties of Norffolk, Suffolk and York and elsewhere, excepting the aforesaid tenements in the City of York, and
the towns of Leycestre and Notyngham, were to be sold at the
discretion of John Gra, her husband, and the proceeds to be turned
to his use.

Given in the Priory of Nocton, Wednesday 5 October 1429.

Proved before the Official of the Archdeacon of Stowe in the
chapel of Ingylby on 22 October in the year aforesaid. The executors
were to produce an inventory of the goods of the deceased on the
next law-day after the feast of the Epiphany.   [Latin]

---

[53] *capitia*: hood or other item of a woman's dress.

Assize of Fresh Force.[54]

On Monday in the fifth week of Lent 1 Henry VI [22 March 1423], the plaintiffs named below presented a bill of assize of fresh force to Thomas Esyngwald, Mayor, and William Craven and Thomas Kyrkham, Sheriffs, as follows: —

John Talbot, Lord de Fornyval, Thomas de Dacre, Lord of Gildesland [Gilsland, parish of Waterhead, Cumberland], William de Haryngton, knight, Richard Hawnserd, knight, Edmund Fitz-William and Geoffrey Lowther, complained that they had been dispossessed within the last forty days of their freehold in York, by Christopher Spencer, esquire, and Margaret, his wife, formerly the wife of Walter Askham; pledges for the prosecution were Thomas Santon and John Hexham, merchants. The sergeants at mace to the Sheriffs were ordered by the Mayor and Sheriffs to summon twenty-four free and law-worthy men, mistrusted by neither party, to give evidence before the Mayor and Sheriffs in the *Guyhalda* on Monday in the sixth week of Lent [29 March]. And they put the said Christopher and Margaret on bail to ensure that they or their bailiffs should be there (f. 71v) to hear the inquest. The plaintiffs were ordered to appear on the same day and they appointed John Alman as their attorney.

On the said day [29 March] John Alman complained on behalf of the plaintiffs that they had been disseised of the twenty-eight messuages by the defendants within the last forty days. The defendants did not appear but Nicholas Tunstall, their bailiff, replied for them and gave no reason why the assize should be stayed. It was therefore ordered to be taken but was deferred in default of the jurors. The sergeants at mace were ordered to distrain their goods to ensure their presence on Monday, the day after the first Sunday after Easter [12 April]. The same day was given to both parties.

On that day, Nicholas Tunstall, attorney for the defendants, claimed that the plaintiffs had never been seised of the messuages and therefore could [not] have been dispossessed. The defendants had caused no injury or disseisin to the plaintiffs and requested that the matter be tried by assize, and the plaintiffs did likewise. The jurors, Robert Fereby, Richard Lucas, Henry Rothewell, John Hesyll, John Garston, Adam Lytster, Thomas Holbek, John Thornton, cordwainer, Thomas Bryght, goldsmith, Henry Skyrmer, Robert Thresk, walker, and John Skyrmer, declared on oath that

[54] Faded in parts.

the plaintiffs had been seised of all the messuages until Christopher Spencer and Margaret, his wife, wrongfully dispossessed them within the forty days before the complaint was made, causing damages to the plaintiffs of 100s. The Court enquired whether the disseisin was made with force and arms, to which the jurors replied that it was not. It was ordered by the Court that the plaintiffs should recover seisin of the messuages together with damages of 100s. assessed by the jurors, and that the said Christopher and Margaret should be amerced. The plaintiffs freely forgave the 100s.

Given under the official mayoral seal, date as above [12 April 1423].   [Latin]

(f. 72) FEOFFMENT.
    John Dodyngton, citizen and merchant of York,
    to Henry Percy, Earl of Northumberland, John Southwell, clerk, William Swerd, and John Dunkan, chaplains,
lands and tenements in the City and suburbs of York.
    Witnesses. Richard Russell, Mayor, John Lillyng, John Gascoigne, Sheriffs, John Moreton, John Aldestanemor, Thomas Holbek, William Brandesby.
    Given at York, 5 July 9 Henry V [1421].   [Latin]

GIFT.
    John Dodyngton,
    to Henry Percy, John Southwell, William Swerd, and John Dunkan,
all his good and chattels, in return for a certain sum of money paid by them.
    Witnesses. Richard Russell, Mayor, John Lillyng, John Gascoigne, Sheriffs, John Aldestanemore, William Brandesby.
    Given at York, 5 July 9 Henry V [1421].   [Latin]

(ff. 72-72v.) AGREEMENT.
    between Robert Howm, citizen and merchant of York, Robert Holme, apprentice in the law, and Agnes, widow of the late John Kenlay of York,
on the division of the lands and tenements which belonged to the late John Kenlay. Agnes, his widow, was to have his lands and tenements in Huntyngton as dower; Robert Howm, citizen and merchant, by the right and title of Margaret, his wife, daughter and

one of the heirs of John Kenlay, was to have a tenement in Ousegate, another tenement in Castlegate and all rents-seck[55] specified in
a deed; and Robert Holme, by the right and title of Katherine,
his wife, daughter and one of the heirs of John Kenlay, sister of
the aforesaid Margaret, was to have all the lands and tenements
which belonged to John Kenlay in Coppergate.

[Undated.] [Latin]

ACKNOWLEDGEMENT OF TRUST.

William Revetour, chaplain, and Robert Neuton, executors of
the will of Alice Coker,
to Agnes Burn and Isabel Blakburn, daughter of the said Agnes
and of Ed. Blakburn, her late husband,
testifying that William Revetour held in safe custody for the use
of the said Isabel, the following items which the said Alice Coker
left to her in her will; a bowl worth 26s. 8d, a piece of silver with a
cover worth 20s, six silver spoons worth 12s, a silver girdle worth
5s, a silver ring worth 9d, a wool-fell worth 3s. 4d, a bronze pot
worth 5s, a plate worth 12d, a grid-iron with a *creset*[56] worth 8d, a
feather-bed with a *bolster* worth 5s, a pair of *blanketts* worth 2s, a
pair of sheets worth 3s, a blue bed with a coverlet worth 13s. 4d, a
red bed of *say*[57] without a coverlet worth 4s, a crucifix worth 20d,
two amber jars worth 12d, a chest worth 6d, a towel worth 3s, and
a linen cloth (*mappa*) worth 20d.

Further, that the said William had £7. os. 3d of the said
Ed[ward's] goods which belonged to Isabel, and which he agreed
to pay to her or her attorney when she should become of age.
Agnes and Isabel affirmed that William Revetour had never had
any other goods or chattels belonging to them.

Given, 7 April 10 Henry VI [1432]. [Latin]

RECEIPT AND ACQUITTANCE.

Agnes Burn, daughter of William Coker, late of York, girdler,
to William Revetour, chaplain, and Robert Neuton of York,
girdler, executors of the will of Alice Coker, widow of the said
William Coker,
for a bowl, a piece of silver, six silver spoons, a girdle ornamented

---

[55] *rent-seck*, rent reserved by deed but without any clause of distress.
[56] *cresset*: fire-basket.
[57] *say*: fine, serge-like cloth.

with silver and £13. 9s. 2d which Alice, her mother, had bequeathed to her; and acquittance from all actions or demands.

Given, 7 April 10 Henry VI [1432].

Subscribed. Burton.   [Latin]

(f. 73) QUITCLAIM.

John Beverlay, citizen and merchant of York, son and heir of John Beverlay, son and heir of William de Beverlay, late of York, spicer, and of Alice, his wife,

to Nicholas Wyspyngton, citizen and merchant of York,

lands, tenements, and messuages in the Thoresdaymarket, which the said Nicholas Wyspyngton had by the gift and feoffment of John Spanyell, George Helmesley, chaplains, and Nicholas Girlyngton, gentleman, and which William de Beverlay, his grandfather, gave to John Wilton and Agnes his wife.

Witnesses. Thomas Snawdon, Mayor, Thomas Roderham and Thomas Kyrk, Sheriffs, William Ormeshede, William Bowes.

Given at York, 8 October 11 Henry VI [1432].   [Latin]

BOND.

Thomas Ridlay, citizen and alderman, John Thrysk, merchant, and Ralph Clyfton, gentleman, all of York,

in 20 marks each,

to ensure that Nicholas Blakburn junior, merchant, citizen and alderman, would keep the king's peace towards Thomas Mody of York, walker.

Nicholas Blakburn, junior, was similarly bound in 40 marks, before William Bedale, Mayor, and the Aldermen, Justices of the Peace for the city.

Given, 12 April 15 Henry VI [1437].   [Latin]

(f. 73v) FEOFFMENT.

John Brygnall of York, chaplain,

to Joan Halyday, daughter of John Halyday, formerly of Akworth,

lands and tenements in the Marsh in the City of York, lying in width between the lane which leads to All Saints' Church in Havergate and the land which formerly belonged to Thomas Bracebryg, citizen and merchant, and in length from the high street in front as far as the land of William Alne, late citizen and merchant.

Rent. 40s. p.a.

If the rent was forty days in arrears, John Brygnall was to have distraint; if it was a year in arrears and sufficient distraint could not be found, or the property was not adequately maintained and repaired he was to have repossession.

Witnesses. Thomas Snawdon, Mayor, William Bowes, junior, John Esyngwald, Sheriffs, Richard Russell, Thomas Bracebryg, John Ward, William Holme.

Given at York, the Wednesday after the feast of the Assumption of the Blessed Virgin Mary, 10 Henry VI [20 August 1432].

[Latin]

(f. 74) GIFT.

William Hovyngham of York, butcher,
 to Peter Huton, Nicholas Bewe, clerks, and John Emondson,
all his goods and chattels.

Witnesses. Thomas Snawdon, Mayor, Thomas Kirke and Thomas Rotheram, Sheriffs, Nicholas Blakborne, William Bedale, and John Wigane.

Given at York, 10 October 11 Henry VI [1432].   [Latin]

The said William Hovyngham came before Thomas Snaudon, Mayor, and acknowledged the deed to have been made by him without fraud or any evil intent, in the presence of Thomas Ryddelay, William Barton, Chamberlains, Roger de Burton, Common Clerk, on the feast of St. Lucy the Virgin, 11 Henry VI [13 December 1432].

Subscribed. Burton R.   [Latin]

LIVERY OF SEISIN.

William Nauton, Katherine, his wife, and Hamon Askham,
 to William Roucliff,
of an annual rent of 40s. from eighteen messuages in York of which they were the tenants, by the payment of 2s.

Reciting the fine levied in the king's court at Westminster, 6 Henry VI, by which Joan, the widow of John Werkesworth, had granted the rent to William Roucliff.

Witnesses. William Ormesheede, Mayor, Thomas Kyrke and John Rokeby, Sheriffs, Richard Russell, John Bolton.

Given, 12 March 11 Henry VI [1433].

On 5 May 11 Henry VI [1434], William Nauton, Katherine his

wife, and Hamon Askham came before William Ormesheede, Mayor, John Thresk, Chamberlain, and Roger de Burton, Common Secretary, and acknowledged the deed to have been made by them.

It was enrolled at their request.   [Latin]

(f. 74v.) DEED TO LEAD THE USES OF A FINE.[58]

between John of Thwaittes of the one part, and John Hewyk of Westminster and Emmotte his wife, Walter Loffe of Ramsebury in Wiltshire, and Joan (John), his wife, of the other part.

John Hewyk and Emmotte, Walter Loffe and Joan, were to convey to John Thwaittes at the latter's cost, a sure estate in law by a fine in a court of record, in a *mese* in Skeldergate and in three *meses* on Bysshophill which formerly belonged to William Aglande of York, merchant, and two acres of meadow *a stang*[59] *less* in the meadow of Acastre Malbych.

Consideration. 133 marks to John Hewyk and Emmotte, Walter Loffe and Joan; 53 marks was to be paid in hand, and £26. 13s. 4d. [40 marks] of the 133 marks to be paid to John Gascoigne of York, merchant.

John of Thwaittes was then to receive all the bonds and sureties in which the said Walter Loffe and Joan were bound to John Gascoigne, and to deliver the same to them. He was to pay a further 20 marks on both the feast of St. Hillary next and the Quindene of Easter.

John of Thwaittes was to receive from John of Laweton of York, tenant of the messuage in Skeldergate, 7 marks owed for the previous year's rent, if the latter would pay it to him. Otherwise John Hewyk and Emmotte, Walter Loffe and Joan would allow him it in his last payment.

John of Thwaittes was to receive all deeds and muniments relating to the messuages and meadow, namely twenty-six deeds in the hands of John Gascoigne and two indentures and a testament in the hands of John Topclyff. He had received the deeds of the meadow.

He was to enfeoff Dame *John* Graystok of half a garden which she had bought of Walter Loffe and Joan, and to take an obligation in 20 marks out of the hands of the said Joan, in which sum Walter and Joan were bound to Sir Rauf Graystok and Dame Joan his wife,

[58] Faded in parts.
[59] *stang*: measure of land, a rood.

as surety for half of the garden. Should the value of the messuages prove to be less than 8 marks p.a., the said John Hewyk and Emmotte, Walter Loffe and Joan would reduce the consideration of 133 marks in proportion. John Gascoigne was to release his right in the messuages to John of Thwayttes before Easter next and to receive the said sum of £26. 13s. 4d.

Given, 26 November 10 Henry VI [1431]. [English]

(f. 75) QUITCLAIM.

Nicholas Westfield, clerk, of the County of York, and Joan his wife, daughter and heir of John Bode, former burgess of the town of Cales [Calais], and Margaret, his wife,

to the said Margaret Bode, widow and executrix of the will of John Bode,

lands and tenements, rents and services which formerly belonged to John Bode, father of the said Joan, in the town of Cales. Because his seal was unknown to many, and for greater security, he had caused the official mayoral seal to be affixed to the deed.

Given at York, 23 August 1433, 11 Henry VI. [Latin]

(ff. 75-75v) QUITCLAIM.

John Lancastre, citizen and tailor of York,

to John Austanemore, merchant, and William Holbek, mercer, citizens of York,

an annual rent of 40s. from the five tenements which Adam Wygan, late Rector of St. Saviour's Church, and Ellis Yong, chaplain, had by the gift and feoffment of Thomas Holbek, late citizen of York and Matilda, his wife, in Mikelgate and without the *Mikellyth* in the suburbs of York. John Lancastre, together with John Dunkan late of York, chaplain, had the rent of 40s. by the grant of the said Adam Wygan and Ellis Yong by a fine levied in the king's court.

Witnesses. William Ormeshede, Mayor, Nicholas Wyspyngton, Nicholas Usflete, Sheriffs, John Moreton, William Bedale, Nicholas Louth, William Stokton.

Given, 4 January 12 Henry VI [1434].

On 7 January 12 Henry VI, John Lancastre came before William Ormesheved, Mayor, and in the presence of John Thresk, one of the Chamberlains, and Roger Burton, Common Clerk, acknowledged that the deed had been made by him. [Latin]

On 15 April 12 Henry VI [1434], John Apilton, Abbot of Neubo [Newbo], came before Thomas Gare, Mayor, and acknowledged, in the presence of Roger de Burton, Common Clerk, and others, that the deed shown by Robert Arthyngton, gentleman, was made by him, John Apilton, and was sealed with his seal, the tenor of which follows: —   [Latin]

"Wytt all men that I Johne Apilton, Abbot of Neubo, sumtyme Vicar of Acastre Malbys, confessour and executor to Nicholas Northfolk of Naburne, wyttnes that the forsayd Nicholas in hys lyve at the tyme of his dying, prayd and charged me als I wald answar to God at the day of dome that I sould gyve none of hys moveable godys nor herelomes to Cateryn and Johne, doghtiris of Thomas, his son, yf so were that the same Thomas happynd noght to cum home beyonde the see bot thar to dye, for, he sade, the forsade Cateryn and Johne sowlde inheret all hys land in Nabourn and others plass, for he saide he myght noght put it fro thame, nor he wald noght dame his sall nor charge his consiens saveyng the land that he gafe to hys othir childyr for terme of thar lyve, and this I wyttnest and rehersed before Johne Portyngton and William Wylesthorp, arbetrores chosyn on the parte of Johne Northfolk. In wyttnes of this, to this present wrytyng wryten by my nowyn hand, I have sett my sele. Wrytyn at Yorke, the 11 daye of Marse in the yer of Oure Lord 1427".

(f. 76) On 12 June 12 Henry VI [1434], John Bryan of Swynton in Rydale in the County of York, gentleman, came before Thomas Gare, Mayor, in the Council Chamber on Ouse Bridge, and declared on oath in the presence of Guy Roucliff, Recorder, William Stokton, one of the Chamberlains, and Roger de Burton, Common Clerk, that he did not know of any entail of those lands and tenements in Seynt Savourgate which John Thresk, citizen and merchant of York, had lately bought from him nor of any impediment to John Thresk's right to those lands and tenements in the future; but that he, John Bryan, had full right and title to them at the time of the grant, and would fulfil any agreements then made with John Thresk.

Subscribed. Burton, R.   [Latin]

(ff. 76-76v) FEOFFMENT.

Master Richard Arnall, Official of the Court of York, Robert

Alne, Parson in the Church of York, John Spanyell, chaplain, and William Stokton, citizen and mercer,

to Joan, widow of William Neusom, esquire, for life without impeachment of waste, and after her death to Master Thomas Hebbeden, her son, and the heirs of his body, remainder to John Hebbeden, her son and the heirs male of his body, remainder to Joan Fitling, her daughter and the heirs male of her body, remainder to Matilda, her daughter, widow of John Hothome, knight, for life, and thereafter to John Hothome, her son, and the heirs male of his body, remainder to William Ingleby and the heirs male of his body, remainder to the right heirs of Joan, widow of William Neusom,

lands and tenements, rents and services in the City and suburbs of York, together with the advowson of the chantry of the Blessed Katherine the Virgin in the Church of St. John the Evangelist at Ouse Bridge in Mikelgate, which the feoffors had by the gift and feoffment of the said Joan, widow of William Neusom.

Tripartite indenture.

Witnesses. John Austanemore, Mayor, John Brounflete, William Gyrlyngton, Sheriffs, John Dodyngton, William Brandesby, William Rodes, Thomas Holbek.

Given at York, 11 September 6 Henry VI [1427].   [Latin]

On 1 September 14 Henry VI [1435], John Hebden, esquire, came before Thomas Kyrkham, Mayor, and there sealed a deed of acquittance and handed it to Master Robert Alne, named in the following deed.

RECEIPT AND ACQUITTANCE,

John Hebden of Hebden, esquire,

to Master Robert Alne, co-executor of the will of Master Thomas Hebden, deceased, brother of the said John,

for a chest containing a knife with a black striped (*virgatum*) handle in the form of a dog at the end, and various deeds, muniments, bonds, acquittances and other sealed evidences of title to the number of two hundred and thirteen, relating to the inheritance of the said Master Thomas and himself, John Hebden, and their heirs, and various messuages, tenements, rents and services in the City of York and in other towns in the County of York. The said Master Thomas Hebden had delivered the chest and contents to Master Robert Alne for safe keeping to the use of himself and John

Hebden and their heirs. John Hebden also acknowledged receipt from Master Robert Alne and Master John Artas, co-executors, of a bed with appurtenances, a vessel in the form of a chalice, gilded and with a cover, and a hood of *gray*[60] bequeathed to him and his wife in the will of the said Master Thomas.

Given at York, 30 August 1435, 14 Henry VI [sic].   [Latin]

(ff. 76v-77) FEOFFMENT.

The first deed of the foundation of the benefice or chantry of William Grenefeld, late Archbishop of York

Joan de St. Oswald of York,

to Master Philip Mauleverer of Bolton, clerk,

a tenement with shops, cellars, and upper storeys in Ousegate, which the feoffor had by the gift and feoffment of John Gra, citizen of York, lying in width between the tenement of John de Selby, chaplain, and the tenement of the said Master Philip Mauleverer, which he had of Nicholas de Appelby, citizen of York, and extending in length from Ousegate in front as far as Coppergate behind.

Witnesses. Nicholas de Langeton, Mayor, John de Craik, John de Acum, John de Ripon, Bailiffs, Thomas Durant, Richard de Leycestr, John Durant, Hugh de Miton, Peter le Pulter, William Ablot, Nicholas de Appelby, Alan de Quixelay, Robert de Sallay, Robert de Applegarth, John de Shirburn.

Given at York, the feast of St. Martin in Winter [11 November] 1340.   [Latin]

FEOFFMENT.

Nicholas, son of John de Appelby, citizen of York,

to Master Philip [Mauleverer] of Bolton, clerk,

a tenement with shops, cellars and upper storeys in Ousegate, lying in width between the land of Joan de St. Oswald on the one side, and the land of Robert de Appelgarth which formerly belonged to Ray Robert on the other, and in length from Ousegate in front to Coppergate behind. The feoffor had the tenement by the gift and feoffment of John son and heir of Matthew de Merston.

Witnesses. Nicholas de Langeton, Mayor, Ralph de Stayngreve, William de Holm, John de Sourby, Bailiffs, Thomas Duraunt, Richard de Leycestre, Hugh de Miton, Peter le Pultere, Alan de

[60] *gray*: grey material or fur, usually of badger skin.

Quixley, Robert de Sallay, William de Shirburn, William de Neuton, William de Appelby, clerk.

Given at York, 5 March 1338/9, 13 Edward III.   [Latin]

(ff. 77-77v) FEOFFMENT.

Philip Mauleverer of Boulton, clerk,

to Thomas de Mikelfeld, of Boulton, junior,

lands and tenements which he had by the gift and feoffment of Nicholas son of John de Appelby of York and Joan de St. Oswald of York, in Ousegate, lying together in width between the land of Robert del Appelgarth, formerly of Ray Robert on the one side, and the land of John de Seleby, chaplain, on the other, and in length from Ousegate in front as far as Coppergate behind.

Witnesses. Nicholas de Langeton, Mayor, William de Sutton, Thomas de Estrington, and John de Essheton, Bailiffs, Richard de Alverton, senior, Richard de Brigenall, Walter de Kelstern, John de Soureby, William Gra, William de Holm, Robert de Sallay, John Duraunt, Peter le Poletier, citizens of York, Thomas Deymle of York, clerk.

Given at York, the Friday after the feast of St. Luke the Evangelist [19 October] 1341, 15 (France 2) Edward III.   [Latin]

FEOFFMENT.

Thomas de Mikelfeld of Boulton, junior,

to Master Richard de Chester, canon in the Church of St. Peter of York,

lands and tenements in Ousegate, which he had by the gift and feoffment of Master Philip Mauleverer of Boulton, clerk [as above].

Witnesses. Nicholas Fouks, Mayor, Robert le Walsshe, Richard le Ferrour, William Fox, Bailiffs, Hamon de Hessay, William Gra, Richard de Laycestre, John de Selby, William de Holm, John Duraunt, Robert de Sallay, Peter le Pulter, Nicholas de Appelby, Robert de Dalby, William de Appelby, clerk.

Given at York, 16 January 1342/3, 16 Edward III.   [Latin]

(f. 78) FEOFFMENT.

Hamon de Hessay, executor of the will of Master Richard de Chester, late canon in the Cathedral Church of St. Peter of York, with the consent of the Chapter of that Cathedral and in accordance with the king's licence, to William Gryme, chaplain of the chantry established by the will of the said Master Richard de Chester in the Cathedral Church of St. Peter and parson thereof,

two messuages in Overousegate, lying together in width between the land of John de Middelton on the one side and that of Robert del Appilgarth on the other, and in length from Overousegate, in front, as far as Coppergate behind.

Reciting that Master Richard de Chester, in his will, had desired that a perpetual chantry be founded in the Cathedral Church of St. Peter and a suitable chaplain instituted and inducted to celebrate mass for the souls of William de Grenefelde, late Archbishop of York, of himself the said Master Richard, and for the souls of Vivian, his father, and Margery, his mother, and of all archbishops and canons of the said church. For this purpose, he had devised the said tenements in his will.

The feoffment was made according to the terms of a licence granted and conferred by the king to Richard de Hasthull, Peter de Hynkeleye, Master Richard de Snoweshull, Parson of the Church at Huntyngton, Hamon de Hessay of York, Master Robert de Abirfford and Robert de Hethton, executors of the will of the said Master Richard de Chester, and to the chaplain ordained to the chantry, notwithstanding the Statute of Mortmain and the fact that the messuages were held in burgage of the king.

Witnesses. John de Langton, Mayor, Ralph de Horneby, Robert de Ampilfford, William Frankisshe, Bailiffs, Hugh de Miton, John de Acastre, William de Beverlay, Robert de Bridsall, Richard de Willesthorp, John Hode, William de Chester of York, clerk.

Given at York, the Wednesday after the feast of St. Barnabas [17 June]1360, 34 Edward III. [Latin]

Memorandum[61] that the preceding five deeds relate to the foundation of a benefice or chantry for the soul and to the memory of William Grenefeld, former Archbishop of York, at the altar of St. Nicholas in the Cathedral Church of York. [Latin]

(f. 78v) QUITCLAIM.

Stephen Rudstane, Rector of the Church of Brandesby, to Christopher Spencer, esquire, and John Askham, son and heir

---

[61] Written large and badly faded.

of Walter Askham, and the heirs of the said John,
three messuages in the parish of Holy Trinity in Mikylgate.
Witnesses. Thomas Kyrkham, Mayor, John Thresk, Richard
Bukden, Sheriffs, John Bolton, William Craven.
Given at York, 31 January 14 Henry VI [1436].   [Latin]

[Another copy of the above quitclaim].

FEOFFMENT.
Roger Straunge, clerk,
to Richard Straunge, chaplain,
lands and tenements in Bouthom in the suburbs of York.
Witnesses. John Griseley, Thomas Montagu, Alexander Saddeler.
Given at London, 20 January 14 Henry VI [1436].   [Latin]

(f. 79) GRANT.
John Carleton, clerk, William Ormesheved and John Bolton, citizens and aldermen of York, and William Revetour of York,
chaplain,
to Nicholas Wyspyngton and John Thresk, citizens and merchants of York, Thomas Teryngham, gentleman, and William
Hovyngham, of York,
the reversion after the death of Joan, widow of John Blakburn,
of lands and tenements in Haymangergate, otherwise called Flesshamels or Nedelergate, except a room lately belonging to Agnes
Wandesford, above the tenement built on the ground lately of
Richard Barneby, facing the high street, and except part of the
land of Nicholas Blakburn, senior, late citizen and merchant of
York, enclosed with a stone wall built at the cost of the keepers
of the fabric of the Cathedral Church of St. Peter of York, at the
end of the tenement of Richard Barneby.
    The said tenements had been recently built and lay together be-
tween the tenement of the Cathedral Church of St. Peter, lately of
the said Richard Barneby, on one side, and Swythynlane on the
other, and in length from the high street in front as far as the king's
ditch behind.
    The reversion of the lands and tenements after the death of
Joan, widow of John Blakburn, late citizen and merchant of York,
was devised to the grantors by the will of the said Nicholas Blakburn.

Witnesses. Richard Warter, Mayor, Richard Bukden, Sheriff, Thomas Gare, and Nicholas Usseflet, Thomas Ryddelay, John Lofthouse, Robert Chapman.

Given at York, 17 September 15 Henry VI [1436].   [Latin]

(f. 79v) GRANT OF ANNUITY.

Henry, Earl of Northumberland and Lord of the Honour of Cokermouthe,
to Richard Pinchebek, his valet, in reward for good service,
100s. p.a. to be paid on Whit Sunday and the feast of St. Martin in Winter each year, by his receiver, bailiff or farmer of his lands and tenements in the City of York.

Given at London, 25 February 15 Henry VI [1437].   [Latin]

WRIT.

Henry, Earl of Northumberland and Lord of the Honour of Cokermouth,
to his receiver, bailiff or farmer of his lands and tenements in York,
to pay Richard Pinchebek an annuity of 100s., granted as above.

Given at London, 25 February 15 Henry VI [1437].   [Latin]

The above two deeds were enrolled on request, 31 May 15 Henry VI [1437] in the mayoralty of William Bedale.   [Latin]

(ff. 80-80v) GRANT OF OBIT.[62]

The Master and Brethren of St. Leonard's Hospital, York,
to Master Robert Esyngwald, clerk,
to celebrate an annual obit for John Smyth and Alice, his wife, parents of Master Robert Esyngwald, and for Hawisia, his wife, on the fourth of the nones of October [4 October] during the lifetime of the said Master Robert, and after his death for his soul and those aforesaid, with the *Placebo, Dirige* and Requiem Mass, and with due ringing of the great bells; and to pay to the chaplains of the hospital, viz. to each brother 6d, to each novice 4d, to each sister of the hospital 2d, to the chaplain of the infirmary 3d, to the clerk of the church 2d, also to the clerks and choristers ringing the great bells 8d, to the sacristan of the hospital for wax to burn at the funeral services and mass 6d, and to the bell-ringers of the City of York for proclamation of the obit 4d. The Master and Brethren

---

[62] The original indenture belonging to the Mayor and Commonalty is preserved amongst the York City Archives. [G.41:6]

of St. Leonards were to enter a bond in 40s. to the Mayor and Commonalty for the fulfilment of the premises.

Consideration. £20 and other gifts from Master Robert Esyngwald to the hospital.

Tripartite indenture.

Given in the Chapter House of St. Leonard's Hospital, 1 October 1436. [Latin]

ACQUITTANCE.

John Byrscowe, citizen and merchant of York,

to Henry Market, citizen and merchant of York,

of all actions or demands whatsoever.

Given 1 July 15 Henry VI [1437]. [Latin]

This deed was enrolled at the wish of the parties before William Bedale, Mayor, 2 July 1437. [Latin]

(ff. 80v-81) FEOFFMENT.

John Carleton, clerk, junior, Robert Rudestane, Thomas Warde and William Revetour of York, chaplain,

to Roger Salvayn, esquire, and Margaret Bolton, daughter of John Bolton, Alderman of the City of York, and the heirs of their bodies, remainder to the right heirs of Roger,

the manors of Herswell [Harswell], Holme in Spaldyngmore and Thorp in Strata [Thorpe le Street] and other lands and tenements in Ottryngham in Holdernesse; an annual rent of £20 from the manor, lands and tenements in Northduffeld which Lady Alice Salvayn had by the grant of the said Roger for the term of her life; the tenements in Northduffeld which Thomas Salvayn held; and all other manors, lands or tenements in the County of York which the feoffors had by the gift and feoffment of the said Roger.

Witnesses. Robert Ughtred, knight, Robert Constable, Robert Elys, esquires, William Hundgate, Robert Stodehowe.

Given, 15 November 13 Henry VI [1434]. [Latin]

(ff. 81-82) LETTERS PATENT.[63]

Henry VI, at the request of the commons and with the assent of the lords spiritual and temporal,

to the Mayor and Commonalty of the City of York,

granting a pardon and release from:—

[63] The original is amongst the York City Archives (A17).

[1] all transgression, offence, misprision, contempt or impeachment before 2 September 1431 against the Statutes of Liveries, punishable by fine, relief or other money penalty or by imprisonment;

[2] all murder, rape, rebellion, insurrection, felony, conspiracy and other transgression, offence, negligence, extorsion, misprision, ignorance, contempt, concealment, and deceit committed before 2 September 1431.

[3] all outlawry, except of counterfeiters and multipliers of money, washers and clippers of gold and silver, common thiefs and notorious felons.

[4] all escapes of felons, chattels of felons and fugitives and felons *de se*, deodands, wastes, impeachments, articles of eyre, destruction, trespass of vert and venison, sales of wood within and without the forest and other offences committed within the realm of England and parts of Wales before 2 September 1431, punishable by demand, debt, fine, ransom or other pecuniary penalty, forfeit of goods, imprisonment, amerciament of the community or the individual, or charge upon the free tenure of those who never offended, such as heirs, executors, or tenants of lands of escheators, sheriffs, coroners and others;

[5] all gifts and alienations and purchases of land and tenements, held by the king in chief or lands acquired in mortmain without licence; all intrusion and entry into hereditaments, without due procedure, upon the death of ancestors, and all issues and profits accruing therefrom in the meantime;

[6] all fines, assessments, amerciaments, issues, forfeits, reliefs, scutage and all debts, accounts, loans, arrears of farms and accounts before the day of coronation, excepting always such debts and accounts as are owing in respite by virtue of Letters Patent or writs of privy seal whether by installment or assigment;

[7] all actions and demands that the king may have against them for these fines and all outlawry for any of the above offences before the day of coronation;

[8] all penalties forfeit before the king, his council, chancellor, treasurer, or any of his justices, due to the present king or his father, before the day of coronation;

[9] all writs of *securitatis pacis* lying for entry into royal lands within the realm;

[10] all escapes of prisoners to be guarded by a minister of the

king or a member of the Record of Commissions and Freedoms; with the exceptions of all offences against the Statute of Praemunire [1392] by obtaining Papal bulls, and the offence of remarriage of widows of noble rank without royal licence;

[11] all prests and pledges of war, the thirds and thirds of thirds in the spoils and prisoners of war due to Henry V up to the day of his death;

[12] all jewels mortgaged to Henry V by the Mayor and Commonalty for their pledges of war in support of the voyages against the town of Harflewe [Harfleur] etc, if full satisfaction for them had not been rendered within the year following 27 March 1437, with the proviso that in the future the Mayor and Commonalty should not exact or be able to exact from the king or his heirs any further debt, security, regard, demand, charge or pledge of war by reason of retinue of war with Henry V or any other pretext of war that causes or is likely to cause such voyages—always excepting any debt or charge appropriate to the said Mayor and Commonalty for the defence of the castle and town of Calais and its marches.

Given at Westminster, 18 June 18 Henry VI [1437].

Subscribed: by the king himself in parliament.

Normanton. [Latin]

(ff. 82-82v) PAPAL MANDATE.
Pope Eugenius [IV]
to the Prior of Holy Trinity, York, and the Dean of the Church of St. Peter's, York,
to command publicly in the churches that various lands, property, goods and chattels belonging to the Mayor and Commonalty by legal right, and wrongfully withheld from them, be restored within a certain time to be fixed by the said Prior and Dean. If their command was not obeyed within that time they were to bring a general sentence of excommunication against the offenders until full satisfaction should be made.

Issued at the request of the Mayor and Commonalty.

Given at Florence, 1435/6, 14 of the Kalens of January, [19 December] in the 5th year of the pontificate.

Subscribed. N [?] de Carbonibus. [Latin]

WRIT OF *Supersedeas.*
Henry [VI]

to William Bowes, Mayor of the City of York, and the Justices of the Peace,

to stay all actions against John Bolton, merchant, Robert Middilton, mercer, William Holbek, mercer, and Richard Stowe, vintner, all of York, who were each bound in £20 before Peter Bukcy, former Mayor of York, as sureties that William Bedale would keep the peace towards Hawisia, wife of William Selby of York; and to release William Bedale from prison if they had arrested him for that reason alone.

Witnessed at Westminster, 18 June 6 Henry VI [1428]. [Latin]

(ff. 82v-83) WRIT OF *Supersedeas.*

Henry VI

to the Mayor of the City of York and the Justices of the Peace, on behalf of the sureties of William Bedale, mercer, reciting their bond, [as above].

Witnessed by Humphrey, Duke of Gloucester, Regent (*custos*) of England,[64] at Westminster, 21 November 10 Henry VI [1431].

[Latin]

PRESENTATION.

James Baguley, Rector of All Saints' Church in Northstret, Nicholas Blakburn and Thomas Redley, Aldermen, William Marshall and Robert Chapman, parishioners of All Saints, patrons of the chantry of Adam de Bank, late citizen and dyer of York, founded at the altar of St. Nicholas in the said church,

to William Bedale, Mayor,

of John Redley, chaplain, to the vacancy caused by the death of John Richemond, the last chaplain of the said chantry.

Given at York, 9 January 1437/8, 16 Henry VI.   [Latin]

ADMISSION.

William Bedale, Mayor,

of John Redley, chaplain,

to the chantry of Adam de Bank, [as above].

Given at York, 20 January 1437/8, 16 Henry VI.   [Latin]

(f. 83v) FEOFFMENT.

Ralph Clyfton, son and heir of John Clifton, late of Clifton near

---

[64] Regent during Henry VI's absence in France from April 1430 to February 1432 (F. M. Powicke and E. B. Fryde, *Handbook of British Chronology*).

York, and of Margaret his wife, and Thomas Clyfton his son,
to Richard Neuland, citizen and tailor of York,
an acre of land in the *mylnefeld* in Clyfton near Bouthom, lying
between the land of the Abbot and Convent of St. Mary's and
the land of the late William Wandesford of York, and in length
from the high street in front to a certain footpath behind.

Witnesses. Thomas Roderham, Henry Forester, Richard Neuland, John Staynburn, William Galbike, John Neuland, William
Pryns.

Given at York, 12 February 1432/3, 11 Henry VI.   [Latin]

QUITCLAIM.
Ralph Clyfton and Thomas Clyfton, his son,
to Richard Neuland,
an acre of land in the *mylnefeld* in Clyfton [as above].

Witnesses. Thomas Roderham, Henry Forester, Richard Neuland, John Stayburn, William Galbeke, John Neuland, William
Pryns.

Given at York, 14 February 1432/3, 11 Henry VI.   [Latin]

(f. 84) WRIT OF *Supersedeas.*
Henry VI
to his Justices of the Peace and the Sheriffs of the City of York,
to stay all proceedings against John Cotyngham, gentleman, John
Preston, ironmonger, John Lancastre, tailor, and William Wollay,
tailor, all of York, who on 5 January last were each bound in £10
before Thomas Ridley, Mayor, as sureties for Richard Crull of
York, merchant, and the same Richard in £20, to ensure that he
would keep the peace towards Richard atte the Ende.

Given at Westminster, 8 June 18 Henry VI [1440].
Subscribed. Morton.   [Latin]

(ff. 84v-85) On 19 September 16 Edward IV [1476], William Claxton of Brekynberyburn in County Durham, esquire, came before
Thomas Wrangwish, Mayor of the City of York, in the Council
Chamber, affirmed that he had issued a deed to Ed. Hastynges and
others, and that it was sealed with his seal.

He sought that it be enrolled as follows: —

LEASE.

William Claxton of Brekynberyburn in County Durham, esquire, son and heir of the late William Claxton of Brekynberyburn, esquire, and Matilda, daughter of Ralph Heton,[65] esquire, wife of the said William Claxton the son,

to Ed. Haystinges, knight, John Haystynges, John Hoton, and Robert Percy, esquires.

a messuage called *Hurdhous* and lands, meadows and pastures in the tenure of Thomas Nicholson, as enclosed with hedges and ditches, in the manor of Brekynberyburn,[66] lying on the west side of the common way which leads from the City of Durham as far as the bridge called *Brounebrigg.*

Term. The life of the said Matilda, without impeachment of waste.

Rent. 13s. 4d. p.a. during the life of Matilda.

If the rent was in arrears William Claxton was to have distraint.

Appointment of William Ragett and Thomas Watson as attorneys to deliver seisin.

Witnesses. Thomas Asper, Master Nicholas Lancastre, clerk, Thomas Yotten, Adam Gunby.

Given, 16 September 16 Edward IV [1476].   [Latin]

LETTERS OF ATTORNEY.

Ed. Hastynges, knight, John Hastynges, John Hoton and Robert Percy, esquires,

to John Redemayn, William Philipp and John Gollen,

to receive seisin of the messuage and lands in Brekynberyburn [as above].

(f. 85v) Given, 16 September 16 Edward IV [1476].   [Latin]
(f. 86) [Blank.]

(f. 86v) On 6 February 17 Henry VI [1439], Ralph Clyfton of Clyfton near York, son and heir of John Clyfton of Clyfton, came before Thomas Reddeley, Mayor of the City of York, in the Council

[65] Spelt Hoton in Letters of Attorney, f. 85.

[66] Not identified. Hurdhous [Herd's House] lies on the A1 road north of Sunderland Bridge. Brounebrigg [Browney Bridge] is where the main road crosses the river Browney about 150 yards south of Herd's House. About 2 miles to the N.W. is a farm called Bracken Hill, and in the immediate area is the estate of Burnhall. The lessor is probably William Claxton of Holywell, in the parish of Brancepeth, about 1 mile S.W. of Herd's House. He was Constable of Brancepeth Castle 1461, died 1496. (Information supplied by W. A. L. Seaman, County Archivist, County Record Office, Durham.)

Chamber, affirmed that he had made and sealed with his own seal, deeds of feoffment and quitclaim and letters of attorney as follows, and sought their enrolment in the common register of the city.

[Latin]

(f. 87) FEOFFMENT.

Ralph Clyfton of Clyfton near York, son and heir of John Clyfton of Clyfton,
to William Scargill, senior, and William Scargill, junior, esquires, a messuage and an oxgang of land in Tollerton which formerly belonged to William Ray, alias William Haldenby of Clyfton.

Witnesses. John Langton, Thomas Saynell, knights, William Mirfeld, Guy Fairfax, Robert Ingilby, esquires.

Given at Wakfeld, 12 October 17 Henry VI [1438].   [Latin]

QUITCLAIM.

Ralph Clyfton
to William Scargill, senior, and William Scargill, junior,
lands and tenements in Clyfton and Tollerton and elsewhere in the County of York which formerly belonged to William Ray, alias William Haldenby of Clyfton.

Witnesses. John Langton, Thomas Saynell, knights, William Mirfeld, Guy Fairfax, Robert Ingilby, esquires.

Given at Wakefeld, 20 October 17 Henry VI [1438].   [Latin]

(ff. 87-87v) LETTERS OF ATTORNEY.

Ralph Clyfton of Clyfton,
to John Scargill, Robert Derkyn, John Jacson, or William Paget, to deliver seisin to William Scargill, senior, and William Scargill, junior, of a messuage and oxgang of land in Tollerton [as above].

Given at Wakefeld, 12 October 17 Henry VI [1438].   [Latin]

On the last day of February 17 Henry VI [1439], Guy Fairfax of Walton in the County of York, esquire, came before Thomas Rydley, Mayor, in the Council Chamber, acknowledged certain letters of attorney to Nicholas Louth to have been made and sealed by him and the late Master Thomas Cleveland of York, clerk, and sought their enrolment as follows.   [Latin]

LETTERS OF ATTORNEY.

Guy Fayrfax of Walton in the County of York, esquire, and Thomas Cleveland of the City of York, clerk,
to Nicholas Louth of York, merchant,

to receive all goods and chattels, which they, together with John
Bolton and William Bowes, Aldermen, had by the gift of Robert
Louth of York, merchant, deceased.

Given, 27 October 16 Henry VI [1437].   [Latin]

(f. 88.) *The enrolment of an indenture for Jaspar Grondman and J.
Denom of sale of a shipe.* On the last day of June 17 Henry VI
[1439], Jaspar Gronndman of Dansk [Danzig] in *Prucia* and John
Denom, merchant of York, came before Thomas Ridley, Mayor of
York in the Council Chamber, showed an indenture made and
sealed by them and sought its enrolment as follows.   [Latin]

BILL OF SALE OF A SHIP.

This indentoure witnesse howe that Shipper Jasper Gronndman
of Dansk in Pruceland has made sayle to John Denom of York,
merchaunt, and John Texton, merchaunt of Beverlay, a quarter of
a ship cald James, for £26 13s. 4d sterling and al the fische that
the said Shipper Jasper has in the said ship. And as for the quarter
of the shipp parte, the forsaid John Denom has content unto the
said Shipper Jasper and paide hym in cloth and money in the Cite
of York; forthermore as for the fische, what tyme the said Shipper
Jasper or his attournay delyvers to forsaid John Denom als mekel
fische as thai delyverd, than the said John Denom shall pay for
every ilke last[67] £7 forthermore, so as the said Shipper Jaspar has
full promyst afor the Maire of the Cite of Yorke to the said John
Denom to save hym harmelesse for the forsaid quarter of the shipp
for al maner of accionns a yere and a day efter this dat. Also the
same Shipper Jasper has loved and made ful promyst to bringe a
generall acquietance undir the toun seal of Dansk unto the said
John Denom for the said quarter of ship and fische, for al manere
of accions that may be asked bi the said Shippar Jasper and Hance
Droutheman and thair heires and assignes and al maner of men
that has with it to do. And who so bringes the said acquietance
under the toun seal of Dansk unto the said John Denom, that than
the said John Denom shall pay for the said fische, the whilk thai
make deliverance of in cloth and money, like as ther forwarde is
afore writen. To whilke witnes the forsaid parties to thise inden-
toures ther seales sonderly has putt. Dat at York the last day of
Juyn in the 17 yere of Kyng Henry Sext that nowe is.

Subscribed. Misne.

[67] *last*: a variable weight; of fish, equivalent to twelve barrels.

(f. 88v) THE CITY'S SWORDS.[68]

In the name of the Lord, Amen. Whereas many Catholic kings in exercise of their most valued prerogative of love, have in former times granted insignia of honour to their cities and other places, yet it happens that with the lapse of years not only the names of such grantors, but often the dates of their gifts, have passed away from the minds of men. That such noble grants might be more firmly held in remembrance, the wisdom of our ancestors devised a precaution of this kind, namely that what is worthy of commendation should be reduced into writing, so that by frequent perusal it might obtain more serious attention, and by the aid of consideration this present slight written memorial may be impressed upon the minds of posterity.

That most vigorous prince and illustrious lord Richard the second, late King of England and France and lord of Ireland, wishing to confer honour on his City of York before all others, in the year of our Lord 1388, in the twelfth year of his reign and in the mayoralty of William Selby, granted and confirmed amongst other gracious gifts for himself and his heirs to the citizens of the City of York and their heirs and successors, that the Mayor for the time being should have the sword first given by the king himself, or another sword as he pleased, carried before him with the point erect in the presence of all magnates and lords of the realm who were his kinsmen, except only in the presence of the king himself and his heirs, as was contained in the charter granted by him to the citizens.

Later, in the year of our Lord 1421 and the eighth year of the reign of King Henry V, that most serene prince Sigismund, Emperor of Germany and King of the Romans, came to England and was forthwith constituted a knight and brother of the military order founded in the royal chapel of St. George at Wyndesor, where all knights of the order upon their reception offer their swords to be suspended there during their lifetime. After their death the swords were at the disposal of the dean of the chapel for the time being, according to the custom of the chapel hitherto observed. On the death of the said Emperor the dean of the chapel presented the sword offered by him to that discreet person, Master Henry Hans-

---

[68] Somewhat faded in parts. Transcribed in Ll. Jewitt and W. H. St. John Hope, *Corporation Plate and Insignia of Office*, Vol. II pp. 448-9, and discussed and translated by R. Davies. *The State Swords of the York Corporation*, Yorkshire Philosophical Society, Annual Report, 1868, pp. 27-32.

lap, canon of the same chapel and prebendary of the prebend of Skipwith in the collegiate church of Houeden and Rector of the Church of Middelton near Pykering not far from the City of York, from whence he sprang, as it pleased him to say. Therefore, the aforesaid Master Henry, preferring in his mind as a man of much gratitude to distinguish his own country by such a gift, (f. 89) on the fifth of May in the year of our Lord 1439 and the seventeenth year of the reign of King Henry the Sixth, came to the City of York as the chief place of all the north and delivered the sword formerly of the said Emperor, covered with ruby coloured velvet on the scabbard together with ruby scorpions worked in silk thereon, and gladly presented the same to that honourable man Thomas Ridley, then Mayor of the city to be carried before every Mayor of the city for the time being at his pleasure. So that every Mayor in his time should rejoice in the variety of so many principal swords and thence praise and honour to the citizens should multiply and increase and the people in passing might exclaim in praise "Behold the two swords of the City of York, the first of King Richard and the other of the Emperor."

There is also a third sword carried in daily use which was not obtained by the gift of a king but truly provided at the citizens' expense. And thus the City of York is adorned with three swords, each with two edges.

Subscribed. Burton, Roger.   [Latin]

FEOFFMENT. [Partially affected by damp]

Robert Rilleston, son of John Rilleston, [? omission] in the County of York,

to Henry Drynghouse, citizen and brazier of York,

a tenement in Mikelgate, lying in width between the tenement lately of John Elvyngton on the east, and the tenement belonging to the chantry at the altar of St. Mary and St. John the Evangelist, founded in the Cathedral Church of St. Peter of York, on the west, and extending in length from Mikelgate in front as far as North-strete behind.

Witnesses. Thomas Ridley, Mayor, William Northeby and John Croser, Sheriffs, William Craven, Richard Shirwod, John Clarell.

Given at York, 18 May 17 Henry VI [1439].   [Latin]

(ff. 89-89v) QUITCLAIM.

Robert Rilleston, son of John Rilleston in the County of York, to Henry Drynghouse,

the tenement in Mikelgate [as above].

Witnesses. Thomas Ridley, Mayor, William Northeby, John Croser, Sheriffs, William Craven, Richard Shirwod, John Clarell.

Given at York, 23 May 17 Henry VI [1439]. [Latin]

(ff. 89v-90) GIFT.[69]

Roger Burton of York, clerk,

to Robert Danby of Yafford [Yafforth], and Thomas Wytham of Corneburgh [Cornbrough] in the County of York, esquires, and William Vescy of York, gentleman,

all his goods and chattels.

Witnesses. William Girlington, Mayor, William Holbek and Thomas Danby, Sheriffs, Thomas Brereton, Thomas Sargeantson, Robert Brereton, Thomas Sutton, citizens of York.

Given, 1 April 18 Henry VI [1440]. [Latin].

GIFT.

Robert Danby and Thomas Witham

to William Vescy,

the goods and chattels which they had by the gift of Roger Burton of York, clerk.

Given, 1 June 18 Henry VI [1440]. [Latin].

BOND.

Thomas Saunderson of Kyngeston on Hull, merchant,

to John Bedale, John Caulton and William Catryk, citizens and merchants of York,

in 100 marks to be paid on Whit Sunday next, to save harmless the said John Bedale, John Calton and William Catryk from all sums paid to Richard Myndrom, John Redale,[70] Thomas Hobson and Richard Dolfynby of Berwik on Tweed, merchants, by the said Thomas Saunderson on behalf of William Bedale, late citizen and merchant of York.

Given, 8 April 19 Henry VI [1441]. [Latin]

---

[69] See also f. 96v.
[70] *Redale*: also spelt Redell.

(f. 90v) ACKNOWLEDGMENT made in the Council Chamber
before Thomas Kirke, Mayor,
  by William Northffolk, gentleman,
  to John Grene and Katherine, his wife, daughter of Thomas
  Northfolk, brother of the said William,
that the reversion of tenements in the City and suburbs of York,
which he held jointly with Robert Northfolk, his brother, and
Elizabeth, his sister, for the term of their lives by the gift of Nicholas Northfolk their father, belonged to Katherine, wife of John
Grene. He paid 1d. as acknowledgment of his life tenancy.
  Given, 21 August 19 Henry VI [1441].   [Latin]

ACQUITTANCE.
  Thomas More, citizen and mercer of York,
  to John Dubber, citizen and merchant of York,
of all actions and claims whatsoever.
  Given, 30 September 20 Henry VI [1441].   [Latin]

ARBITRATION.[71]
(f. 91) This judgment was returned by the searchers of the masons
and carpenters, namely John Ampilford and John Bould, masons,
John Bolron and William Warte, carpenters, before Thomas Kirke,
Mayor of York, on the last day of January in the twentieth year of
the reign of King Henry VI [1442].   [Latin]
  Memorandum that this is jugement and award of John Ampilford,
John Bould, masons, John Bolron and William Warter, carpenters
and serchours of the same craftes, that is to say that the stone wall
bi twix the tenement of John of Bolton, citisin and marchant of
York on that oon party, and tenement of thabbot and convent of
Cristall [Kirkstall] on that other party, in Mikelgate in York, is
holy and fully the wall of the said John of Bolton, and that al the
ease that the said abbot has of the said wall is thurgh sufferance
and patiens of the same John of Bolton. And the same day and the
same yere Alice Semer, neuly awner and possessor of the said
tenement of John of Bolton, swore and opinly affermed for treweth
that John Lofthouse and others of the deputz of the said abbot
and convent withdrewe the said wall unknawinge to the said Alice.
  And the same day we the said serchours were [sic] and serched a
tenement of the said John of Bolton in Petergate in the tenure of

[71] Printed by James Raine in *English Miscellanies* p. 18.

John Wetelay, and we fynd that the same place has taken mikel herm for defaut of a gutter the whilk shuld be betwix the said place and tenement of Thomas Holme, the whilk gutter the same Thomas Holme shuld make and reparell to save and isshewe the watter fro the said place of John of Bolton.

The enrolment of evidence in the time of John Thresk, Mayor of the City of York, elected on the day of St. Blase [3 February]1441.
[Latin]
(f. 91v) On 6 April 20 Henry VI [1442], Matilda del Clay came before John Thrisk, Mayor, sealed two deeds of quitclaim made by her and sought their enrolment: —

QUITCLAIM.
Matilda del Clay, widow, daughter and elder heir of Brian son of Isolda, daughter and heir of John de Holme,
to John de Clyff and Nicholas de Clyff, chaplains,
the manor of Northolm in Rydall [North Holme in Ryedale] in the County of York, formerly of the said John de Holme.
Witnesses. John Thrisk, Mayor, Richard Warter, Thomas Ridley, Aldermen, Thomas Gray of Barton in Rydall, Robert Thornton of Newton, Thomas Clay, Stephen Edenham.
Given, 6 April 20 Henry VI [1442].   [Latin]

(ff. 91v-92) QUITCLAIM.
Matilda del Clay
to William Holthorp,
the manor of Magna Edston [Great Edstone] in Rydall in the County of York, which formerly belonged to John de Holme.
Witnesses. John Thrisk, Mayor, Richard Wartre, Thomas Ridley, Aldermen, Thomas Gray of Barton in Rydall, Robert Thornton of Newton, Thomas Clay, Stephen Edenham.
Given, 6 April 20 Henry VI [1442].   [Latin]

QUITCLAIM.
Roger Hay, citizen of York,
to John de Ask, esquire, and Alice de Miton, widow of Germain Hay, brother of the said Roger.
lands and tenements in Aughton, Iverthorp [Everthorpe] North Cave, Est Elvelay [Kirk Ella] and West Elevelay [West Ella] in the County of York.

Witnesses. Thomas de Meteham, Peter del Hay, Robert Rud-stane, John Portyngton, Thomas Wilton, Robert de Santon, Richard de Santon.

Given at Aughton, 26 November 1427, 6 Henry VI.   [Latin]

On 16 May 20 Henry VI [1442], William Lyon and Joan Lyon, his sister, and also William Galby and Agnes, his wife, came before John Thrisk, Mayor, sealed two deeds of quitclaim made by them and sought their enrolment:—

(f. 92v) QUITCLAIM.

William Galby of Wystowe, yeoman, and Agnes his wife, formerly the wife of William Lyon, and the daughter and heir of Thomas Lynelandes,
to John Cateryk, citizen and mercer of York and John Killyng-holme,
a messuage in Fossegate lying in width between the tenement of the late Richard Knyght of York, chandler, and the tenement of the Abbot and Convent of Meaux (*Melsa*), and in length from Fossegate in front as far as the River Foss behind. The said John Cateryk and John Killyngholme had the messuage by the gift and feoffment of William Lawton, John Russhden and John Bell, citizen of York.

Witnesses. John Thrisk, Mayor, Thomas Crathorn, John Turpyn, Sheriffs, William Barley, John Gudale, citizens and mercers of York.

Given at York, 14 May 20 Henry VI [1442].   [Latin]

(ff. 92v-93) QUITCLAIM.

William Lyon of York, baxter, son and heir of William Lyon and Agnes his wife, and Joan Lyon, daughter of the said William and Agnes, his sister,
to John Cateryk and John Killyngholme,
a messuage in Fossegate [as above].

Witnesses. John Thrysk, Mayor, Thomas Crathorn, John Turpyn, Sheriffs, William Couper, pinner, William Marsshall, merchant, citizens of York.

Given at York, 16 May 20 Henry VI [1442].   [Latin]

THE JUDGMENT OF THE SEARCHERS appointed to view a sewer, enrolled at the instance of the Abbot and Convent of Furness (*Fournas*), with the consent of the Mayor and Commonalty of York.[72]

John Ampilford and John Boulde, searchers of the masons, and John Bolron, one of the searchers of the carpenters, reported that the Abbot and Convent of Furness should, by right and custom, maintain and repair the half of the sewer on the east side thereof, opposite their tenement without Mikillith Barr, from the corner of the tenement of John Hemelsay as far as the old course of the said sewer between the tenement of the Abbot and Convent and that of John Rayneshawe; and the said John Rayneshawe should maintain the other half of the sewer, on the west side as far as the old course aforesaid. Further, the Abbot and Convent should henceforth repair the sewer or water course crossing or flowing next to their land entirely at their own costs because they stopped up the course of the sewer, in exoneration of a certain annual rent of 4d, previously paid by them to the Commonalty.

Sealed with the official mayoral seal.

Given, 5 August 20 Henry VI [1442].   [Latin]

(f. 93v) WRIT OF HABEAS CORPUS.

King [Henry VI]

to the Sheriffs of the City of York,

to cause John Patryngton, citizen and skinner, to appear before his justices at Westminster in the octave of St. Michael, to reply to the plea of Thomas Beverlay and John Bristowe that he should pay the 113s. 8d. which he owed them and unjustly retained.

Given at Westminster, 28 June 20 [Henry VI] [1442]. [Latin].

By virtue of the said writ, John Patryngton was attached by Thomas Crathorn and John Turpyn, Sheriffs, on the feast of St. Peter Ad Vincula 20 Henry VI [1 August 1442]. On the same day, Robert Maulyverer, senior, of the court of John [Kempe] Archbishop of York, came before John Thresk, Mayor, and alleged that the said John Patryngton had been summoned by an official of the Archbishop to reply——[blank] to a plea of debt in the Archbishop's Court in his palace at York. The Sheriffs replied that from time immemorial all Bailiffs and Sheriffs of the City of York had obeyed the orders of the king under his seal and were bound by law to execute them. The said John found Henry Market, mercer, and William Gayte, cordwainer, to indemnify the Sheriffs from

72 Faded in parts.

the return of the writ, and he was then freed from the city gaol.

[Latin]

EXPENSES INCURRED IN OBTAINING A NEW CHARTER.[73]

Firstly, in various expenses incurred this year by Thomas Redley and William Girlyngton, Aldermen of this city, at the king's parliament held in London, in the writing, conception and making of various bills and supplications presented to the king for confirmation and augmentation of the charter of the city's liberties.   30s.

In the expenses of John Shirwod on two journeys to London for obtaining the said charter, in going, staying there and returning, for 29 days in May and June this year.   [no sum stated]

As a gratuity to Peter Erden for his advice, favour and work in the said matter.   13s. 4d.

As a gratuity to Nicholas Girlyngton, lawyer, for the above reason.   6s. 8d.

As a gratuity to James Hopwod, lawyer, for the same reason.   3s. 4d.

In the expenses of Peter Erden in sailing from London to Chelcheife [Chelsea] to converse with the Cardinal of York[74] about the matter.   16d.

In wines, cherries and other things bought and given to the said lawyers for their advice.   2s.

For a gift to the doorkeeper at the king's chancery for allowing Peter Erden to enter.   4d.

Item, paid for engrossing the charter anew.[75]   35s. 4d.

(f. 94) Item, paid for the enrolment of the charter in the king's rolls.   20s.

In one silk cord (*lase de cerico*) bought for the charter.   20d.

Item, paid to the king for the fine of the grant and confirmation

---

[73] Faded in parts. The entry is undated but from the persons named and the handwriting probably relates to the inspeximus charter granted by Henry VI, 24 April 1442 (C. Ch. R. 1427-1516, pp. 30-31). Thomas Ridley, merchant, was appointed Chamberlain in 1432, Sheriff 1434-5, Lord Mayor in 1439 and died before 1456; William Girlyngton, draper, was a Chamberlain in 1421, Sheriff 1426-7, Lord Mayor 1440 and died in 1444. John Shirwood was appointed as Common Clerk on 3 Feb. 1441/2. Expenses of obtaining the charter are not, however, included in the Chamberlains' Roll for 1442-3, and the accounts for other years in the mid-fifteenth century in which charters were granted are not available.

[74] John Kempe, Archbishop of York, was appointed a cardinal in 1439.

[75] literally, for writing the charter anew, by agreement made *in grosso*.

of the charter together with certain additions and clauses newly
granted and confirmed this year.   £13. 6s. 8d.
  Item, the fee paid for sealing the new charter.   £8. 9s.
  Item, paid to the scribe's clerk for his assiduous and speedy work
in examining the charter.   2s.
  For a wooden box for keeping the charter in.   4d.
                                                                    [Latin]

RESOLUTION TO VIEW THE CITY BOUNDARIES.

The Monday after the feast of the Conception of the Blessed
Virgin Mary, 21 Henry VI [10 December 1442].

Assembled in the Council Chamber—John Thriske, Mayor, Nicho-
las Blakburn, senior, John Bolton, Richard Wartre, Nicholas Us-
flete, Thomas Ridley, Aldermen, Guy Rouclyff, Recorder, Nicholas
Wyspyngton, Richard Bukden, and William Stokton, Aldermen,
Henry Thwaytes and John Stafford, lawyers, Henry Merket and
Thomas Barton, Sheriffs, William Craven, John Croser, William
Holbek, Thomas Danby, William Habirford, Thomas Crathorn,
and John Turpyn of the Twenty-Four, William Clyff, Thomas
Neleson and Robert Colynson, Chamberlains.

  And afterwards on the same day, the searchers and many of the
craftsmen came before the Mayor, Sheriffs, Aldermen and others of
the Council, in the Council Chamber, and it was unanimously
ordained with the consent of the counsel and lawyers and agreed
that the Mayor, Sheriffs, Aldermen and others should, on the Tuesday next following, view the limits and bounds between the
franchises and liberties of the County of the City and the County
of York and should make note of all alterations or destructions of
any of the limits or bounds.   [Latin]

(f. 94v) *The bounds and metes of the City.*[76]

  On the said Tuesday all the aforesaid persons and several other
citizens began to note and view the bounds and limits aforesaid,
from the River Ouse on the north as far as a certain bridge in the
Fetesenge, called in English Littilenge; and so extending by a

---

[76] Partially faded. The earliest account of the riding of the boundaries, in the
mayoralty of Thomas de Howom, 1374-5, is printed in *York Memorandum Book* I,
pp. 20-22. A very similar description is assigned to the year 1413-14 by Drake, who
also prints the boundaries of 23 Henry VII, 1507 (ff. 180v-181 below) under the date
23 Henry VI, 1445 (*Eboracum*, pp. 244-5). A list, map and comparison of all surviv-
ing descriptions of the boundaries, 1374-1819, appears in *The Victoria County History*;
The City of York, pp. 315-8.

ditch and a marsh (*mere*) next to the Spetelwell by a way next to the mill of the Abbot of St. Mary's of York. And thence as far as the Maudeleyn Spetell[77] in the highway which leads from York to Clyfton. And so as far as the mill formerly of John de Rouclyff but now of the heir of William Ingleby, knight. And thence by the way next to the gallows of the Abbot of St. Mary's aforesaid, where there was formerly a *watergate* in the *outegange* which leads to the forest of Galtres, as far as a certain wooden bridge there. And so by the marsh as far as Whistanecrosse above Astilbrig.[78] And so by a great stone as far as the River Foss, descending alongside the river on the west side as far as the water mills of the aforesaid Abbot. And thence beyond the River Foss next to the mills on the south side, extending as far as a certain place where a wooden cross stands on Heworthmore next to the way which leads to Stokton. And thence next to the stone cross at the west end of the town of Heworth as far as the Theefbrig. And so by a way to the wooden cross in the way which leads to Osbaldwyk, so proceeding along the highway which leads to Kexby as far as the cross next to the bridge beyond the mill of St. Nicholas's [? hospital]. And so returning from the cross next to the mill by a way as far as the [Grenedykes] next to the close of the hospital of St. Nicholas aforesaid. And thence as far as the cross in the Grenedykes next to St. Leonard's gallows. And thence beyond Tylmyre by a certain way leading to the wooden cross in the way which leads to Fulford next to Algarthsyke. And so extending directly to the River Ouse and beyond the River Ouse as far as a certain cross called Haydale-crosse in the way which leads from the City of York to Bisshopthorp. And thence directly [beyond] the field called the Nenfeld [sic] as far as Knaresmyre beyond the gallows standing there, on the south side of the said gallows as far as the Outegange leading to the moore called Yorkesm[ore]. And thence by a certain rivulet as far as the stone bridge at the end of the town of Holgate, descending always by a ditch there on the west side as far as [Fletebrig] in the Bisshopfeld on the west side of the River Ouse.[79]   [Latin]
(f. 95) [Blank]

---

[77] *the Maudeleyn Spetell*: the hospital of St Mary Magdalene (A. Raine, *Mediaeval York*, p. 257).

[78] Astilbrig: Yearsley Bridge (Raine p. 258).

[79] There follow approximately three more lines, detectable only by ultra violet light, of which the only words legible are *Registrum* and *consilii*.

(f. 95v) On 26 January 21 Henry VI [1443], Roger Aunger came before John Thriske, Mayor, in the Council Chamber, showed various deeds made and sealed by him, and sought their enrolment in the common register of the city, as follows. [Latin]

(ff. 95v-96) FEOFFMENT.

Roger Aunger, son of Thomas Aunger of Redenesse, and Isabel, his wife, daughter of John Neusom, esquire,
to John Bell of Walmegate, citizen and chapman of York, and Isabel, his wife,
a piece of waste land in Walmegate, lying between the tenement of the feoffors in the tenure of Thomas Thresk, shearsmith, and the tenement of the Prioress and Convent of Swyne [Swine], and containing in length along the churchyard of St. Dennis in front 11½ ells and behind 11½ ells, and in width from the east side 6½ ells and from the south side 6 ells.

Rent. 3s. 4d. p.a.

If the rent was forty days in arrears, the feoffors were to have distraint.

Witnesses. Thomas Rydley, Mayor, William Holbek, Thomas Danby, Sheriffs, Thomas Lyverton, Thomas Thresk, shearsmith.

Given, 24 January 18 Henry VI [1440]. [Latin]

LETTERS OF ATTORNEY.

Roger Aunger and Isabel, his wife,
to Thomas Thresk, shearsmith, and Robert Makeblyth of Heslyngton, husbandman,
to deliver seisin to John Bell and Isabel, his wife, of a piece of land in Walmegate.

Given, 24 January 18 Henry VI [1440]. [Latin]

GRANT.

Roger Aunger,
to John Bell and Isabel, his wife,
an annual rent of 6s. 8d. from a tenement and eight acres of land in Redenesse, in the tenure of William Cawkewell, situated between the land of the Abbot and Convent of St. Mary's, York, on the west and the land of John Estofte on the east, and abutting on the highway on the north and on the *Grypedyke* on the south.

If the rent was not paid, John Bell and Isabel, his wife, were to have distraint.

The grantor gave them 1d. as seisin.

Given, 26 January 18 Henry VI [1440].   [Latin]

(ff. 96-96v). DEFEASANCE.
    John Bell and Isabel his wife,
       to Roger Aunger,
of his grant of 6s. 8d. p.a. rent [as above], provided they might
build on the waste piece of land in Walmegate, which they had by
the feoffment of the said Roger Aunger and Isabel, his wife.

    Given, 28 January 18 Henry VI [1440].   [Latin]

GIFT.[80]
    Roger Burton of York, clerk,
       to Robert Danby, sergeant at law to the king, Thomas Wytham,
       esquire, John Warter, Rector of the Church of Goldesburgh,
       William Vescy of York, and Alice Burton, the donor's daughter,
all his goods and chattels.

    Witnesses. William [? Stanes],[81] William [? Gowle], Adam
Gunby, clerk, John Walker, John Lownd, citizens of York.

    Given, 20 December 25 Henry VI [1446].   [Latin]

(ff. 97-97v) LEASE.
    Robert Loncaster and John Loncaster, clerks, sons of John Lon-
       caster, late citizen and tailor of York,
       to Margaret Loncaster, widow of the said John Loncaster, tailor,
       for life,
all their lands and tenements in the City of York, which they had
jointly with John Loncaster, tailor, and Alice his wife, their parents,
now deceased, by the gift and feoffment of Thomas Ricall, chaplain.

    Witnesses. John Croser, Mayor, Thomas Scauceby, Richard
Thornton, Sheriffs, John Catryk and John Bedale, citizens and
mercers.

    Given, 26 July 25 Henry VI [1447].   [Latin]

QUITCLAIM.
    Margaret Loncaster
       to Robert Loncaster and John Loncaster,

---

[80] Partially faded. See also f. 89v.
[81] A William Stanes, clerk, was admitted to the freedom in 1429, and a William
Stanes, brewer, was one of the Chamberlains in 1440.

lands and tenements in the City of York which belonged to the said
John Loncaster, tailor, her late husband.

Witnesses. John Croser, Mayor, Thomas Scauceby and Richard
Thornton, Sheriffs, John Catryk and John Bedale, citizens and
mercers of York.

Given, 23 July 25 Henry VI [1447].   [Latin]

FEOFFMENT.

William Nevile, esquire, son and heir of Alexander Nevile of
Thornton on Swale, knight, Thomas Marsshall of Cundall, chaplain, and Alexander Pode of Studeley, yeoman,
to Richard Bedford, son of John Bedford of Kyngeston on Hull,
merchant, and Margaret, his [Richard's] wife, and her heirs,
lands and tenements in the City and suburbs of York which lately
belonged to the said Margaret.

Witnesses. John Croser, Mayor, Thomas Scauceby, and Richard
Thornton, Sheriffs, John Marton, John Shirwod, and William
Marsshall, citizens of York.

Given, 4 September 26 Henry VI [1447].   [Latin]

(ff. 97v-98) QUITCLAIM.[82]

Alexander Nevile of Thornton on Swale, knight,
to Richard Bedford and Margaret, his wife, and her heirs,
lands and tenements [as above].

Witnesses [as above].

Given, 8 September 26 Henry VI [1447].   [Latin]

QUITCLAIM.[82]

William Nevile, Thomas Marsshall and Alexander Pode,
to Richard Bedford and Margaret, his wife, and her heirs,
lands and tenements [as above].

Witnesses [as above].

Given, 8 September [? 26] Henry VI [1447].   [Latin]

(ff. 98-98v) FEOFFMENT.[83]

[Alexander Nevile]
to Richard Bedford and Margaret, his wife, and her heirs,

[82] Partially faded.
[83] Four lines at the foot of f. 98 are completely illegible, except for the words
Omnibus hoc scriptum visuris vel audituris——.

the manor of Skelton in the forest of Galtres with appurtenances in the County of York, lands and tenements in Skelton, common pasture in the forest of Galtres and also a close called *Corteburn* with a wood called *Hordern* in the said county, which he had by the gift and feoffment of the said Margaret in her widowhood.

Witnesses. Thomas Wytham of Corneburgh, Thomas Gower of Stitnam [Stittenham], esquires, Christopher Willesthorp of Roclyff, John Thwenge, John Shirwod of York, gentlemen, John Bolton of Huntyngton.

Given, 4 September 26 Henry VI [1447].   [Latin]

(ff. 98v-99v). CONFIRMATION AND QUITCLAIM.[84]

William Nevile, son of Alexander Nevile,
    to Richard Bedford and Margaret, his wife, and her heirs,
the manor of Skelton [etc], which they had by the gift and feoffment of Alexander Nevile, his father [recited verbatim as above].

Witnesses. Thomas Wytham of Corneburgh, Thomas Gower of Stitnam, esquires, Christopher Willesthorp of Roclyff, Robert Home, John Thwenge and John Shirwod of York, gentlemen, John Bolton of Huntyngton.

Given, [?8] September 26 Henry VI [1447].   [Latin]

QUITCLAIM.[85]

Alexander Nevile,
    to Richard Bedford and Margaret, his wife, and her heirs,
the manor of Skelton [etc., as above]
    Witnesses [as above].
Given, 8 September 26 Henry VI [1447].   [Latin]

(ff. 99v-100) QUITCLAIM.[85]

Thomas Marsshall of Cundall, chaplain, and Alexander Pode of Studeley,
    to Richard Bedford and Margaret, his wife, and her heirs,
the manor of Skelton [etc].
    Witnesses [as above].
Given, 8 September 26 Henry VI [1447].   [Latin]

The aforesaid Alexander [Nevile], William his son, Thomas Marsshall, and Alexander Pode, sought the enrolment of the pre-

[84] Partially faded.
[85] Partially faded.

vious seven deeds in the common register of the city, on 10 October 26 Henry VI [1447]. [Latin]

(ff. 100-101) GRANT OF OBIT.

The Master and Brethren of St. Leonard's Hospital,
to Isabel, the widow of Thomas Karre, late Sheriff of York, John Karre, a former Sheriff, his son, John Marton and John Stayneburn, executors of the will of the said Thomas Karre,

in consideration of 100 marks paid by the said executors for the use of the hospital, undertake to celebrate an obit with music, in the conventual church of the hospital, annually on 1 May, beginning in 1446, for Thomas Karre and Isabel his wife, and also for the souls of the said Isabel, John Karre and Joan, his wife, after death, with the *Placebo* and *Dirige* and the requiem mass. The bells of the hospital were to be rung beforehand and proclamation made by the city bellman. The Master and Brethren were to pay to each brother present at the mass, not excluding the sick or those occupied in the business of the hospital, 6d, to each sister present, not excluding the sick, 4d, to the chaplain of the infirmary 3d, to the clerk of the church 2d, and also to all clerks and choristers of the hospital ringing the great bells, 6d between them, to the city bellman for proclamation of the obit 4d, and 13s. 4d. to be divided equally among the poor in the said hospital. They were bound to the Mayor and Commonalty in £40 to fulfil the above premises, with power of distraint for default.

Tripartite indenture, sealed with the common seal of the hospital, the seals of the said executors and the seal of the Mayor and Commonalty.

Given in the Chapter House of St. Leonard's Hospital, 26 July 1445, 23 Henry VI. [Latin]

(ff. 101v-102v) LETTERS PATENT[86] of Henry [VI], granting a pardon and release to Richard Litster of Wakefeld in the County of York, junior, yeoman,

[1] from all transgression, offence, misprision, contempt or impeachment before 9 April last [1446], against the Statutes of Liveries, punishable by fine, relief or other money penalty or by imprisonment;

[2] all treason, murder, rape, rebellion, insurrection, felony, conspiracy, champerty, maintenance of suits, bribery and other trans-

[86] Not printed in Calendar of Patent Rolls.

gression, offence, negligence, extorsion, misprision, ignorance, contempt, concealment, forfeit or deceit committed before the said 9 April;

[3] all outlawry, provided the said Richard had not committed treachery against the king's person;

[4] all escapes of felons, chattels of felons and fugitives, chattels of outlaws and felons de se, deodands, wastes, impeachments, articles of eyre, destruction, trespass of vert and venison, sales of wood within the forests and without and other offences committed within the realm of England and march of Wales before the said 9 April, punishable by demand, debt, fine, relief or other pecuniary penalty, forfeit of goods and chattels, imprisonment, amerciament of the community or the individual, or charge upon the free tenure of those who have never offended such as heirs, executors or tenants of the lands of escheators, sheriffs, coroners, etc.

[5] all gifts, alienations and profits of lands and tenements held of the king in chief and all gifts made in mortmain without the king's licence; all intrusions and entry into hereditaments without due procedure on the death of ancestors, before the said 9 April, together with all rents and profits received therefrom in the meantime.

[6] all penalties forfeit to the king, his council, chancellor, treasurer, or any of his justices, due to the present king or his father before 9 April last and all writs of *securitatis pacis* before that date.

[7] the thirds and thirds of thirds of the prisoners of war due to the king before 9 April 1446, and all transgression, offence, misprision, contempt and impeachment, before that date contrary to the Statutes of Provisors concerning the acceptance, reading, publishing, notifying and execution of various letters and Papal bulls, and all suits under a writ of *praemunire*.

[8] all fines, assessments, amerciaments, issues, forfeits, reliefs, scutage and all debts, accounts, loans, arrears of rent and accounts before 1 September 20 Henry [VI, 1441], and all actions and demands that the king might have for the same, and all outlawry for the above offences, excepting always such debts and accounts as are owing in respite by virtue of letters patent or royal writ under the great or the privy seal whether by instalment or assignment. Proviso that the present pardon should not conspire to anyone's prejudice, and that it should not affect or extend to Eleanor Cobeham, daughter of Reginald Cobeham, knight, John Bolton of

Bolton in the County of Lancaster, bladesmith, William Wyghale, late warden of the king's gaol at Notyngham or to the felonious slaying of Christopher Talbot, knight; nor to any wool or wool-fells, or any merchandise of the staple conveyed to any parts beyond the realm of England, contrary to the statute made in the parliament at Westminster on the day after the feast of St. Martin 18 Henry VI [12 November 1439], nor to the exoneration and acquittance of any person from the fines to be made according to the same statute. The pardon should not affect the royal auditors, namely, at the treasury at Calais (*Cales*), and the victuallers of the royal household at Calais, the Chamberlains of Chester, North Wales and South Wales, the keepers of the wardrobe in the royal household, the keepers of the great wardrobe, or the keepers or clerks of the wardrobe, the clerks of works, the constables of Bordeaux (*Burdegal*), the treasurers of Ireland and the receivers of the duchies of Lancaster and Cornwall.

Witnessed by the king at Westminster, 28 July 24 Henry [VI, 1446].

Subscribed. By the king himself in parliament.

Preston. [Latin]

(f. 103) FEOFFMENT.

William Bowes, citizen and merchant of York, and Agnes, his wife,
    to William Fallan, clerk, Roger Yarom, chaplain, and John Knapton, chaplain,
messuages, lands, tenements, rents and services in the City and county of York.

Witnesses. William Girlyngton, Mayor, John Carr and William Haberforth, Sheriffs, John Bolton, merchant, Robert Hasyngwold, notary, Nicholas Romlay, William Kyselay.

Given at York, 4 June 19 Henry V [1441]. [Latin]

(f. 103v). FEOFFMENT.

Richard Hamerton, Rector of a moiety of the Church of St. Mary the Elder in York, Thomas Howren, Rector of All Saints' Church in Northstrete and William Hancok of York, chaplain,
    to Thomas Scauceby, citizen and merchant of York,
lands and tenements in Mekilgate, lying in width between the tenement of John Karr, citizen and merchant, on the one side, and the tenement of the chantry founded at the altar of St. John the

Evangelist in the Cathedral Church of St. Peter on the other, and in length from Mekilgate in front as far as Northstrete behind. The feoffors obtained the property by the gift and feoffment of Robert Lede, late citizen and tailor of York.

Witnesses. William Holbek, Mayor, Nicholas Holgate, Robert Perte, Sheriffs, William Clyff, William Shirwod, Henry Drynghouse, Richard Claybruke, citizens of York.

Given, 28 May 27 Henry VI [1449].   [Latin]

(f. 104) On the last day of July 27 Henry VI [1449], Alice del Pole brought the following deed before William Holbek, Mayor, in the Council Chamber, affirmed that it had been made and sealed by her and requested its enrolment in the common register of the city.

(ff. 104-104v) FEOFFMENT.

Alice del Pole of York, widow, daughter and heir of John Brathwayte, late citizen and draper of York,

to Brian Medcalff, gentleman, and Joan his wife, and the heirs of the said Joan,

lands and tenements, rents and services in the City and suburbs of York, which descended to her by hereditary right on the death of John Brathwayte, her father, with the exception of a tenement in Conyngstrete in which she dwelt, which was to remain after her death to the said Brian and Joan, and the heirs of the said Joan.

Rent. 66s. 8d. p.a. to be paid in equal portions on Whit Sunday and the feast of St. Martin in Winter, during the life of the said Alice del Pole.

The feoffees were to make an obit annually, on the vigil or the feast of St. Andrew the Apostle, in the Church of St. Martin the Bishop in Conyngstrete, for the souls of the said John Brathwayte and Marion his wife, of John Raghton, late husband of Alice del Pole, of Ed. de la Pole, her late husband, and of John Raghton, her son, and for her soul after death.

Alice del Pole was to have the right of re-entry in default of the obit and annual rent.

Witnesses. William Holbek, Mayor, Nicholas Holgate, Robert Perte, Sheriffs, Thomas Barton, citizen and Alderman, William Shirburn, bower.

Given, 24 July 27 Henry VI [1449].   [Latin] (ff. 105-106) INSPEXIMUS.

Concerning the chantry at Thorne

by Thomas [Arundel], Archbishop of York, of the foundation deed of a perpetual chantry in the chapel of Thoren [Thorne], as follows:—

> Richard de Thoren, canon of the Cathedral Church of St. Peter of York, with the consent of King Richard [II] and Thomas, Archbishop of York,
>
> to Thomas Broune, chaplain in the chapel of Thoren, in the diocese of York, and his successors,

the site of the chapel as enclosed, together with various lands, tenements and rents granted by him to the chapel, in frankalmoign. The said Thomas Broune and his successors were to reside personally and continuously in the said chantry, no dispensation from a superior being valid, and were to celebrate mass daily for the souls of the founder, and of Edward de Wyndesore, late King of England, of Thomas de Arundell, Archbishop of York and of the founder's parents, friends and benefactors. They were to say the *Placebo* and *Dirige* with Commendation of the dead each day, ill health only excepted, and were to be obliged on oath before the Archbishop on their admission or institution to the chantry, to perform their office faithfully. Should the chaplain be prevented from performing his duties by serious infirmity, he was to find another in his place, as long as the rent of the chantry amounted to £6. He was to swear that he would not sell the lands and tenements or lease them for more than five years, but would maintain them in the condition in which he received them, and that he would not sell the books, chalices, vestments or other ornaments pertaining to the chantry, mortgage them nor lend them for use outside the chapel, under penalty of being deprived of the chantry. The institution or admission of a chaplain was to be of no effect unless the said oaths were taken. He was to cause a trental to be celebrated annually for the founder's soul in the Church of the Friars Preachers of Beverley, from the rents pertaining to the chantry, so long as the said friars should be content with 5s. for the celebration. After the death of each chaplain, an assessment of the defects in the houses and tenements belonging to the chantry was to be made by the most law-worthy and discreet men of the neighbourhood, and all the money raised from the premises was to go to the churchwarden of the collegiate church of St. John of Beverley. The latter, with the consent of the chaplain of the chantry, should not fail to spend the money so received without loss of time on repairs and necessary rebuilding, previously considered and assessed, to which they should be compelled if necessary by the ordinary of the place by sentence of greater excommunication, preceded by lawful warning. If any chaplain should be publicly defamed for intemperance or be convicted as a common frequenter of inns and could not clear himself, the Archbishop for the time being should remove him from the chantry and choose another suitable and honest chaplain in his place. The presentation of a chaplain to the chantry was to belong to the said Richard de Thoren during his liftetime. After his death, the nomination was to belong to the Archbishop of York or in the case of a vacancy in that office, to the Chapter of York. The nominee was to be presented by the Mayor of the City of York to the Archbishop or Chapter and by him admitted and instituted. If it should happen that there was no Mayor of York, then the collation and institution should belong solely to the Archbishop or the Chapter.

Witnesses. Master William de Kexby, precentor, John de Shirburn, Chancellor, Thomas de Dalby, Archdeacon of Richemond, Nicholas de Feriby and Thomas de Walworth, canons residentiary in the Cathedral Church of St. Peter of York.

Given at York, 11 June 1390.

Confirmed by the Archbishop at his manor of Rest,[87] 17 August 1390, in the third year of his translation.

Subscribed. Burton Roger.   [Latin]

(f. 106) NOMINATION.[88]

John [Kempe], Archbishop of York,

to the Mayor of the City of York,

of Richard Sutton, chaplain, to the chantry founded in the chapel of Thorne, following the death of Thomas Broune, the last holder of the office.

Given in the hospital at Leicestre, 14 August 1426, in the second year of his translation.   [Latin]

PRESENTATION.

Peter Bukcy, Mayor of the City of York,

[87] Rest Park, near Sherburn in Elmet.
[88] A later nomination of a chaplain to the same chantry appears on f.120v.

to John [Kempe], Archbishop of York,
of Richard Sutton, chaplain, to the chantry in the chapel at Thoren.
    Given at York, 20 August 1426.   [Latin]

[ff. 106v-111v. relate to the foundation of the hospital in honour
of Jesus Christ and the Blessed Virgin Mary in Fossgate, later the
Merchant Adventurers' Hall.]

[ff. 106v-107] LETTERS PATENT.[89]
    Edward III
granting licence, on the surrender by John de Rouclyf and other
brethren [not named] of the fraternity of the guild in honour of
Our Lord Jesus Christ and the Blessed Virgin Mary, in the City
of York, of previous letters patent, and in consideration of 40s.
paid to the king, to change their guild into a hospital; and for the
appointment of a chaplain to be presented by the said John to the
diocesan for admission, a chaplain being presented in all vacancies
by the said John and his heirs, to be instituted and inducted as
perpetual warden, having the care and keeping thereof and being
called warden; also for them to grant the rent of 16s. 8d, belonging
to the guild under the royal licence to acquire lands and tenements
to the value of £10 p.a. in York held of the king in burgage, and
the remaining £9. 3s. 4d. of land and rent when acquired, to the
warden, brethren and sisters of the hospital, for their maintenance
and that of the chaplains to celebrate divine service in the hospital
for the good estate of the king, and the brethren and sisters and
their souls after death, and for the souls of Philippa, late Queen, his
consort, and of all the poor and infirm of the hospital; and for the
warden to implead for lands and possessions of the guild. Also
annulling the said guild.
    Witnessed at Westminster, 12 February 45 (France 32) Edward
III [1371].   [Latin]

(f. 107-108v) ARCHIEPISCOPAL LICENCE,
    of John [Thoresby], Archbishop of York.
        Reciting that a guild had been founded in Fossegate by citizens
        of York, with the licence of Edward [III], and that, by a
        further royal licence, it had been transformed into a hospital for
        chaplains and poor and infirm persons.

[89] Also calendared in C.P.R. 1370-74, p. 47. A complete transcript is printed by
M. Sellers, York Mercers and Merchant Adventurers, pp. 27-30.

Reciting also the following proxy: —

John de Rouclif, clerk, late master of the guild in honour of
Our Lord Jesus Christ and the Blessed Virgin Mary, and Ralph
de Romundby, Richard de Thursby, John de Beverley, Robert
de Pothow, Peter de Thorpe, Joan de Brystowe of York, Enota,
widow of John de Crome, and John de Thorneton, spicer,
brethren and sisters of the guild,

to John, Archbishop of York,

submitting the guild and all lands and tenements acquired by
royal licence, in order that he might transform it into a hospital
in accordance with the royal charter; and appointing William
Brunby, chaplain, to act on behalf of the guild.

As their seal was unknown to many, they had caused the
official seal of the Dean of Christianity of York to be affixed.

Given at York, 24 August 1373.

Now ordaining that: —

[1]. A hospital should be founded in Fossegate in honour of Our
Lord Jesus Christ and the Blessed Virgin Mary, endowed
with the houses and possessions of the said guild.

[2]. There should be a suitable chaplain appointed to administer
and govern the hospital, its revenues and goods, and to distribute the revenues to the poor.

[3]. A chaplain was to be presented by Master John de Rouclif
and his heirs within one month of a vacancy occurring, and
admitted by the Archbishop, or, in the event of a vacancy
in that office, by the Dean and Chapter, or by the Chapter.
If a chaplain was not presented within one month, the presentation was to go firstly to the Mayor of the City of York,
then, if no presentation were made within the following
month, to the Official of the Court at York, and finally to
the Archbishop or, if the see were vacant, to the Dean and
Chapter or the Chapter alone.

[4]. Each warden on admission should take an oath to use the
goods to the benefit of the hospital and avoid all waste, to
make an inventory of the goods, to render account within
a month after Whit Sunday and to reside continuously and
personally in the hospital. Should he squander the goods,
turn them to his own use, or otherwise neglect the administration, he should be removed from office and another more
suitable chosen.

[5]. There should be thirteen poor and weak persons, and also two poor student clerks chosen by the warden, each of whom was to receive 4d. weekly from the warden. If any of the brethren, sisters or benefactors should be in need and sought a place in the hospital at a convenient time, they should be preferred to others.

[6]. The master or warden of the hospital should have 10 marks p.a., and no more, from the revenues.

[7]. When the revenue of the hospital was 6 marks more than the aforesaid payments, another suitable chaplain should be appointed by the warden on the nomination of Master John de Rouclif and his heirs. He should receive the 6 marks p.a. from the warden in equal portions on each of the following four feasts, All Saints, the Purification of the Blessed Virgin Mary, Philip and James the Apostles, and St. Peter ad Vincula. He was to reside continuously and personally within the hospital.

If the revenue of the hospital further increased, the number of poor should be increased accordingly.

[8]. The warden and chaplain were to recite daily the office of the dead, and three times every week seven penitential psalms with the litany. Masses were to be celebrated daily for King Edward, the Archbishop, John de Rouclif, the Mayor of the City of York, the Official of the Court of York, the brethren, sisters and benefactors of the hospital and the poor residing there, for their souls after death, and for the soul of Philippa, late Queen.

[9]. Any warden or chaplain proved guilty of incontinency should be removed from his office and another suitable and honest person appointed in his place.

Given at Thorp near York [Bishopthorpe], 27 August 1373, in the 21st year of his translation. [Latin]

(ff. 109-109v) LETTERS PATENT.[90]

Richard [II]

granting licence to William de Ottelay, chaplain, William de Touthorp, chaplain, John de Dernyngton, Richard de Alne, John de Quyxlay, John de Stokwyth, and William Celer, citizens of York, to give and assign fourteen messuages, seven shops, and 32s. rent in

[90] Also calendared in C.P.R. 1396-9, p. 67.

York and its suburbs, held of the king in burgage, to the warden, brethren and sisters of the hospital in honour of Our Lord Jesus Christ and the Blessed Virgin Mary, in full satisfaction of the licence granted to them by Edward III, to acquire [further] land and rent to an annual value of £9. 3s. 4d., notwithstanding the Statute of Mortmain.

Consideration, 20 marks paid in the hanaper.

Reciting the licence of Edward III [as above, ff. 106v-107].

Witnessed at Westminster, 11 February 20 Richard II [1397].

(ff. 109v-110) LETTERS PATENT.[91]

Edward [III]

granting licence to Robert de Smeton to alienate in mortmain to John Freboys, master, and the brethren and sisters of the guild of Our Lord Jesus Christ and the Blessed Virgin Mary, a messuage and 10s. rent, held of the king in burgage by the payment of 4d. p.a. in *husgabul*, above which, and other services due, the messuage was of no annual value, according to an inquisition made by Peter de Nuttle, late escheator of the said county; the messuage to be held as of the value of 6s 8d yearly, together with the rent aforesaid, in part satisfaction of the £10 p.a. of land and rent which they had licence to acquire for the daily celebration of mass in the parish church of St. Crux or elsewhere in the city.

Reciting briefly the terms of the grant of licence for the incorporation of the guild and for lands and rents worth £10 p.a. to be acquired.[92]

Witnessed at Westminster, 16 February 32 (France 19) Edward [III] [1358]. [Latin]

(ff. 110-110v) *The will of John Freboys*, citizen of York, as contained in the register of wills of the Court of York. Desiring burial in the church of St. Mary, Castlegate, next to Agnes, his late wife, and making the following bequests:—to the fabric of that church, 13s. 4d; to the rectors for his forgotten tithes from the time when he became a parishioner of that church, 13s. 4d; to the high altar of the church of St. Michael de Belfrey, as a mortuary gift, his best robe with a lined cloak; to the fabric of All Saints' Church, Pavement, 6s. 8d; in wax for burning around his body on the day of

---

[91] Also calendared in C.P.R., 1358-61, p. 9.

[92] Calendared in C.P.R., 1354-58, pp. 517-18; transcribed by M. Sellers, *York Mercers and Merchant Adventurers*, pp. 1-3.

burial, 30s to be divided into three parts, one for the Rector of the church of St. Michael le Belfrey, the second for the Rector of All Saints' Church, Pavement, and the third for the Rectors of St. Mary's Church, Castlegate; for his funeral expenses and for calling together his friends, £3; to poor clerks and widows, 10s; to Robert Caperon, 6s. 8d; to the four leper-houses in the suburbs of York, 4s, in equal portions; to the clerks imprisoned in the Archbishop's prison 12d; to the prisoners in the gaol on Ouse Bridge 12d, to the prisoners in York Castle, 3s; to the poor in the hospital on the bridge 12d; to two anchoresses in York 2s, in equal portions; to the four orders of mendicant friars in York, 40s, in equal portions; pro[93] marks to Brother John Freboys for his habit and other necessities fitting to his work; to William, his brother, £15; to two suitable chaplains to celebrate divine service for the souls of himself, Alice Frankyssh and Agnes, her daughter, for one year after his death, £8 to provide a salary of 6 marks each; to William, his brother, for life, remainder to Emma, his wife, for life, remainder in frankalmoign to the master, brethren and sisters of the Guild of the Blessed Mary in Fossegate, a tenement with a croft in Munkgate which the testator had by the bequest of Agnes de Eberston and of Ellen, his mother;

to Emma, his wife, the tenement with a shop in which he lived in Petregate, which formerly belonged to Robert del Isle, late citizen of York, and which he had by the gift and feoffment of Henry de Raghton, Rector of All Saints' Church, Pavement, and William de Grengham, chaplain; to John de Qwarrom, 20s; to Ellen, wife of John Tuke of York, 20s; to Matilda, wife of William Fox, goldsmith of York, 20s; to Thomas, the brother of Emma, his [the testator's] wife, £3; to Thomas de Duffeld, citizen of York, 20s; to John de Staunton, clerk, if he should draw up his inventory, 6s. 8d;

to Emma, his wife, and William, his brother, whom he appointed his executors, the remainder of his goods; to Matilda and Isabel, his servants, 13s. 4d, in equal portions.

Given at York, the Thursday after the Epiphany of the Lord [7 January] 1360/1.

Inspected and sealed by the Official and Commissary General of the Court of York, 4 October 1362. [Latin]

[93] It seems that the scribe must have been thinking ahead and inserted pro instead of the amount.

(ff. 110v-111) LETTERS PATENT.[94]

Edward [III]

granting licence for the alienation in mortmain to the master, brethren and sisters of the guild in honour of Our Lord Jesus Christ and the Blessed Virgin Mary, of a messuage and toft by William de Huntyngdon, citizen of York, a messuage by John Neuton, and another messuage by John de Lasseles, in satisfaction of 10s. of the land and rents to the annual value of £10 which they had licence to acquire. The three messuages and the toft were held in burgage of the king and were of a clear annual value of 6s. 8d, according to an inquisition taken by William de Nessefelde, escheator in the County of York.

Witnessed at Westminster, 6 June 33 (France 20) Edward [III] [1359]. [Latin]

GRANT.

William Waselyn and Agnes, his wife,

to William de Selby, Richard de Waune, Nicholas Warthyll, and John Dernyngton, citizens of York, and the heirs and assigns of the said Nicholas,

the advowson of the hospital of the Holy Trinity and Saint Mary, in Fossegate.

Witnesses. William Frost, Mayor, Thomas de Ruseton, William de Alne, Sheriffs, Thomas Gra, John de Houeden, Thomas Smyth, John de Barthwayte, Robert de Talkan of York.

Given at York, 6 September 1396, 20 Richard II. [Latin]

LETTERS OF ATTORNEY.

William Waselyn and Agnes, his wife,

to Richard Mekyn of Fangfosse, chaplain,

to deliver seisin to William de Selby, Richard de Waune, Nicholas Warthill and John Darnyngton, of the advowson of the hospital of the Holy Trinity and St. Mary in Fossegate.

Given at York, 6 September 20 Richard II [1396]. [Latin]

(f. 111v.) FINAL CONCORD.

William de Selby, Richard de Waune, Nicholas Warthyll and John Dernyngton, citizens of York, plaintiffs,

and William Waselyn and Agnes, his wife, deforciants,

[94] Also calendared in C.P.R. 1358-61, pp. 227-8.

concerning the advowson of the hospital of the Holy Trinity and St. Mary at York, which the plaintiffs had by the grant of the said William Waselyn and Agnes.

Fine. £20.

Given, the octave of St. Hillary 20 Richard II [20 January 1397].

[Latin]

(ff. 111v-112) GRANT.[95]

The Mayor and Commonalty, in consideration of 500 marks given by Robert Howme, merchant, former Mayor of York, to the use of the commonalty, undertake to pay a suitable chaplain 10 marks p.a., payable in two equal portions by the Chamberlains in the *chambre of the mayralte* on Ouse Bridge, for the celebration of divine service for the souls of the said Robert and Agnes and Joan, his wives, his parents and benefactors and those from whom he had any goods undeservedly. The masses were to be celebrated in the parish church of St. Maurice in the suburbs of York during Robert Howme's lifetime and after his death at the high altar in the recently founded chapel of St. Anne on Foss Bridge, in the nomination and gift of the said Robert and his heirs.

Should the 5 marks not be paid within forty days after Whit Sunday and the feast of St. Martin in Winter, an additional 6s 8d was to be paid to the chaplain and the same amount to the Dean and Chapter of St. Peter's, York, for all of which payments the said Robert Howme and his heirs, the chaplain and the Dean and Chapter might have recourse to temporal or ecclesiastical law.

Quadripartite indenture, the four parties being Robert Howme, the chaplain [unnamed], the commonalty of York and the Dean and Chapter.

Given at York, 4 February 1427/8, 6 Henry VI. [Latin]

(ff. 112-114v) GRANT.[96]

Robert Howme, citizen and merchant and former Mayor of York, son and executor of Robert Howme, late citizen and merchant.

Reciting the grant of the Mayor and Commonalty, as above, but stating that the masses were to be said for the souls of Robert Howme, his father, William and Isabel, the latter's parents, and Katherine and Margaret, his wives, for his own soul and the souls of his mother and Agnes and Joan, his wives.

[95] The original is preserved amongst the York City Archives (G70: 34).
[96] York City Archives (G70: 35).

And ordaining that: —

[1] The chaplain, who was to be a secular chaplain, was to celebrate masses and the offices of the dead daily with the Commendation of souls, according to the custom, time and form of the York ordinal, and a mass of Requiem weekly on the most convenient day, and was to make mention in the masses, canonical hours and certain prayers of Robert Howme's good estate while he lived and after his death of his soul and of those aforesaid. He was to celebrate mass in the chapel on all feast days and Sundays between the ninth and tenth hours before lunch. If he wished to absent himself with the licence of his patron, he should arrange at his own expense for another chaplain, secular or regular, to celebrate mass.

[2] Each chaplain should have a place at the altar and his own key for keeping his books, chalice, vestments and other ornaments.

[3] If the number of priests, clerks and other ecclesiastical ministers endowed in the same chapel should increase so that there were sufficient to sing with music at divine service, the chaplain should attend personally, wearing a surplice and help with the singing.

[4] The chaplain was not to hold any other ecclesiastical benefice or temporal office, or celebrate any pecuniary or peculiar masses outside the chapel. If any chaplain was legally convicted of incontinency, theft, robbery, perjury or any other canonical offence, or was unable through his own fault to take care of the said celebration, he was to be removed from his duties as unsuitable, and another chaplain was to be appointed by the said Robert during his lifetime or, after his death by Thomas, his son, and the heirs of his body in succession. If he died without such heirs the appointment was to be made by any other sons he might have, and the heirs of their bodies or, for want thereof, by Katherine, his daughter and the heirs of her body, or if she died without such heirs, then by any other daughters he might have and the heirs of their bodies. In default of all such heirs, the Mayor was to appoint a chaplain.

[5] The chaplain was to say the *Placebo* and *Dirige* and the Commendation of souls daily, and make an annual obit for the souls of the founder's father and of others aforesaid in the church of St. Maurice during his lifetime and afterwards in the said chapel, to the value of 6s 8d; namely, 4d to each of six chaplains present at the offices for the dead and the mass celebrated therein, 4d. to the city bell-ringer for proclaiming the obit and 4d to the parish

clerk for ringing the bells, 2d each to four boys attending and wearing surplices, and for buying two wax candles weighing three pounds, to burn during the obit each year and as long afterwards as they would last at the high altar of the said church, and after his death at the high altar of St. Anne's chapel. Immediately after the mass on the day of the obit the chaplain was to give 20d for his father's soul. The obit was to be on the day after the feast of St. Anne.

[6] The chaplain was to celebrate all the divine services in the said church during Robert Howme's lifetime and in the chapel after his death. He was to take an oath to observe all the ordinances herein made, not to alienate, mortgage, destroy or waste the books, chalices, vestments and other ornaments but to make an inventory and deliver them to his successor, and to find sufficient security for them on his admission to office. If it should happen that bread, wine and candles could not be had from the said church or chapel, the chaplain was to provide them at his own expense.

[7] The chaplain was to receive 10 marks p.a., payable twice yearly by the Chamberlains, as was determined in the above deed. When a chaplain resigned, died or was expelled for some just cause, Robert Howme or his heirs, in the aforesaid order, were to nominate another honest and suitable chaplain, within forty days of being notified of the vacancy. If his son Thomas, or any of his heirs neglected to nominate a chaplain within forty days, the Mayor was to do so within the twenty days next following, all future appointments being reserved to Robert Howme, Thomas Howme or their heirs. The Mayor and Commonalty were likewise to nominate the chaplain if Robert Howme's son, Thomas, and daughter, Katherine, and any other children he might have, died without heirs of their bodies. If they failed to appoint within forty days, then the Dean and Chapter were to name the next chaplain.

Quadripartite indenture.

Given at York, 14 February 1427/8, 6 Henry VI.   [Latin]

Subscribed: And if anyone should wish to know in future how the 500 marks were spent for the benefit of the commonalty, it shall be known by this that in the mayoralty of William Bowes [1428], a tenement in Conyngstrete in the tenure of John Farnelay, spurrier, was bought of John Ellerker, sergeant at law, for 100 marks. It renders to the commonalty 6 marks p.a. besides 11s. p.a. to the Vicars Choral of the Cathedral Church of St. Peter and 2s. p.a. to

Thomas Neuport in part payment of the salary of the said chaplain.

[Latin]

[At the head of f. 114 is also a copy of part of the licence of John, Archbishop of York, relating to the foundation of the guild of Our Lord Jesus Christ and the Blessed Virgin Mary. It ends abruptly in the middle of a sentence, and bears the marginal note, *void*. The full text appears on f. 108.]

(ff. 114v-115) ROYAL WRIT.

Henry [VI]
to the Mayor, Sheriffs and Commonalty of the City of York, reciting that by Letters Patent of 26 February 8 Henry VI [1430],[97] made with the consent of the lords spiritual and temporal and the commons of the realm and for 5 marks paid in the hanaper, he had granted denization to Henry Market, born in the parts of Almain, and his heirs. Charging them to allow him all privileges, offices and customs within the city.

Witnessed at Westminster, 18 October 20 Henry VI [1441].

[Latin]

(ff. 115v-116) GRANT.

Marginal note: Concerning the payment of 18 marks at the high altar in the Cathedral Church of St. Peter at York, to Master Thomas Haxhey.

The Mayor and Commonalty of York,
to the Dean and Chapter of the Cathedral Church of St. Peter, York,

an annual rent of 18 marks, to be paid at the high altar of the said church, in two equal portions on the feasts of Whit Sunday and St. Martin in Winter or within one month after each feast, for which they were to receive from the Dean and Chapter or from the Chapter alone, should the office of Dean be vacant, an acquittance given in the Chapter House. In case of default, the Mayor and Commonalty would pay an additional 10 marks as a penalty. Any acquittance or exoneration other than one given in the Chapter House was to be void. Each Mayor and Chamberlain on the day of his election or institution to office was to swear on oath in the

[97] C.P.R. 1429-36, p. 43.

Common Hall before the Dean and Chapter, that he would pay the rent as abovesaid.

Proviso that if the Dean and Chapter refused to give an acquittance, the rent for that term was to be respited until they did so.

Given at York, 8 March 6 Henry VI [1428]. [Latin]

(f. 116v) ACQUITTANCE.
The Dean and Chapter of St. Peter's, York,
to the Mayor and Commonalty,
of the rent of 9 marks received for the term of St. Martin in Winter last past, part of the rent of 18 marks p.a., granted as above.

Given in the Chapter House, on the vigil of St. Andrew the Apostle, 7 Henry VI [29 November 1428]. [Latin]

(ff. 116v-116Av) *A plea heard at Westminster before William Babyngton and others of the King's Justices of the Common Bench in the Michaelmas term, 7 Henry VI.*[98]

Marginal note: Concerning the rent of 9 marks to the Dean and Chapter of York.

The Mayor and Commonalty of the City of York were summoned to reply to the Dean and Chapter of the Cathedral Church of St. Peter at York, on a plea that they should pay them the 9 marks' arrears which they owed of an annual rent of 18 marks. The Dean and Chapter, per Thomas Sutton their attorney, affirmed that the Mayor and Commonalty had withheld the annual rent and refused to render the same on Whit Sunday in the sixth year of the reign; and that they still refused to do so, by which they suffered a loss of £100. They showed in the court the counterpart of the deed testifying to the grant of the said annual rent, [here recited as above].

The Mayor and Commonalty, per Robert Den, their attorney, said that they could not deny the charge of the Dean and Chapter, that they had made the deed in question, or that 9 marks of the rent was in arrears, but said that they had been prepared to pay the 9 marks on Whit Sunday and ever since. It was considered that the Dean and Chapter should recover the annual rent from the Mayor and Commonalty. The latter who came on the first day by summons should not be amerced. The attorney of the Dean and Chapter received 9 marks' arrears in court and thereupon the Mayor and Commonalty were acquitted. [Latin]

[98] Partially damaged by damp.

(f. 116Av-117v) GRANT.[99]

Marginal note: concerning the shrine which is carried annually on the feast of Corpus Christi.

The Mayor and citizens
to the keepers of the guild of Corpus Christi.

Whereas from time immemorial a community of men and women known as the Corpus Christi guild had existed in York, for the due honour of the Eucharist and the feast of Corpus Christi, and now John Bolton, Mayor, and the citizens, all being members of the guild, proposed [to provide] from their own resources, a shrine splendidly worked in carved wood embossed with gold and thereafter, with God's help, enriched with finest silver and gold and decorated more preciously still; and they desired that each year on the feast of Corpus Christi, weather permitting, or otherwise on any more convenient feast day following, it should be carried publicly through the streets and squares of the city by priests in solemn procession, bearing within itself the sacrament of Corpus Christi, visible to men's gaze through crystal or glass or other material and preceded by the lights of torches held by good citizens and members of the fraternity;

now grant that a special place in the chapel on Ouse Bridge, dedicated to the Holy Confessor, William, sometime Archbishop of York, should house the shrine from year to year; that the six chaplains, currently the keepers of the guild, should have authority of the shrine, to enter and remove it as necessary and especially on the feast of Corpus Christi, to carry or see that it was carried out of the chapel (without interference from the Mayor or citizens, to hold the procession)[1] and later to replace the shrine; that they should also hold the keys of the enclosed reliquary, provided that one key for the exterior cover and veil of the shrine should always remain in the Council Chamber of the city in the possession of the Mayor, so that any Mayor could, without enquiry or delay, arrange for the shrine to be shown, unadorned, to distinguished persons.

Sealed with the common seal of the city and the seals of the keepers of the guild, John Bernyngham, Roger Bubwyth, John de

[99] The original is preserved amongst the City Archives (A15), and is transcribed by R. H. Scaife, *The Guide of Corpus Christi, York*, pp. 251-3.
[1] Words in brackets are omitted from the Memorandum Book but appear in the original grant.

Grymesby, John Craven, John de Sutton and William Bryg, chaplains.

Given at York, 16 January 1431/2, 10 Henry VI.

Subscribed, Burton, Roger. [Latin]

(ff. 117v.-119) GRANT.

Marginal note: concerning two chantries in the conventual church of the Friars Preachers of York, for Nicholas Blakburn and Margaret, his wife.

The Prior and Convent of the Friars Preachers of York, in consideration of the great beneficence of Nicholas Blakburn, senior, former Admiral of the King of England and Mayor of York, with the consent of Brother John Rokell, Doctor of Theology and provincial prior, and of all the brethren,

to the said Nicholas Blakburn and Margaret, his wife,

[1] A perpetual chantry of one priest, a brother of the house, to celebrate daily for the said Nicholas and Margaret in the conventual church at the altar of St. Mary Magdalene, situated on the south side of the nave. The altar should be provided at the friars' expense with ornaments and all things necessary for a priest celebrating there, viz. a chalice, book, bread, wine and wax.

A suitable brother was to celebrate at the altar for the said Nicholas and Margaret and others named below, first ringing the chapter bell for the mass in like manner as it was rung daily for high mass. He was to pray daily, Sundays and principal feasts excepted, for the said Nicholas and the health of his estate while he lived, and was to celebrate a mass of the Holy Spirit, saying the collect *Deus qui caritatis* with the Secret and post communion; after his death he was to celebrate a mass of Requiem for the souls of Nicholas and of Margaret after her death, and of all their family and benefactors. On Sundays and feast days the priest was to say the *Deus qui caritatis* or, after Nicholas's death, the *Inclina* with the Secret and post communion; excepting also Maundy Thursday, Good Friday and the Saturday before Easter day, on which days according to the statutes of the order, no masses ought to be celebrated at the lower altars. On all other days, the brother deputed to do so, or another in his place, was to celebrate for the said Nicholas and Margaret or their souls unless prevented by fire, infection or repair of the church, in which case the prior might assign another suitable place for the celebration. The masses were not to be omitted on any day, the said three days excepted, and excepting only any case, general interdict or suspension and similar inevitable causes.

[2] another perpetual chantry at the high altar for the daily celebration of a mass of the Blessed Virgin Mary. During Nicholas's lifetime, the prayer *Deus qui caritatis* was to be said at the mass and after his death the prayer *Inclina domine*. Immediately after the mass at the high altar, all the brethren in the choir should say the psalm *De profundis* with the *Pater Noster* and *Ave Maria* and other prayers, the *Inclina* and *Fidelium Deus* etc. These masses were to be celebrated daily with the exception of the three days [named above].

[3] an obit, after the death of the said Nicholas and Margaret, to be publicly proclaimed throughout the City of York by the common bellman and celebrated in the said church, with the offices of the dead and nine lessons on the feast of St. James the Apostle, and a mass of Requiem on the feast of St. Anne, sung by the choir wearing their copes. The obit was not to be omitted any year, for any reason, a general interdict or similar inevitable case only excepted.

Each prior on his first day in office and all those under his authority were to promise on oath to fulfil the premises. Each prior should likewise warn, exhort and by virtue of the holy spirit and holy obedience enforce on all those under his authority, that they should observe inviolate the chantries, masses, obits and funeral services according to the premises, and should be bound to issue sentence of greater excommunication, judicially and in accordance with the rules of the chapter, against any offending brother. In the event of default, the prior and brethren were to pay, on the following day, 40s in equal portions to the Mayor and Commonalty and the heirs and executors of Nicholas Blakburn, to be employed by them in pious uses for the souls of the said Nicholas and Margaret. They were to have the right of distraint and, if the 40s was not received within forty days, the right to sell the goods distrained.

Confirmed and sealed by Brother John Rokell, professor of theology and provincial prior of the Friars Preachers of England.

Tripartite indenture.

Given at York, in the Chapter House of the friars, the feast of St. Blase the Martyr [3 February] 1431/2, 10 Henry VI.

Subscribed. Burton, Roger.   [Latin]

(f. 119v) PETITION OF THE VINTNERS.[2]

To thair worshipfull lord the Mair of the Cite of York and all Aldermen and the Consell of the same, shewes mekely we your concitezeyns vynters that we haf diverse tymes shewed to you that men of other craftes that selles swete wynes and other wynes for thair wynes be retail wythin the franchese of this Cite, whilk swete wynes are pertenand to us als a parcelle of oure crafte, suld and awe after custume of this Cite be contributory to us in bryngyng furthe of our pagent in Corpus Christi play, lyke als merchantz makes us to pay to tham when we mell[3] wyth Pruys, Flanders and other place, of whilk sw[e]te wynes we haf yit no answer nor remedy. And, worshipfull lord and sirs, like you to consider that we haf bene in possession of swete wynes sald be retaill in so mykill that Richart Russell, when he was our pageant maister, receyved pageant silver of Thomas Dam and all other after thair afferant for sellyng of swete wynes at that tyme, and so evermore other men when thay occupied the same office. And also be alde custume and usage of this Cite for serchyng of swete wynes pertyens to the serchours of the vynters and to no nother, in so mykill that noght lang tyme passed our sercheours at commandement of the Mair at that tyme and hys consell serched swetewynes and other thurgh thys cite. And at that tyme our shercheours, in presence of the mair, fand in the house of John Asper in Stayngate, a vessell of swete wyne unabell to be sald, and in other places also, the whilk war forfet and the hevedes[4] smyten oute openly in syght of the poeple. And thare-fore worshipfull lord and sirs we beseke you to considre this mater tenderly and that we may be so demened that we may contynue furth in our ald possession and noght be put thair fro more nowe than we haf bene in tyme passed. And who so will wythstand or agaynesay this, lat tham prove whether thair swetewynes that thay sell be grewyng of grape or elles wynes made wyth spicery or other crafte wyth outen grape.

(ff. 119v-120)[5] The petition was read and agreed to in the Council Chamber, on 19 September 12 Henry VI [1433], before William Ormesheved, Mayor, Richard Russell, William Bowes, senior, John Moreton, Thomas Bracebrig, John Aldstanmore, Nicholas Blak-

---

[2] Printed in *York Civic Records*, Vol. II, pp. 85-6. Ordinances of the vintners, dated 1482-3 are printed in *York Memorandum Book* II, pp. 275-7.

[3] *mell*: mix, deal, treat.

[4] *hevedes*: heads.

[5] The last ten lines of f.119v are very faded.

burn, John Bolton, Thomas Snaudon, Thomas Gare, John Louthe,
and Thomas Kyrkham, Aldermen, Thomas Kyrke, John Rukby,
Sheriffs, Thomas More, Robert Yarom, John Warde, Richard
Louthe, John Dodyngton, John Brounflete, William Grillyngton,
Thomas Karr, William Belford, William Bowes, junior, and John
Ratclif of the Twenty Four. The searchers of the vintners were to
have the search of sweet wines sold by retail in the liberty of the
city, and all who sold sweet wines were to contribute to the vintners'
pageant in proportion to the sweet wine they sold.   [Latin]

(f. 120) PETITION OF THE SPICERS.[6]

Shewes full mekely to your ryght hygh worthynesse Mair, Aldermen and the wyse Counsell of the Chaumbre, the pore crafte of the
spicers. Whar as we haf hadd wyth outen tyme of mynde the sherch
of swet wynes alswele grewand as confect, ypocras,[7] clarr[et] and
all other, that nowe late be the suggestion of diverse persones the
whilk never hadd als be thair craft knawlege of swilk wynes, to
tham ys supposyd grauntyd the sherch of the same wynes wythin
this cite, in grete harme wyth grevows hynderyng to the losse of
our crafte of spicers, als wele in our said craft as to our pageant, for
sen the tyme at the play was begun in thys cite, all the sellers be
retaill [of] swete wyne grewyng and confect has payed to our craft
of spicers and to non other as for that merchandyse. Wherfore we
be sek your hegh worthynesse, seyng our predecessours Mairs,
Aldermen and other of the Counsell of the Chambre be thair hegh
and discrete wytts hasse ever latyn us be in possession of swylk serch
wyth takyng to our pageant of all the sellers of swete wyne, that
ye will consider thair wytts and apply your worthy wytts unto
thairs that precessed yowe in tyme, for trewly yt warr full hevy to
us your citezeins of the pure crafte of spicers oft said to seke any
remedy bot of your ryght hegh worthynesse. Thys we beseke yowe
als for our ryght and in way of charite.

The petition was read, 6 November 12 Henry VI [1433], before
William Ormeshed, Mayor, William Bowes, senior, John Moreton,
Richard Russell, John Aldestanemore, Nicholas Blakburn, John
Bolton, Thomas Snaudon, Thomas Gare, Richard Warter and
William Bedale, Aldermen, Robert Yarom, John Gascoigne, John
Warde, Richard Louthe, John Brounflete, William Grillyngton,

---

[6] Printed in *York Civic Records*, Vol. III, p. 176.
[7] *ypocras*: Hippocras, a cordial drink of wine flavoured with spices.

John Raghton, William Bowes [junior], John Esyngwald, Thomas Catryk, Thomas Kyrke and John Rukeby of the Twenty-Four. It was unanimously agreed that the previous decision on the petition of the vintners should be observed unless any statute of the realm should be discovered to the contrary. [Latin]

(f. 120v) PRESENTATION.[8]

John [Kempe], Archbishop of York,
to Thomas Kyrkham, Mayor of York,
of William Routh, chaplain of the chantry in the chapel of Molsecrofft, to the chantry in the chapel of St. Mary at Thurne near Beverley, [lately] held by Richard Sutton.

Given in the Hospital of St. James near Westminster, 13 December 1435, in the 11th year of his translation. [Latin]

On 1 April 23 Henry VI [1445], Richard Straunge, chaplain, sought the registration of the following deed in the common register of the city, before Thomas Crathorn, Mayor, and other worthy men in the Council Chamber.

(ff. 120v-121) FEOFFMENT.

Richard Straunge, chaplain, brother and heir of Roger, the son and heir of Hugh Straunge,
to William Gawke, senior, and William Gawke, junior, his son, and Juliana, wife of William Gawke, senior, one of the daughters of the said Hugh Straunge, and the male heirs of the body of William Gawke, junior, remainder to Joan, widow of John Burton, another daughter of the said Hugh, and the heirs of her body, remainder to the feoffor and his heirs,
thirteen messuages and six strips of land in Bouthom in the suburbs of the City of York.

Witnesses. Richard Bukden, Mayor, William Clyff, Richard Claybroke, Sheriffs, John Bedale, Edmund Pole, William Stanes, litster, Richard Neuland, draper, Thomas Atkynson, armourer.

Given the day after the feast of St. Michael the Archangel 23 Henry VI [30 September 1444]. [Latin]

(f. 121) ORDINANCES OF THE ARMOURERS.[9]

[8] See also ff. 105-6.
[9] Printed in York Civic Records, Vol. III, pp. 176-7. See also ordinances of 1475, ff. 139v-140 below.

To thaire ful honorable and gracious lorde the Maire of the Citee of York.

Besekes ful humbly your tendre lordship your trewe herted servauntez at our simple power the hole craft of armorers of this Citee of York, graciously to considre the nowne powere and insufficience and ful fewe of craft in nowmbre, that we suffice not to mayntene nor uphalde the charges and costes that we bere yerely about the bringyng furth of our pageant and play upon Corpus Christi day with mony other costes, olesse than it may lyke you to provyde som other meen to our succour and supportacion. And for asmuch as your said besekers have noon ordenauncez nor rewle to be governed after, for lake of which mekell evell chaffer is made and uttred within this citee to grete disworship thereof, sklaunder to the said craft and grete dissaite to the kyngs poeple, we beseke mekely that thies ordenauncez undre writen may be entred into your boukes of recorde bothe for the worship of this citee and for the wele of the said craft and kynges poeple.

First, if ther be eny man that wil occupie as maister in the said craftes within this citee, the serchours of the same craft shal have ful power to serche hym if he be sufficient in connyng to occupie as maister and save the worship of this Citee. And if thay fynd hym not able thay shal warne hym to sesse of that occupation (f. 121v) unto the tyme that he have lernede his craft better to occupie as maister. And if he will not sesse at the first warnyng, at the second he shall lose 40s, that oon halfe to the commonalte of this citee and that other halve to the said craft.

Item, if ther be eny man that will occupie as maister in the said craft that has not bene apprentice within this citee and wele and dewely fulfilled the terme of his printeship, that he shal pay at his first settyng upp 13s. 4d in the manere aforsaide.

Item, that no man of the said craft shal take no man to servant nor to pryntice bot hym that is ane Inglisshman born, uppayn of 40s. to be paide in the manere and fourm afore writen.

[Undated, but written in the same hand as the previous and succeeding entries, both dated 1445.]

(ff. 121v-122v) GRANT OF OBIT.

The Master and brethren of St. Leonard's Hospital,
to Isabel, formerly the wife of William Lee, Thomas Karr, late Sheriff, Richard Russell and Robert Gaunte,

bind themselves, in consideration of £45, to perform an obit with music, the *Placebo* and *Dirige* and other services of the dead, annually on 14 August in the choir of the hospital church, for the souls of William Lee, Thomas Karr, Richard Russell and Robert Gaunte, her late husbands, and especially for the soul of the said Isabel after her death. The great bells of the hospital were to be rung and the obit proclaimed by the city bellman. They were to pay annually on the day of the obit to each brother of the hospital 6d, to each sister 2d, to the clerks and choristers ringing the great bells 6d, to the bellman for proclaiming the obit throughout the city 4d; and 8s. ——d.[10] p.a. to provide and maintain a lamp burning before the sacrament in the choir of St. Helen's Church in Staynegate. They were to pay a penalty of £40 to the Mayor and Commonalty in case of default, for which the latter should have distraint. Any goods distrained were to be returned as soon as the premises were fulfilled.

Tripartite indenture, the several parts remaining with the said Isabel, the Mayor and Commonalty, and St. Leonard's Hospital.

Given in the Chapter House of St. Leonard's Hospital, 17 April 1445, 23 Henry VI. [Latin]

(ff. 122v-123) QUITCLAIM.

John Askham, son and heir of Walter Askham, late sergeant at law,

to William Killom, son and heir of William Killom, late citizen of York,

a messuage in Haymangergate, now called Nedillergate, and an annual rent of 40s. from the same messuage which lay between St. Crux Church in Fossegate and the land formerly of John Cawod, butcher, and which the said William Killom the son had by the grant and release of Christopher Spenser of the County of York, esquire, and Margaret his wife, mother of the said John Askham.

Witnesses. William Bowes, Mayor, John Cateryk, John Gudale, Sheriffs, Thomas Crathorn, John Radclyff, Patrick Bradley.

Given at York, the last day of November 22 Henry VI [1443].
[Latin]

QUITCLAIM.

Christopher Spenser of the County of York, esquire, and Mar-

[10] Omission.

garet, his wife, formerly the wife of Walter Askham, sergeant at law,

to William Killom, son and heir of William Killom,

the messuage and annual rent [as above] which Christopher Spenser held for life in the right of his wife, Margaret, and which the said Walter Askham had together with other lands and tenements in the City and suburbs of York by the gift and feoffment of Thomas Leycestre, formerly of London, grocer, and Alice his wife, daughter and heir of William Durant, late citizen of York.

Witnesses. William Bowes, Mayor, John Cateryk, John Gudale, Sheriffs, Thomas Crathorn, John Radclyff, Patrick Bradley.

Given at York, 27 November 22 Henry VI [1443].   [Latin]

(f. 123v) LETTERS OF ATTORNEY.

Christopher Spencer and Margaret, his wife,

to William Couper, citizen and pinner of York,

to recover from the administrators of the goods of John Waghen, late citizen and mercer of York, £20 owed for ten years' arrears of rent at 40s. p.a. for a messuage in Haymangergate alias Nedillergate; to implead the administrators if necessary, and deduct his expenses from the amount received.

Given at York, 27 November 22 Henry VI [1443].   [Latin]

(ff. 123v-124) FEOFFMENT.

William Kyllom, son and heir of William Kyllom, late citizen of York, and of Alice, his wife, daughter and heir of William Durant, late citizen of York,

to William Couper, citizen and pinner of York,

the messuage in Haymangergate [as above] which descended to the feoffor by hereditary right after the death of Alice his mother, and which lay between the Church of St. Crux in Fossegate, on one side, and the land formerly of John Cawod, butcher, and afterwards of Thomas Snowdon, alderman, late citizen and pewterer, on the other.

Witnesses. William Bowes, Mayor, John Cateryk, John Gudale, Sheriffs, John Radclyff, Thomas Crathorn, Patrick Bradley.

Given at York, 1 December 22 Henry VI [1443].   [Latin]

QUITCLAIM.

William Kyllom, son and heir of William Kyllom,

to William Couper, citizen and pinner,
the messuage in Haymangergate [as above].
Witnesses. William Bowes, Mayor, John Cateryk, John Gudale,
Sheriffs, John Radclyff, Thomas Crathorn, Patrick Bradley.
Given at York, 3 December 22 Henry VI [1443].   [Latin]

(ff. 124-124v) AGREEMENT.

that William Couper, citizen and pinner of York, and Ellen
his wife, and their executors, should provide William Killom of
York, saucemaker, with food and drink at their own table every day
during his life, except when he should be ill or when neighbours
and honest persons dined with them, together with woollen and
linen clothes, a bed and shoes. He was to bear himself well and
honestly towards the said William Couper, Ellen his wife, and their
servants, and utter no scandal.
Witnesses. Peter Fryston, clerk, Thomas Curteys, William
Owesby.
Given at York, 22 August 22 Henry VI [1444].   [Latin]

ACQUITTANCE.

Robert Warde of Boynton on the Wolds, gentleman, and Joan,
his wife, daughter and heir of John Helmeslay, formerly of
Gysburn [Guisborough] in Cleveland, son and heir of William
Helmeslay, late citizen and draper of York,
to John Bedale, William Catryk, Agnes his wife, daughter of
William Bedale, alderman, late citizen and mercer of York, and
John Calton, executors of the will of the said William Bedale,
from all actions for repair of a tenement with buildings and appur-
tenances in the Thoresday market, which the said William Bedale,
father of John Bedale, had by the lease of the said John Helmeslay
for forty-two years.
Sealed for greater security with the mayoral seal by John Croser,
Mayor.
Given at York, 17 February 25 Henry VI [1447].   [Latin]

(ff. 125-6) INSPEXIMUS AND CONFIRMATION.

by Henry VI, of previous grants and confirmations of the liberties
of Whitby Abbey, reciting briefly:—
[1] The charter of William [I], late king, granting to the Church
of Whiteby, Serlo the prior and the monks thereof, all liberties

for their lands and men, and freedom from all customs and dues
of kings, earls, barons, lords and their bailiffs wherever they
travelled, bought or sold.[11]

[2] A further charter of the same king, granting to the Church
of St. Peter of Prestby[12] and Whitby, to Serlo the prior and the
monks, the same laws and customs as were enjoyed by the
Church of St. John of Beverley, the Church at Ripon and St.
Peter's, York.[13]

[3] The grant by Richard I to the Church of St. Peter [of
Prestby] and St. Hilda of Whiteby, and to the abbot and monks,
of all the liberties and customs which the Churches of St. John
of Beverley and St. Wilfrid of Ripon enjoyed.[14]

[4] The confirmation by Henry VI, 3 December 1445,[15] of the
above grants to Hugh the abbot and the convent of Whiteby.

Witnessed by the king at Westminster, 8 July 24 Henry VI
[1446].   [Latin]

(ff. 126-127v) INSPEXIMUS AND CONFIRMATION.[16]

Henry [IV] to the Dean and Chapter of St. Peter, York,
of the charter of Richard [II][17] reciting that the king's progenitors by charters which the king has confirmed, gave to the
Dean and Chapter aforesaid various franchises, liberties, privileges, immunities and acquittances, and that lately in a parliament at Winchester the king granted to the Mayor and citizens
of York that the justices of the peace and of labourers and
artificers in the three *thrithings* of the County of York should
not intervene in the city, its suburbs or liberty or without them
in any matter done or arising therein; and that the Mayor and
twelve Aldermen, or four, three or two of them with the Mayor
should have power to correct, punish, enquire, hear and determine all matters within the city, suburbs or liberty just as the

[11] The complete charter is transcribed in *Whitby Cartulary*, ed. J. C. Atkinson,
Vol. I, p. 147.

[12] Prestby: name now lost, the district being absorbed into Whitby (ibid. I,
xiv-xv).

[13] Ibid. II, 530-1.

[14] Ibid. I, 150-2.

[15] Ibid. II, 535-51; C. Ch. R., 1427-1516, p. 51.

[16] C. Ch. R. 1341-1417, pp. 403-4. The original charter also confirms a previous
one dated at Westminster, 1 February 3 Richard II [1380], not mentioned in the
present volume.

[17] C. Ch. R. 1341-1417, pp. 337-8.

justices of the peace, labourers and artificers had without the same, as is more fully contained in the said charter.

The king of his special grace and for the greater security, quiet and tranquillity of the said Church and the Dean and Chapter now declared that at the time of the grant to the Mayor, Aldermen and citizens it was not his intention that under colour of the grant they should enter the close or cemetery of the said Church or the bedern of the vicars, or the dwelling houses, inns or houses without the close and cemetery belonging to the dignities, canonries and prebends, and being in the hands of their owners or occupied by the officers or ministers of the Church by the lease or licence of their owners, or that they should intervene or have cognizance, correction or jurisdiction within the said close, cemetery, bedern or houses.

The king also granted that the Dean and Chapter and their successors should have correction and punishment and authority and power to hear and determine by their steward all matters arising in the close, cemetery, bedern, houses and inns, just as the Mayor and Aldermen had by their grant in the city, suburbs and liberty and as the justices of the peace, and of labourers and artificers had in the *trithings*, so that neither the said justices, the Mayor, Aldermen and citizens, nor any other of the king's ministers should interfere with the jurisdiction hereby granted to the Dean and Chapter, to whom were reserved all the liberties granted to them by the king and his progenitors.

Witnesses. W[illiam Courtenay] of Canterbury and Th[omas Arundel] of York, Chancellor, Archbishops, R[obert Braybrooke] of London, W[illiam of Wykeham] of Winchester and J[ohn Waltham] of Salisbury, Treasurer, Bishops, John of Acquitaine and Lancaster, Edmund of York, Thomas of Gloucester, Dukes and uncles of the king, Edward Rutland, Richard Arundel, the king's brother, and John de Holand of Huntingdon, Chamberlain, Earls, Thomas de Percy, Steward of the Household and Master Edmund Stafford, Keeper of the Privy Seal.

Given at Westminster, 24 July 17 Richard [II, 1393].

Witnesses to the confirmation. Thomas [Arundel] of Canterbury, R[ichard le Scrope] of York, Archbishops, R[obert Braybrooke] of London, W[illiam of Wykeham] of Winchester, H[enry Beaufort] of Lincoln, E[dmund Stafford] of Exeter, Bishops, Edmund, Duke of York, uncle of the king, Henry de Percy, Earl of Northumberland. Constable of England, Ralph de Nevyll of Westmorland, Marshall of England, the king's brother, John Somerset, Chamberlain, Earls, John de Scarle, clerk, Chancellor, John Norbury, Treasurer, William de Roos of Hamelak, Reginald de Grey of Rutbyn [Ruthin], William de Wilughby, Thomas Rymston, Steward of the Household, Richard Clifford, Keeper of the Privy Seal.

Given at Westminster, 1 July 1 Henry [IV, 1400].

Subscribed: By writ of privy seal and for £10 paid in the hanaper.

Enrolled on the third part of the charter roll of 1 Henry [IV].

[Latin]

(ff. 127v-128) *The grant of privileges enrolled at Westminster before John Prisot and other justices of King's Bench, in the Trinity term, 27 Henry VI [1449]. Ro. 405.*

The Mayor and citizens of York per William Stillyngton, their attorney, seeking to defend their liberties produced the following royal grants before the justices on the quindene of St. John the Baptist [8 July 1449].

[1] Letters Patent of Henry VI [11 February 1449]. The king had learned from a petition of the Mayor and citizens of the City of York, that the city, suburbs and precinct thereof were a county in themselves, separate from the County of York, and called the County of the City of York, etc. as appeared more fully in the said charter.[18]

[2] Letters Close of Henry VI to the justices of King's Bench, mentioning Letters Patent of 11 February last by which the king, considering that the City of York was too grievously charged, paying a great fee farm and taxes and other charges, was at present diminished and in decay and for a long time had not been helped or relieved by the presence of the king, his courts, councils or parliaments; had therefore granted to the Mayor and citizens without payment of any fine or fee that the hundred or wapentake of Aynsty should be annexed to the County of the City of York, and that the city, suburbs, precinct and hundred and all contained therein, except the Castle of York with its towers, ditches and dykes, should be the County of the City of York; that all bailiffs of franchises within the County of the City should obey the Sheriff of the same; and that the Mayor and citizens should have the

18 C.P.R. 1446-52, pp. 221-2.

hundred or wapentake with all its appurtenances, privileges and franchises, and that all Sheriffs of the County of the City should have full power, jurisdiction and authority within the hundred. Ordering the justices that the Mayor and citizens should not be molested, contrary to the tenor of the said grants.

Witnessed at Westminster, 4 July 27 Henry VI [1449].

The Mayor and citizens sought that they might exercise their power, jurisdiction and authority within the said hundred or wapentake according to the grant, as they were accustomed to do in the County of the City. [Latin]

(f. 128v) LETTERS CLOSE.[19]

Henry [VI]

to all sheriffs, mayors, bailiffs and ministers, to suffer all tenants of the honour of Eye [Suffolk], free men and others, to be quit of toll, stallage, chiminage, pontage, pavage, picage, murage and passage throughout the realm, as they had been from time immemorial.

Witnessed at Westminster, 14 February 17 [Henry VI, 1439].
Subscribed: Stopyndon. [Latin]

COMMISSION.[20]

Henry VII

to William Todde, Mayor, John Vavasour, Richard Yorke, Thomas Wrangwysshe and Thomas Asper,

to deliver the gaol of the city, reserving all amerciaments due to the Crown. The Sheriffs were to cause all prisoners to come before them on a day to be appointed by the said justices.

Witnessed at Kenelworth, 17 May 2 Henry VII [1487].
Subscribed. Bacheler. [Latin]

(f. 129) [Address of a royal grant, apparently an unfinished copy of Letters Close concerning the tenants of the honour of Eye, as on f. 128v.]

[The remainder of f. 129 and part of f. 129v are blank.]

(f. 129v) ROYAL MANDATE.

Edward [IV]

to the Mayor and Sheriffs of York,

---

[19] C. Cl. R. 1435-41, pp. 202-3; see also f.153v below.
[20] C.P.R. 1485-94, p. 179. This entry is in a later hand than those immediately preceding and following.

ordering that the Prior and monks of the Church of St. Cuthbert of Durham should not be molested, under penalty of £10, in their enjoyment of the privileges granted by Henry II and which the king had confirmed.[21] Reciting the charter of Henry II by which he granted their liberties and customs throughout England and Normandy and all ports of the sea, and freedom from toll, passage and customs in all ports and markets of the realm.

Witnessed by the king at Westminster, 3 June 4 Edward [IV, 1464].   [Latin]

On 20 September 1 Richard III [1483], Alison Spynney, daughter of Richard Rawdon and sister and heir of Alexander Rawdon, son and heir of the said Richard, came before John Newton, Mayor, Richard York and Robert Hancok, Aldermen, in the Council Chamber on Ouse Bridge. She declared that a deed of feoffment and a deed of release, then read, had been made and sealed by her. The Mayor, at her request, granted that they should be enrolled in the common register of the city, as follows.   [English]

(f. 130) FEOFFMENT.
    Alice Spynney, widow, daughter and heir of Richard Rawdon, late of Abirford in the County of York, gentleman,
    to Richard Scott of York, merchant,
lands and tenements in Berwyk on Tweed which belonged to Richard Rawdon, her father.
    Witnesses. Thomas Tubbak, Roger Brere, William Barker, John Boon, Thomas Cok, citizens of York.
    Given, 28 August 1 Richard III [1483].   [Latin]

QUITCLAIM.
    Alice Spynney,
    to Richard Scott,
lands and tenements in Berwyk on Tweed [as above].
    Given, 6 September 1 Richard III [1483].   [Latin]

(ff. 130v-131v) ASSIZE OF FRESH FORCE.
    The king's court for the City of York held at the *Guyhald* before

---

[21] The Inspeximus and Confirmation of the same date to the Prior and monks of St. Cuthbert's are calendared in C.P.R. 1461-1467, pp. 392-3.

William Stokton, Mayor, Thomas Scauceby and Richard Thorn, Sheriffs, 20 December 25 Henry VI [1446].

John Nevyll, William Everyngham and Christopher Dransfeld, esquires, made complaint that Edward Bethom, esquire, and Thomas Gayte, chaplain, had unlawfully disseised them within the past forty days of a messuage in the City of York. The plaintiffs found John Garnar and William Hunt as sureties and appointed Hugh Hurlork, Richard Lasset and Adam Gunby as their attorneys. The sergeants at mace to the Sheriffs, John Sharpe, John Rillyngton, John Ledes and Robert Burgys, were ordered to summon by good summoners, twenty-four law-worthy men as jurors.

At the Court held at the *Guyhald*, the Monday before the feast of the Conversion of St. Paul [23 January 1447], the sergeants at mace returned a list of the jurors, summoned by John Feld and Richard Bouges for each of whom John Londe, William Marr, James Hunt and Ralph Mond acted as sureties. The sergeants at mace reported that neither of the defendants owned anything within the city by which they could be attached, and that they could not be found. They did not appear in court, but the assize was postponed in default of jurors until the Monday before the feast of the Purification of the Blessed Virgin Mary [30 January 1447].

On that day the sergeants at mace reported that the jurors were mainprized by James Fynche, Edmund Saynte, Robert Love and Richard Lang. Twelve of them, namely, Thomas Rawdon, John Wady, William Shirwod, William Barlay, John Bukcy, William Coverham, Robert Harwod, Robert Garton, Richard Croull, Thomas Atkynson, John Lynton, and John Lyllyng, affirmed on oath that the plaintiffs had been seised of the messuage until they were wrongfully dispossessed by Edward Bethom and Thomas Gayte. They assessed damages at £4 and costs at 20s.

Verdict: the plaintiffs should recover seisin of the messuage and receive 100s. and the defendants be placed at the mercy of the court.   [Latin]

(ff. 131v-133) ASSIZE OF FRESH FORCE.

Pleas in the king's court of the City of York held in the *Guihald* before John Gillyott, Mayor, and Henry Williamson and Thomas Maryott, Sheriffs, on Monday, 21 March 14 Edward IV [1474].

Richard, Duke of Gloucester, John Shirwod, Archdeacon of Richmond, Thomas Midelton, Miles Willesthorp, John Neviell,

Henry Rokeley, William Marsshall, Giles Newton, and John Newton, made complaint that John Hemylsey of York, gentleman, had
unlawfully disseised them within forty days, of six messuages in
the City of York. The plaintiffs found Thomas Colynson and
Thomas Wright as sureties, and appointed Adam Gunby as their
attorney. The sergeants at mace to the Sheriffs, John Russell, John
Aldefeld, Richard Coltman and John Alnewyk, were ordered to
summon by good summoners twenty-four law-worthy men as jurors.

At the Court held in the *Guihald* on Monday, 28 March 14
Edward IV [1474], the sergeants at mace returned a list of the
jurors summoned by John Russell and John Aldfeld for each of
whom John Hunt, Richard Child, Henry Monnde and William
Flynt acted as sureties. They reported that John Hemylsey was
attached by a bronze jar worth 4s. John Hemylsey did not appear
in court but was represented by John Gray, his bailiff, and denied
that he had dispossessed the plaintiff of the messuages. He put himself on the assize and the plaintiffs did likewise. The assize was
postponed in default of jurors.

On Monday 4 April [1474], the sergeants at mace returned the
names of the jurors each of whom was mainprized by Richard Dent,
William Flynt, Richard Faildon and Simon Baildon. The jurors
did not appear so their sureties were fined and the assize postponed.

On the Monday after Easter [11 April 1474], the sergeants at
mace reported that they had distrained the goods of each of the
jurors to the value of 12d. and that each was mainprized by Richard
Fyn, William Gyn, Simon Dale and Robert Failbe. Twelve of
them, namely William Croft and Thomas Maners, esquires, Richard
Claybruke, Robert Harwod, William Scauceby, John Birdsall, William Warde, John Bell, tailor, Thomas Beverley, Guy Fraunkeleyn,
Robert Appilby and Thomas Appilton affirmed on oath that the
plaintiffs were seised of the six messuages in demesne as of fee until
John Hemylsey wrongfully dispossessed them within the forty
days last past.

They assessed damages to the plaintiffs at 6s. 8d. and costs at 10s.

Verdict: the plaintiffs should recover seisin of the six messuages
and 16s. 8d. costs and John Hemylsey should be placed at the
court's mercy.

Sealed with the mayoral seal.

Given at York, 1 January 14 Edward IV [1475].   [Latin]

(ff. 133-134) ASSIZE OF FRESH FORCE.

Pleas in the king's court for the City of York held at the *Guyhald* before William Lambe, Mayor, John Newton and William Chymnay, Sheriffs, on Monday, 29 May 15 Edward IV [1475].

Thomas Neleson, Alderman, citizen and merchant of York, and William Neleson, his son, made complaint that Thomas Wady had unlawfully disseised them in the last forty days of eight messuages in the City of York.

The plaintiffs found Brian Conyers and Robert Danby as sureties and appointed Adam Gunby their attorney.

The sergeants at mace to the Sheriffs, Thomas Messyngham, William Sawer, John Hardwyk and Richard Bery were ordered to summon by good summoners twenty-four law-worthy men as jurors.

On Monday, 5 June, the sergeants at mace returned a list of jurors summoned by Robert Mudd and Richard Fayldon, each mainprized by John Fyn, Robert Rudd, William Thomson and Thomas Styrton. They reported that Thomas Wady owned nothing within the city by which he could be attached, nor could he be found in the city, but the assize was postponed in default of the jurors.

On Monday after the feast of St. William, Archbishop of York [12 June], the sergeants at mace reported that each of the jurors was mainprized by James Lutton, Edmund Saynton, Robert Lowe and Geoffrey Styrton. Twelve of the jurors, namely, Thomas Maners, esquire, John Hemylsay, William Crofte, esquire, John Birdsaull, William Scauceby, Thomas Beverley, fishmonger, William Wallay, John Scalby, Henry Fawsett, Robert Appylby, John Burton, barker, and Richard Croklyn, declared on oath that the plaintiffs had been seised of the eight messuages until Thomas Wady had disseised them of one of them within the forty days last past. They assessed damages at 26s. 8d. and costs at 13s. 4d.

Verdict: the plaintiffs should recover seisin of the messuage and the 40s. assessed by the jurors and also 53s. 4d. as damages in triplicate according to the royal statute, a total of 93s. 4d. Thomas Wady was to be arrested. [Latin]

(f. 134v) [Blank].

(f. 135) AN EXPLANATION OF THE USE OF ROMAN AND ARABIC NUMERALS.[22]

It is to be noted[23] that numbers are not always represented by their names, but that all numbers can be represented whenever these [seven] figures are placed by themselves, with others, or repeated— *i, v, x, l, m, c, d.* Whenever a lesser number is placed before a greater, take away so much, if placed after it, add so much. So that if *x* is placed before *l*, take away ten and if it is placed after, add ten. The simple names of numbers from three to one hundred are of neuter gender and indeclinable, according to the grammarians.

The cardinal numbers. [All numbers from one to a hundred and also the hundreds and thousands to ten thousand are written, in Latin, in black ink with their equivalent above in Roman numerals, in red ink. For the numbers from two hundred to nine hundred, which are declinable, the alternative endings —*i,—e,—a* are given in each case].

It is to be noted that whenever *centum* is compounded with words ending in *m* or *n*, the *c* is changed to *g*, as in *quadringenti*. The change is not made in *sexcenti* because *sex* has no *n*.

The ordinal numbers.

Primus,—a,—um, Secundus,—a,—um, Tertius,—a,—um. [etc] ——*Vicesimus,—a,—um, Vicesimus primus* [etc] —— *Tricesimus, Tricesimus primus* [etc] —— (f. 135b) *Centesimus, Decentesimus* [sic], *Trecentesimus* [etc] —— *Millesimus.*

[The Roman numerals are added above the Latin in red ink].

The numbers of division or distribution.

Singuli bini terni, [etc] —— *viceni, trigeni,* [etc] —— *Centeni, ducenteni,* [etc] —— *milleni.*

Adverbial Numbers.

Semel, bis, ter [etc] —— *vicesies, tricesies* [etc] —— *centies, millesies.*

Numbers of weight.

Simplum, duplum, triplum [etc] —— *vicicuplum, tricicuplum,* [etc] —— *centuplum, millecuplum.*

There are other numbers known as Arabic which have special figures called Jewish characters. There are nine of these numbers 9, 8, 7, 6, 5, 4, 3, 2, 1 and also a cipher 0, which placed alone

[22] A literal translation is given wherever possible. The editor's descriptions appear within square brackets.
[23] The first word is quite clearly *Otandum* but Notandum seems to be implied.

signifies nothing, but when occupying a place gives significance to other figures. These figures should be taken from right to left as above, the first signifying unity, the second the number two, the third the number three etc. Every figure in the first place signifies itself, in the second place, ten times itself, and in the third a hundred times and in the fourth (f. 136) a thousand times, and so on, so that each place is always ten times the preceding one.

[There follow the Roman numerals in black ink, with the equivalent Arabic numerals below them in red; 1—106, 200—203, 300—305, 400—403, 500—504, 600—604, 700—704, 800—804, 900—903, 1000—1003, 2,000, 3,000 [etc]—10,000, 20,000, 30,000 [etc]—100,000. Finally, written in Latin, with the equivalent Arabic numerals beneath, *centiesmillemilia deciesmillemilia millemilia centiesmilia decemilia mille centum decem unum* 111, 111, 111 and likewise 222, 222, 222 [etc] —— 999, 999, 999].

Note that in the last table each figure, reckoned from right to left, represents the various kinds and denominations of numbers.

[Latin]

(ff. 136v-138) ASSIZE OF FRESH FORCE.

Pleas held in the king's court at York in the *Guihald* before William Lam, Mayor, John Newton, and William Chymnay, Sheriffs, on Monday, 10 April 15 Edward IV [1475].

Henry Fawsett of York made complaint that John Lowes and John Turnbull, and Katherine, his wife, had unlawfully disseised him within the last forty days of a messuage in the City of York. The plaintiff found Robert Storme and William Bernyngham as pledges, and appointed Adam Gunby as his attorney.

The sergeants at mace, Thomas Messyngham, William Sawer, John Hardwik and Richard Bery were ordered to summon by good summoners, twenty-four law-worthy men as jurors.

On Monday, 17 April, the sergeants at mace reported that the jurors had been summoned by Richard Bery and William Sawer, each of whom was mainprized by John Le, Richard Page, Thomas Norton and William Fytt, and that the defendants had nothing within the city by which they could be attached, nor could they be found in the city. The defendants did not appear but a certain Thomas Blanfrount made essoin for them. Henry Fawsett, per Adam Gunby, his attorney, said that by the law of the land there should be no essoin in this assize, and sought that the assize should be taken against the defendants by default, and that the jurors be caused to appear in the court. The court agreed. The jurors did not appear and the assize was postponed.

On the Monday after the feast of St. George the Martyr [24 April], the sergeants at mace returned the names of the jurors, each mainprized by John Le, William Fox, Henry Gray and Richard Page. The jurors did not appear, the sureties were amerced and the assize was postponed.

On Monday, the feast of the Apostles Philip and James [1 May], the sergeants at mace reported that the jurors had each been distrained to the value of 12d. and each was mainprized by Laurence Lynton, Geoffrey Joy, Simon Pille and Walter Gayte. Again they failed to appear and the assize was postponed until the Monday after the Invention of the Holy Cross [8 May]. Each of the jurors had then been distrained to the value of 20d. and was mainprized by Thomas Mudd, Richard Joynour, Robert Patryk and Dennis Stiward. Twelve of the jurors, namely Thomas Maners, esquire, William Croft, esquire, William Scauceby, Thomas Holtby, Thomas Knollez, Thomas Beverley, fishmonger, John Burton, barker, William Wallay, John Scalby, John Couper, merchants, Nicholas Thornton and John Croull, said on oath that the said Henry Fawsett was seised of the messuage in demesne as of fee until the defendants had recently and unlawfully dispossessed him, and that the assize was brought within forty days after disseisin. They assessed damages at 10s, and costs at 20s.

Verdict: Henry Fawsett should recover seisin of the messuage and the 30s. The defendants were placed on the court's mercy.

[Latin]

On 15 October 15 Edward IV [1475], Margaret Lee brought a deed and a quitclaim before William Lambe, Mayor, for his examination and asked that they should be enrolled in the common book of the city.

(ff. 138-138v) FEOFFMENT.

Margaret Lee of York, widow, daughter and heir of Thomas Duffeld, son and heir of Richard Duffeld, late of York, gentleman,

to Thomas Neleson, citizen and merchant of York and William Neleson, his son,

her capital messuage and also lands and tenements, closes,

meadows, pastures, rents and services in Skelton in the forest of Galtres.

Appointment of Robert Danby, chaplain, as her attorney to deliver seisin.

Witnesses. Thomas Asper, George Lovell, gentlemen, William Kydhall, William Richardson, yeoman, Adam Gunby of York.

Given, 8 April 14 Edward IV [1474].   [Latin]
Subscribed. Gunby.

(ff. 138v-139) QUITCLAIM.

Margaret Bedforde, widow, lately the widow of John Liegh, deceased,

to Thomas Neleson, citizen and Alderman of York, his heirs and assigns,

her capital messuage, lands and tenements in Skelton in the forest of Galtreys [as above].

Witnesses. Thomas Asper, gentleman, William Hayward, chaplain, John Thwyng of York, weaver.

Given, 22 September 14 Edward IV [1474].   [Latin]

(ff. 139-139v) A VIEW OF THE BOUNDARIES OF A PIECE OF GROUND BEHIND COPPERGATE.[24]

The decision of the searchers named below, returned in the Chamber of the City of York before William Lam, Mayor, on Wednesday, 23 October 15 Edward IV [1475].   [Latin]

The 23 day of the moneth of Octobre in the 15th yere of Kinge Edward the Fourth, William Hyndeley, John Shupton, masons, John Hirste and Christopher More, carpentours, 4 serchiours within the saide cite, cam in thair propre personnes in the Counsail Chambre afore the Maire abouvsaide, and there and thanne made thaire bodelye othez upon the Holy Evangelist truely forto serche the metez ande boundez of a certayn grounde of John Gillyot of Yorke, Aldreman ande merchaunt, adionyng upon ane othere grounde of William Rakett thelder and Thomas Aslacby. Whereapon ande incontinent after the saids daye ande yere the forsaide serchiours, accordinge to the custume of the same cite ande by thassents ande desiers aswele of the forsaid John Gillyott as also of Sir Thomas Hambald, attourney of the forsaidez William Rakett and Thomas Aslacby, thanne there also presente in the saide Coun-

---

[24] Printed by James Raine in *English Miscellanies* pp. 19-20.

sail Chambre, yode[25] unto the grounde of the said John Gillyott, lyynge at the baksyde of the saide John Gillyott's tenement, wherin he than dwelled in Coppergate towards the king's water of Fosse, in the parisshe of Alle Halows upon the Pavement within the saide cite, betuyx a tenement in the haldyng of Henry Williamson on that one side and a tenement of the saids William Rakett and Thomas Aslacby, late in the haldyng of Robert Amyas, on that othere syde, ande the same grounde ther and than the same serchiours diligently serched and mesured by gode deliberacion. And incontinent the same daye and yere, the saide serchiours after thair serche so made cam in the saide Counsail Chambre afore the saide Mayre, (f. 139v) and there ande thanne saide in vertu of thair othe, that the saide grounde conteyneth in lengthe at the ovirsyde in breede frome the tenement of the saide Henry Williamson unto the grounde of the saidez William Rakett and Thomas Aslacby, 6 yerds ane ynche lakk, ande at the netheresyde 5 yerds halfe yerde and halfe quarter ande more by ane halfe ynche as to thair estimacion etc. Memorandum that the saidez day, yere, presence and place, the foresaide John Gillyott promised for his partie that if the saidez William Rakett ande Thomas Aslacby will at any tyme hereafter have a newe serche of the saide grounde, that than he will beere his due parte of alle suche costs as shall be requisite in that behalfe, etc.

(ff. 139v-140) *The Constitution of the Armourers made 20 October 15 Edward IV* [1475], *in the time of William Lam, Mayor.*[26]

[Latin]

Item, it is forthermore ordeyned in the tyme of William Lam, Maire of the said cite, aswele by his assente as by thassent ande consente of all the godemen of the same crafte, that is to say, William Spence, John Denny, Thomas Hogeson, Gawdy Shawe, Robert Dowe, Roland Robson, John Garthe ande Thomas Sandall, citisyns of the same cite, that whatsomever he be of the saide crafte that will not obbey his serchiours for tyme beynge in alle thyngs that ben reasonable concernynge the same crafte, shall forfayt every tyme 12d to the crafte ande to the chambre by even porcions withoute pardone.

[25] *yode*: past tense of *go*.
[26] Printed in *York Civic Records*, Vol III. pp. 177-9. See also undated ordinances of the guild, ff. 121-121v above.

Item, it is forthermore establisshed, ordayned ande ennacted that what maister so ever he be of the saide crafte that commys not to his serchiours for tyme beynge at every reasonabill tyme when he therunto shall be reasonablye ande convenyently warned, shall forfaite 6d. in maner ande forme abovesaide, withoute he have a reasonabill execuse.

Item, it is forthermore ordayned for gode rule of the same crafte, that if there be any debate or variance moved betuyx any tweyne of the saide crafte for any thynge that belangs to the same crafts, that thanne the same tweyne so standinge at variance shall abyde ande therin stande to the rule and ordynance of the same serchiours for tyme beynge ande of othere tweyne of the moste honest personnes of the same crafte within the same cite. And who so ever that it be that disobeyeth him therunto at eny tyme hereafter shall forfaite in fourme abovesaide 20d, withoute pardone in any wise.

Item, it is forthermore ordayned that if any maner of man of this cite frome nowefurth take apon hym to wirke as maister in any poyntez perteynyng or belongynge to the crafts of armourers or fourbours[27] within this Cite of Yorke, ande stands unffraunchised ande unadmitted for a brothir of the same crafts, that thanne he shall be ffraunchised, firste pay[ing] his upsett according as is abovesaide, if he therto be foundon able by the serchiours for tyme beyng, or els be discharged as afore ys saide. Ande if there be any othere man of this cite that frome nowefurth exercisez or haunts[28] to occupy any maner of poyntes (f. 140) belongynge to the saidez crafts ande therfore taks or shall take any salarye or payment therfore, that thanne he that so dothe shall be contributorie yerely unto the saide crafts in thair chargs berynge, als lange tyme as he so occupyez or shall occupy in that feate or feats, to be therunto assessed by the saide serchiours for tyme beynge. And if so be that the saide serchiours will hereafter at any tyme ovir charge any man in that behalfe, that thanne it shall be myttegate ande eased by the Mayre's discrecion for tyme beynge.

Item, it is ordayned forthermore that all ande every maister of that occupacion within this cite for tyme beynge shall mete in a convenyent place within this saide cite yerely fro nowefurth, the second Sonday next aftre the feste of *Corporis Christi*; and there and thanne to elect ande chuse thair sercheours ande pagende

---

[27] *fourbours*: furbishers, burnishers.
[28] *haunt*: to practise habitually.

maisters for the yere folowynge. And who it be that fayleth to com whan he is reasonably warned shall forfaite in that behalfe 6d in fourme beforesaide. And the same day there the sercheours ande pagend maisters to make there rekenyngs.

Item, what maister of the same crafte that hereafter taketh any apprentez shall take that apprentez for the termes of 7 yerez and no les ande that by indentourz, ande that the same indenturz be shewed to the sercheours of the same crafte for tyme beynge within 10 dayes next aftre the makynge of the same indenturz, under the payne of forfaitour of 20d to be payde in maner ande fourme afor-saide by every maister that offendeth in this behalfe hereafter.

Item, that alle the maisters of the same crafte frome nowefurth yerely on Corpus Christi day in the mornyng be redy in thair owen propre personnez, every one of thayme with ane honest wapyn,[29] to awayte apon thair pagende maisters ande pagende at the playnge and settyngefurth of thair saide pagende at the firste place where they shall begyns, ande so to awayte apon the same thair pagende thurgh the cite to the play be plaide as of that same pagende. And who it be of the saide maisters as hereafter makyth defalt in this partie shall forfait 6d to be paide in fourme before writen withoute he have a reasonable excuse.

[30]Item, if ther be any man of the said occupacion, maister, ser-vante or prentys, that with drawith any man's goods falsely, he for to be forsworn this citie and never to come therein to wyrk of the said occupacion and it be knowen, to the value of thyrteyn pens hal-peny.

Item, if that any of the said crafte within this citie goo aither within this said citie, suburbs of the same, or into the contre for to desyer any knyght, gentylman or [any] other of what degree soever he be, that he may clense his harnes or any thyng that belongs the said occupacion, withoute he be sent for, he shall forfait for every tyme 3s. 4d. as is abovesaid.

Item, that noen of the said occupacion make no skalberds but of good stuf and warkemanlyke, uppon payn to forfait and pay 6d as is abovesaid for every defaute.

Item, that no man of the said occupation dight[31] no swerds but warkmanlyke with all things belongyng the same, uppon payn of

---

[29] *wapyn*: weapon.
[30] The last four paragraphs are written in a later hand.
[31] *dight*: dress, make ready.

4d. a pece for as many as is found fawte.

(f. 140v) ORDINANCES OF THE GLOVERS.[32]

In the vigill of the feste of Whitsonday in the 15th yere of King Edward the Fourth [13 May 1475], at the instance ande prayer of alle the godemen of the saide crafte, thees ordynances underwriten were ordayned to be observed within this cite by thassente of William Lambe, than Maire of the said cite, William Holbek, John Gillyott, Christopher Marsshall, John Tonge, John Fereby, Aldremen, Thomas Kaytour, John Towthorp, Thomas Maryott ande John Newton of the nombre of the 24 in the Counsaile Chambre of the same cite there assembled, the day and yere abovesaide.

In primis, it is ordayned than who so ever sells openly within this cite in thaire shoppez any glovez, pursez or keybands called Ynglisshware shall paye yerely to the pagende maisters of the saide pagende ande crafte, that is to seye, of a deynsyn[33] 2d, ande of a straunger 4d, to the sustentacion ande uphalding of the pagende of the forsaide crafte yerely, alle the brether and susters of the fraternyte ande gilde of the Blissed Trinite[34] within the saide cite maynteyned by the merchaunts of the saide cite allway except, ande also all maner of men sellyng London ware like wise to be excepted.

Item, it is forthermore ordayned that every glover that shall set upp for him silfe ande halde a shoppe within this cite as a maister, firste he shall be serched by the serchiours of the saide crafte for tyme beynge, ande if [he] be foundon able so to do that thanne he so do payyng his duete as afore ys saide, ande if he be not foundon able that thanne he to surcease to the tyme that he be foundon able, upon payn of forfeytynge of 6s 8d in maner and fourme aforesaide, als ofte tymez as he occupyez or shall occupye within the saide cite as maister after that he be warned to leve by the serchiours for tyme beynge.

Item, that ilke maister that taks a prentez he shall pay for him to the said crafte the firste tyme that he settes him on werk, 12d.

Item, it is ordayned that what maister of the saide crafte as here-

[32] Printed in York Civic Records Vol III pp. 181-3. Earlier ordinances are printed in York Memorandum Book I, pp. 48-50, 81-2. See also ordinances of 1500, ff. 170-170v. below.
[33] deynsyn: denizen, inhabitant.
[34] the merchants' guild, (M. Sellers, York Mercers and Merchant Adventurers, 1356-1917, p. x)

after within this cite setts a Scottisshman on werk within that crafte in any maner wise, shall forfeyte 6s 8d in fourme aforsaide.

Item, that no man of the saide crafte fro nowfurth hynge no skynnez by the nekks to shue in thaire wyndous, upon payne of forfettyng 20d in maner ande fourme abovsaid.

Item, where in thordinance of the craft [of] glovers abovesaid, in the lesse registre the 17th lefe of the same, is asigned that if any of the same craft hast set up as a master after he be abled by the serchours therof, he shall pay for his upset to thands of the chamberleyns of this citie for the tyme being 3s 4d, and to the said craft of glovers 5s. as more at large appereth in the said ordinance, whereby it is foundon that a foryene comyng to this citie and abled to set upp as a fre man of the same in the said craft of glovers, hath asmoch availe and libertie as he which hath be apprentise within this citie at the said craft ayenst all good ordour of reason. Wherfor in the tyme of the right honourable Sir William Todde, knight, Maire of the Cite of York [1487], by the consent of all the craft of glovers forsaid, it was ordaind and enacted from hensfurth to be observed and kepid that evere foryene comyng to this citie and abled to set up as a master within the same in the said craft of glovers, shal pay for his upset to the chambre and craft equally to be devided 13s 4d without any delay.

(f. 141) Item, that no man of the saide crafte frome nowe furth sett no stall in the high waye withoute there wyndows for sellyng of thair chaffer,[35] apon payne of 40d to be payde in fourme abovesaide.

Item, that no maner of man of the saide crafte within this cite from nowefurth be rebell unto the serchiours of the saide crafte for tyme beynge in any thynge tochinge the wele ande honestye of the saide crafte, apon the payn of 40d to be forfayte in fourme abovesaide.

Item, that if any maister of the saide crafte, duely warned at enny tyme commynge by the sercheours of the same crafte, com not withoute he hase a reasonable cause in that behalfe, [he] shall forfayte 4d.[36] at every tyme.

Item, that no maister of the same crafte, neyther by him silfe nor by his servants, hawke his ware to be soolde here in this cite fro nowefurth, apon the payne of forfeytur of 6d, to be forfayte in

---

[35] chaffer: wares.
[36] Altered to 8d in a different ink.

fourme abovesaide als ofte tymez as any truspas in that behalfe.

[37]It is ordenyd, enact and stablyshid, be the autorite of the holl Counsell of thys c[ity], the 30th of the moneth of Januari in the secud tym of the mairalte of Richard York, in the 22 yere of the reing of King Edward the Fourth [1483] : —

Furst, that it shallnot be lefull to ony maister of the said craft of glovers from this day forward to gyff ony wark to ony man of the said craft inhabityng within the Mynstir Garth, Saint Mary Gate, Saynt Leonards or odyr placez wher the seircheours of the same may have no seirch, what maister that heraftir offends in that behalve to forfate and lese 6s 8d withouete pardon to the chambyr and craft by evyn porcions. And yf the seircheours for the tym beyng bere ony man that offends in that behalf ony favour and willnot present it to the Maior and Chamberlayns for the tym beyng, to ryn in the same contemp withoute pardon.

Item, for somuch as diverse tymys of the yere, much unabill ware belongyng to the said craft of glovers is broght by forents to thys cite to be sold, the wich ware is bowght for lytill valeu by certen cocitesyns of the said occupacion and utyrd agayn by tham to the comon people in grete hurt unto tham, for somuch as the same ware is unabill, for wych caus and for the commun wele, it is ordenyd and enact that no cocitesyn of the said occupacion take apon hym to by ony ware so broght unto thys cite to be sold belonoyng unto the said craft of glovers, unto the tym it be seen by the seirchours of the same for the tym beyng and admittid for gude and able. And he that doeth contrarie thys to forfet and pay 6s 8d in maner and form above said to the chambre and 3s 4d to the craft.

(f. 141v) ORDINANCES OF THE MILLERS.[38]

[Present]. William Lam, Maior, William Snawsell, Christopher Marsshall, Thomas Wrangwissh and John Tonge of the 12 [Aldermen], Richard Claybruke, John Letheley, Robert Amyas, Thomas Alayn and Thomas Maryott of the 24.

The 20th daye of the moneth of Novembre in the 15th yere of Kinge Edward the Fourth [1475], alle abov saide were assembled in the Counsaill Chambre apon Ouse Brigge, where ande thanne it was feremely ordeyned, ennacted and establisshed by alle abov sayde att the speciall instance, request ande prayer of John Longe and

---

[37] The remaining ordinances are written in a later and more cursive hand.
[38] Printed in *York Civic Records* Vol III, p. 180.

Richard Bell, serchiours of the crafte of milners within the Cite of Yorke, made by thaym in the name of all the godemen of the saide crafte, for evermore hereafter to be observed, obbeyed ande kepped within the same cite: —

Firste, that it shall not be levefull to any estraunge man to sett up as maister within this cite ande suburbez of the same in that crafte tofore he have ben serched, examynde ande approved for able ande connyng in that feate, to pay than 13s 4d, to be payde unto the chambre of this cite ande to the crafte aforesaide by even porcions.

Item, in like case, that every apprent[i]s in that crafte that of newe shall sett upp for him silfe as maister in the same crafte, pay at his firste upsettyng 3s 4d to the chambre and crafte abovesaide in maner aforesaide.

Item, that he that comyth not to assemble when he is warned by his serchiours for tyme beyng for mater touching the wele of this cite, oles thanne he have a reasonable cause of excuse, forfayte every tyme 6d to be payde in fourme aforesaid.

Item, that it be not levefull for none alyen borne oute of the obbeysance of the King of England to occupy as maister within this cite in that crafte frome nowfurth, and also that it be not leful to no maister of the said craft to leid eny baxster sekks,[39] appon the payn of forfatour of 3s 4d *tociens quociens* to be payd in fourme aforsaid.

(f. 142) Item, if any maister or servante of the saide crafte from nowefurth be foundon untrue in any poynte of that saide crafte, and therof convicte by due serche of the serchiours of the same crafte for tyme beynge or by anye othere lelemen[39] of the saide cite, shall forfayte the firste tyme 2s, to be payde in fourme abovesaid, and over that to make condigne satisfaccion to the partye to whome the offense is doon to, ande if he afterwards be convict in that behalfe that reasonably may be proved, than he to ... [erasure] forswere after the cite for ever. And over this if eny maister of the same be owing eny money for grynding by baxster or eny other man and goeth to a other man to grynd, and the same man unpaid and that shewed by the seirchours, he that grynds that man so known to forfet 2s in maner abovesaid.[41]

Item, if any man of the saide crafte be rebell or assemble any personnes ayenste his serchiours of the same crafte for tyme beyng,

---

[39] *baxter sekks*: baker's sacks.
[40] *lelemen*: honest, true men.
[41] This sentence is interlined in a somewhat later hand.

in any poynte belongyng to the wele ande honesty of the same crafte, that thanne he so rebellyng forfayte 3s 4d to be payde in fourme aforsaide.

ORDINANCES OF THE PLASTERERS AND TILERS.[42]

Be it had in mynde that aswele by the assente ande consente of William Lam, Mair of the Cite of Yorke [1475], as also by the full consente ande assente of all the godemen of the saids crafts, thes ordynauncs ben made to ben observed ande kepped within the same cite for evermore hereafter by thayme of the same crafts.

Firste, what persone sum ever he be of the saids crafts that is warned by the sercheours to com to thair assemble ande commys not without he hase a resonable cause, he forto pay 6d to the chambre ande to the crafte by even porcions.

Item, that what maister of the saids crafts as hase hereafter any straungers wirkyng with hym or thaym in the same crafts or in any of thaym, awnswere for his pagend silver to the craft apon payn of 12d to be paide in fourme beforesaid.

Item, it is ordayned that if any man of the saide crafts be foundon inobedyent or rebell unto the sercheours of the saids crafts for tyme beynge in ther occupacion mynistryng that may be evidently proved, he shall lese and forfayte at every tyme 3s 4d in fourme beforesaid.

(f. 142v) [43]Item, it is ordaned that ther shall noo man of the saids crafts hafe noo prentes but one at ones, ande that for 7 yerez. Ande when that prentez hath seruffed 4 yerez of the saide terme that than it shall be levefull to the maister to take a nother prentes. Ande who that dothe contrarye of this ordynaunce shall forfayte 6s 8d in maner ande fourme aforesaide.

Item, it is ordayned that everilke maister of the forsaide crafts havyng any apprentes, shall bringe in his indenturez of covenants tofor the sercheours of the same crafts for tyme beynge within 14 dayes next after the makyng of thaym, apon the payne of 3s 4d to be payde in fourme beforesaide.

Item, it is ordaned that whatt man of the said crafts that withdraweth eny maner of gude owt of eny gudeman or woman, place or placs, within this said citie, suburbs and precincts of the same, unto the valew of 13½d and that proved, shalbe deiect and put owt

[42] Printed in *York Civic Records*, Vol III pp. 179-80. For earlier ordinances of the guild see *York Memorandum Book* I, pp. 59-60, *ibid* II, 125-8. See also ordinances dated 1572, ff. 229-231v. below.
[43] The whole paragraph has been crossed through.

of the craft and no more to wirk within the said citie.[44]

(f. 143) *Taxes of the City of York payable to the king.*[45]

	According to the books of the city.	According to the rolls in the Exchequer
St. Mary in Castlegate.	£6-10s.	£7-10s.
St. Michael at the Bridge.	£13	£14
All Saints in Ousegate.	£8	£9
St. Peter the Little.	£4-10s.	100s.
St. Martin in Conyngstrete.	£8	£10
St. Helen in Staynegate.	£6	100s.
St. Wilfred.	£3-10s.	60s.
St. Michael de Belfrey.	£11-16s.	£11
Holy Trinity in Gotheromgate, St. John del Pyke.	£8	£7
St. Andrew, St. Helen at the Walles, St. Maurice, St. John in Hundegate, St. Mary in Layrethorp, St. Cuthbert, and All Saints in Peseholm.	60s.	40s. (St. John in Hundegate 3s. 4d.)
St. Sampson.	£8	£8
Holy Trinity in King's Court.	£14	£14
St. Crux in Fossegate.	£14	£14
St. Saviour.	£5	100s.
St. Dennis.	£6-10s.	110s.
St. Margaret, St. Laurence, St. Peter in the Wylughes, St. Edward, St. Nicholas in Walmegate, St. George, St. Helen and All Saints in Fisshergate.	60s.	40s.

[44] This sentence is written in a later hand.

[45] This list and the explanation on f. 143v of the total and the 44s. customarily collected from the inhabitants of Bootham also appear in the Memorandum Book A/Y f. 71 (old numeration f. 57). John Rumby is there named as one of the collectors of the king's taxes but is omitted from B/Y f. 143v. (*York Memorandum Book* I, pp. 178-9 where the date 1397 is wrongly assigned to the entry, although the Mayor is named as Thomas Gare. He held office in 1420, his son of the same name in 1434. William Frost was Mayor in 1397.)

An assessment of the parishes under the grant of parliament, 6 Henry VI [1428], of a tenth from every parish containing ten households, of which the church was of the yearly value of 20s. is printed in *York Memorandum Book* II, pp. 130-4.

See also the accounts of the fifteenths and tenths for the city, 1564, on f. 192v below.

St. Mary the Elder and Clementhorp.	£7-10s.	£9-10s.
St. Mary of the Bishop.	25s.	20s.
St. Nicholas in Mikelgate.	£4	60s.
St. Martin in Mikelgate and St. Gregory.	£8	£8
St. John at the Bridge.	£10	£9
All Saints in Northstrete.	£8-10s.	£11
Total	£162-12d.	Total £162
		[sic] [46]

[Latin]

(f. 143v) Of the total of £162-12d. collected for the king's taxes according to the books of the city, the collectors were answerable to the king in the Exchequer for the whole tenth of the City of York, £162. And so they collected more than they paid to the value of 12d. They were accustomed to collect 44s. from the inhabitants of Bouthom, a suburb of the city, which seemed to the Mayor and Council to be the 44s. which the collectors of the *Northrithinge* claimed from the men of Bouthom. The Council therefore considered that the collectors, when they had collected the tax for the city, should hand 44s. to the Chamberlains to acquit the city towards the *Northrithing*. Certain pledges were then taken of Thomas Kirkham, mercer, Thomas at Esshe, baker, and Henry Estby, collectors of the king's taxes in the said city in the time of Thomas del Gare, Mayor, [1420 or 1434].

Subscribed. Burton R.   [Latin]

The deduction of £16-19s. 7¾d. from the tax of the city deducted by the grant of parliament, 15 Henry VI, in the time of Richard Wartre, Mayor, [1436].

St. Mary, Castlegate.	16s.
St. Michael at the Bridge.	20s.
All Saints, Ousgate.	17s. 4d.
St. Peter the Little.	9s. 8d. [?]
St. Martin in Conyngstrete.	17s. 4d.
St. Helen in Staynegate.	13s.
St. Wilfrid.	7s. 4d.
St. Michael de Belfrey	24s.
Holy Trinity in Gotheromgate and St. John del Pyke.	} 17s. 4d.

[46] The figures given total £163 10s.

St. Sampson.	16s.
Holy Trinity in King's Court.	34s. 10d.
St. Crux.	30s. 4d.
St. Saviour.	20s.
St. Dennis.	14s.
St. Mary the Elder and St. Clement.	16s.
St. Nicholas in Mikelgate.	8s. 8d.
St. Martin in Mikelgate, and St. Gregory.	19s. 4d.
St. John at the Bridge.	20s.
All Saints, North Street.	18s.

The total deducted above, £16-19s. 6d. And so there remained 1¾d. not deducted.[47]   [Latin]

(f. 144)

St. Mary, Castlegate.	4s.
All Saints, Pavement.	2s. 8d.
St. Peter the Little.	12s.
St. Helen in Staynegate.	7s.
St. Martin in Conyngstrete.	4s.
St. Wilfrid.	9s.
St. Michael de Belfrey.	13s. 4d.
Holy Trinity in Gotheromgate and St. John del Pyke.	10s. 8d.
St. Sampson.	4s.
Holy Trinity, King's Court.	5s. 2d.
St. Crux.	9s. 8d.
St. Saviour.	4s.
St. Dennis.	8s.
St. Mary the Elder and St. Clement.	34s.
St. Martin in Mikelgate, and St. Gregory.	14s.
St. John at the Bridge.	6s. 8d.
All Saints, North Street.	21s. 8d.

Total of the last deduction.[48]
Total of both deductions.
And so the parishes aforesaid
paid to each tax, the said allowances
having been deducted.   [Latin]

[47] Some of the figures for the individual parishes are not clearly legible. The total of those given is in fact £16 19s 2d.
[48] No totals have been inserted.

(f. 144v) The taxes paid to the king by the parishioners of the City of York in addition to the aforesaid deductions.

St. Mary at Castlegate.	110s.
St. Michael at Ouse Bridge.	£12.
All Saints, Ousegate.	£7
St. Peter the Little.	68s. 4d.
St. Martin in Conyngstrete.	£6-18s. 8d.
St. Helen in Staynegate.	100s.
St. Wilfrid.	53s. 8d.
St. Michael de Belfrey.	£9-18s. 8d.
Holy Trinity in Gotheromgate, and St. John del Pyke.	} £6-12s.
St. Andrew (15s.) St. Helen at the Walles (15s.) St. Maurice (26s. 8d), St. John in Hundegate (3s. 6d.), St. Mary in Layrethorpe (4s.) St. Cuthbert (4s.) and All Saints (3s. 6d.) in Peseholme.	} 71s. 8d.
St. Sampson.	£7
Holy Trinity in King's Court.	£12
St. Crux in Fossegate.	£12
St. Saviour.	76s.
St. Dennis.	108s.
St. Margaret (35s. 8d.) St. Laurence (20s.) St. Peter in the Wylughes (12s.) St. Edward (7s.) St. Nicholas in Walmegate (5s.) St. George (2s.) St. Helen (2s. 6d.) and All Saints in Fysshergate (2s. 6d.)	} 86s. 8d.
St. Mary the Elder and St. Clement.	100s.
St. Mary of the Bishop.	25s.
St. Nicholas in Mikelgate.	71s. 4d.
St. Martin in Mikelgate and St. Gregory.	£6-6s. 6d. [?]
St. John at the Bridge.	£8-13s. 2d. [?]
All Saints in Northstrete.	£6-10s.

      Total of this tax £136-11s. 8d.[49]
      The collectors were answerable to
      the king for only £136-10s. 7d.
      And so they had for their expenses

[49] The figures given total £138-9s. 8d.

13d. as long as the aforesaid
deductions should endure.

Marginal note: See more of this material in book 'Gil' f. 68.[50]

[Latin]

City of York.	The cost of a whole 15th & 10th. £136-10s. 8d.
	The cost of a whole 15th and 10th of the town of Halifax. 8s.
[County of] York	The cost of a whole 15th and 10th of the town of Leyds. 40s.
	The cost of a whole 15th and 10th of the town of Wakefeld. £3-14s. 4d.
	The cost of a whole 15th and 10th of the town of Bradfurth. 20s.

[Latin]

(f. 145)   Wapentake of Aynsty.

Askham Bryan.	30s.
Acastre Selby.	25s.
Acastre Malbys.	20s.
Bisshopthorp.	13s. 4d.
Helagh.	15s.
Wighale.	16s.
Colton.	18s.
Thorp Arch.	28s.
Willesthorp.	17s.
Bekerton [Bickerton].	14s.
Folifat [Follifoot].	10s. 6d.
Appilton.	23s.
Bilburgh.	20s.
Rughford with the holding of St. Leonard's.	18s.
Munkton.	10s.
(nothing because 11s. 1½d. elsewhere)	
Styvton [Steeton].	24s.
Coupmanthorp.	23s. 4d.
Walton.	15s.
Bolton Percy.	26s. 8d.
Bilton.	8s.
Marston.	22s.
Tokwyth.	8s.

[50] Not identified; see note on f. 143 above.

Hoton [Hutton]	20s.
Oxton.	8s.
Chatherton [Catterton] with the holding of St. Leonard's.	7s.
Drynghous.	6s. 8d.
Skakilthorp [Scagglethorpe]	3s.
Askham Richard.	15s.

Total £23-4s. 6d./5s. 7½d.[51]

The liberty of St. Leonard's
Hospital in Cramworth Parva,[52]
Ribston, Nappay [Nappa], Coupmanthorp,
[Copmanthorpe] Haghalthwart,[52] Letheley
[Leathley], Stokyld, [Stockheld, parish of
Barwick in Elmet], Midelton, Urhhton [?][53]
and Doncastre.
} 73s. 4d.

The liberty of St. Mary and St. Peter [in] Hesay,
Monkton, Knapton, Appilton and Acastre.
} 30s.

Popilton, Upper.	48s.
Popilton, Lower.	43s.
Acome with Holgate.	68s.
Uskleffe [Ulleskelf].	26s.

Total £9-5s.
Sum total £37-12s. 10d.
half of which is £18-16s. 5d.[54]   [Latin]

(f. 145v) ROYAL GRANT.[55]

Richard [II], following complaints from the Warden and Friars
Minor of York,
to the Sheriff of York and the Mayor and Bailiffs of the city,
granting his special protection to the Warden and Friars Minor.[56]

[51] 5s 7½d added in a different ink.
[52] Not identified.
[53] Not identified
[54] The totals £37 12s 10d and £18 16s 5d show evidence of having been erased and re-written.
[55] C. P. R. 1377-81, p. 458.
[56] There were disturbances in the city in 1380 with riots between the supporters of John de Gisburn, the deposed Mayor, and Simon de Quixley who was forced to take office. The above grant suggests that the Franciscan friary was damaged early in that year as well as in 1381, when it is known that St. Leonard's Hospital, St. George's Chapel and the Dominican and Franciscan friaries were attacked and subsequently received redress from the city. [York Memorandum Book I pp. xiii-xiv; Victoria County History, the City of York, p. 81].

Their walls were not to be forcibly entered nor their walls, gardens or houses broken or trodden down, nor their celebration of divine services disturbed. No violence or sacrilege was to be committed after entering their walls and no injury was to be caused to the Warden, the friars or their servants or to their goods, under penalty of a heavy forfeiture.

(f. 146) Witnessed by the king at Westminster, 14 April 3 Richard [II, 1380].

Subscribed. Waltham.　　　　　　　　　　　　　　　　[Latin]

(f. 146v) ORDINANCES OF THE FLETCHERS.[57]

[Present] Thomas Wrangwishe, Maior, Thomas Neleson, John Marshall, William Snaweshill, Richard Yorke and John Glasen [Aldermen], Richard Cleybroke, Thomas Mariot, Robert Amyas, John Lightlop of the 24, Alan Wilberfosse and Thomas Scotton, Sheriffs. The 3rd day of the moneth of Aprill in the yere of the reigne of King Edward the Fourth the sixteenth [1476], were assembled in the Counsaile Chaumbre upon Ouse brig, and there and then it was fermely ordeined, enacted and stablished by alle abovesaide, at the request and praier of all the goode men of the hole craft of the flechers, for evermore after this to be observed, fulfilled and keped: —

First, that noman of the saide craft of the flechers shall presume upon hym to occupie as a maister in the saide craft nor to setupp any shop in the citie, to the tyme that the sersours of the saide craft have examend hym and founden hym able to be a maister of the saide craft, and who so doose contrarie to this ordinance sall forfet 6s 8d, the oone half to be paied to the commonaltie of this cite to the use of the chaumbre of the same, and the other half to be paied to the same crafte by even porcions.

Also it is ordeined and agreed that no maister of the saide craft nor his servantz shall wirke no manere stuffe belonging to the saide craft but goode and able stuffe for the wele of the king's people. And whosomever shalbe foundon defective therin by the sersours of the saide craft, at every tyme that he shalbe sersed and so founden in defaute, to paie 6s 8d in manere and fourme abovesaide.

And that no man of the saide craft within this citie and subburbes

---

[57] Printed in *York Civic Records* Vol. III, p. 181. For earlier ordinances, see *York Memorandum Book* I, 110-12.

of the same sett no man to wirke in the saide craft to [he] be examened and abiled by the sersours of the same craft, and who somever dooith the contrarie to paie 6s 8d as it is aforsaide.

(f. 147) Also that every apprentice of the saide craft at his first settyng upp shalbe examened and abled by the sersours of the saide craft, and then for to paie 6s 8d, wherof the oone half to the chaumbre and use of this citie and the other half to his saide craft.

Also that noman of the saide craft shall uppon the Sonday or other festivall day shafe and waxe fethir nor glewe, but if it be in a tyme of necessitie to feste downe a fethir or two that is lowse. And who so doose contrarie to this ordinance, at every tyme he is founden and knowne defautie in the same, to paie 6s 8d in the fourme above-saide.

Also it is fully agreed and ordeined that no man occupieing as maister in the saide crafte shall take to hym any apprentice in the saide craft for les terme than 7 yers. And whosomevere doothe the contrarie this ordinance to paie 6s 8d in manere and fourme afore writen.

(f. 147v) ORDINANCES OF THE PORTERS.[58]

The following constitutions and ordinances were constituted and ordained in the time of Thomas Wrangwishe, Mayor [1476], by the assent of the whole chamber and also of all the porters of the city. [Latin]

First, it is ordeined and enacted that no persoune of what degree or condicion he be of take upon hym to bere any manere graynes, coles, turffs, or any other manere stuff that belonges unto the saide porters of this citie to bere, upon the payne of forfaiture of every suche berer 12d, the one half unto the chaumbre of this citie and the other half unto the sustentacion of the torches and lightes of the saide craft.

Item, that no sleddman nor other persoune carie by cart, slede nor horse, any thing that belongis to the saide porters to bere, upon payne of forfeture every persoune so dooing 2s at every tyme that he shall so carie contrarie the saide ordinance to paie in manere and fourme aforesaide. Provided allwey that if the saide porters or any of theyme be called or warned by any persoune to bere any manere graynes, coles, turffs or any other thing belonging unto

---

[58] Printed in *York Civic Records*, Vol. III, pp. 185-6. For ordinances of 1495 and 1587, see also *York Civic Records*, Vol. II, pp. 122-3 and *ibid* Vol. III, p. 143.

theyme, and be noe redie, refuse or willfully absent hym self frome
the executeing of his office and bereing of the same, that then it
shalbe lefull to any persoune to take and accepte whosomevere shall
please theyme for that season to bere or carie all suche graynes,
coles, turff, or any othering in defaute of the saide porters. And
also it shalbe lefull to every persoune of what degre or condicion
he be of, by hym self or his servantz to bere or carie all manere
graynes, coles, turff and all other things for his propir use when
and what tyme somevere it shall please hym, the forsaide ordinance
in anything not with standing.

Item, that every kidberer[59] within this said citie and fraunches
from hynsfurth yerely shall paie unto the sustentacion of 4 torches
yerely to be founden and borne by the saide porters in the procession of Corpus Christi 2d.

(f. 148)[60] Item, that every porter that shal of new begyn in the
same shal pay 5s. in fourme folowyng, that is to say 40d to the
said occupacion of porters and 20d. to the Chaumbre.

Item, it is ordeined and enacted in the tym of Richard York, Mair
[1482], with the concent of John Baylye, John Davyson, John
Grayson, John White, William North, Thomas Wryght, Roland
Herryson, John Waker, Robert Marshall, William West, John
Fysher, John Magone, John Williamson, Robert Otley, and John
Newall, porters of the said cite, that no porter when he has taykyn
hys byrdyn at the shipp or at the stayth, beyt colls, turffys or odyr
thyng, shall not set up hys said byrdyn in hys awn hows or odyr
place ne the stayth or ferre, bot evyn furthwyth when he has
rescevyd it at the shipp or at the stayth he shall beere it immediately
to hys hows in whos name it was bowght at the stayth or at the
shypp, apon the payn of forfatour of 18d, that is to say 12d to the
chambyr and 6d to the uise of the lyght of the said porters.[61]

Also, in the tyme of Sir William Todde, knight, Maier of the Cite
of York [1487], by thauctoritie of the counsaill of the chambre, the
upset of the porters above writyn was canceld by the said Sir William
Todde. And that from hensfurth evere porter that shall of new
begyn in the same shall pay for his upset 3s 4d, that is to say
20d to the chambre and 20d to the occupacion of porters.[62]

---

[59] kidberer: carrier of faggots, bundles of twigs.
[60] The whole paragraph has been crossed through.
[61] This paragraph is in a later, more cursive, hand.
[62] Written in a third hand.

(f. 148v) ORDINANCES OF THE BOOKBINDERS.[63]

First, it is ordeined and enacted in the tyme of Thomas Wrangwishe, Maire of the Citie of Yorke [1476 or 1484], by the hole assent of all the craft of the bookebynders of the Citie of Yorke, that it shalbe levefull to the sersours of the saide craft for the tyme being to serse allmanere of bokes putto selle within the saide citie and all othir things belonging unto thaire craft, and the defautes therin to presente unto the chaumbre, there to be corrected and punyshed at the will of the Maire by thadvise of the saide sersours. And whosomevere is therin rebell unto the saide sersours and willnot suffir the saide serse dewly and trewly to be doone, to forfet at every tyme 40d, and that to be paied unto the saide chaumbre and craft be evene porciones.

Item, that no man of the saide craft take none apprentice for lesse terme then 7 yeres, uppon payne of 10s to be paied in manere aforesaide.

Item, that no man take uppon hym to settup as a maister in the saide craft to he be abled by the sersours of the same craft, upon payne of forfeture of 20s to paie as is aforesaide. And that every apprentice within the citie paie at his upset as a maister in the saide craft 40d, and every foreine that hath not be apprentice within the citie paie 13s 4d at his upset as is abovesaide.

Item, that no maner man, religious or secular, that is not fraunchesed nor abled by the saide craft and sersours take upon hym to bring in or sett oute any werke of this citie or fraunches, upon payne of 6s 8d as is abovesaide.

Item, that no man of the saide craft frome hynsfurthe take upon hym for to teche any persoune his craft or science for any money, withoute it be his apprentice, upon payne of 10s to paie unto the chaumbre and crafte abovesaide.

Item, whosomevere of the saide craft frome hynsfurthe that at all suche tymes as he is warned to apere at suche tyme and place as he is warned by his sersours, for the honour and wele of his saide craft, and absent hymself withoute a resonable and sufficiant excuse, to paie unto the chaumbre and craft by evene porcions 8d.

[63] Each ordinance has the marginal note *vacat*, void. Printed in *York Civic Records*, Vol. III, p. 184. See also ordinances of 1554, ff. 211v-212 below.

(f. 149) *Thordinance of Textwriters, Lominers,*[64] *Notors,*[65] *Tournours*[66] *and Florisshers*[67] *of the Citie of York.*[68]

At thinstant supplicacion and request of thool company of textwriters, lominers, notours, tourners and florisshers within the Citie of York, suburbs and fraunchies of the same, willing to be corporate as other crafts within the said citie, and also for the puplique wele and prouffit of thinhabitants of the same, it was ordigned, ennact and establisshed inviolate to be observed and kepid for ever by the right honourable and worshipfull Sir William Todde, knight, Maier of the citee forsaid [1487], his bretherern Aldremen and Commune Counsaill of the same as it apperith in statutez herafter ensuyng.

First, it is ordand that fromehensfurth yerely there shalbe elect amongs the company of textwriters, lominers, noters, tournours and florisshers, two suffisaunt and able men to be serchours in that craft for oone yere complete, under the payne of forfaitour of 3s 4d to be employed to the chambre.

Also that noo persone within the said citie set upp a shopp to write, lomine, note, turne or florisshe, or within the suburbs or fraunchise of the same opynly or coverdly, unto suche tyme he be foundon able to exercise that occupacion by the serchours forsaid, undre the payne of forfaitour of 3s 4d to be devided equally to the use of the chambre and the said craft.

Also that evere apprintice which hath well and truly served his yeres within this citie shall pay at such tyme as he shall set upp for himself in the same craft 20d, to be devided as is toforesaid. And if ther be any such that hath not beene apprintice within the said citie at the forsaid craft that entendeth to set upp as a master in the same, [he] shall pay for his upset 3s 4d to be devided as is toforesaid.

Also that noone of the same craft take his apprentice for lesse termes than for 6 yeres[69] and that he be of age 16 yeres[69] complete, and that his indentours be shewed within 3 weks after he be fest unto the serchours of the same craft for the tyme being. And that noo man of the craft forsaid lerne noo persone of othr craft any

[64] *lominers*: illuminators.

[65] *notors*: writers of musical scores, annotators.

[66] *tournours*: turners, translators.

[67] *florisshers*: those who embellished writing with 'flourishes', flowing curves.

[68] All the ordinances are crossed through. Revised ordinances appear on ff. 161-2.

[69]—[69] Interlined.

part therof bot oonely his apprentice, under the payne of forfaitour of 40d to be devided equally to the chambre and the craft.

Also it is ordand asfar as is in the said Maier, Aldremen and Counsellours forsaid, that noo prest within this citie, suburbs and fraunchesse of the same, having a competent sallary, that is to say 7 marks or above, exercise the craft of textwritters, lominers, noters, tournours and florisshers within the same for his singuler prouffit and lucour, nor take noone apprentice, hirdman or other servant into his service, (f. 149v) nor make noo bargans or cov[en]ants to that entent undre the payne of forfaitour of 13s 4d to be devided as is abovesaid. Provided alway that it shalbe lefull to any prest to write, lomine, tourne or florisshe any maner of books to his propre use or to distribute to any place in way of elmose.[70] And that it be lefull to evere prest not having a competent sallary within the citie, suburbs and fraunchise of the same to exercise the craft of text-writing, lomine, note, tourne and florisshe any books at his pleaser for his singuler availe, prouffit and lucour with his owne hands, not taking apprentise or hirdman to hyme in any wise, undre the payne of forfaitour of 13s 4d to be devided as is toforesaid.

Also if an aliene wolde set upp as a master in the craft abovesaid after he be foundon able by the serchours of the same for the tyme being, he shall pay for his upset of the said craft to the chambre and the same to be devided, 20s.

Also if ther be any apprentice or hirdman in the said craft that withdraweth any goods to the value of 12d frome his master or othr he shalbe warned to leef, and if he eftsones doo asmoch, he shall never occupie within the citie, suburbs and fraunchise of the same. And what master of the same craft that taks hyme to his service and setts hyme on wark within this citie, suburbs and fraunchesse of the same shall forfet to the use of chambre and craft forsaid 10s.

And that noo master, apprentice or hirdman of the said crafte be rebell or otherwise mishave theme self unto ther sherchours for the tyme being, them lauffully and curtasly serching in ther occupacion, upon the peyne of 12d to be paid as is toforesaid.

Also it is ordand that evere foryene using any part of the said craft that cometh into this citie to sell any books or to take warke to wirk shall pay to the upholding of ther padgeaunt yerely 4d.

Also it is ordand that if any master of the said craft having a

---

[70] *elmose*: alms.

prentice desese, the which apprentice hath not fulfilled his yeres
with his said maister, he shall continewe still during his [?heyeres]
with the wif of the said master aslong as she kepith hur soole,[71]
except his said master pardon hyme his yeres unserved, which if he
soo bee and be foundon able by the serchours, he shall pay for his
upset 3s 4d to be devided in maner and forme abovesaid. And if he
be not foundon able by the said serchours he shall serve furthe his
yeres as is afforsaid with what master hyme best shall seme, under
the payne of forfaitour of 10s. to be paid in maner and fourme
afforsaid.

(f. 150)[72] Also if ther be any master that be warned by the serchours to come to what place as is assigned for the well of our science,
he that comez not at the oure that is assigned shall pay 4d as oft
tymes as he doth the contrary. And if any discover[73] the counsaill
ther had, he shall forfet to the chambre and craft by evene porcions
12d.

Also it is ordand that what master or servaunt be rebell ayenst
the serchours tham lauffully serched shall forfet to the chambre and
craft by evene porcions 12d.

ARBITRATION IN A DISPUTE BETWEEN THE SCRIVENERS AND TEXTWRITERS AND SIR WILLIAM INCECLYFF, PRIEST.[74]

Memorandum that it is aggreed, ordand and establisshed by the
right worshipfull Sir William Todde, knight, Maier of the Citie
of York [1487], arbiter indifferently named and chosen betwix
the scryveners and textwriters of that oone partie and Sir William
Incecliff, prest, of the same of that othr partie, in and upon all
maner of maters of variauncs and debats hanging in demaunde
betwix theme, frome the begynnyng of the world unto the dait
herof, aswell by the free consents and wolls of the said scryveners
and textwriters as the said Sir William; that he by hymself, hired
man, servant or other shall finissh and make up twoo books which
he hath in hand at the making herof, wherof oone boke belongeth to
his chauntery within the Chapell of Fossebrig and the other apper-
tigneth to hymself, of the which 12 pesez is writyn the day of the

[71] *kepith hur soole*: remains unmarried.
[72] f. 150 is only about two-thirds the normal width.
[73] *discover*: reveal.
[74] Printed by R. Davies in *A Memoir of the York Press* (1868), pp. 3-4. A further
award between the parties appears on ff. 162v-163.

yeving herof. And also to have with hyme after finisshing of the said books, during his woll and pleaser at all tymes herafter, a child and oone after an other to put to what lernyng or use hyme shall best seme without any interupcion, let or trouble of any of the said scryveners or texwriters or ther successors. And that the said Sir William shall sell such boks as shalbe maid by hyme and his said child at any tyme herafter, oonely to and for thexhibicion and costs of his said child and none other wise to his singuler avauntage and prouffit.

(f. 150v) And that the said Sir William shalnot be named or elect any padgeant maister, sersour, or put in any office or charge by the said scryveners and textwriters at any tyme herafter ayenst his woll and pleaser, bot oonely to bere his charge as oone of them doth yerely toward the cost of ther play in the fest of Corpus Christi.

[The remainder of f. 150v is blank].

(f. 151) On 2 March 29 Henry VI [1451], William Bolton came into the Council Chamber before Richard Warter, Mayor, and sought the enrolment of the following deed which he acknowledged to have been made and sealed by him.

FEOFFMENT.

William Bolton, son and heir of Adam Bolton, kinsman and heir of Alice Crauncewyk,
to Simon Olyver of York, joiner, and Margaret, his wife,
a messuage and garden lying without Mikillyth in the suburbs of York, in length from the high street in front as far as the king's ditch behind, and in width between the tenement of the late Stephen Lytster of York on the one side and the tenement of William Selby, formerly of Nicholas Foule, on the other.

Witnesses. Thomas Barton, Mayor, Thomas Beverlay, William Barlay, Sheriffs, William Craven, William Crathorn, William Couper.

Given at York, 9 November 29 Henry VI [1450].

Subscribed. Freman. [Latin]

(f. 151v) AGREEMENT CONCERNING GROUND IN BOOTHAM.

Memorandum that it is agreid betwix Thomas Wandesford of the Cite of Yorke, gentilman, and Herry Fox of Pannall in the Countie of Yorke, yoman, the 18 day of Marche in the thirde yere of the reign of our most redoubted sovereyn lige lorde King Herry the Sevent [1488], in and apon certan variaunce of ground depending betwix the said parties, lying in Bouthom in the suburbs of the said Cite of Yorke, by the honorable Sir Robert Hancok, Maior of the same cite, and Peris Cooke, John Pety, Chamberleyns of the same, and other wirshupful persones of the said cite being present of the ground aforsaid, that the hege of whiksall[75] late set by the said Thomas with whitethorn, that the said Herry shall up hold the same of his own propre costs and chargs during his naturall lieff, and efter his disseise the said heige to be upholden for ever with whitethorn by the heires or assignes of the said Herry. And if the said heige at eny tyme herafter in defalt of upholding of the same the said Thomas Wandesford, his heirez or assignes, tak eny hurt at eny tyme herafter, that laufully and of right can be proved, that than the said Herry woll and graunts for hym, his heires and assignez, to content and pay 2s of lawful money of England, that is to say 12d to the said Thomas Wandesford, his heire or assignez, and 12d to the behufe of the commonaltie of the said cite by even porcions *tociens quociens* withoute pardon.

(ff. 152-3) On 14 January 30 Henry VI [1452], John Dale of Kingeston upon Hull, merchant, came before Richard Wartre, Mayor of the City of York in the Council Chamber, and sealed and acknowledged the following six bonds.

BOND.
    John Dale of Kyngeston upon Hull, merchant,
    to Thomas Shalcok, citizen and baker of York,
in 20s to be paid to the said Thomas, his executors or his attorney, in equal portions on the feasts of St. Peter ad Vincula and the Nativity of Our Lord next.
    Given, 14 January 30 Henry VI [1452].
    Subscribed. Gunby.   [Latin]
[The other five bonds are identical except that John Dale bound himself by them to pay 20s each year on the said feasts during the succeeding five years.]
[f. 153 is blank except for the final line of a bond.]

(f. 153v). *Evidence shown by Henry Gascoigne concerning the*

---

[75] *whiks, quicks, quickset,* cuttings of plants, especially whitethorn, of which hedges are made.

*nonpayment of toll by his tenants in Naburn, enrolled in the time
of Thomas Danby, Mayor, 30 Henry VI [1452].*[76]

All tenants of the honour of Eye, freemen and others, are and have
been from time immemorial, quit of toll, murage, etc., in all cities,
towns and elsewhere in the realm of England. William Fairefax
holds the manor of Acastre which extends into Acastre, Naburn and
Bisshopthorp, as parcel of the said honour; and Henry Gascoigne
holds of the said William certain lands and tenements in Naburn,
as part of the manor of Acastre, for an annual rent of 4s. paid to
William Fairefax as chief lord of the fee called *Malbyssh fee.* That
the said William is the possessor of that fee is proved by the following deeds.   [Latin]

DECLARATION.
  William Colby,
    to Sir John Malbys,
that he would not give to the church his land in Holtby which he
had of Richard Maunsell for homage, service, and a sum of money,
and for which he had a confirmation from Sir John Malbys, chief
lord of the land.
  Witnesses. Brian son of Alan, William de Tameton, Jord Harom,
Richard Maunsell, Thomas Parson of Acastre.
  [Undated].   [Latin]

(ff. 153v-154) ACQUITTANCE.
  Richard Malbys,
    to Edmund Maunsell and his heirs,
of suit of court at Acastre, held every three weeks, for the tenement
which Edmund Maunsell held of him in Naburn. Edmund Maunsell had brought a royal writ against him before the justices of
[Common] Bench because he had distrained him for suit of court
as above, contrary to the form of the feoffment. The said Edmund
was to make suit of court twice each year, at the courts next after
Michaelmas and Easter when summoned, and perform all other
services due to Richard Malbys. He might appoint attorneys for
the purpose.
  Witnesses. Sir John Meens, Sir William Ryther.
  [Undated].   [Latin]

Memorandum that Henry Gascoigne is seissed in demean and

[76] See also f. 128v.

service of 7 meesses, 6 cotages, 133 acre of arrable lande, 7 acre medewe, 60 acre wod, 200 [acres] more, with the appurtenance in Naburn, in the name of the thrid parte of the hole maner of Naburn, as parcell of the maner of Acastre of the honor of Ey, by the whilk honor the seid Henry and al those whose estate the saide Henry hase in the said thrid parte of the manere, and the tenants therof, has had and used to be and goo toll free thurowe out the reame of England without tyme of mynde, and the names of the tenants that haldes and er dwellyng of the saide thrid parte er thies:

Rauff Cromwell, knight, Thomas Maners, Ralph Aclom, John Morton, John Cawod, William Couper, Nicholas Chapman, William Johnson, John Ferrour, Margaret Letters, William Holme, Janet Russell, Thomas Mathewe, Thomas Couk, Thomas Norton, Henry Langwath, John Wenslagh, Adam Hirde, John Purdon.

[Undated]

Marginal note: To the king 8d, to William Fairefax 2s. [Latin]

On 20 January 31 Henry VI [1453], John Thwenge of York, gentleman, and Joan, his wife, came before Thomas Danby, Mayor, in the Council Chamber and sought the enrolment of the following deed.

(ff. 154-154v) FEOFFMENT.

John Thweyng of York, gentleman, and Joan, his wife,

to the Master and Brethren of St. Leonard's Hospital, York,

two messuages in York. One, in which they then lived, lay in the parish of St. Dennis in Walmegate, in width between the tenement of John Bell on the south and the tenement of the late William Broket on the north, and in length from Walmegate in front to the Foss behind. The other messuage, in the tenure of John Loufthouse, parchmentmaker, lay in Gotheromgate in the parish of Holy Trinity, in width between the tenement of John Stafford on the east and the tenement of Thomas Howme on the west, and in length from Gotheromgate in front to the garden of the said Thomas behind.

Rent. 4 marks p.a. during the lives of John Thweynge and Joan, his wife. If the rent was ever in arrears, they were to have distraint.

Witnesses. Thomas Danby, Mayor, John Strensall and Thomas Danyell, Sheriffs, Thomas Belford, gentleman, John Bell, John Coupeland.

Given at York, 12 February 30 Henry VI [1452].   [Latin]

(f. 155) On the day after the feast of Simon and Judas the Apostles, 32 Henry VI [29 October 1453], Christopher Blakburn came before John Catryk, Mayor, showed a deed and a release, and asked that they should be enrolled in the common book of the city.

FEOFFMENT.

Christopher Blakburn, late of Sandwyche in the County of Kent, gentleman, one of the sons of Nicholas Blakburn, late citizen and merchant of York,

to Thomas Wandesford and Agnes, his wife, sister of the said Christopher Blakburn, and the heirs of their bodies, with the reversion, in default thereof, to the said Christopher and the heirs of his body,

the capital messuage and the two tenements annexed to it, in Northstrete, which formerly belonged to Nicholas Blakburn, citizen and merchant of York, his grandfather.

Witnesses. John Catryk, Mayor, William Craven, John Craven, Thomas Hemylsey, William Shirborn of York.

Given on the feast of Simon and Judas the Apostles 32 Henry VI [28 October 1453].   [Latin]

(f. 155v) QUITCLAIM.

Christopher Blakburn,

to Thomas Wandesford and Agnes his wife, and the heirs of their bodies,

the capital messuage and two tenements [as above].

Witnesses. Thomas Barton, Thomas Danby, citizens and Aldermen, John Hemylsay, John Strensall, John Punderson, of York.

Given on the day after the feast of Simon and Judas the Apostles 32 Henry VI [29 October 1453].   [Latin]

(ff. 155v-156) ROYAL PRECEPT.[77]

[Edward I]

to the Sheriff of York, escheator in that County, to cause the brethren of St. Nicholas's Hospital, York, to have seisin again of 1½ acres of meadow near the king's fish-pond in the suburbs of York, on the condition by which they had previously held the land. Reciting that the king had learned from an inquisition taken by Wythard and William de Norburg[78] that the 1½ acres were not

[77] C.Cl. R. 1272-9, p. 280.
[78] Guyschard de Charron and William de Norb[ury] in Calendar of Close Rolls.

ancient demesne of the Crown, nor arrented at the Exchequer, but that Empress Matilda, late Queen of England, bought a carucate of land and the meadow aforesaid and gave them to the brethren, on condition that they should provide all lepers coming to the hospital on the eve of the feast of the Apostles Peter and Paul with the following victuals, bread, ale, a mulvel,[79] butter, salmon and cheese.

Given at Kenington, 28 April 5 Edward [1] 127[7].[80]   [Latin]

(ff. 156-156v) On the feast of the Assumption of the Blessed Virgin Mary 34 Henry VI [15 August 1456], Thomas Fulthorp, knight, one of the king's justices of Common Bench came before John Carr, Mayor, showed various deeds made and sealed by him and asked that they should be enrolled in the common book of the city.

GIFT.

Thomas Fulthorp, knight, one of the king's justices of Common Bench,

to Margaret Soureby, Roger her son, Isabel and Anne, her daughters,

all his goods and chattels, except a piece of silver-gilt with a cover, and another piece of silver without a cover, twenty cows, two hundred ewes, sixteen oxen, two carts and two ploughs which he wished Thomas, son of the said Margaret, to have after his death; except also another piece of silver, two cows and twenty ewes which he wished Margaret Fulthorp, his sister, to have after his death; and except his arms which he desired to be divided by the said Margaret, their mother, between Roger and Thomas his sons; also to the said Margaret, for one year after his death, his house at the *Groyne*, which he had of Thomas Lomeley, knight, with all his salt and wool.

Witnesses. John Thresk, citizen and merchant of York, John Gook, Rector of the parish Church of St. Cuthbert in Peseholme, William Hayton, chaplain, John Thwynge, gentleman, Adam Gunby.

Given, 4 August 34 Henry VI [1456].   [Latin]

(ff. 156v-157) QUITCLAIM.

Thomas Fulthorp,

---

[79] *mulvel*, cod.
[80] 27 April 1276 in Calendar of Close Rolls.

to Margaret, daughter of Robert Soureby, and Thomas and
Roger, her sons,
the manors of Thorptheweles [Thorpe Thewles], Hurworth on
the Moor and all lands and tenements, rents and services in Thorpe-
theweles and Hurworth aforesaid, Aldakris [Oldacres] and But-
tirwyk in the County of Durham.
Given, 4 August 34 Henry VI [1456].   [Latin]

QUITCLAIM.
Thomas Fulthorp,
to Margaret Soureby, and Roger and Thomas, her sons,
lands and tenements, rents and services in Thorpbulmer, Greteham
[Greatham], Brountofte [Bruntoft], Wolstone [Wolviston],
Norton, Owton, Preston and Hertilpole [Hartlepool] in the County
of Durham.
Given, 4 August 34 Henry VI [1456].   [Latin]

(f. 157v) QUITCLAIM.
Thomas Fulthorp,
to Thomas and Roger, sons of Margaret Soureby,
the manor of Tunstall, and lands and tenements, rents and services
in Tunstall aforesaid, Thorleston and Morleston in the County of
Durham and wapentake of Sadberg.
Given, 4 August 34 Henry VI [1456].   [Latin]

(f. 157v) WILL OF THOMAS FULTHORP.[81]
   To all thoos that this present writyng heres or sees, Thomas Fulthorp, knyght, one of the Justices of the Comon Place, sendes
gretyng in God. Be it knawen to all Christen men, I beyng in clere
mynde and understandyng ordaynes and makes this for my full
and playne will withoutyn any variance. That is to say, it is my
will that Thomas, the son of Margarete Soureby, take and receyve
the one halfe of the profettes and revenous of my maners and townes

---

[81] Another will of Thomas Fulthorp, knight, in Latin but of the same date, is
printed in *Testamenta Eboracensia* II, p. 203. In it he desired burial in the Cathedral
Church of St. Peter of York, bequeathed his best gown as a mortuary gift to the
Rector of St. Cuthbert's Church in Peasholme, York, and made bequests to various
religious houses. Money due to him was to be delivered to Margaret Soureby to the
use of herself and of Roger, Isabel and Anne, her children.
   The will was proved on 3 May 1457.

of Tonstall, Hurworth, Thorleston, Morleston, Aldakirs and Hertilpole to his awne propre use, and the othir halfe there of is my will to be takyn and receyved by the said Margarete to the mariages of Roger, Isabell and Anne, childre to the said Margarete, broder and sisters to the said Thomas, unto tyme that the said Thomas come to the age of 18 yere. Also it is my full will as for the revenous of my maner of Seint Elyn Aukeland [St. Helen's Auckland] and other landes and tenementez that I have in the same towne, yerely shall be takyn and rererde 20 marcs of thaime by the said Margarete to the mariages and releve of Roger, Isabell and Anne, childer un to the said Margarete, unto the tyme that 200 marcs of thaime be made levy, and (f. 158) overe that it is my will that my maistre Sir Thomas Nevile, broder to the Erle of Westmorland have yerely all profettes and revenous of the said maner, landes and tenementes overe the said 20 marcs to be goode maistre and supporter, as my full triste is in him and ay hath been, to the said Margarete, Roger, Isabell and Anne, agaynes my wyfe and othir persones for she wold nevere be reuled by me bot ay contrary my will. Tharefore it is my will that she have none of my landes nor goodes nor entermettyng of thaime in any wyse, for in trouthe she hath more goodes of myn than evere I had of hirs. Providyng alway that it is my will that if the said Roger, Isabell and Anne or any of thaime be maried agaynes the will and aggrement of the said Margarete, their modir, than I will that he or she, son or doghter, so maried have no parte of the revenous of this my said will, bot alonely the profettes and revenous of thaime shall return to the said Margarete and thoos of hir childer that will be reuled by hir. Into witnes of this my present will indented I have setto the seall of myn armes. Yeven the 13 day of the moneth of Auguste in the yere of the reign of Kynge Henry Sext 34th [1456].

On the eve of St. Matthew the Apostle and Evangelist 35 Henry VI [20 September 1456], Thomas Turpyn came before John Carr, Mayor, in the Council Chamber and asked that the following quitclaim should be enrolled.

(ff. 158-158v) QUITCLAIM.

Thomas Turpyn, son and heir of John Turpyn, late citizen and litster of York,

to Thomas Clerke, citizen of York,

a messuage in Northstrete, lying between the messuage of the

Mayor and Commonalty in which Thomas Neweton, shearman, lately dwelt, on the one side, and the messuage of William Kendale, late citizen and merchant of York on the other, and extending in length from Northstrete in front to the messuage of William Holbek, citizen and merchant, occupied by William Warde, behind.

Witnesses. Thomas Howren, clerk, William Gaunt, merchant, Christopher Dobley, John Tydeman, John Lese, chaplains,

Given, 12 August 34 Henry VI [1456].

Subscribed. Gunby.   [Latin]

On the penultimate day of January 36 Henry VI [30 January 1458], William Stokton came before Robert Colynson, Mayor, and asked that the following deed should be copied and enrolled in the common book of the city.

(ff. 158v-159) FEOFFMENT AND GIFT.

William Stokton, citizen and merchant of York,

to John Ince, citizen and merchant,

lands and tenements, rents and services in the City of York, and suburbs thereof, together with all his goods and chattels and all debts owed to him.

Witnesses. Robert Colynson, Mayor, Thomas Brounflete, John Marsshall, Sheriffs, Richard Lematon, citizen and Alderman.

Given at York, 1 January 36 Henry VI [1458].

Subscribed. Gunby.   [Latin]

On 10 September 37 Henry VI [1458], John Peghan, senior, came before William Holbek, Mayor, and asked that the following deed should be enrolled in the common book of the city.

(ff. 159-159v) GRANT.

John Peghan, senior,

to Roger Fulthorp, son of Margaret Soureby, daughter of Robert Soureby, and the male heirs of his body, remainder to Thomas Fulthorp, brother of the said Roger, and the male heirs of his body, remainder to Isabel and Anne, their sisters, their heirs and assigns,

the reversion of the manor of Bekhawe [Becca Hall] and lands and tenements, rents and services, in Abyrforth [Aberford] and Luttryngton [Lotherton] in the County of York. Reciting that he, John Peghan, and William Hardyng had leased the aforesaid manor, lands, tenements, rents and services to Thomas Fulthorp, knight, deceased, and Margaret Soureby for life, reserving the reversion to him the said John Peghan, as contained in a fine in the king's court.

Witnesses. John Thrisk, Alderman, Christopher Spenser, esquire, John Thwenge, gentleman.

Given, 4 April 36 Henry VI [1458].   [Latin]

(ff. 159v-160) GIFT.

Margaret Sourby of York,

to William, Prior of Holy Trinity Priory in Mekilgate, John Thresk, citizen and merchant of York, Christopher Spenser, esquire, and John Thwenge of York, gentleman,

all her goods and chattels and all debts owed to her.

Given, 4 April 36 Henry VI [1458].

Subscribed. Gunby.   [Latin]

LEASE.[82]

The Mayor and Commonalty of York,

to John Long, senior, of York, miller,

a piece of land at the end of Castilgate, one part lying along that street as far as the dike of the king's tower, and containing in length from north to south thirty-nine yards, and the other part lying from the high street abutting on the wall of the garden of the Friars Minor as far as the dike of the tower of the king's castle, in length, from east to west, seventy yards.

Term. 101 years from the feast of St. Martin next.

Rent. 2s. p.a. payable to the Wardens of Ouse Bridge.

If the rent was ever half a year in arrears, the Mayor and Commonalty were to have re-entry.

The lessee was to enclose the land at his own expense.

The indenture was made on 8 November 22 Edward IV [1482] and sealed by both parties on 9 January 22 Edward IV [1483].

[Latin]

(f. 160v) [Blank].

(f. 161) *Thordinance of the Science of Tixtwryters, Lominers, Noters, Turners and Florisshers whithin the Citie of York, suburbs and fraunchesse theroff*.[83]

---

[82] In a later hand than the preceding entry.

[83] Printed, in part, in *York Civic Records*, Vol. II, pp. 78-80. Earlier ordinances are to be found in *York Memorandum Book* I, pp. 56-7.

Memorandum, that where it was agreid and graunted in the tyme of the right wurshipfull Sir William Tod, knyght, late Maire of the Citie of York [1487],[84] aswelby thassent and concent of the same Maire as by thassent and concent of all other Aldermen and Common Counceil of the same citie, at the especiall instance and request of all thoccupacionz and sciencez of the tixte writers, luminers, noters, turners and florisshers of the same citie, certein ordinancez concernyng the publique common well of the said citie and the prosperoux continuaunce of the same occupacions and scienciez fermely to be observed and keped, and the same ordin- ancez to be regestred in the regestre of the said citie, which graunte notwithstonding, the regestering of the same ordinancez for certein concideracionez was deferred and prolonged to the tyme of the right worshipfull Sir William White, Maire of the said citie, in whos tyme of maraltie, that is to say the 18th day of January, the 7th yere of the reign of Kyng Herry the 7th [1492], it was agreid and clerely determyned in the Counceil Chaumbre of the said citie by thassent and concent of all the presens undre written, that is to say William White, Maire of the said citie, Richard York, knyght, Nicholas Loncastre, William Chymney, William Tod, knyght, Robert Hancok, John Gilliot, Aldermen, William Fairfax, Re- corder, John Stokdale and John Huton, Shereffs of the same citie, Thomas Alayne, William Tayte, William Barker, Richard Clerk, John Shaw, Robert Johnson, Alexandre Dauson, John Elwald and John Norman of the 24, that all such articlez comprysed within a sedule of parchement which the said tixtwryters, luminers, noters, turners and flurisshers shewed tofore the said presens concernyng the said ordinancez shuldbe registred in the common registre of the said citie, the tenour of which ordinance enseweth.

Furst, it is ordand, enact and establisshed by the said Maire, Aldermen and Common Counceill toforesaid, at the humble sup- plicacion of the company of the sciencez above written, that from hensforth yerely there shalbe elect emongs tham two sufficient and able men to be serchours in the same crafts for oon hole yere com- plete, undre the payn of 3s 4d to be forfeit holy to the chambre by the said craft.

Also, that noon of the said craft or science set up a shop to write, lumin, note, turne or flurissh within the citie, suburbs or fraun- chesse of the same openly or cuvertly unto such tyme he be found

[84] The ordinances of 1487 appear on ff. 149-150.

able to exercise that occupacion by the serchourz forsaid, undre the pein of 13s 4d to be devided equally unto the use of the chambre and the said craft.

(f. 161v) And that every apprentice which haith well and truelie served his yeres within this citie, shall pay at such tyme as he shall set up for hym selff in the same craft 3s 4d, to be devyded as is to foresaid. And if their be ony such that have not bein apprentice within the said citie in the forsaid craft, that intendeth for to setup as a maister in the same, shall pay for his upset 13s 4d to be devyded as is to forsaid.

Also that noone of the said craft take his apprentice for lesse termez then for 7 yeres complete, and that his indentourz be shewed within thre weiks after his band unto the serchours of the same craft for the tyme being, undre the pain of 10s. And that no man of the craft forsaid lerne no person of other craft any part theroff, but onlie his apprentice, under the pein abovesaid to be devided as is abovesaid.

Also it is ordand as fare as is in the said Maier, his bredre Aldermen and other of the Commune Counceill of the Citie of York, that noo preste within this citie, suburbs and frraunchesse of the same havyng a competent salary, that is [to] say 7 marks or above, exercise the craft of tixtwryters, luminers, noters, turnourz or florisshourz within the same for his singler prouffit and lucour, nor take noon apprentice, hierdman or other servant to his service nor make no barganes or cov[en]auntz with ony person to that entent, undre the pain of 40s. to be devyded as is to foresaid. Provided always that it shalbe lefull to any preste to write, lumine, note, turn or florissh any maner buks to his propre use or to distribute to any place in way of almuse,[85] and that every preiste not havyng a competent sallary within the said citie, suburbs and fraunchiesse of the same shall exercisse the craft of tixtwryting, luminyng, notyng, turnyng and florisshing any buks at his pleasour for his propre availe and prouffite with his awn hands, not takyng apprentice or hierdman unto hyme in any wies, under the pein of 40s to be paied as is to fore said.

Also, if any aliene would settup as a maisteir in the craft abovesaid, after he be foundon able by the seirchours of the same for the tyme being, he shall pay for his upsett forsaid to the chambre and craft forsaid, equallye to be devided, 40s.

[85] *almuse*, alms.

(f. 162) Also, if there be any apprentice or hierdman in the said craft that withdraweth ony goods to the valour of 12d from his maister or ony other persone, he shall be warned to leif and if he eftsones doe asmuch he shall never occupy within the citie, suburbs and fraunchiesse of the same. And whate maister of the same craft that taks hym to his service and setts hyme on wark within the citie, suburbs and fraunchiesse of the same, shall forfeit to the use of the chambre and craft foresaid 10s.

Also, that no master, apprentice, nor hierdman of the said craft be rebell or otherwies mysbehave hym unto the serechourz for the tym being, hyme lawfully and curtasely serching in there occupacion, uppon the payn of 12d to be payd as is to foresaid.

Also, that every forein using any parte of the same craft that cumyth into this citie to sell any buks or to take any warke to wurk, shall pay to the upholding of their padgiant yerelie, 4d.

Also, it is ordand that if any master of the said craft havyng apprentice discesse, the which apprentice haith not served hole his yeres with his said master, he shall continowe duryng his yeres with [the wife]⁸⁶ of his said maister as long as shee kepith hir soole, except his said master pardone hym his yeres unserved, which if he so be and founden able by the serchourz he shall pay for his upsett 3s 4d in maner and fourme to be devyded as is abovesaid. And if he be not[founden]⁸⁶ able by the said serchourz upon the said pardone he shall [serve]⁸⁶ furth his yeres with what master as hyme shall best seme, undre the payn of 10s to be paid in maner and fourme abovesaid.

Also, if any master of the said craft, lawfully warned by his serchours of the same for the tyme being or ther depute to cume to any assemble at any place and houre appointed for the well of the said craft, absent hymselff willfully, [he] shall forfeit without pardone 4d as oftymes as he is so warnyd, except he can shewe a resonable excuse in that behalve. And whatsoever he be that discovers the counceill at any such assembles, if it can be proved apon hym by ony master of the same craft or any other person, he shall forfeit as oft tymez as he soo doith 12d, to be devided as is afforesaid.

(f. 162v) *Thaward of George Kyrk, merchaunt, Robert Johnson, grocer, Thomas Graa, goldsmith, and William Baker, merchaunt, maid and awarded by thaim as arbitrourz indifferently chosen be-*

⁸⁶ The omissions are supplied from the ordinances of 1487 on ff. 149-50.

*twix the tixtwriters, luminers, noters, turners and florisshers on
that oon partie, and Sir William Inceclyff, preist, on that other
partie ensewith*:—[87]

Memorandum that where diverce variauncez, controverciez and
disordes wer of late depending, stirred and moved betwix the tixtwriters, luminers, noters, turners and flurisshers of the Citie of
York on that oon pairtie, and Sir William Incecliff, preist, on that
other partie, apon which premissez the said parties, by the commaundment of the right reverent fadre in God tharchbisshop of
York, haith pitt and compremitt theim to abide the reule, award
and jugement of George Kirk, merchaunt, Robert Johnson, grocer,
Thomas Graa, goldsmyth, and William Barker, merchaunt, arbitrourz indifferently elect betwix the said parties, takyng upon the
charge of the said award and jugement after the compleints,
awnswers and replicacions of the said pairties ripelie hard and examined, by good deliberacion, awardez and demes, that almaner
accions, trespasses, debats, quarellez and demaundez dependyng
or moved betwix the said pairtez afore the day of this award, be
clerely lade oparte and forgiffin apon both parties. Also we awarde
that as for the forfett which [was] presented by the serchourz of
the said occupacion agayn the said Sir William Inceclyff be clerely
pardoned, for by our mynds we fynd hyme not lawfully warned
therof by the said serchours. Also wee deme and award that the
said Sir William and all other prestes within this citie, suburbs
and fraunchiesse of the same frome hensforth take noon apprentice
ne hiredman to set on wark in the said occupacion, apon the payn
of 40s. as oft tymez as thei or any of thame ar founden defective,
whereof the oon halff to be imploid to the common well of this
citie and the other halve to thoccupacion of tixtwriters abovesaid.
Provided alway that the said Sir William Inceclyff, and all other
prestez that haith any wark or buks in wrytyng at the tyme of
makyng of this award, have respeit to finysh all such books afor the
feist of Purificacion of Our Lady next ensewing after the date of
this award. (f. 163) Also we awarde and deme that it be leffull to
the said Sir William Inceclyff and all other preists within this
[citie], suburbs and fraunchiessez of the same, to write and make
books to ther awn proper use or to giffe in almose and charitie at
ther pleasour, so that the same bukez or ony of thame by the same

---

[87] An earlier award between the parties appears on ff. 150-150v.

Sir William or ony of the said preists or any other in his or ther namez colurable be not put to any sale undre the payne toforsaid. In wittnes of this our award wee have subscribed our namez the [blank] day of [blank].

(ff. 163v-164v) Blank.

(f. 165) On 14 March 9 Henry VII [1494], Ralph Clyfton came into the Council Chamber before Michael White, Mayor, and caused the following quitclaim to be read aloud.

QUITCLAIM.

Ralph Clyfton, son and heir of Thomas Clyfton, late of Bisshopthorp, deceased,

to Thomas Dayvell, esquire, and Elizabeth his wife, and the heirs of the said Thomas,

lands and tenements, rents, reversions and services in Bisshopthorp, Middilthorp and Bustardthorp in the County of the City of York, which lately belonged to Thomas Clyfton, his father.

Given, 14 March 9 Henry VII [1494].

The Mayor ordered the above deed to be enrolled at the request of the said Ralph Clyfton. [Latin]

(f. 165v) On 18 May 10 Henry VII [1495], Thomas Bradeley of Worssop [Worksop] in the County of Nottingham, yeoman, came before George Kyrk, Mayor, in the Council Chamber, showed the following gift made by William Metham to Elizabeth his wife and to him, Thomas Bradeley, and sought its immediate enrolment in the common book of the city.

GIFT.

William Metham of Cadeby in the County of York, gentleman,

to Elizabeth Metham, his wife, and Thomas Bradeley of Worssop in the County of Nottingham, yeoman,

all his goods and chattels and all debts owing to him.

Witnesses. Robert Holt, chaplain, William Holt of Doncastre, baxter, John Bryd of Cateby, husbandman.

Given at Cateby, 27 April 10 Henry VII [1495]. [Latin]

(ff. 166-7) On 11 June 11 Henry VII [1496], John Wyclyff of

Hornby, gentleman, and Robert Wycliff of Ellerton in Swaldale, gentleman, came into the Council Chamber on Ouse Bridge before Robert Johnson, Mayor, William Chymney, Michael Whyte, George Kirk, Thomas Gray, and John Metcalfe, Aldermen, William Neleson and Richard Thornton, Sheriffs, Thomas Alayn, Thomas Fynch, Thomas Foulneby, John Stokdale, Peter Cooke and John Pety of the Common Council, and sought the enrolment of the following two deeds in the common register of the city.

FEOFFMENT.[88]

William Marschall, Rector of the church of Wicliff and Thomas Ermyn, chaplain,

to Robert de Wycliff, clerk, and the heirs of his body, remainder to Thomas Pykworth, knight, and his male heirs begotten by Ellen, his late wife, sister of the said Robert, remainder to John, son of John de Ellerton and the male heirs of his body, on condition that he and his male heirs should be called by the name of Wyclyff and bear the arms used of old by his ancestors, the lords of the manor, remainder to Robert son of John de Langton, and the male heirs of his body, on the same condition, remainder to Thomas son of John de Lamore and the male heirs of his body, on the same condition, remainder to the said John de Langton and his heirs, on condition that he should sell the property immediately, for the greatest sum possible, and distribute the money realised in alms to the poor, for the good of the souls of the said Robert de Wiclyff, and John de Langton and their ancestors, the manor of Wycliff and the advowson of the church of Wycliff, together with all services of the free tenants of the manor and all other lands, tenements, rents and services, in Wycliff, Thorp [Thorpe, in the parish of Wycliffe], Westlaton [West Layton] and Barton in the County of York, and lands and tenements in the County of Lincoln, all of which they had by the gift and feoffment of Robert de Wycliff.

Tripartite indenture, the respective parts being sealed by William Marshall and Thomas Ermyn, Thomas Pykworth and John de Langton, and Robert de Wycliff.

Given, 20 April 13 Henry IV [1412].   [Latin]

---

[88] The descent of the manor of Wycliffe is given in the Victoria County History of the North Riding, Vol. I, p. 139.

(ff. 167-8) LEASE.

Robert Wycliff, clerk, and Thomas Pykworth, knight,

to John de Ellerton, senior, and Matilda, his wife, John son of John de Ellerton, Robert de Norton, William de Katryk and Matthew de Ellerton and the male heirs of the body of the aforesaid John son of John,

the manor of Wycliff, advowson of the church of Wycliff and lands and tenements, rents and services [as above], which they had by the feoffment of William Marshall and Thomas Ermyn, except the rights of wardship, marriage, relief and escheat of the free tenants, and all large trees growing in the wood called *Wycliffwod* and in the village and lands of Wycliff, and reserving free entry and exit to fell and remove the trees at all times of the year to the said Robert Wycliff for the term of his life.

Term. The lives of Robert de Wycliff and Thomas Pykworth, the lessors.

Rent. 20 marks p.a. to Robert de Wycliff for life, during the lifetime of Constance, widow of Nicholas de Wycliff, and 10 marks p.a. to the said Constance, and £20 p.a. to the said Robert after the death of Constance. After the death of Robert de Wycliff, 20 marks p.a. were to be paid to Thomas Pykworth during the life of Constance, and £20 p.a. after her death.

Reserving to the lessors the right of distraint in the said property and all lands and tenements of the said John de Ellerton in the liberty of Richemond, if the rent was six weeks in arrears, and the right of re-entry if the rent was a whole year in arrears and sufficient distraint could not be found, or if the said John son of John de Ellerton should die without male heirs of his body during the lifetime of either of the lessors.

The aforesaid John de Ellerton and Matilda, his wife, Robert de Norton, William de Katryk and Matthew de Ellerton were to return the manor, lands and tenements at the end of the year after the death of John son of John de Ellerton without male heirs of his body, and were afterwards to be exonerated from all rents, saving only to him and his executors all crops of corn, free entry and exit to the same, and all his goods and chattels.

Given, 6 June 13 Henry IV [1412]. [Latin]

The above deeds were enrolled at the special instance and request of John and Robert Wycliff and by order of the Mayor, Aldermen, Sheriffs and others of the Common Council. [Latin]

(f. 168) *The obit of William Spencer and others in the church of St. Martin in Conyngstrete in the City of York.*   [Latin]

This indenture tripartite maid the 10th day of the moneth of Decembre the yere of Our Lord God 1496, and where as the right wurshipfull Sir William Spencer of Bristowe, merchaunt, of his almose and charitie hath giffen and delivered to the church wardaynes of Seynt Martyn Church in Conyngstrete within the Citie of York, £20 of money toward the supportacion of divyne service within the same churche, witnesseth that the churche wardaynes graunteth, and by thes presents bynd theym and theyr successourz, yerely in the said churche to make or cause to be maid an obite, the Monday next after the Trenite Sonday, the dirige, and on the Tuesday next the obite masse, solemply with note and belles roungen as custome is in the said citie. For whiche dirige and masse the parysh prest shall perceyve of the said churche wardaynez 6d, and every other prest of the same churche personally beyng at the said dirige and masse 4d, the parysch clerk for ryngyng 6d, the under clerk 2d and for 2 lightez apon the herse 8d, and to 4 of most poure persones in the same parysche 4d, and the belman for publishing of the day tofore the said obite 4d.

At whiche masse the Maier and Shireffs of York for tyme beyng yerely shall personaly come and offer ychone of theyme 1d, to thentent to see the said obite be yerely duely performed. And the Maier for his said comyng shall perceyve of the said churche wardaynes 12d and either of the Shireffs 6d.

And for mor suertie for performaunce of the said obite in maner and forme abovesaid, the said parochaynes hath purchassed with the said money, lands and tenementez in Yapham, Meltonby and Wighton [Market Weighton] in the Counte of York to the yerely value of 30s over almaner chargez and [? sessez], in whiche lands and tenementez John Metcalff, Notarie Publik, James Sheffeld, William Mason, William Skypton, Roger Breer, Robert Grenebanke, Robert Skypton, Richard Scott and Richard Makblith ar enfeffed and full poscescion hath of the same to thentent abovesaid. And if it happyn 6 or mo of the said feoffes to discese, then the other cofeoffez beyng over liff and havyng the survivour shall enfeffe in the (f. 168v) said lands and tenementez other 9 discrete persons of the said parysche, and so infenytly to succede to thentent that they shall suffr the church wardaynes of the said church for tyme beyng yerely to perceyve and take almaner rents and profitez comyng and growyng of and in all the said lands and tenementez and every parcell therof, to thentent to performe the said obite in maner and forme abovesaid. And the superplusage and residue of the said rents and profitez over the said obite and necessarie reparacionz savely to be kept and emploied to adornaments or other necessarie chargez within the same churche.

And the said parochianez graunteth by thes presentez that the parysch prest every Sonday shall specially pray for the prosperite and welfare of Johnet Spencer, William Chymney, Alderman, and Dame Margaret his wiff, and after their discesez for theyr saulez and for the saulez of Richard Spencer, sometyme Shireff of York and Alison, his wiff, of William Hovyngham and Alison, his wiff, of William Spencer and Alison, his wife, and all cristen saulez. And iff the said church wardaynes and parochianez and their successours be remysse and necligent and performe not yerely the obite in maner and forme abovesaid, then it shalbe laufull unto the Mayre of the said citie and his successours so often tymez to entre into all the said lands and tenements and every parcell therof and theym to hold and have, and all the rents and profitez therof comyng and growyng to resceyve and take theym for that yere, and to make the said obit in maner and forme abovesaid, and the residue therof to convert and emploie to the comon well of the said citie for the said yere.

In witnes of the premysses wel and treuly to be observed and performed as is abovesaid, to one partie of this tripartie indenture remanyng with the said Janet Spencer and hir coexecutours, the seale of thoffice of marialtie of the said citie and the sealez of the said John Metcalfe, James Sheffeld, William Mason, William Skipton, Roger Breer, Robert Grenbank, Robert Skypton, Richard Scot and Richard Makblith ar put. And to an other part of the same indentur remanyng within the tresorie and registred in the registre of the said citie, the sealez of the said Janet and hir coexecutours and John Metcalfe [etc., as above] ar put. And to the third part of the same indenture remanyng with the said church wardaynes and parochianez and theyr successours, the sealez of thoffice of the said marialtie and the said Janet and hir coexecutours ar put. Written and delivered the day and yere abovesaid.

(f. 169) *The judgment of the searchers [in the dispute] between*

*the Prioress and Convent of Nonmonkton and Elizabeth Laton and
William Thorp, her son.*   [Latin]

Robert Baynes and Christopher Horner, searchers of the stone-
cutters and masons, and John Couper and William Chambre,
searchers of the carpenters, were chosen impartially by Thomas
Gray, Mayor, in the dispute between the Prioress and Convent of
Nonmonkton and Elizabeth Laton, widow, and William Thorp,
her son, as to the ownership of a wall of wood, plaster and tiles
lying between their tenements, in the parish of Holy Trinity in
Gotheromgate.

The searchers found that the wall belonged to the Prioress and
Convent and their tenement as of right, and that it was lawful
for them to demolish and remove it; also that a lead *gutter* adjacent
to the wall belonged to the tenement of the said Elizabeth and
William.

28 January——[year omitted] Henry VII.   [Latin]

(ff. 169-70). ORDINANCES OF THE BUTCHERS.[89]

18 December 14 Henry VII [1498].

John Metcalf, Maior; William Chymney, John Gilliot, William
White, Michael White, George Kyrke, Thomas Gray [Alder-
men]; Brian Palmes, Recorder; John Elwald; John Byrkhede and
Richard Wynder, Sheriffs; Thomas Alayn, William Tayte, John
Hagge, Miles Grenebank, William Berker, baker, John Shawe,
William Berker, mercer, John Stokdale, Peter Cooke, Edward
Foster, John Custaunce, John Pette, Richard Thornton, Bertram
Dawson of the Twenty Four.

Assembled in the Counseill Chambre within the Comon Hall,
for asmyche as divers persons enfraunchest as buchers and other
of this citie apon credence takez stuff and other goods of other
fraunchest men and foreyns, for whiche stuff and goods when theyr
credetours askez or sewez for theyr duetez the said persons, aswell
by proteccions as by letterz under the captaynes sealez of Calice
[Calais], Berwicke, or of other places privleged, delayes and barres
ther said creditours of theyr detts and duetez to ther utter undoyng
and to the gret (f. 169v) sclaunder and infamye of this wurshipfull
citie. For refomacion herof it is ennacted and ordayned by the said

[89] Printed in *York Civic Records*, Vol III pp. 187-8. For earlier ordinances see
York Memorandum Book I, pp. 57-9, 83-4, and for those of 1528, *York Civic
Records*, Vol. III, p. 115.

presence, that if any maner fraunchestman of this citie herafter pur-
chace any proteccion or other letter of Calice, Berwike or of any
other place priveleged, and allege and shewe theym in court or out
of court within this citie, to thentent to delay and barre any crede-
tour or man or woman of this citie of suche duetez and detts as
they awe unto ther credetours or of any parte therof, that every such
person so doyng to forfette and leese his fraunches and libertiez
within this citie.

Item, it is ordayned that the Maier and Chamberleyns for the
tyme beyng shall comaund the sersors of the buchers to attend
open theym and every market day to serche all foreyn buchers, and
no foreyn bucher to putt to saile any flesche tofore he come to the
Maier and Chamberleyns for his serse. And that every foreyn
bucher bryng his stuffe and ware to the Thuresdaymarket, levyng
none of his flesche in any house or hosterie within the citie or
suburbs, and they to depart furth of the said market by 4 of the
cloke at efternone every market day from All Halow mes unto
Candelmez, and by 6 of the cloke at efternone from Candelmes unto All Halowmes, and that he hawke no maner flesche within this
citie, suburbs of the same, apon payn of forfetour of his flesche and
40d to the chambre and craft by even porcions, for every tyme he
doth contrary to any article heroff.

Item, if a woman that was a bucher wif within this citie herafter
happen to take to husband a man of any other occupacion, the said
husband not to occupie any thyng bylongyng to the occupacion of
buchers tofore he have maid fyne and agrement with the chambre
and craft after the discreccion of the Maier for tym beyng.

Item, that no bucher take none apprentice bot by indenture and
that for terme of 7 yere and that he shewe his indenture to his
sersours within 14 daies next after he be fest apprentice, apon payn
of 40d to the chambre and craft.

(f. 170) Item, if any bucher be disobedient or rebell unto his
sersors in theyr due and lawfull serche makyng, to forfett every
tyme 6s 8d to the chambre and craft.

Item, if any bucher be found with any falshed or untreuth to the
value of 12d or more, he to forswere the said occupacion for ever
within this citie.

Item, it is ordayned that no bucher, nor none other man or
woman of this citie, herafter at any tyme of the yeer shall not kep no
swyn in swynstyes or in any other house or place within the citie

or suburbs of the same, for the foule corrupcion that cometh of theym, apon payn of forfetour at the first tyme for every swyn 40d, the second tyme 6s 8d and so every tyme for every swyne to double theyr forfettour to the chambre toward the comon well of this citie.

(f. 170). *The Ordinance of Glovers and Perchmyners.*[90]

Memorandum that the 18th day of Marche the yere of the reign of King Henry VII after the conquest the 15th [1500], in the tyme of marialtie of the right wurshipfull Sir William Neleson, then Maier of this wurshipfull Citie of York, Nicholas Lancastre, John Gilliot, William White, Michael White, George Kyrk, John Metcalf, John Elwald, John Stokdale, Aldermen, Alan Staveley, Robert Pette, Shireffs of the said citie, William Tayte, Miles Grenebank, William Barker, baker, John Shaw, Thomas Foulneby, William Berker, mercer, Edward Foster, Thomas Derby, John Custaunce, John Pette, Richard Thornton, Miles Arawme, Bertram Dawson, Thomas Jameson, John Doggeson, John Byrkhede, Richard Wynder, assembled opon Ousebrigge at the especiall request and prayer of the hole craftez of glovers and parchemeners within the said citie, in reformacion of the breke of the comon lawe emong other thyngs. It was ennact, ordeyned and established by the said Maier, Aldermen, Shireffs and the Comon Counseill of this abovesaid citie, fermely hereafter to be kept and observed, that for so myche as the buchers of this citie by many and diverse yerez hertofore past hath used to cut of the hedez, chekez and erez and a gret part of the neke of all suche shep skynnes as they have sold to the said glovers (f. 170v) and parchemeners, or to any other man contrary to the ordinance of our soveraigne lord the kyngs lawez in that behalve provided, for which theyr wrongfull and mysdemeanour in that byhalf, the said day and yere it was ennacted by the said Maier and by thassent and consent of the said Aldermen, Shireffs and Comon Counseill, that the said buchers shall pay and delivere unto the hands of my Lord Maier and his chamber toward the common well of this citie,——[blank]. And that from hensforth the said buchers nor theyr successors sell no shep skynne that any burchers

[90] Printed in *York Civic Records*, Vol. III pp. 183-4. See also ordinances of the glovers, dated 1475 and 1483, ff. 140v-141 above. Earlier ordinances of the parchment makers are printed in *York Memorandum Book* I, pp. 67, 81-2; *ibid* II, pp. 128-9, 237-8.

of this citie sells contrary to this ordinance of 12d to the comon well of this citie. And if any glover and parchemener of this citie or any other person by and resceyve any maner of shep skynnes that hase not the hole chekez and eyrez, to forfett to the common well of this citie for every shep skynne so bought and ressavyd by theym 12d. And that no glover, puchemaker, sadiler, cutler, armorer ne shomaker of this citie from nowfurth wirk no sheyp skynnes barked[91] opon payn of every shep skynne of 20d to the common well of this citie.

(f. 171)[92] *Memorandum that thys ys parte of the ordynans of the Skynners.*[93]

Primo, that all the forfetts that er dewe in the skynner craft and schalbe in tyme comynge be raisyd, and the tone half of them be paid to the chambre and the oder half unto the craft for to maynteyn ther pagent and ther light.

Item, yf any wyll sell old furrs for newe or put lambe fell or porcion of lambe fell in furrs of boge[94] or scherlyngs[95] in lambe-furrs, or sell any old pellour[96] for newe, or put in any newe furr old pellour, that he pay half a marke to be payd in maner abowe said. And that noo perfornesyng[97] be put in newe pelluz and sold for newe but if yt be hale,[98] brode[99] and clene ledder, apon payne of the forsaid payne.

Item, that all the uphalders[1] that sells furrs within this cittye or subberbs be contributarye and pay unto the pagant of the skynners in the play of Corpus Christi.

---

[91] *barked*: tanned.

[92] f. 171 is a larger folio than normal with writing in two columns on one side only. It was apparently folded and inserted when the volume was rebound.

[93] Printed in *York Civic Records*, Vol. III pp. 189-90. Similar, though presumably earlier ordinances are to be found in *York Memorandum Book*, I, pp. 60-1, 63-7, and more detailed ones, dated 19 Oct. 1582, in House Book 28 ff. 69v-72 (*York Civic Records*, Vol. VIII pp. 61-3).

[94] *boge*, budge: imported lambskins. Derived from the place name Bougie in N. Africa, a flourishing trading centre from the eleventh to the early fourteenth century. In the fourteenth century, the term was extended to include lambskins from other Mediterranean lands, in particular, the fine Spanish lambskins. (Elspeth M. Veale, *The English Fur Trade in the Later Middle Ages*, glossary).

[95] *scherlyng*, shearling: the fleece of a sheep that has been once shorn.

[96] *pellour*, pelure: furs, also used in a more limited sense to indicate lamb and sheep skins (E. M. Veale).

[97] *perfornesyng*, performing: trimming.

[98] *hale*: whole, sound.

[99] *brode*: broad.

[1] *uphalder*, upholder: a dealer in second hand clothing and bedding (E. M. Veale).

Item, if any of the skynners befor said be rebell, dystrobe[2], mys-say or dysabay any of the sersors or the pagent masters of ther craft that schalbe for the tyme in doyng of ther office dewly, that he pay 6s 8d in the maner aforsaid.

Item, if it soo be that any body wyll compleyn them of any maner of furr to be sessyd, that they come unto the serssors of the said craft that schalbe for the tyme, within the fyrst quarter of a yere next after the delyverance of the furre, and than the serssors schall have power to serche that furr within the said fyrst quarter and to cause correke and amend dewly the defawtts yf any be, and after the said quarter the serssours schall noght be compellyd to serche in no suche caise.

Thes to be the taske of our crafte[3]

Primo, for weshynge and fleschynge of 100 lame skynnys, 4d
Item, for 100 tewynge[4], 16d
Item, for a tymmer[5] of fechys[6] tewyng 8d
Item, for a tymmer of martrones[7] tewyng 12d
Item, for a tymmer of mynkys tewyng 12d
Item, for a tymmer of bevers tewyng 20d
Item, for a tymmer of otters tewyng. 3s 4d
Item, for a tymmer of foxes tewyng 3s 4d
Item, for a tymmer of catts tewyng 20d
Item, for 1000 graywarke[8] tewyng 5s
Item, for 1000 calabar[9] tewyng 5s
Item, for a tymmer of armyns[10] tewyng 6d
Item, for a tymmer of letys[11] tewynge 3d
Item, for 100 conys[12] tewyng 20d

[2] *dystrobe*, distrouble: disturb, trouble greatly.
[3] Printed in *York Civic Records*, Vol. III, p. 190. The list is identical, except for variations of spelling, to that dated 1582 and printed in *York Civic Records*, Vol. VIII, pp. 62-3.
[4] *tew*, taw: to dress skins (E. M. Veale).
[5] *tymmer*, timber: originally the boards between which skins were packed, but later a bundle of 40 skins (E. M. Veale).
[6] *fechys*, fitches: skins of the polecat (E. M. Veale).
[7] *martron*: marten.
[8] *graywarke*, greywerk: winter squirrel skins with the grey back (E. M. Veale).
[9] *calabar*, calabre: squirrel skins, originally from Calabria, S. Italy (E. M. Veale).
[10] *armyns*: ermines.
[11] *letys*, lettice: skins of the snow-weasel; more valuable than minever, less expensive than ermine for which it was often used as a substitute (E. M. Veale).
[12] *conys*: rabbits.

Item, for 100 lambe betyng and sewyng	4d
Item for 100 hoppyng and schapyng	8d
Item, for 100 palestryng[13]	12d
Item, for a dossen tavillions[14]	4d
Item, for 1000 graywarke wanyng and brayng[15]	2s
Item, for the potyng of pynshyng[16] of rightyng of womes and riggez[17]	2s
Item, for warpyng of all maner of furrs of riggez and womes of furre.	2d
Item, for testyng of a furre.	2d
Item, for the semyng and travesyng and the casyng[18] of a furre.	6d
Item, for 50 purde[19] semys sewyng	1d
Item, for 100 putts[20] schapyng and sewyng	6d
Item, for a tymmer of cropps[21] makyng	3s 4d
Item, for a tymmer of putts sewyng the overquart[22] semys.	1d
Item, for a fur of cropps and a fur of putts travesyng, sewyng and casyng.	4d
Item, for 100 conys cuttyng, betynge, sewyng and swarynge[23]	10d
Item, for a furr of schanks[24] makyng	6d
Item, for a furre of purde maid owt of tavillions of 4 yerds wyde and i yerd depe.	8d
Item for a fur of brode menevere[25] makynge of tavilions.	6d

(f. 171v) [Blank].

---

[13] *palestryng*: ? stitching in *tiers* or vertical strips (E. M. Veale).

[14] *tavillions*, tavelons: 1. the boards between which 4 skins were packed. 2. bundles of 4 skins. 3. possibly strips of squirrel scraps (E. M. Veale).

[15] *wanyng and braying*: processes in the preparation of squirrel skins, probably after tawing: beating? (E. M. Veale).

[16] *pynshyng*: folds, gathers, pleats.

[17] *womes and riggez*: bellies and backs, 2 types of hides of different thicknesses.

[18] *casyng*: to stitch skins together in a rectanglar shape (E. M. Veale).

[19] *purde*, pured: trimmed (E. M. Veale).

[20] *putts*, potes etc: furs made of the paws of an animal—squirrel unless the animal is named (E. M. Veale).

[21] *cropps*, croupes: furs made of skins from the heads of animals. If the animal is not named squirrel is probably to be understood (E. M. Veale).

[22] *overquart*, overthwart: transverse, cross.

[23] *swarynge*, squaring: same meaning as casyng, see note 18. (E. M. Veale).

[24] *schanks*: furs made from skins of legs of *budge*. (E. M. Veale).

[25] *menevere*, meniver: not ermine, less expensive than ermine (E. M. Veale).

(f. 171A) *The ordinance of Skynners.*[26]

Memorandum that the last day of Aprile the yere of the reign of King Henry VIIth after the conquest of Yngland the 15th [1500], in the tyme of the marialte of the right wurshipfull Sir William Neleson, then Maier of this wurshipfull Citie of York, Nicholas Lancastre, John Gilliot, Michael White, George Kyrk, Thomas Gray, John Metcalff, John Elwald, John Stokdale [Aldermen], Alan Staveley, Robert Petty, Shireffs of the said citie, William Taite, Miles Grenebank, William Barker, baker, Thomas Fynch, John Shawe, William Barker, mercer, Edward Foster, Thomas Darby, John Custaunce, John Pette, Richard Thornton, Thomas Jameson, John Doggeson, Richard Wynder assembled on Ousebrige at the especiall request of the hole crafte of skynners within this citie and suburbs.

It was ennacted by the said presence fermly hereafter to be observed, that no taillour nor any other person within this citie, suburbs and precincts of the same, from now furth fure no man's ne woman's gownes, colers ne cuffez, or any garments of any person or persons, opon payn of forfettour for every tyme 6s 8d, wherof 5s to the chambre and 20d to the craft of skynners. Provided allway that the skynners of this citie that nowe ar and theyr successours foure to every fraunchest person of this citie a gown or other garment of two yerds for 8d, of 3 yerds for 12d, of 4 yerds for 16d, and so after the rate. And the said skynners to fure to all foreyns and unfraunchest persons as thei and the said skynners can agree to ther most avauntage. And that no skynner ne any other person of this citie from hensfurth wirke no stuffe tawed by any glover, apon payn of forfettour for every tyme 6s 8d in maner and forme abovesaid.

Item, that no skynner ne non other person of this citie wirk ne tawe no prest stuff that is bought rawe, ne fure no prest gownez or garments in theyr chambres, opon payn off forfettour for every tyme 20s, wherof 13s 4d to the chambre and 6s 8d to the craft of skynners.

And the grauntez and ordinauncez abovesaid to be kept ferme and stable, the said skynners byndeth theym and ther successours to make and sustene yerely of ther costs and charges a hate of

[26] Also entered in House Book 8, f. 79v. and printed in York Civic Records, Vol. II. pp. 151-2.

mayntenaunce of good, fyne and pure gray for the honour and wurship of this citie.[27]

(f. 171Av.) On 25 April 16 Henry VII [1501], George Daddy, gentleman, and Sybil, his wife, came into the Council Chamber before John Stokdale, Mayor, showed two deeds and asked that they should be enrolled in the common register of the city. The said Sybil, questioned by the Mayor, declared that she had made and sealed the deeds of her own free will.

(ff. 171Av-172) FEOFFMENT.

George Daddy of Somercotez in the County of Lincoln, gentleman, and Sybil, his wife,
to George Kyrk, citizen and Alderman of York,
messuages, lands and tenements in the Flesshamels alias Nedelergate, which formerly belonged to John Newton, late citizen and dyer, and also four cottages in Peesholme, lying in width between the tenement of Thomas Fryston, chaplain of the chantry founded in the church of St. Saviour in honour of St. James the Apostle, on the west, and the tenement of William Long, chaplain of the chantry in the Cathedral Church of St. Peter, founded in honour of the Blessed Mary Magdalene, on the east, and in length from Peesholme in front as far as the king's dyke behind.

Witnesses. John Stokdale, Mayor, Nicholas Lancastre, Doctor of Laws and Alderman, George Essex, and Thomas Bankhous, Sheriffs, Thomas Folnetby, Edward Foster, John Shawe.

Given at York, 20 April 16 Henry VII [1501].   [Latin]

QUITCLAIM.

George Daddy and Sybil his wife,
to George Kyrk,
messuages, lands and tenements in the Flesshameles and four cottages in Peesholme [as above].

Given, 22 April 16 Henry VII [1501].   [Latin]

(f. 172v) GRANT.

George Daddy and Sybil, his wife, kinswoman and heir of John Newton, late citizen and Alderman of York,

[27] The Cap of Maintenance is worn by the sword-bearer on state occasions and is never doffed even in the presence of the sovereign. The first one is said to have been given by Richard II in 1393 and a later cap, made in 1580, is still preserved in the Mansion House. The one in current use was presented by George V in 1915.

to George Kirk,
the reversion after the death of Matilda Newton, widow, of a
messuage in Northstreyt, lying between the land of William Neleson, Alderman, and the land formerly of Thomas Wrangwisch,
late Alderman; and also of two tenements in Northstreyte between
the land of Richard Garnett, citizen, on either side.

Witnesses. John Stokdale, Mayor, George Essex, and Thomas
Bankhouse, Sheriffs.

Given at York, 25 June 16 Henry VII [1501].   [Latin]

(ff. 172v-173) CONFIRMATION.

Matilda Newton, widow,
    to George Kirk,
of the reversion after her death, of a messuage and two tenements
in Northstreyte [as above], granted to him by George Daddy and
Sybil, his wife.

Given at York, 27 June 16 Henry VII [1501].   [Latin]

(f. 173v.) PROCLAMATION.

William Dorham, late Abbot of Saynt Mare Abbay nyghe York.

Yff there bee any marcer, grosser, draper or othyr marchaunt, or
any fyschemonger, bucher or any other vitellour, or any other maner
of person or personez, what degre or estate so ever he or they be off,
within the Citie of York or the suburbez of the same, or yit in the
countre, that is awyng any maner of dett of dewtie for any maner
of vitell or any other stuffe what so ever it be, takyn by my Lord
William, Bischop of Dorham that nowe is and late the Abbot of
Saynt Mary Abby, or by any of his predecessours abbotts of the
said monestery, from the begynnyng of the warld unto Michelmesse
even last passyd, or takyn by any of theyr servaunts or officers to
the use of the said abbay, or yit any dett or dewtie d[e]we to any
servaunt or warkeman for theyr warke or service doyne at the said
abbay, lett theym come to the said Lord of Dorham to Overton at
any tyme within these 10th days next folowyng and desyre the
said dewtie and detts, and they shalbe resaved thankfully, and the
said detts and dewtyes shalbe then and there furthwith to theym
content accordyng to ryght and concience, yff any suche be awyng
and so canne be proved of treuth; for hys mynd is to mak that
monestery clere awt of dett frome the begynnyng of that monastery
unto Michelmesse even last past, as well for any detts or dewties of

any of his predecessours as for any thyng by hym takyn in his tyme or by his commaundment, and not allonely within this citie and thys countre bot also within all other placez aswell in the south partez, north, west, or the east partez of this contre. And God save the kyng's grace.

These premysez was proclamyd within the Citie of York uppon Setturday the 12th day of Novembre the 18th yere of the most noble regne of Kyng Henry the VIIth [1502], and then beyng maire of the same citie Maister Thornton, grossour.

(f. 174) On 22 November 18 Henry VII [1502], John Jameson, alias John Bradyffe, came into the Council Chamber before Richard Thornton, Mayor, William Neleson, Alderman, the Chamberlains and Common Clerk, and sought that the following acquittance should be copied in the common register.

ACQUITTANCE.
   John Jameson alias John Bradyffe of Croydon in the County of Middelsex, labourer,
   to Thomas Jameson, citizen and Alderman of York,
of all actions, real and personal, all suits, transgressions, offences, debts and demands.
   Given, 22 November 18 Henry VII [1502].   [Latin]

On 5 April 20 Henry VII [1505], William Neleson, Alderman, came into the Council Chamber before Michael White, Mayor, the Chamberlains and Common Clerk, and sought the enrolment of the following acquittance in the common register.[28]

(ff. 174v-175) ACQUITTANCE.
   William Neleson, citizen and Alderman of York,
   to Thomas Jameson of York, merchant,
of an annual rent of 13s. 4d. claimed by the Prior of St. Mary's, Kyrkham, from a capital messuage with a shop and cellar opposite the great meat market in York, lately in the tenure of Thomas Fynche of York, merchant, and which Thomas Jameson had by the gift and feoffment of the said William Neleson, together with a messuage and the houses appertaining to it in Helkell opposite Holy Trinity Church in King's Court, lately in the tenure of the

[28] This statement, with a number of omissions and corrections, has been crossed through, and repeated below in the same hand.

said Thomas Jameson, but now of Henry Marshall, and also a stone house with buildings and appurtenances there. The said messuages and house were held at an annual rent of 14s. payable to the Mayor and Commonalty and 13s. 4d. to William Neleson, of which latter payment Thomas Jameson was hereby also acquitted.

Given, 3 April 20 Henry VII [1505].   [Latin]

(ff. 175-176) INQUISITION POST MORTEM.[29]

On the estate of Thomas Fayrfaxe, knight, held at the *Guyhald* on 31 May 20 Henry VII [1505], before Michael White, Mayor, the king's escheator, by virtue of a royal writ.

The jurors, William Norton, esquire, Thomas Bankhouse, Richard Russell, Richard Vavasour, Thomas Wandesforth, gentleman, Thomas Hardsang, John Kent, gentlemen, Thomas Hogeson, John Shaw, Richard Blakburn, William Monkton, Thomas Freman of Wighall and Thomas Howe, declared on oath that Thomas Fayrfaxe was seised in demesne as of fee of the manors of Walton, Folifayt [Follifoot], Acastre Malbys and Coupmanthorp [Copmanthorp] in the County of the City of York and of 100 messuages, 300 oxgangs of land, 1000 acres of woodland, 200 acres of meadow, and 1000 acres of moor in the places aforesaid; also of five messuages in the City of York, four messuages in Thorparche and an annual rent of 5 marks from the mills at Thorparche. By a deed dated 27 November 13 Edward IV [1473], he had enfeoffed Robert Sherburn, esquire, John Malyvery, knight, Robert Radclyff, esquire, Richard Shyrburn, Thomas Sherburn, Hugh Ratclyff, Roger Ratclyffe and Roger Singleton of the aforesaid manors, lands and tenements to the use of himself. Richard Shyrburn and Thomas Sherburn, continued to hold them by the right of survivorship.

The manor of Walton and lands and tenements there were held of William Gascoigne, knight, in socage, at an annual rent of a pair of gilt spurs and a pound of cinnamon (*syninum*) for all services; they were worth £10 p.a.

The manor of Folyfate and lands and tenements there were held of the heirs of Alice de Vavasour, in socage, and were worth 20 marks p.a.

The manor of Acastre Malbys and lands and tenements there

---

[29] Printed in *Calendar of Inquisitions Post Mortem*, 2nd Series Vol II, p. 583. For an inquisition on his lands in the County of York, see *ibid* p. 582.

were held of the king as of his honour of Eye, for military service, and were worth £45 p.a.

The manor of Coupmanthorp and lands and tenements there were held of the heirs of Peter de Bruys, for what service the jurors knew not, and were worth £10 p.a.

The four messuages in Thorparche were held of Thomas Earl of Derby as of his manor of Thyrske, but the jurors did not know for what service; they were worth 40s. p.a.

The five messuages in the City of York were held of the king in free burgage as all the city was held, and were worth 4 marks p.a.

Thomas Fairfaxe, knight, held no other manors, lands or tenements in the County of the City of York on the day he died, 31 March last past [1505]. Thomas Fayrfaxe, esquire, was his son and nearest heir and was twenty-nine years of age.

Sealed by the escheator and the jurors.   [Latin]

(ff. 176-176v) On 13 June 20 Henry VII [1505], John Egremond, knight, came into the Council Chamber before Michael White, Mayor, John Beilby, Humphrey Maners, Robert Hastyngs and Richard Hesylwoode, delivered a deed of feoffment and a quitclaim and asked that they should be enrolled in the common register.

(ff. 176v-177) FEOFFMENT.
  John Egremond, knight,
    to Henry, Earl of Northumberland, William Fayrfaxe, sergeant at law, John Hall, clerk, Thomas Fairfaxe and John Pykeryng, their heirs and assigns, to the use of the said Earl,
the manor of Catterton in the County of the City of York and also all lands, tenements, rents, reversions, services, meadows, pastures, woods and commons in Catterton.

Consideration. A certain sum of money [unspecified].

Rent. 40 marks p.a. to be paid by Henry, Earl of Northumberland, during the life of the feoffor.

Appointment of George Bentley and George Battersby as attorneys to deliver seisin.

If the annual rent was not paid, John Egremond was to have re-entry.

Given, 30 May 20 Henry VII [1505].   [Latin]

(ff. 177-177v) QUITCLAIM.

John Egremond, knight,
    to Henry, Earl of Northumberland, William Fayrfaxe, John Hall,
    Thomas Fairfaxe and John Pykeryng,
the manor of Catterton and lands, tenements and appurtenances
there.
    Given, 6 June 20 Henry VII [1505].   [Latin]

(ff. 177v-178) INQUISITION POST MORTEM.[30]

on the estate of Robert Stokys, esquire, held in the *Guihalda* on
24 October 22 Henry VII [1506], before Alan Stavley, Mayor, and
the king's escheator, by virtue of a royal writ.

The jurors, Thomas Bankhouse, John White, William Lund,
Richard Garnet, John Scauceby, John Pie, Richard Blakburne,
Thomas Gudebarne, John Yorke, Richard Russell, Christopher
Gilliot and William Bradley, declared on oath that Robert Stokys
was seised on the day he died of the manor of Bekyrton [Bickerton],
one——[31] of land with a tenement in Thorparche, 1½ acres of
land in Tocwithe [Tockwith] and a waste burgage in York.

He held the manor of Bekyrton of the heirs of Lord de Mow-
bray[32] for what service the jurors knew not, and it was worth
£24.20d. p.a. The land and tenement in Thorparche were held of
William Gascoigne, knight, as of his manor of Thorparche, for
what service the jurors knew not, and were worth 4d. p.a. The land
and tenement in Tocwithe were held of the heirs of Lord de
Trussbutt[33] for what service the jurors knew not, and were worth
16d. p.a. The tenement in York was held of the king in burgage
and was worth nothing.

Robert Stoks was the son and nearest heir of Robert Stoks the
father and was thirty-two years of age.
    Sealed by the escheator and jurors.   [Latin]

(ff. 178-179v) INQUISITION POST MORTEM.[34]

on the estate of Thomas Davell (or Dayvell), held in the *Guihald*

---

[30] Printed in *Calendar of Inquisitions Post Mortem*, 2nd series, Vol. III, pp. 144-5.
[31] Word omitted, given as *rood* in Cal. I.P.M.
[32] *held of John Roucliff, knight*, in Cal. I.P.M.
[33] *held of James Roos, esquire*, in Cal. I.P.M.
[34] Listed as indexed but now missing, in *Calendar of Inquisitions Post Mortem*, 2nd
Series, Vol. III, p. 606.

on 9 August 22 Henry VII [1507], before John Birkhed, Mayor, and escheator, by virtue of a royal writ.

The jurors, William Barker, baker, William Robynson, John Bateman, Richard Blakburn, William Nettilton, Nicholas Johnson, Matthew Cottes, Nicholas Bakster, John Tenaunt, Robert Fonse, Henry Mores, Robert Fraunkesh and Nicholas Maland, declared on oath that Thomas Davell was seised in demesne as of fee tail of the manor of Tokwith, ten messuages, sixteen tofts, a mill, forty ox-gangs of land, fifty acres of meadow, sixty acres of pasture, ten acres of woodland and 15s. rent in Tokwith, a cottage in Marston and 6s. rent in York; that the said property in Tokwith was worth £16 p.a. and was held of James Roos of Ingmanthorp, esquire, for fealty and 1d. p.a. rent for all services. The cottage in Marston was worth 4s. 6d. and was held of the Abbot of Fountains for fealty. The rent in York was held of the king in free burgage.

Recital that by a fine levied in the king's court on the quindene of Easter, 3 Richard III, *nuper de facto et non de jure Regis Anglie*, Thomas Davell had acknowledged that the aforesaid property belonged to Elizabeth, wife of Seth Snawsell, by virtue of a feoffment made by him to the said Seth and Elizabeth and William Snawsell. They had then granted the property to Thomas Davell and the male heirs of his body, with the reversion to them the said Seth, Elizabeth and William Snawsell and the heirs of Elizabeth.

By another fine levied by Thomas Davell and Elizabeth, his wife, in the king's court, on the octave of St. Michael 9 Henry VII [1493], they had acknowledged that eight messuages, two tofts, 120½ acres of land and five acres of meadow in Bishopthorpe belonged to Elizabeth, wife of Seth Snawsell, by virtue of a feoffment made by Thomas and Elizabeth Davell to Seth, Elizabeth and William Snawsell. The latter had then granted the property to the said Thomas and Elizabeth Davell and the male heirs of the body of Thomas, with the reversion to the feoffors. It was worth £6 13s 4d and was held by Thomas Davell of the king in chief, in socage, by fealty and for a rent of 2 marks p.a. for all services.

The jurors stated that Elizabeth, wife of Thomas Davell, Elizabeth, wife of Seth Snawsell, and William Snawsell had died during the lifetime of Thomas Davell, and that the latter had died without male heirs of his body. The property ought to remain to the said Seth for life and afterwards to John Snawsell, son and heir of Elizabeth, his wife.

They also recited Letters Patent dated at Westminster, 28 January 10 Henry VII [1495],[35] pardoning Thomas Dayvell and Elizabeth, his wife, for acquiring the property in Bishopthorpe from Seth Snawsell, esquire, Elizabeth his wife and William Snawsell, his father, without the king's licence.

Thomas Dayvell died on 17 September 22 Henry VII [1506]. John Snawsell was his kinsman and nearest heir, being the son and heir of Elizabeth, daughter and heir of William Dayvell, brother and heir of Thomas. He was twenty-six years of age.

Sealed by the escheator and jurors.   [Latin]

(f. 180) [Blank].

(f. 180v) *Boundaries and Limits of York.*[36]

15 November 23 Henry VII [1507].

John Birkhed, Mayor, Brian Palmes, Recorder, William Neleson, Thomas Jameson, Robert Petty, John Dogeson, John Shaw and Bartram Dawson, Aldermen, Robert Petty, Thomas Bankhouse, Thomas Parcour, John Hall, William Wilson and Thomas Drawswerd of the Twenty Four, Edward Clifford, John Chapman and John Tramell, Chamberlains.

On the said Monday, all the persons named above with several other persons and citizens began to note and view the boundaries and limits aforesaid, from the River Ouse on the north as far as a certain bridge in the Fetesyng, called in English Littelyng; and so extending by a ditch and a *meer* next to the Spitelwell by a way next to the mill of the Abbot of St. Mary's of York, and thence as far as the Mawdleyn Spitell in the highway which leads from York to Clifton. And so as far as the mill formerly of John de Roucliff and now of the heirs of William Yngilby, knight. And thence by a way next to the gallows of the Abbot of St. Mary's aforesaid and where there was anciently a *watergat* in the *outgang* which leads to the forest of Galtres as far as a certain wooden bridge there. And so by a *merr* as far as Whitstoncros above Astilbrig, and so by a large stone as far as the River Fosse, descending always alongside the river on the west side to the water mills of the aforesaid abbot. And

---

[35] C.P.R., 1494-1509, p. 12, where the surname is spelt Daynell.

[36] The description is almost identical to that of 1442, ff. 94-94v. above. It is printed in Drake's *Eboracum*, p. 245, where the date is wrongly given as 23 Henry VI, and translated in Thomas Widdrington's *Analecta Eborancensia*, pp. 129-30.

thence beyond the River Fosse next to the said mills on the south side, extending as far as a certain place where a wooden cross stands on Heworthmore next to the way which leads to Stokton. And thence to the stone cross at the west end of the township of Heworth to the Theyfbrig and so by a way to the wooden cross in the way which leads to Osbaldwik. So proceeding in the highway which leads to Kekysby [Kexby] to the cross next to the bridge beyond the mill of St. Nicholas. And so returning from the cross next to (f. 181) the mill by a way which leads to the Grendiks next to the close of St. Nicholas, and thence as far as the cross in the Grendiks next to the gallows of St. Leonards. And thence beyond Tilmyer by a certain way leading to the wooden cross in the way which leads to Fulforth next to Halgarthsike. And so extending directly to the River Ouse and beyond the River Ouse to a certain cross called Hadilcrosse in the way which leads from the City of York towards Bishopthorpe. And thence beyond the field called the Newfeld as far as Knaresmyer beyond the gallows standing there on the south side of the said gallows as far as the Outgang leading to the moor called Yorkesmyer. And thence by a certain rivulet as far as the stone bridge at the end of the township of Holgate, descending always by a ditch there on the west side to the Fletbrig in the Bishopfeld on the west side of the River Ouse.

These boundaries and limits were assigned by the discretion and advice of the council and lawyers aforesaid, according to the form and effect of old deeds, registers and other writings of the city, in the maner and form drawn up at those times.   [Latin]

(f. 181v) AGREEMENT.

John Birtby, chaplain of the chantry of St. James in St. Mary's Church in Castlegate, and his successors, were to pay 18d annually to the church wardens of St. Margaret's church as his predecessors did, for the provision of two candles to burn before the image of the crucifixion of Our Redeemer in St. Margaret's Church, annually on the feast of St. Peter ad Vincula.

Penalty 2s.

The agreement was reached between the parties, called before John Birkhed, Mayor, in the Council Chamber on Ouse Bridge, 20 January 22 Henry VII [1507].

Sealed with the mayoral seal and enrolled in the small register of the city on the date aforesaid.   [Latin]

(ff. 182-182v). On 10 April 23 Henry VII [1508], Thomas Langton came before John Pette, Mayor, Richard Makblith, Richard Gurnell and John Roger, Chamberlains, read two deeds and asked that they be enrolled in the common register as follows.

FEOFFMENT.

Thomas Langton, senior, of Huddilston in the County of York, esquire,

to Thomas Darcy, knight, Lord Darcy, Thomas Dalby, Archdeacon of Richmond, Thomas Magnus, Archdeacon of the *Estrithing*, John Vavasour, William Eleson, Thomas Meryng, John Pulleyn, Thomas Langton, junior, Roger Wilberfosse and Ralph Auger, gentlemen, in performance of the last will of the said Thomas Langton, senior,

the manor of Huddelston and lands, tenements, rents, reversions and services in Huddelston and Shirburn, and lands and tenements in York.

Appointment of Richard Kendale, clerk, and George Parker as attorneys to deliver seisin.

Given, 24 March 23 Henry VII [1508].   [Latin]

(ff. 182v-183v) DEED TO DECLARE THE USES OF A FEOFFMENT.

Thomas Langton the elder, of Huddelston, squire,

to Thomas Darcy, Thomas Dalby, Thomas Magnus and other feoffees in the manor of Huddelston,

to allow Sir Marmaduke Constable, knight, and others whom he had enfeoffed to the use of Thomas Langton, his cousin and heir apparent, and Elizabeth his wife, with lands and tenements in Fenton, Biggyng, Abirfforth, Ferburn [Fairburn], Barston [Barkston] and Marshland in the County of York, to supplement them, if their annual value was less than £10, with the necessary sum from the lands in Huddelston, Shirburn and York [as above].

Thomas Darcy, knight, and the other feoffees were to suffer his executors or administrators to receive profits to the value of £200 from the manor of Huddelston and lands and tenements in Huddelston, Shirburn and York for the performance of his will and payment of his debts; after which the feoffees were to hold the lands to the use of his right heirs.

Proviso that if his executors or administrators should be hindered in levying the sum of £200 by Sir Marmaduke Constable, knight,

Thomas Rukby, or John Walker, they were to receive £300 of the said revenues.

Further proviso that the feoffees should cause no waste or destruction of any principal woods within the said manor, lands or tenements, but might allow his executors and administrators to fell and sell underwood and to take away free stone.

Given, 26 March 23 Henry VII [1508]. [English]

(ff. 183v-184) On 12 January 24 Henry VII [1509], John Bonfan and Elizabeth, his wife, came into the Council Chamber on Ouse Bridge before John Doggeson, Mayor, Richard Makblith, Richard Gurnell, and John Roger, Chamberlains, and asked that the two deeds which they showed and read should be entered in the common register of the city.

FEOFFMENT.
John Bonfan and Elizabeth, his wife,
to William, Abbot of St. Agatha's monastery near Richmond in the County of York, and the Convent of the same, in frankalmoign,
lands, tenements, rents, reversions and services in Huddiswell [Hudswell] near Richmond.
Appointment of George Warcopp and John Barmeston as attorneys to deliver seisin.
Sealed with the official mayoral seal and those of the feoffors.
Given, 10 January 24 Henry VII [1509]. [Latin]

(f. 184v) QUITCLAIM.
John Bonfan and Elizabeth, his wife,
to William, Abbot of St. Agatha's monastery and the Convent thereof,
lands, tenements, rents, reversions and services in Huddiswell near Richmond, which belonged to William Johnson, William Clynts, Henry Clynts and John Clynts.
Sealed with the official mayoral seal and those of John Bonfan and Elizabeth.
Given, 14 January 24 Henry VII [1509]. [Latin]

(f. 185) On 22 March 24 Henry VII [1509], Leonard Aykers and Joan, his wife, sought the enrolment of the following deed before George Essex, Mayor, George Kirk, Alderman, Thomas York,

Thomas Clerk, Humphrey Maners and John Burton.

FEOFFMENT.

Leonard Aykers of Arkenden [Arkendale], in the County of York, husbandman, and Joan, his wife, daughter and heir of John Mitchell, late of Poklyngton [Pocklington],
to Thomas Bateman of Poklyngton,
a messuage and garden in the town of Poklyngton, lying in width between the land now of Henry Westale on the west and the land formerly of Martin del See on the east, and in length from the high street of Poklyngton in front as far as the land of Richard Goddard behind.

Sealed with the official mayoral seal and those of the feoffors.

Given, 22 March 24 Henry VII [1509].   [Latin]

(f. 185v) On the penultimate day of October 1 Henry VIII [1509], William Gascoigne came into the Council Chamber on Ouse Bridge before George Essex, Mayor, Thomas York, Humphrey Maners, John Burton, John Scawceby, Ralph Batty and William Swale, read a feoffment made and sealed by him, with the intention on the dorse of the same and also a bond, which he asked should be registered in the common register of the city.

(ff. 185v-186v) FEOFFMENT.

William Gascoigne of Abirfourth [Aberford], in the County of York, esquire,
to Anthony Wyndsore, knight, John Vavasoure, esquire, Richard Kighley, esquire, John Kighley, gentleman, John Gascoigne, gentleman, and Ralph Moure, gentleman,
the manors of Lasyngcroft [Lazencroft], Ardeslowe [Ardsley], Westhetton [Upper Heaton, parish of Kirkheaton] and Mirfeld, and lands, tenements, rents, reversions and services in Esthetton,[37] Westgarfourth, and Garfourth Morehous [Moorhouse Farm, Garforth].

Appointment of Robert Harpyng and John Wilson as attorneys to deliver seisin.

Witnesses, Leonard Vavasoure, clerk, Richard Thornton, clerk, Henry Malleverey, chaplain, Percival Moure and William Ledes, gentlemen.

[37] *Esthetton*; probably Kirkheaton, as distinct from West or Upper Heaton, although there is no evidence of the use of the prefix East in the *English Place Name Society's* volume.

Given, 27 October 1 Henry VIII [1509].   [Latin]
Endorsement.

The intention of the feoffment was that the feoffees should hold
the manor of Lasyngcroft to the use of John Gascoigne and Anne,
his wife, and the heirs of their bodies begotten, and the other lands
to the use of the said John Gascoigne and the heirs of his body
begotten, except the lands and tenements in West Garfourth,
Garfourth Morehous and South Milforth [South Milford]. They
were to hold all these said lands and tenements to the use of John
Gascoigne and Anne, his wife, according to the marriage settlement made on 8 October 22 Henry VII [1506], between John
Vavasour, esquire, and Thomas Gascoigne of Lasyngcroft, for the
marriage of John Gascoigne, son and heir apparent of the said
William, and Anne, daughter of John Vavasour.   [English]

(f. 187) BOND.

William Gascoign of Abirforth,
to John Vavasour of York, esquire,
in [? £900] payable on the feast of the Nativity of Our Lord next,
to ensure that John Gascoign, gentleman, son and heir apparent of
the said William Gascoigne, esquire, and Anne, wife of the said
John, should have peaceful possession of the manor of Lasyngcroft
and lands in Shippyng [Shippen] in the County of York, and also
the manors of Ardeslowe, and Westhetton with lands and tenements
in Esthetton, Westgarforth and Garfurth Morehous. William
Gascoign was not to alienate any of the said manors or lands, nor
suffer a recovery to be had against him or any of his feoffees, without the written consent of John Vavasour.
Given, 28 October 1 Henry VIII [1509].   [Latin and English]

(ff. 187v-188) INQUISITION POST MORTEM.[38]

on the estate of John Thwates, esquire, held in the *Guihald* on
28 May 2 Henry VIII [1510], before John Shawe, Mayor and
escheator, by virtue of a royal writ. The jurors, Thomas Bankhows,
John Beysby, John Thornton, Thomas Hoghson, William Robynson, Richard Blakburn, Richard North, John Symson, Thomas
Gudebarn, Thomas Mason, John Huchonson, Thomas Nicholson

[38] Printed in *Calendar of Inquisitions Post Mortem*, 2nd Series, Vol. III, p. 440.
For a later inquisition, held under a Commission of Concealments, see *ibid* p. 170.
A similar, but not identical, inquisition to the above appears on f. 200 below.

and William Shereburn, said on oath that John Thwatys was seized in demesne as of fee of a messuage called *Davyhall* in the City of York, which he held of the king in chief by knight's service, and that it was worth £7.12s. ½d p.a.; and of ten messuages in the city, held of the king in burgage by fealty and worth £3.6s.8d p.a.; 5s p.a. rent from a messuage in Busterdsthorp called *Bustardhall* and 11s rent p.a. from two messuages and twenty acres of land in Angrum, in the County of the City of York, all held of William Yngilby, esquire, as of his manor of Hoton Wandesley [Hutton Wandesley], for what service the jurors knew not.

John Thwatis, son of Thomas Thwatis, son of the said John Thwatis, his grandfather, was the nearest heir and was one year of age when the latter died on 29 January 22 Henry VII [1507].

Sealed by the Mayor and escheator, and the jurors.   [Latin]

On 3 August 2 Henry VIII [1510], William Leyke and Margaret, his wife, came into the Council Chamber before John Shawe, Mayor, and showed the following deed. After the said Margaret had been examined alone, they asked that it be enrolled in the common register.

(ff. 188-188v) QUITCLAIM.

William Leyke and Margaret, his wife,
to John Lyncoln, son and heir of John Lyncoln, late of York, merchant,
a tenement and adjoining garden in Litill Seynt Andrewgate, in the tenure of Alice Lyncoln, widow, mother of the said John Lyncoln the son.

Given, 3 August 2 Henry VIII [1510].   [Latin]

(f. 189) INQUISITION POST MORTEM.

on the estate of Brian Stapilton of Wighall, knight, held in the *Guihald* before William Wright, Mayor and escheator, on 27 October 10 Henry VIII [1518], by virtue of a royal writ.

The jurors, namely John Smythe, John Tong, Robert Johnson, Cuthbert Byrtbek, Anthony Machell, Robert Stewynson, Ralph Neleson, John Northe, William Thomlynson, Peter Esterby, Richard Thomlynson, Henry Hutchonson and Thomas Gudbarn, said on oath that Brian Stapilton was seised in demesne as of fee of the manor of Wighall [Wighill], in the County of the City of York, and of a messuage, three cottages and a toft in the City of

York, of a garden or close in Clementhorpe, and also of three cottages in the street without Michaelgate Bar. He had enfeoffed William Bulmer and Robert Aske, knights, Richard Goldysburght, Robert Roos, Thomas Tempest and William Rokby, esquires, with the manor of Wighall and lands and tenements in Wighall, York and Esedyke [Easdyke], to the use of himself, Brian Stapilton. They had then granted the said manor, lands and tenements to him for life, without impeachment of waste, with the remainder to Christopher Stapilton, his son and heir apparent, and the heirs of his body begotten.

The said manor of Wighall was held of the Earl of Darby as of his manor of Thresk [Thirsk], but for what service the jurors knew not. It was valued at £60 p.a. The land and tenements in York were held of the Mayor and Commonalty in burgage and were worth 13s 4d p.a.

Brian Stapilton died on 18 September last [1518]. Christopher Stapilton was his son and nearest heir and was thirty-three years of age.

Sealed by the escheator and jurors. [Latin]

(f. 189v) ADMISSION.
    by Alan Staveley, Mayor,
    of John Pulley, chaplain,
to the office of chaplain in the perpetual chantry in the chapel of St. William the Archbishop on Ouse Bridge, vacant by the resignation of John Robynson, the last chaplain.

The nomination and presentation were made by William Bulmer, knight, patron of the chantry.

Given at York, 12 October 1519, 11 Henry VIII. [Latin]

(ff. 190-190v) AGREEMENT.
    between Sir Richard Chomley, knight,
    and William Neleson and John Dogeson, Aldermen, made in the presence of Edmund, Abbot of St. Mary's Abbey, York, and Thomas Drawswerd, Mayor.
The said Sir Richard Chomley, with the consent of Janet Wranguays and Agnes Wranguays, daughters of William Wranguays and Anne his wife, daughter and heir of Robert Tuyge of London, merchant, should have the lands and tenements, rents, reversions and services of the said Robert Tuyge in the County of

Kent, which descended to him by the inheritance of Anne Wran-guays, daughter of Robert Tuyge. For these he should pay eighty marks to Janet and Agnes Wranguays on condition that he should recover and hold the said lands and tenements by fine or feoffment.

Also the said Janet and Agnes Wranguays should be conveyed to London at Sir Richard Chomley's expense, and on the latter's return from London each should receive 20s. If he received the lands, the 40s. thus paid should be reckoned as part payment of the 80 marks; if not, the sum of 40s. should be given in reward to the said Janet and Agnes. He was to help them to such goods left, assigned or bequeathed to them in Kent or elsewhere by their father, uncle or any friends.

Given, 11 May 8 Henry VIII [1516].   [English]

BOND.

     Roger Chomley of Pykeryng, esquire,

       to William Neleson and John Dogeson, Aldermen,

in 100 marks to be paid on the next feast of St. Michael the Arch-angel,

to ensure that Sir Richard Chomley, knight, should fulfil obliga-tions mentioned in the said agreement.

     Given, 11 May 7 [sic] Henry VIII [1515].   [Latin and English]

     On 4 August 12 Henry VIII [1520], the said indenture and bond were delivered to Reynold Barlaw attending Master Newport, one of the king's justices of assize, at the desire of the said Master Newport.   [English]

(f. 191) GRANT.

     Simon Vicars, Mayor, at the instance of Richard Rokeby, knight and Recorder,

       to John Chapman, merchant,

exoneration from election to the office of Mayor, Alderman, Sheriff, Constable, Overseer or Warden of the Walls or Collector of Taxes or any other office contrary to his wish. He was not to be com-pelled to attend at parliament or for any other foreign duties.

     Consideration: a certain sum of money [unspecified].

     Given in the Council Chamber at the *Guyhald*, the penultimate day of December 13 Henry VIII [1521].   [Latin]

(f. 191v) ADMISSION.

by Paul Gillour, Mayor,
of John Hutchynson, chaplain,
to the chantry in honour of St. Thomas the Martyr, founded in the
church of St. Nicholas and vacant by the resignation of Thomas
Acryng, the last chaplain.

Salary: 40s. p.a. to be paid by the Chamberlains.

The appointment was in the gift of the Mayor by virtue of his
office.

Given in the Council Chamber on Ouse Bridge, 8 March 13
Henry VIII [1522].   [Latin]

(ff. 191v-192) GRANT.

Thomas Bankhous, Mayor, the Aldermen and Common Council,
to Henry Smyth, formerly clerk of the parish of St. Sampson's,
the office of clerk of St. William's Chapel on Ouse Bridge, with
custody of all ornaments belonging to the chapel. Proviso, that at
suitable times he should sing divine service in the choir of the
chapel, play the organ or teach boys. The said Henry Smyth undertook to perform himself, or by a suitable deputy, all other services
which his predecessors were accustomed to do, in honour of God,
the Blessed Virgin Mary and St. William.

Given in the Council Chamber on Ouse Bridge, 5 August 13
Henry VIII [1521].   [Latin]

(f. 192v) *IN THE ACCOUNT ROLLS OF THE FIFTEENTH
AND TENTH. CITY OF YORK.*[39]

Richard Pease, merchant, Thomas Symson, goldsmith, Thomas
Temple and Robert Tesymonde, butchers, collectors of the first
of two fifteenths and tenths from the laity of the city, 5 Elizabeth
[1562-3], render account for £136.10s.8d, paid into the treasury
on 1 February 6 Elizabeth [1564].

And they were acquitted
by Richard Gudbury,
examined by Thomas Hide.

In the Receipt Rolls of the Exchequer beginning at the Michaelmas
Term 6 Elizabeth, namely after the feast of St. Hillary, Tuesday
1 February [1564].

[39] See also ff. 143-145, for earlier accounts of the Fifteenth and Tenth.

City of York.

From the collectors of the first 〕 on behalf of the
of two fifteenths and tenths   ｜ Mayor and burgesses
from the laity of the city, 5   ｝ by a writ under the
Elizabeth, £50   〕 Queen's privy seal.
    examined by Edmund Baswicke,
    deputy of Robert Hare   [Latin]

(f. 193) *In the Time of John Norman, Mayor of the City of York.*
On 2 April 15 Henry VIII [1524], Christopher Atkynson and
Agnes, his wife, came into the Council Chamber on Ouse Bridge
before John Norman, Mayor, showed the following deeds of
feoffment and quitclaim and sought their enrolment in the common
register of the city.

FEOFFMENT.

Christopher Atkynson of York, armourer, and Agnes his wife,
daughter and heir of John Catur, late of York, merchant, and
Agnes his wife, daughter and heir of John Tong, late Alderman
and merchant,
    to Richard Pawlyng of York, tanner,
a tenement in Walmegayt, lately in the tenure of George Lokeryg,
weaver, and lying in width between the land of St. Leonard's Hospital on the south and the land of the Augustinian Friars on the north,
and in length from Walmegate in front on the east as far as the
land of the said hospital behind on the west.
    Appointment of Nicholas Fishar and John Aklande as attorneys
to deliver seisin.
    (f. 193v) Sealed by John Norman, at the request of Christopher
Atkynson and Agnes his wife, with the official mayoral seal.
    Given at York, the last day of March 15 Henry VIII [1524].
                                   [Latin]

QUITCLAIM.

Christopher Atkynson and Agnes, his wife,
    to Richard Pawlyng,
a tenement in Walmegate, which he lately had by the gift and
feoffment of the said Christopher Atkynson and Agnes.
    Given, 5 April 15 Henry VIII [1524].   [Latin]

(f. 194) BOND.

Nicholas Palmes of Nayburne [Naburn], esquire, and William
Babthorpe of Osgerby [Osgodby], esquire,
to William Bowmer, knight, and Richard Ellys, clerk, executors
of the will of Brian Palmes, esquire, late sergeant at law,
in 200 marks to be paid on the feast of the Nativity of the Lord next,
to ensure that Richard Palmes, gentleman, one of the sons of the
said Brian Palmes, when he reached the age of 21 years should
deliver an acquittance from all manner of actions to William Bowmer and Richard Ellys at their request.
Given, 10 October 16 Henry VIII [1524].   [Latin and English]

(f. 194v-195) ACQUITTANCE.

William Palmes, gentleman, one of the sons of Brian Palmes,
esquire, late sergeant at law,
to William Bulmer, knight, Richard Ellys, clerk, and William
Marshall, gentleman, executors of the will of the said Brian
Palmes,
for his boyhood portion received from them that day, and all other
actions, suits or demands.
Given, 10 October 16 Henry VIII [1524].   [Latin]
Subscribed. Per me William Palmes.
William Bulmer, knight, per Robert Bulmer, gentleman, his
servant, paid to the said William Palmes, gentleman, £56 in full
satisfaction of his boyhood portion, and 10s. of the legacy of Anne
Palmes, widow. He also paid to Richard Palmes, gentleman, for
his boyhood portion, 100 marks, and also 20s. of the legacy of Anne
Palmes.
Witnessed by John Norman, Mayor, 11 October 16 Henry VIII
[1524].   [Latin]

(195v) ORDINANCES OF THE INNHOLDERS.[40]

The ordynaunce of the inholders of this City of York, made in
the tyme of maryalte of the right worshipfull Thomas Mason, Maor
of the sayd city, the 7th day of Marche in the 19th yere of the reyn
of our soveryng lord Kyng Henry the VIIIth [1528], and fully
enacted and determyned by the sayd Mare and his brethern with
the hole consent of the inholders of this citie, and at theyr speciall

[40] The ordinances of 1528 are printed, in part, in York Civic Records, Vol. III,
p. 190; later ordinances, dated 1562 and 1564, in Vol. VI, pp. 44-5, 93-4.

request and desyer, for the gud amendement of their craft and the common well of the king's people to be observed in maner and fourme folowyng: —

Fyrst it is enacted, ordaned and establissed that noo man shall kepe any inns, hostrye, nor take noo hors within this citie or suburbs of the same oonles he have a sign at his dore, uppon payne to forfett and pay for evere hors foundon in his hows or farmeold 12d, als oft and whensoever any such shalbe so founden and knowen, the oon half therof to be emploied to the well of this citie and the other half therof to the seid craft and pageant.

Item, that it shalbe lefull to the sercheourz of the inholders of this citie for to make serche in all things consernyng ther crafte, as well within the howsez of thame that thei suspect or shall know that keps innez, hostriez and takyn in hors which have noo sign at ther dore, as all other inholders, hostillers and takers in of hors that have signes at ther doors, at all tymes for the well and gud order of the same crafte and profett of the king's people. And whooso of the seid inholders, hostillers and takers in of hors that woll not suffer the sercheourz to make due serche as is aforeseid or be rebellion to serchors shercheourz [sic] shall forfett and pay at evere tyme that thei disobey this ordynaunce 6s 8d, to be emploied in maner and fourme aboveseid.

Item that evere inholder and other as is aboveseid, having a sign att his dore, shall com to the serchers att all tymes of reasonable warnyng to gyf his best counsell and help consernyng that crafte, and not to absent hym without a reasonable cause, uppon payne of 12d at evere tyme to be emploied as is aboveseid.

(f. 196) Item, that evere inholder and other that keps inne or hostrie shall have in his hows redy mayd bottells of hey[41] to be shewid to the sercheourz at all tymes when they shall com to make serche, uppon payne of 8d to be emploied as is aforeseid as often as (*tociens quociens*).

Item, that the pageant masters of the innholders for tyme beyng yerely shall make a dew accompt and rekenyng of theyr receyts and payment consernyng theyr pageant and play, before and unto the sercheours of that crafte, the Sonday come a sennett next aftir Corpus Christi day, of payne to forfett and pay 6s 8d to be emploied as is aforesayd.

Item, that noo bayker of this citie shall kepe any inne or hostrie

---

[41] *bottells of hey*: bundles of hay.

nor take in noo hors uppon payn of 20s to be payd as is aforeseid as often as (*tociens quociens*).

20 October 17 Edward IV [1477] in the time of John Tong, Mayor. [Latin]

Item, the day and yere abovesayd it was ordeyned to be observed for ever, that the serchars of the hostelars within this citie shall have full power to make due and true serche in all and every hostery wythin this sayd citie, suburbs and procyncts of the same, of all otes mesures, that is to say buschell, half buschell, poke[42] and half poke and botells of hay. And that all the botells kepe sufficient weight accordyng to the statutes in the chambre. And he or she that is founde culpable in the premisses or any one therof forfait and lose 6s 8d, thone half to the chambre and the other half to the sustentacion of the pageant of the sayd ostelars.

Item, that no man nor woman within this sayd citie, suburbs and procincts of the same, holde no comon ostrye withowte he or she have a signe over theyr doore, and he or she that doeth the contrary to forfayte and pay withowte any perdone 13s 4d, in maner and forme as is abovesayd.

Item, that no baxter that kepith ostery bake none horsebread within hym self, apon a payne in a statute therof ordeyned and provyded.

Item, that all the sayd hostelars and every of theym that holde innes or hostery withowte signe have theyr signes up by the fest of the Natyvitie of Our Lord next ensuyng after this present date.

(f. 195A)[43] ORDINANCES OF THE OSTLERS.[44]

20 October 17 Edward IV [1477]

[Present]. John Tonge, Maior, John Gilyot, John Marchall, Richard Yorke, William Lambe, Thomas Wrangwishe, John Glasyn, William Wellys, John Ferybe, and Robert Amyas of the Twelve, Richard Cleybruke, Thomas Catour, John Lyghtlope, Thomas Meryot, John Newton and Thomas Scotton of the Twenty Four.

[There follows the text of the ostlers' ordinances, as on f. 196,

---

[42] Spelt *peke* on f. 195A (see below). *peck*: a measure, ¼ bushel.
[43] A small parchment folio, apparently inserted when the volume was rebound.
[44] Printed in *York Civic Records*, Vol. III, p. 186. The same ordinances are also entered in House Book I, f. 68 and printed in *York Civic Records*, Vol. I, p. 21.

identical except for minor variations of spelling. It is subscribed *Enrolled in the Register*].

(f. 195Av) [Blank].

(f. 196v) LEASE.
Henry Trewe of Naborne [Naburn], yeoman, and Mercella his wife, widow of the late Edward York, esquire,
to Bartholomew York, merchant,
a capital messuage and the stable behind it, in the parish of St. John the Evangelist at the end of Ouse Bridge.
Term. The life of the said Mercella.
Consideration. £22. 6s. 8d, of which 20 marks was paid by Bartholomew York to Edward York during his lifetime, and the remaining £9 to Henry Trewe and Mercella on the day of the completion of this deed.
Sealed, at the request of the parties, with the official mayoral seal by Henry Dason, Mayor.
Given at York, 9 May 23 Henry VIII [1531]
Date of enrolment, heading the entry 10 May 24 Henry VIII [1532]. [Latin]

(f. 197) QUITCLAIM.
William Faryfax of Steton, esquire, Laurence Morton, Henry Carbott and Thomas Wyereld of the same,
to Thomas Goldthwayt,
the manor of Wolston [Ouston Farm in the township of Oxton] near Tedcastre and lands, tenements, rents, reversions, fisheries and services in Wolston, with appurtenances in the County of the City of York.
Given, 23 October 24 Henry VIII [1532].
Date of enrolment, heading the entry, 24 October 24 Henry VIII. [Latin]

(f. 197v) PRESENTATION.
John Pullayn of Kyllinghall, gentleman,
to John Hall, clerk,
the chantry in St. Anne's Chapel on Foss Bridge founded by Nicholas Blakeburn, senior, now vacant following the death of Robert Atkyrk, the last chaplain, and in his gift by reason of pur-

chase, together with all lands, tenements, rents and services pertaining to the chantry.

John Hall was to reside continually and personally, according to
the wish of Nicholas Blakburn.

Given, the last day of January 25 Henry VIII [1534].   [Latin]

ADMISSION.[45]
by George Gaile, Mayor,
of John Hall, clerk,
to the chantry in St. Anne's Chapel on Foss Bridge.   [Latin]

(f. 198) ADMISSION.
George Gayll, Mayor,
of Robert Keld, priest in holy orders,
to the perpetual chantry at the altar of St. Mary the Virgin in St.
William's Chapel on Ouse Bridge, vacant by the death of Henry
Cukeson, the last chaplain, and in the gift of Edmund Sandford of
Thorp Salvayn [Thorpe Salvin], in the County of York, esquire.

Given in the Council Chamber on Ouse Bridge, 20 May 26 Henry
VIII [1534].   [Latin]

(ff. 198v-199) On 14 March 28 Henry VIII [1537], Thomas
Knolles, late of York, gentleman and public notary, came into the
Council Chamber on Ouse Bridge before Ralph Pullayn, Mayor,
and read Letters Patent of Henry VIII, which he asked should be
enrolled in the common register of the city.

LETTERS PATENT
of Henry VIII,
granting a pardon and release to the aforesaid Thomas Knolles,
late of the City of York, Public Notary, Procurator of the Con-
sistory Court of the Archbishop, and gentleman, from: —
[1]. all treasons and crimes of *lese majeste* and also rebellions,
insurrections, misprisions, treasons and conspiracies against the
crown.
[2]. all murders, homicides, felonies, robberies, and accessories
thereof.
[3]. all illicit misprisions of words, conventicles, illicit assemblies
and confederations, riots, routs, transgressions, contempts and

[45] incomplete.

offences committed against the law or statutes of the realm before
10 December 28 Henry VIII [1536].

[4]. all indictments, penalties, imprisonments, judgments, con-
demnations, executions and penalties of death, adjudged for any
of the aforesaid premises.

[5]. all forfeits of goods and chattels, lands, tenements and hereditaments, fines and penalties occasioned by the said premises,
which should hereby be restored to him.

Witnessed at Westminster, 18 January 28 Henry VIII [1537].
Subscribed. Neuman

> By the king himself on the aforesaid date
> with the authority of parliament. [Latin]

(ff. 199v & 211)[46] On 27 March 28 Henry VIII [1537], Brian
Roclyd [sic] of Cowthrop and Margery, his wife, came before Ralph
Pulleyn, Mayor, and sought the enrolment of the following in-
denture.   [Latin]

DEMISE.

Brian Roclyf of Cowthorp, in the County of York, esquire, and
Margery, his wife,

to Robert Metham of Acom Grange in the County of the City
of York, esquire,

a close called the *West Parke* and another close called the *Esshe
Hagg Feild* in the lordship of Cowthrop, and also three farmholds
in Bykkerton [Bickerton] in the County of the City of York; one,
of an annual value of 28s, in the tenure of James Gybson, another
of an annual value of 32s, lately in the tenure of John Warrynell,
and the third, worth 4s p.a. in the tenure of Richard Greyn.

Term, 17 years.

Rent, nil; consideration unspecified.

Margery, wife of Brian Roclyf, was to acknowledge before the
judge at the next assizes for the County of York, that she made
the demise of her own free will, without any compulsion from her
husband. Brian Roclyf was to be bound in £100 for the due performance of the covenants.

Given, 10 December 26 Henry VIII [1534].   [English]

---

[46] The following deed is continued on f. 211 which seems to indicate that the
folios were wrongly re-arranged when the volume was rebound.

(f. 200) INQUISITION POST MORTEM.[47]

on the estate of John Twhats, esquire, held on [blank] 2 Henry VIII [1510-11], before John Shaw, Mayor and escheator.

Jurors. Thomas Bankhouse, Robert Diconson, William Lounde, Christopher Horner, James Blannde, George Keld, John Bateman, William Lewty, George Barbour, Christopher Payntour, William Cure, Thomas Gudebarn and Thomas Gokeman.

[Details as on ff. 187v-188, except that it is here stated that the messuage called Davyhall was worth 5s. (instead of £7.12.½d) and that John Thwates was also seized in demesne as of fee, on the day he died, of an annual rent of £7.12s.1d. in the city, paid by the Sheriffs of York on the feasts of St. Michael and Easter]. [Latin]

(ff. 200v-201) APPRENTICESHIP INDENTURE.

of Robert White, son and heir of William White, late Alderman and dyer, deceased,

to John White, citizen and grocer,

Term. 7 years from 21 November 2 Henry VIII [1510].

Robert White was to obey his master, keep his secrets and counsel and not to cause him any wilful damage to the value of 6d or more each year, or allow any such damage which he could prevent; not to waste his master's goods nor lend them without permission; to render a faithful account and payment of all money received; not to play at dice, chess or other illicit games; not to withdraw from his master's service nor absent himself by day or night; not to commit adultery or fornication in his house under penalty of doubling his period of servitude, and not to marry unless with his master's consent.

John White was to instruct him in the trade, in buying, selling and trading, to the best of his ability, provide him with food and drink, clothing, a bed and shoes, all necessary expenses and 12d p.a. as a salary.

Given at York, 21 November 2 Henry VIII [1510]. [Latin]

f. 201v. ORDINANCES OF THE HORNERS.[48]

The last day of April 14 Henry VII [1500]. [Latin]

William Neleson, Mayor, Nicholas Lancastre, John Gyliote,

---

[47] A similar, but not identical inquisition to that on ff. 187v-188.
[48] Also entered in House Book 8, ff. 80-80v and printed in York Civic Records, Vol. II, p. 152.

Michael White, George Kyrke, Thomas Gray, John Metcalf, John
Elwalde, John Stokdall; Alan Stavelay and Robert Petty, Sheriffs;
William Tayte, Miles Grenebanke, William Berker, baker, Thomas
Fynche, John Shawe, William Berker, merchaunt, Edward Foster,
Thomas Derby, John Custaunce, John Petty, Richard Thornton,
Thomas Jameson, John Dogeson, Richard Wynder.

Item, the same day at the especiall request of the hole craft of
horners of this citie, it was enacted by the saide presennce fermly
hereafter to be observed, that no horner within this citie, suburbs
or procincts of the same from nowe furthe take upon hym to wyrke
in the craft of horners, or in any poynt of the same, unto tyme he
be infraunchest, examyned, abled and admytted by the sersors of
horners, upon payn of forfetour for every tyme 6s 8d, wherof 5s
to the chambre and 20d to the horners.

Item, that no man of the saide craft from hensforthe wyrke any
maner of thynge longyng to the said craft of horners with any
person of any other crafte or occupacion within this citee, bot with
a maister of the craft of horners, upon payn afforsaide; provyded
alway that the maisters of the craft of horners gife the men of
the same craft resonable hyre and salary as they may deserve and
ellys they to wyrke where they pleas at ther libertie, so that the
Mayre for the tyme beyng have examynacion if the maisterz
proferre resonable hyre and salary.

Item, that no maister of the said craft from nowfurthe take non
apprintice for lese terme then for 7 yere togedder and that by
indentur, and to shew there indenturz unto the sersourz of the saide
craft within 14th dayez next after the date of the same, upon payn
of 6s 8d. in maner abovesaide.

Item, if the sersourz of the saide craft fynde any maner of stufe
or warke longyng to the same craft unably wrought and maide,
then he that maide suche stuffe to forfet for every tyme 3s 4d to
the chambre and craft evenly to be devyded.

Item, it was determyned by the same presennce that horners
from nowfurthe payng pageant money to be contributory with the
cutlers and bladsmythez.

(f. 202) On 16 April 2 Henry VIII [1511], Agnes Bonney and
John Heirfeld came before Bartram Daweson, Mayor, delivered
the following deed and asked that it should be enrolled in the
common register of the city.

FEOFFMENT.[49]

Agnes Bonney, sister and heir of Richard Bonney, gentleman deceased, John Heirfeld, son of Joan Heirfeld, sister of Richard Bonney, and Richard Bylburght and Margaret, his wife, another sister of Richard Bonney,

to John Beylby, gentleman,

lands and tenements with appurtenances in Goudmadame [Goodmanham] in the County of York.

Appointment of William Vicars and Richard Beylby as attorneys to deliver seisin.

Given, 16 April 2 Henry VIII [1511].   [Latin]

(f. 202v) On 14 June 4 Henry VIII [1512], Richard Kendall came into the Council Chamber before George Kyrk, Mayor, John Beylby, John Norman, Richard North and William Esshe, and sought the enrolment of the following two deeds in the common register of the city.

FEOFFMENT.

Richard Kendall, clerk, son and heir of John Kendall, gentleman, deceased,

to John Burton, gentleman, and Alice, his wife,

a messuage or cottage with a garden, an acre of land and half a rood of meadow in Northduffeld, in the County of York and lands, tenements, rents, reversions and services in Northduffeld.

Appointment of Richard Beilby and Robert Gelderd as attorneys to deliver seisin.

Given, 14 June 4 Henry VIII [1512].

Subscribed. Esshe.   [Latin]

(f. 203) QUITCLAIM.

Richard Kendall, clerk,

to John Burton, gentleman, and Alice, his wife,

a messuage or cottage with a garden, an acre of land and half a rood of meadow with appurtenances in Northduffeld.

Given, 1 July 4 Henry VIII [1512].

Subscribed, Esshe.   [Latin]

On 11 October 6 Henry VIII [1514], John Heirfeld came before John Thornton [Mayor] in the *Guyhald* and asked that the follow-

[49] See also f. 203.

ing deed should be enrolled in the common register of the city.

QUITCLAIM.⁵⁰

John Heirfeld, son and heir of Joan Heirfeld, one of the sisters
and heirs of Richard Bonney, deceased,
    to John Beylby of York, gentleman,
a messuage, two tofts and five oxgangs of land with appurtenances
in Goudmadame [Goodmanham], in the County of York.
    Given, 11 October 6 Henry VIII [1514].   [Latin]

(f. 203v) FEOFFMENT.

John Fell of York, chaplain, and John White, citizen and grocer,
    to William Malory, knight, Ralph Constable, esquire, John
Malory, son and heir apparent of the said William Malory, knight,
John Roos, esquire, Robert Johnson and Thomas Grey, citizens
and Aldermen, Miles Willesthorp and William Fairfaxe, esquires,
to the use of William White, citizen and Alderman, and Margaret, his wife, and the heirs of their bodies begotten, remainder
to the said feoffees to the use of the right heirs of the said William White,
a messuage in Northstreit, in the parish of St. John the Apostle
and Evangelist near Ouse Bridge; another messuage in Mekilgate in the said parish, in the tenure of Richard Thornton,
citizen and grocer; also a capital messuage and six messuages
lying together in Colergate in the parish of Holy Trinity, King's
Court, and all other lands, tenements, rents and services which the
feoffors had by the gift and feoffment of William White, citizen
and Alderman.
    Witnesses. Richard Yorke, knight and Alderman, Michael White,
Alderman, Richard Thornton, citizen and grocer, John Clerk and
Richard Garnet, citizens.
    Given at York, 14 May 11 Henry VII [1496].   [Latin]

(f. 204) [Blank, except for the date 16 February 6 Henry VIII
[1515], and the name Esshe.]

(f. 204v) INQUISITION POST MORTEM.

on the estate of John Metcalf, gentleman,
held at the *Guihald*, on —— [blank] day of March 6 Henry VIII

⁵⁰ See also ff. 202, 216v-217.

[1515], before Thomas Drawswerd, Mayor and escheator, by virtue of a royal writ. The jurors, John Besby, Richard North, Robert Dyconson, Thomas Mason, Thomas Gilbanke, Robert Fons, John Tramell, John Smyth and Thomas Gokman, John Symson, Robert Conant, William Smyth and Thomas Gudbarn, declared on oath that John Metcalf was seised in demesne as of fee on the day he died of nine messuages in York, held of the king in free burgage. Of these six were in decay and were worth nothing. The other three were worth 26s 8d p.a. He was also seised of a messuage lately built on a toft in Bischopthorp, and of an acre and three roods of land there, part of fourteen tofts and fifteen oxgangs of land, held of the king in socage for a rent of 4 marks for all services. The said messuage, one acre and three roods of land were valued at 6s p.a.

John Metcalf died on 29 June last [1514].

Thomas Metcalf was his brother and nearest heir and was twenty-three years of age.

Sealed by the escheator and jurors.

Subscribed. Esshe.

(f. 205) INQUISITION POST MORTEM.
on the estate of Ralph Bygod, knight,
held on 24 July 7 Henry VIII [1515], before Thomas Drawswerd, Mayor and escheator, by virtue of a royal writ.

The jurors, William Huby, William Cure, John Chapman, Christopher Horner, James Blades, John Rasyn, Thomas Mason, William Harryngton, Thomas Jameson, Thomas Thornton, Thomas Dawson, Thomas Stavelay, Richard Plompton, William Sawer, Robert Bokyngham and Luke Gybe, said on oath that Ralph Bygode was seised in demesne as of fee, on the day he died, of a tenement in the parish of St. Cuthbert. After his death the tenement descended to Francis Bygode, his grandson, son of John, his son. The tenement was held of the king in free burgage and rendered 12d p.a. to the Mayor and Commonalty. It was worth 13s 4d p.a.

Ralph Bygode died on 22 April 6 Henry VIII [1514].

The said Francis Bygode was his nearest heir and was seven years of age.

Subscribed. Esshe.   [Latin]

(f. 205v) WRIT OF *SUPERSEDEAS*.

Henry VIII

to Thomas Drawswerd, Mayor and escheator,

to stay the demands made on John Metcalf, junior, for rents arising from nine messuages in York, a messuage lately built on a toft in Bischopthorpe and 1 acre 3 roods of land there, and to restore any distraint taken, following the judgment reached by the Barons of the Exchequer.

Reciting the Inquisition post Mortem on the estate of John Metcalf, senior, held at the *Guihald* before Richard Thornton, Mayor and escheator, on 10 June 17 Henry VII [1502].[51] Ellen, wife of John Metcalf, senior, late Alderman, was seised of the said premises in demesne as of fee, and so seised took to husband the said John, by virtue of which he was seised of them in fee in her right, and they had issue, namely one John Metcalf. Ellen died and her husband survived her, seised of the premises as tenant in his demesne as of freehold, with the reversion thereof expectant to the said John Metcalf, as her son and heir. The nine messuages in the city were held of the king in free burgage. John Metcalf the father died on 8 February last [1502]; John Metcalf was the son and heir of the said John and Ellen and on 8 August last was thirteen years of age.

Witnessed by William Hody, knight, at Westminster, 12 November 7 Henry VIII [1515], by the memoranda roll for that year.

Subscribed, Blagge. [Latin]

(ff. 206-206v) INQUISITION POST MORTEM.

on the estate of George at Kyrk, citizen and Alderman, deceased, held in the *Guihald* on 31 March 7 Henry VIII [1516] before John Hall, Mayor and escheator, by virtue of a royal writ.

The jurors, namely John Beisby, merchant, Nicholas Ratclyfe, gentleman, Thomas Mason, glover, William Harryngton, John Berker, notary, John Smythe, John Tonge, Luke Gybe, John Richardson, Thomas Custaunce, Cuthbert Byrtbek and Thomas Gudbarn, stated on oath that George at Kirk was seised in demesne as of fee, on the day he died, of:—

[1] a messuage, twenty acres of land and twenty acres of meadow in Bilburght in the County of the City of York, which were worth

---

[51] *Calendar of Inquisitions Post Mortem*, 2nd Series, Vol. II, pp. 334-5.

20s p.a. and were held of the heirs of Willesthorpe, for what service the jurors knew not.

[2] three messuages in York and the advowson of the chantry of St. Katherine in the Church of St. Mary the Elder; one messuage lay in Mekilgate and was worth 20s p.a., a second was situated in the Flesshamels in the parish of St. John the Evangelist [sic][52] and was worth 40d p.a, and the third, in Nedlergate, was worth 20d p.a.

[3] nineteen messuages in the City of York and suburbs thereof devised in his will, which was shown at the inquisition, as follows: —

six tenements in the Flesshamels and two tenements in St. Swythune Layn, worth 53s 4d p.a, to Matilda, his wife, for life, remainder in equal portions to Anthony at Kirk and George at Kirk, his sons, and the heirs of their bodies, with the reversion to the right heirs of George at Kirk, senior;

four tenements within Layrthorpe Posteron, worth 8s, to William at Kirk, his son, his heirs and assigns;

one tenement in Petergate and one tenement in Gotheromgate, worth 20s p.a, to the said Anthony at Kirk, his heirs and assigns;

one tenement without Mykylbarre near Baggergate, worth 13s 4d p.a, to the said George at Kirk, junior, his heirs and assigns;

one messuage or tenement in Northstret, worth 10s p.a, to the said William at Kyrk, his heirs and assigns;

one tenement on the corner of Northstret, worth 3s p.a, to Anthony at Kirk, his heirs and assigns;

one tenement in Northestret, next to the one on the corner, and worth 4s p.a, to George at Kirk, junior, his heirs and assigns;

one tenement in Skeldergate in the parish of St. John the Evangelist, worth 20d p.a, to William at Kyrk, his heirs and assigns.

All the tenements in the city and suburbs were held of the king in free burgage.

George at Kyrk, senior, died on 29 January 5 Henry VIII [1514].

William at Kirk was his son and nearest heir and on the day of his father's death was twenty-one years of age.

Sealed by the Mayor and escheator and the jurors.

Subscribed. Esshe.   [Latin]

(f. 207) On 1 March 7 Henry VIII [1516], John Hage late of

---

[52] The tenement in Micklegate may have been in St. John's parish, but not that in the Shambles.

the City of York, clerk, and John Weddell of the same, merchant, came before John Hall, Mayor, in the Council Chamber on Ouse Bridge, and asked that the following deed of feoffment should be enrolled in the common register of the city.

FEOFFMENT.

Richard Dene of York,

to John Hage of York, merchant, and Agnes his wife,

a messuage or tenement called *Yathouse* with the adjacent garden, lying in the parish of St. Mary the Elder, in width between the land of James Danby, knight, on one side and the tenement of the chaplain of St. Anne's chantry in the church of St. Saviour on the other, and in length from the high street in front as far as the great messuage called *Hothom Place*, lately belonging to John Hothom, knight, behind;

and six acres of land and six acres of pasture lying together in a close called *Gyebes* without Mikkalith next to Holgate Layn, which the feoffor had by the gift and feoffment of the said John Hage.

Witnesses, William Chymney, Mayor, Nicholas Vicars, and Roger Appelby, Sheriffs, Richard York, Nicholas Lancastre, and William White, Aldermen.

Given at York, 4 August 1 Henry VII [1486].

Subscribed, Esshe.   [Latin]

(f. 207v) AGREEMENT.[53]

This present indentour, maide at York in the fest of Saint Mathie Appostell, yere of the reign of Kinge Henry the VIIth after the conquest of Englonde the second [24 February 1486/7], betwixt Freer William Bewyk of the house of the order of Freers August within the Citie of Yorke and the Convent of the same of the oon partie, and Richard Bischope, John Couper, serchourz of the occupacion of the carpenterz within the said citie, James Wynffell, Michael Clerk, William Johnson and Thomas Hunt, keepers of the Holy Fraternite of the Resurreccion of Our Lord mayntened by the carpenterz of the said citie on that other partie.[54]

Witnesseth that the said Prior graunts tham to syng every yere two trentall of messez for the saulez of all the brether and systers of

---

[53] Printed in *York Civic Records*, Vol. III, pp. 186-7.

[54] The carpenters' attendance at meetings of the fraternity in the Augustinian friary was regulated in their ordinances of 1482 (*York Memorandum Book*, Vol. II, pp. 278-9).

the said fraternite, and that the said Prior and Convent of ther hole assent and consent graunts them to syng 5 trentall of messez for every brother of the said fraternite that truly doeth his dutye, after his disceasse, uppon resonable warnyng of his discease. And the forsaid kepers and serchourz, of the hole assent and consent of them and ther occupacion, fastly bynds them and ther successourz sersourz and kepers of the said occupacion of carpenterz for the tym beyng, to pay to the said Prior and Convent and ther successourz yerly for evermore 10s of lawfull money of Englonde, for syngyng of the forsaid two trentalles as affore it is rehersed at two termez of the yere, that is to say at the fest of the Invencion of the Holy Crosse and of All Halows by ewyn porcionz, and for every trentall of messez for every brother disceased as afore it is expressed 5s of lawfull money of England, and for contentacion and payment of 6s 8d, parcell of the said 10s yerely to be paid as affore is specified, we the said serchourz and kepers, of the hole assent and consent of us and all our said occupacion, grauntez and by thes presents letts to ferme to the forsaid Prior and Convent, two measez with ther appertenauncez upon the corner of the lendyng next Saynt Leonards to the watter of Ouse, adioynyng to the forsaid house of freers and conteigneth in lenght 9 yerds and in breid 8½ yerds. To have and to holde the said two meases with ther appertenauncs to the forsaid Prior and Convent and ther successourz from the forsaid fest of Saint Mathie the yere abovesaid, unto the ende and terme of 99 yerez fully complet. And the forsaid Prior and Convent and ther successourz the forsaid two measez with the appurtenancs during the terme afforsaid of ther own propre costagez and chargez shall reparell and uphold. Provyded alway that if the forsaid Prior and Convent and ther successors fall of syngyng (f. 208) of the said two trentallez of messez yerely as affore it is expressed, that then it shalbe lefull to the said serchourz and kepers and ther successourz to entre into all the forsaid 2 measez with the appurtenancs in ther olde estate and tham to occupie, thiez presents indenturez not with- standyng. In witnes wherof to the oon partie of thiez indentourz to the forsaid Prior and Convent remanyng the said serchourz and kepers haith setto ther sealez.

Yeven the day, yere and place abovesaid.
Subscribed. Esshe.

On 5 August 8 Henry VIII [1516], William Anlaby of Thorp-

basset, gentleman, came into the Council Chamber on Ouse Bridge
before John Hall, Mayor, read the following deed of feoffment
made between himself and Robert, his eldest brother, and sought
its enrolment in the common register of the city.

(ff. 208-208v) FEOFFMENT.

Robert Anlaby, son and heir of John Anlaby, late of Thorpbasset,
gentleman, deceased,
to William Anlaby, his brother,
a messuage in Thorpbasset now in the tenure of Thomas Lanwythe,
lying between the tenement of the Prior of Malton on the north
and a waste called *Marohill* on the south, and a toft opposite
the door of the said messuage between the toft of Lord Graystoke
on the south and the toft of the Prior of Malton on the north;
three tofts in the same town, one called the *Viber Close*, another
Kilnhouse Garthe and the third the *Overclose*, lying between
Fylalands on the south and the land of the Prior of Malton on
the north, and abutting on *Bidellgate* towards the west and on
Maroffleshbek towards the east; a piece of meadow called *Bradeng*,
lying between the tenements of Lord Graystoke on either side and
abutting on *Stowbreksike* towards the east and on *Maroffleshbek*
towards the west; two oxgangs of land lying between the land of
Lord Graystoke and the land which the feoffor gave to Thomas
his brother, and the reversion thereof.

Proviso that this feoffment should not be prejudicial to the rent
belonging to his mother as of right.

Consideration. Unspecified.

Witnesses. Ralph Bygod, knight, Ralph Eure, knight, John Bygod, William Eure, esquires, William Lutton, Thomas Heslarton,
Robert Hunter, and John Waren.

Given at Thorpebassett, 5 May 20 Henry VII [1505].   [Latin]
Subscribed. Esshe.

(ff. 208v-209)[55] On 8 November 10 Henry VIII [1518], John
[? Deryk] and Margaret his wife, daughter and heir of Nicholas
Johnson, deceased, came before William Wright, Mayor, in the
Council Chamber on Ouse Bridge and sought the enrolment of the
following two deeds of feoffment and quitclaim, made by Robert
Herryson to Nicholas Johnson.

[55] The remainder of f. 208v is almost entirely illegible without the aid of ultra
violet light.

FEOFFMENT.

Robert Herryson of York, walker,

to Nicholas Johnson of York, yeoman,

a tenement with a garden or orchard adjacent, which the feoffor had by the gift and feoffment of Richard Monkton, pykemonger, and Alice, his wife, lying in Fisshergate in the suburbs of the City of York, in length from Fisshergate in front as far as the highway ——[56] to Fulforth behind and in width between the land ——[56] and the land of Brian Metcalf, gentleman, on the other side.

Witnesses. Richard Thornton, Mayor, William Skypton and Thomas Freman, Sheriffs, Anthony Welburn and William Sawyer.

Given at York, 6 February 17 Henry VII [1502].   [Latin]

QUITCLAIM.[57]

Robert Herryson

to Nicholas Johnson,

a tenement with a garden or orchard adjacent, which he had by the gift and feoffment of Richard Monkton of York, pykemonger, and Alice, his wife, lying in Fisshergate, in length from Fisshergate in front as far as the highway leading from Walmegate Barr to Fulford behind, and in width between the land of the Prior and Convent of the Holy Trinity of York——[58] Metcalf, gentleman on the other side.

Witnesses. Richard Thornton, Mayor, William Skypton and Thomas Freman, Sheriffs, Anthony Welburn and William Sawyer.

Given at York, 10 February 17 Henry VII [1502].   [Latin]

(ff. 209v-210) FEOFFMENT.[59]

John Bollyng, clerk,

to Brian Palmes, sergeant at law, Nicholas Palmes, gentleman, William Gyliott, gentleman, George Palmes, gentleman, Brian Grene, gentleman, Brian Duffeld, clerk, William Sherburn, clerk, John Newton, chaplain, Martin Anderson, chaplain, and William Marchall, to the uses specified in a schedule annexed to this deed.

lands, messuages, tenements and gardens in the City of York, which the feoffor lately had by the gift and feoffment of Margaret Rygge,

[56] Illegible.
[57] Badly faded.
[58] Illegible
[59] Faded in parts.

widow, and Christopher Eltofts, esquire.

Witnesses. George Kyrke, Mayor, John Chapman and Christopher Horner, Sheriffs, William Harnesse and Robert Spoford, chaplains.

Given, 8 October 4 Henry VIII [1512].

Subscribed. Esshe.   [Latin]

The said feoffees were to suffer Sir John Bollyng to receive the issues and profits of those lands for the term of his life. After his death, Sir Martin Anderson, chantry priest of the chantry of St. Thomas of Canterbury in the Church of St. Saviour in the City of York, was to receive them upon condition that he and his successors should cause a solemn *Derige* to be celebrated annually on the last day of January and a solemn mass of Requiem on 1 February for the souls of the said John Bollyng, his parents, Dame Margaret Rygge, widow, and Christopher Eltofts, esquire. Sir Martin Anderson was to give to every priest incumbent within the said church and present at the mass and *Derige* 4d, to the parish clerk 4d, and to the city bellman *to go aboute the Citie prayng for my saule accordyng to the auncient and lawdable custome of the said citie,* 2d.

Should it happen that the said Sir Martin or any of his successors was not content to cause the *Derige* and mass to be celebrated as aforesaid, the feoffees were to suffer the church wardens to receive the issues and profits, to cause the obit to be performed and employ the residue to the use of the said church until the chantry priest was content to perform the services.

Subscribed. Esshe.   [English]

On 1 September 9 Henry VIII [1517], Thomas Thornton, son and heir of Arthur Thornton, came to the house of John Dogeson, Mayor, and sought the enrolment of three deeds in the common register of the city as follows.

(f. 210v.) FEOFFMENT.

Thomas Thornton

to Robert Radclyf and William Radclyf,

a close called *Keygarth* in Over Catton, in the County of York.

Appointment of John Hunter as his attorney to deliver seisin.

Given, 22 August 9 Henry VIII [1517].   [Latin]

QUITCLAIM.

Thomas Thornton

to Robert Radclyf and William Radclyf,
a close called *Keygarthe* in Over Catton, which they had by his
gift and feoffment.

Given, 24 August 9 Henry VIII [1517]. [Latin]

RECEIPT AND ACQUITTANCE.

Thomas Thornton
to Robert Radclyf of Tadcastre,
of the sum of £8 paid for the sale of the close called *Keygarthe* in
Over Catton.

Given, 22 August 9 Henry VIII [1517]. [Latin]

Subscribed. Esshe.

(f. 211) Continuation of the demise on f. 199v. above.

(f. 211v) *Ordynauncs of the Bookebyndars or Stacionars*[60] of the
Citie of York, dyvysed, stabisshed and made by the right worshipfull John North, Mayour of the saied Citie, George Gale, Robert
Hall, Robert Heckilton, John Beane, William Watsone, Robert
Pacocke, Thomas Appleyard, Richard White and William Bek-
with, Aldremen, William Harper, Martyne Sosa, Thomas Stand-
even, James Symsone, James Harington, Parsivall Crawforth,
Rychard Golthrop, John Shelytoe, Raulfe Hall and John Hargill
of the 24 of the Counsell of the saied Cytie, at the instance and
humble request of Thomas Rychardson, John Typlady and otherz
of that craft at their assemble on Ousebrige, the 9th of Novembre
in the first and secund yere of the reignes of our soveraigne lord
and lady Philip and Marie by the grace of God, Kinge and Quene
of Englande, Fraunce, Naples, Jerusalem and Ireland, defendars
of the feyth, Princes of Spayne and Cicilie, Archidukes of Austria,
Dukes of Milayne, Burgundye and Brabant, Countes of Haspurge,
Flaundars and Tyrol [1554]. Whiche ordinaunces, for good ordre
of the saied occupacion and common profite of the Kinge and
Quenes people, are now ratified and aggreed alsoo by the saied
worshipfull presence wyth the whole consent of the goodmen of the
saied craft to be ever hereafter firmely observed and kept as hereafter foloweth.

First, that no man of the saied occupacion shall take any to be
apprentice for lesse terme than for seven yeres to be fully ended,
apon peyne of forfatinge twenty shillings, thone halfe therof to be

---

[60] Also entered in House Book 21, ff. 63v-64 and printed in *York Civic Records*
Vol. V, p. 111. See also ordinances of 1476 or 1484, f. 148v. above.

to the chambre of the sayed cytie use and thother halfe to the needes and behoofe of this occupacion.

Item, that no man shall sett up ne occupie of the saied craft within this cytie neyther for himselfe nor none other, except he hayth ben seven yeres apprentyce wythin the saied citie at that occupacion or ells doo aggree therfor with the chambre and occupacion, apon peyne of fourty shillings to be forfayted, thone halfe to the chambre of this cytie and thother halfe to the said occupacion.

Item, yf soo be that any apprentice doeth uniustly bribe or convey of his maisters goodes to the valewe of twelve penyes, and it sufficiently proved, than he to occupie no moare of the occupacion within the Citie of York, apon peyne of forefayture fourty shillyngs as is aforesaied.

Item, if that there be any of the saied occupacion that doo rebelle and will not obey the head serchars of thoccupacion in their lawfull serche, or ells call or rayle apon theym other (f. 212) wise than become theym to doo, for every suche offense shall loose three shillings foure penyes as ys aforesayed, halfe to the chambre and halfe to thoccupacion.

Item, that no stranger or forynar shall sell any booke or bookes wythin this citie except free men of the same citie, apon peyne of forefature of the saied bookes so sold, thone halfe to the chambre and thother halfe to the occupacion.

Subscribed. T. F.

(f. 212v) FEOFFMENT.

Thomas Clerk of York, gentleman,

to William Pullay, tailor, and Thomas Williams, tanner,

a tenement in Northestrete, lying in width between the land of the Mayor and Commonalty of York on the south and the land of Christopher Neleson, gentleman, on the north, and in length from Northestrete on the east as far as the land of John Bacheler, cordwainer, on the west.

Proviso that William Pullay and Thomas Williams should convey the said tenement within four days to Thomas Clerk and Catherine his wife for the term of their lives, in satisfaction of Catherine's dower in all the lands and tenements of the said Thomas Clerk in York, and after their death to the use of John Clerk, his son, and the heirs of his body, remainder to the right heirs of the said Thomas Clerk.

Given, 7 May 36 Henry VIII [1544].   [Latin]

(f. 213) FEOFFMENT.
William Pullay and Thomas Willyams,
to Thomas Clerk and Katherine, his wife, for life, in satisfaction
of Katherine's dower in all the lands and tenements of her husband in York, remainder to John Clerk, son of Thomas, and the
heirs of his body, remainder to the right heirs of Thomas.
a tenement in Northestrete [as above].
Given, 9 May 36 Henry VIII [1544].   [Latin]

(f. 213v) [Blank].

(f. 214.) *Judgment of the Searchers*   [Latin]
This is the award, order and judgement of us, Edward Tarne,
Thomas Barroby and Bryan Mauxwell, serchers of the carpenters,
Thomas Yaits and John Awdcorne, serchers of the tylers, mayd
apon oure corporall othes, appon certen contraverses in buyldings
and other noysances dependyng betwixt Isabell Nyccolson, wyddo,
of thone partie and James Wylkynson, gyrdler, of thother partie,
the second day of August anno 1571, as followeth: —
In primis, we do fynde that James Wylkynson haith stoppyd upp
a dowerstead wich was a way to come to the grate head. Also our
order is that there shall be a way mayd there agayn as it was accustomyd before, for the dightyng[61] of the grate head at the Shamyls
end.
Also we do award that James Wylkynson shall cast nothing furth
of the baksyde but that he shall bryng it downe to the grate head.
Also we do fynd that nether James Wylkynson, Martyn Marshall
nor Mestres Nyccolson shall have any wyndo or synke to cast any
thyng furth to corrupte the said dyke.
And also we do fynd that one corner of Mesteres Nyccolson wall
stondyth to moche into the said dyke by half a foote.
And also we do fynd that it is laufull for Mestres Nycholson to
buyld upon her wall accordyng to her tymbre, withoute any lett or
stopp of James Wylkynson.
And also we do agree that James Wylkynson shall make his
gutter over his grate head to fall into the quenes dyke, whereby
that naither Mestres Nyccolson nor no other neghtbors shall have

[61] *dight*: put in order, make, construct.

no harme by it, or ells to pull is [sic] downe immedyatly.

Also we do agre that Mestres Nyccolson, James Wylkynson, Rychard Noble and Martyn Marshall shall helpe to make clean the same dyke as ofte as neyd shall requyer.

Also we doo demaund for our serche whiche is our dewtye, 6s 8d to be paid betwixt James Wylkynson and Mestres Nyccolson, aither of theme 3s 4d.

(f. 214v) On 5 April 16 Henry VIII [1525], William Maleverer, knight, came before William Barker, Mayor, Miles Newton, the Mayor's clerk, John Shawe, Ralph Symson and John Rychardson, Chamberlains, in the Council Chamber on Ouse Bridge and sought the enrolment of the following deed in the common register of the city.

DEED TO DECLARE THE USES OF A RECOVERY.

of William Maleverer, knight.

Reciting that he and Robert Barker, clerk, had suffered a recovery by Thomas Middilton, esquire, William Thwayte the younger, esquire, Ralph Hopton, esquire, James Strangweys, esquire, and Robert Curteys, chaplain, in the king's court at Westminster, in the Trinity term 16 Henry VIII [1524], by diverse writs of entry *uppon disseison in the post*, of the manor of Eltoft [Eltofts] with appurtenances in the parish of Thorner, eleven messuages, 500 acres of land, 116 acres meadow, 300 acres pasture, 70 acres wood, 400 acres moor, and 13s 4d rent in Eltofte in the parish of Thorner, Dryghtlynton, [Drighlington] Adwalton, Clawcroft,[62] Folyfate [Follifoot] and Newby in the County of York; the manors of Ernclyff [Arncliffe] and Daulton [Dalton] with appurtenances, 60 messuages, 300 acres of land, 100 of meadow, 200 acres pasture, 80 acres wood, 1000 acres moor, 1000 acres heath and 40s. rent with appurtenances in Erneclyff, Daulton, Ingleby, Westleyfeld,[62] Traynham [Trenholme], Thorner, Clyfforth [Clifford], Tadcaster, Stutton, Potter Newton, Elaydall,[62] Moreallerton [Moor Allerton], Chapeltown, Hawkesworth, Rawdon, Rigton, Bramham, Billesdale [Bilsdale], Otteley,[63] Shadwell, Downkeswyk [Dunkeswick], Birtby [Birkby], in the County aforesaid, the manor of Walkryngham [Walkeringham] with the appurtenances, 100 acres of land, [? 20 acres] meadow, 100 acres [pasture] and 20s.

[62] Not identified.   [63]—[63] Legible only under ultra violet light.

rent [with the appurtenances] .....⁶⁴ and Bekyngham [Beck-ingham] in the County of⁶³ Nottyngham; and the manor of Butyll [Bothel] with appurtenances, ten messuages, 100 acres of land, 60 acres meadow, 100 acres pasture, one water mill, and 20s rent with appurtenances in Butyll, Spyndelstane [Spindelston] and Alknewyk in the County of Northumberland. He, William Maleverer, was also seised of the manor of Woddersom [Wother-some] in the County of York to him and the heirs male of his body begotten according to the old entails of the same. Further, he had suffered a recovery by Thomas Middlyton, esquire, John Gascoigne, esquire, Ralph Hopton, (f. 215) esquire, and Henry Ardyngton, esquire, in the Court of the Bishop of Duresme, 16 Henry VIII, by writ of entry *upon disseisin in the post*, of the moiety of the manor of Seynt Elyn Aukland with appurtenances and also 30 messuages, 200 acres of land, 100 acres meadow, 200 acres pasture, 60 acres wood, 500 acres moor and 10s rent with appurtenances in Seynt Elyn Aukland, Bisshopaukeland, and Bishopton in the County of Duresme.

William Maleverer wills that his recoverers should—

[1] Make estate to Anne Malleverer, widow of James Malleverer, for life without impeachment of waste, *voluntary* [wilful] waste excepted, of the manor of Eltoft and messuages, land [etc., as above] in Eltoft in the parish of Thorner, Dryghtlyngton, Ad-walton, Claucroft, Folyfate and Newby.

[2] Make estate to himself and Joan his wife, for the term of their lives, without impeachment of waste, of the manor of Ern-clyf and all the messuages, lands [etc.] in Ernclyff, Ingleby and Westleyfeld.

[3] Make estate to William Ingilby, John Rouclyff, Henry Wombewell, esquires, John Markynfeld, gentleman, Thomas Sparlyng and their heirs, of lands and tenements to an annual value of £20, part of the manor of Daulton, to be held to the use of Robert Malleverer, his eldest son and heir apparent, and Alice Markynfeld, daughter of Sir Ninian Markynfeld, knight, and the heirs male of the body of Robert, in default thereof to the use of William Malleverer, his second son and the heirs male of his body begotten, (f. 215v) in default thereof to the use of Leonard Malleverer, his third son and the heirs male of his body begotten, in default thereof,

⁶⁴ Two words illegible.

to the use of Henry Malleverer, his youngest son and the heirs male of his body begotten, and in default thereof, to the use of his [William Maleverer's] right heirs.

Proviso that if Robert Malleverer should die leaving only female issue of the said Alice, the said feoffees should stand seised of those lands and tenements to the uses declared in a marriage settlement made between him, William Maleverer, and Sir Ninian Markynfeld on the marriage of the said Robert and Alice, and after the sums specified therein had been levied, the residue should be held to his use for life, remainder to the use of the heirs male as aforesaid.

[4] The recoverers were to be seised after his death of other lands and tenements of the manor of Dailtown, of an annual value of £4, now in the tenure of Ralph Harkay, to the use of Henry Maleverer, his youngest son, for life.

[5] The recoverers should be seised of the moiety of the manor of Seynt Elyn Aukland with appurtenances and lands and tenements in Seynt Elyn Aukland, Bishopaukland and Bishopton in the County of Duresme, to the use of William and Leonard Maleverer, two of his younger sons, severally for the term of their lives.

[6] After the decease of the said Anne and Joan, Henry, William and Leonard and all others afore-named having life interests, the recoverers should be seised of the manors, lands and tenements, parcel of the premises, to the yearly value of 40 marks (f. 216) not put in feoffment to any of the aforesaid uses, to the use of him to assign, give or grant for life or for payment of his debts and performance of his will.

[7] The recoverers were to be seised of the reversion of the said lands and tenements to the annual value of 40 marks, of the reversion of the manors of Eltoft, Ernclyff, Dailtown, Walkryngham, Butill and Seynt Elyn Alkland, and the reversions of lands and tenements in Eltoft, Drightlyngton, Adwalton, Clawecroft, Folyffate, Newby, Ernclyff, Dailtown, Ingilby, Westleyfeld, Trayngham, Thorner, Clyfforthe, Tadcaster, Stutton, Potter Newton, Elaydall, More Allerton, Chappelltown, Hawkesworthe, Rawdon, Rigton, Bramham, Billesdayll, Otley, Shadwell, Downekeswyk, Birtby, Walkryngham, Bekyngham, Butill, Spyndyllsteyn, Awnewyk, Seynt Ellyn Aukland, Bishop Aukland and Bishopton, and also of the manor of Woddersom, to the use of himself for life, remainder to the use of Robert Maleverer, his son and heir apparent, and the heirs male of his body begotten, in default thereof to the

use of William Maleverer, his second son and the heirs male of his body begotten, in default thereof to the use of Leonard Maleverer, his third son and the heirs male of his body begotten, and in default thereof to the use of Henry Maleverer, his youngest son and the heirs male of his body begotten, and in default of such issue to the manors of Woddersom, Eltoft and Thorner, to the use of the old entails of the same, and in default of such issue to the use of the right heirs of him, Sir William Maleverer.

Given 24 October 16 Henry VIII [1524].   [English]

(f. 216v) On 4 December 17 Henry VIII [1525], John Beilby, citizen and gentleman of York, came before William Barker, Mayor, Miles Newton, Common Clerk, John Shawe, Ralph Symson and John Rychardson, Chamberlains, in the Council Chamber on Ouse Bridge, read a deed of feoffment and the schedule annexed thereto, and asked that they should be enrolled in the common register.

(ff. 216v-217) FEOFFMENT.[65]

John Beylby, gentleman,
to Brian Higdon, clerk, Dean of the Metropolitan Church of York, William Clyffton, clerk, John Acclome, esquire, Robert Challoner, gentleman, John Mores, yeoman, and John North, yeoman, to the use of John Beylby, his heirs and assigns,
the manor of More Monkton [Moor Monkton], and messuages, lands, tenements, rents, reversions and services, meadows, pastures, woods and commons in More Monkton and Wyllesthorp [Wilstrop] in the County of the City of York; lands, messuages, gardens and tenements in the City of York and also messuages, lands, tenements, rents, reversions and services in Naburn and Goudmadame [Goodmanham] in the County of York.

Appointment of Henry Mores and John Beyn as attorneys to deliver seisin.

Given 18 January 16 Henry VIII [1525].   [Latin]

(f. 217v-218) DEED TO DECLARE THE USES OF A FEOFFMENT.

The feoffees were to be seised of the manor of More Monkton and premises in More Monkton and Wyllesthorp, to the use of John Beylby, the feoffor and his assigns, for the term of his life,

[65] See also ff. 202, 203.

allowing him to receive the issues and profits without impeachment of waste, and after his death to the use of William Fayrfax of Steton in the County of the City of York, esquire, his heirs and assigns, according to the terms of an indenture made between William Fayrfax and John Beylby, 30 October 17 Henry VIII [1525], concerning the bargain and sale of the reversion of the said manor and other premises. They were to stand seised of the other lands and tenements specified in the feoffment to the use, hereafter to be declared, of John Beylby, his heirs and assigns.

Given, 7 November 17 Henry VIII [1525].   [English]

(f. 218v) APPOINTMENT OF A RECORDER.

15 April 25 Henry [1534].

[Present] George Gayle, Maior; George Lawson, knight, William Barker, William Wryght, Henry Dayson, John Hogeson, John Shawe, William Harryngton, John Beylbe, Robert Elwald, William Dogeson and John North, Aldermen; Robert Hall and John Plewman, Sheriffs; Thomas Dawson, Robert Fons, Roger Geggs, Thomas Baylay, John Lytster and John Collyer of the 24.

Assemblyd in the Counsell Chamber within the Comon Hall of the said citie, the day and yere abovewryttyn, when and where it was fully agreyd and determynyd by the said presents for dyvers consideracions thayme then movyng, that Maister John Pullayn, lernyd in the comon lawe, late deputy unto Sir Richard Page, kyght, lait Recorder of this saide citie, who haith nowe surrendred into the hands of the Mayer and Commonaltie of this said citie the office of Recordership of this said citie for dyvers consideracions, and esp[ec]ially for that he cowld not be present in his owne person with the said Mayer and his bredren at all tymes neydfull to viewe and survey the defauts of the fishegarthes within the water of Owse, and in dyvers other placs within the Countie of the said Citie of York and the Countie of Lyncoln, according to the king comyssion.

Whereuppon the said presens, the day and yere aforesaid, haith frely gyvyn and grauntyd unto the said John Pulleyn the office of the recordership of the said citie, peseably to have, hold and excercyse for the terme of his lyf naturall, and fyve pounds of lawfull Englishe money to be payd hym yerely duryng his said lyf furth of the coffers of the comon chamber of the said citie by the Chamberlayns of this said citie for the tyme beyng, that is to say fifty shyllyngs at the feast of Pentecost and other fifty shyllings

at the feist of Saynt Martyn in Wynter by evyn porcions. Also it
is agreyd by the said presens that the said John Pullayn shall have
yerely frome nowfurth of the Shyrryfs of the said citie for the tym
beyng, the clothing accustomyd before the rydyng day of the
Shirriffs when that thay shall make proclamacion for the kyng within the said citie by vertue of ther office, lykwise as other Recorders
of this said citie haith had in tymes past accordyng to the auncyent
custom of this said citie and for the wirship of the same citie. And
where as the said Sir Richard Page haith yerely oone annuytie of
£12 of the said Mayer and Commonaltie for the terme of his lyf, for
the resynyng of his said office for the consyderacion abovesaid, that
if it forton the said Sir Richard Page to dye then it is fully agred,
(f. 219) concluded and determynyd by the said presents that the said
John Pullayn shall have the old fee that dyd belong unto the
Recorders of this said citie in tymes past, that is to say of the
Shyrryfs of the said citie for the tyme beyng twelve pounds in money
and the said clothyng, and to be payd furth of the said common
chamber by the Chamberlayns for the tyme beyng 26s 8d. In wyt-
nesse hereof etc.

(f. 219v) AGREEMENT BETWEEN YORK AND HULL ABOUT WEIGHTS AND MEASURES.[66]

Be it had in mynde that apon complaynt made by the Mayour
and citizens of York for sundrie wrongs, newe imposicions and
displeasures ageynst the same citizens of late done and practised
by the Mayour and Aldremen of Kyngeston apon Hull, soo it is that
as well the right worshipfull Richard Goldthorp, Lord Mayour
of the saied Citie of York, the Recordar and Aldermen of the same,
as Walter Jobson, Mayour of Hull aforesayd, the Recordar, certayne Aldremen and Commons of the same towne, the 14th day of
Decembre in the yere of our lord God a thowsand fyve hundred
fyfty and sex, at the saied Citie of York, did all personally come
before the right honorable the Lord President and other the Kyng
and Queenes Maiesties Counsell establisshed in the north parties.
And than and there the same Lord Mayour and citizens of York,
by the mowth of their Recordar, complayned theym that the said
Mayour and Aldremen of Hull nowe alate wold not suffre the

---

[66] Petitions from the Mayor and Commonalty to the Archbishop of York and the
Earl of Shrewsbury, asking for their assistance in this dispute with Hull, are printed
in York Civic Records, Vol. V, pp. 150-1.

merchantz and citizens of York to weigh at the common beame there and carie away lead bought of the men of Peake, nor to have and carie away thens their coales, there or ells where bought of the men of Newcastell. And alsoo for that the Mayour and Aldremen of Hull aforesayd have compelled some of the saied citizens to delyver certayne their grayne there by a watir measure beyng of a greater quantitie than it ought to be, contrary to the kyng and queenes gracs lawes and statuts in suche case provyded, and to the great hyndrans and losse of the sayd citizens. Wherunto the saied Mayour and Aldremen of Hull by their Recordar than and there made certayne allegacions and answer whiche the saied Lord President and Counsell thought neyther to be sufficient ne lawfull, and after the matter beyng there soo arguued and debated of bothe parties, the Counsell declared to theym of Hull that they ought to have and use and alsoo suffer to be occupied by any the kyng and queenes subiects, common weights, measures and other things appoynted by the lawes and statuts of this realme, and willed bothe the parties to goe lovyngly togiders and fall to ordre and aggreament emongs theymselfs, and if not they wold to their displeasure. And therapon both the saied parties doyng ther dewties to the saied Lord President and Counsell went forth immediatly thens. And soo endevoryng theymselfs no more to trowble the said Consell with that matter, did descretely and with good deliberacion treat of commune and reasone all the premisses emongs theymselfs, and at last than and there did quyetly and lovyngly conclude and aggree eyther partie with thother in maner and forme folowyng. That is to saye, first that the citizens of York at all tymes from hensforth shall have all suche their lead as nowe is or herafter shalbe brought to the towne of Kyngestone apon Hull (f. 220) or there bought, readely taken up at the common weighows there, comonly called the Woollhows, weighed and striken at their pleasure, payeng onely the accustomed dewties for wyndyng, strikyng and weigheng of the same, and payeng for hows rowme and ligheng of all suche lead as the saied citizens or any of theym shall buye or gett of any of the Peake, onely tenne penyes for every fudder[67] and not above, ligh it there never soo short a tyme or long tyme as they list. And for lyke hows rowme of all suche other leade as the saied citizens or any of theym shall sende or bryng from York and take up at the said weighows only twoo pens for every fudder and not above,

[67] *fudder, fother*: a definite weight, of lead 19½ cwt.

ligh it there never soo short or long tyme as they will. Furthermore, that the saied citizens and every of theym shall not onely be per- mytted and suffred from tyme to tyme quyetly to passe away from Kyngestone apon Hull aforesaid with all suche their coales as shalbe thither brought, but alsoo shall have their reasonable and con- venyent part of any coales there to be solde withowt any lett or denyer of the Mayour or any thenhabitants of Hull aforesayd. And the sayd citizens therin to be bettar entreated than they have ben heretofore. And as towchyng the watir measure ther, the saied Mayour and Aldermen of Hull doo nowe soothly affirme that the same is allready reformed and that whan any of the saied Aldermen of York come to Hull they shall see in dede that it is soo.

Fynally, as for all suche other poysable goodes or wares as any of the said citizens of York shall chanse to take up at Hull, it shalbe lykewise taken up and weighed at their common weighows afore- sayd as they have ben accustomed, and other their goodes where then can aggree or fynde and gett place. And if it happen any one or more [? busye] or querelouse persones of eyther partie to offende in any of the premisses, than the saied Mayours apon re- lation to theym therof made shall by their discretion see reformation and punysshement therin soo that no breache of frendship by any suche occasion shalbe betwene the saide parties. All whiche aggrea- ments, condicions and articles well and [? fermlie] to be performed, fullfylled and kept of eyther parties and——[68] successours for ever, not onely the said Lord Mayour and——[68] of York for theym and their successours, but alsoo the said Mayour and Aldermen and comons of Hull for theym and their successours have made their promise thone to thother of their worship and honesties and——[68] lovyngly takyng leve every of thothers they departed.

Subscribed. By Thomas Fale, Common Clerk.

(f. 220v) ORDINANCES OF THE GOLDSMITHS.[69]

The ancient ordynancs of the mystery or occupacion of golde- smythes of the Citie of York, diligently perused and examyned by the right worshipfull Parsyvall Craforth, Mayour, the Aldermen and Pryvay Counsell of the said Citie, at their assembly in the

[68] Word illegible.
[69] Also entered in House Book 23, ff. 11v-13 and printed in York Civic Records, Vol. VI, pp. 9-12. For earlier goldsmiths' ordinances see York Memorandum Book, I, pp. 74-77.

Counsell Chambre apon Ousebrig, the tenth day of Aprile in the thridde yere of the reigne of our most gracyouse soveraigne lady Queene Elizabeth [1561], and by the said Mayour, Aldremen and Counsell at instans and with full consent of Thomas Symson and Robert Gylmyn, serchars, and other the good men maisters of the said craft beyng present, were than and there dewly reformed, approved, ordeyned and stablished to be frome thensforth firmely observed and kept forever to the worshippe of the said citie, common profitt of the people and honestie of the said occupacion.

In primis, accordyng as it was ordeyned the 5th day of Marche in the 12th yere of the reigne of Kyng Henry the 4th [1411] by the Lorde Mayour, Aldremen, Shirefs and sundrye other the most honest persones of the said Citie of York, with the full aggreament of the wholle occupacion of goldesmythes, it is now ratified and confirmed by all the said assemble that frome hensforth there shalbe twoo serchars to be yerely chosen of the said occupation, Englisshe men borne, and no moe.

Item, that the said goldsmythes shall bryng every of theym their towche[70] and marke so that their works may be approved and towched with the pounce[71] of this citie called the half leoparde heade and half flowre de luyce,[72] accordyng as the statute purporteth. And if any have not a towche or pounce that then they shall cause one newe towche or pounce to be made in accomplishment of justice as the lawe it demandeth. And that every goldsmyth shall make his proper towche or marke to be knowne to the serchars for the tyme beyng, apon payne to forfayte 3s 4d, thone half therof to the use of the Mayour and Commonaltie of this citie and thother half to the profite of the said craft.

Item, that no goldsmyth shall work any worse golde than the towche of Paryse, apon payne of forfayture of the stuff soo wrought, onlesse it be in rynges or other small iowell that may be suffred to be wrought of the same that is brought to theym.

Item, that no goldsmyth shall worke worse alaye than sterlyng apon peyne of forfayture the duble valewe, and that it be not delyvered untill it be serched by the serchars and the said towche of the citie and his marke sett to. And that no serchar sett the

---

[70] *towche*, touch: an official mark or stamp on gold or silver indicating that it has been tested.

[71] *pounce*: die, stamp or punch for impressing marks on metal.

[72] *flowre de luyce*: fleur de lis.

citie towche to worse than sterlyng apon like payne, (f. 221) except there nede sowder in the makyng whiche shalbe allowed accordyng as the sowdre is necessarie to be wrought in the same.

Item, if any maister of the said craft sell or putt to sale any thyng of golde or sylvar whiche belong to their said craft, before it be towched with the common towche of the said citie and also the marke of hym that the said thyng will sell, than he to forfeyte 6s 8d to be equally dyvided in forme aforesaid; except harnesses of girdles, daggars, collers of gentles and other thyngs under the weight of an unce that may not suffyce to beare the said towche, whiche shalbe towched onely with the marke of hym that make it apon payne abovesaid, and to be payde in forme aforesaid at every tyme that any of theym doeth contrarie to this ordynance. Soo that every thyng made within this citie may be knowne from other thyngs made in other places within the realme of England.

Item, it is further ordeyned and aggreed that if any man of the said craft worke any evyll golde or sylvar, that thyng that is soo made shalbe broken and putt ageyne into the fyre to purifie and to fyne and to be made ageyne perfectly. And he that trespased shall forfayte and lose 20s to the chambre and craft by even porcions, and at the secunde tyme 40s, and the thrid tyme 100s. And if he will not soo be chasticed, he shall abiure the craft or be putt forth of the citie.

Item, that accordyng to the statute none of the said artificers or any other shall gilde or sylvar any rynges, beades, harnesse for girdles or suche other made of copre or latyn[73], except ornaments of holy cherche, soo that in the fote or some other part of every suche ornament the latyn or copre appere playnly, and except alsoo spurres for knights and apparell that belongeth to a baron and above that estate, apon peyne to forfeyte 100s in forme aforesaid.

Item, that no goldsmyth sett any counterfait stone in golde except it be a naturall stone, apon payne of imprisonment.

Item, that the serchars of the said occupacion shall dewly make searche as oft as they shall thynk necessarie and trewly present the defaults to my Lord Mayour according to their oathe.

Item, that no man denie the serchars at any tyme to make searche nor revile theym at any tyme, neither in their shoppe nor in any other place whill they be serchars, in peyne of forfayture

---

[73] *latyn*, latten: brass.

6s 8d as oft as they soo doe, to be levied and payed in forme above-said.

(f. 221v) Item, if their be cause why that occupacion sholde mete for the weale of the said citie and be warned by the serchars to mete at a place convenyent at a certayne howre, he that is away without reasonable cause to paye 12d in forme aforesaid.

Item, that no goldsmyth shall sett any iornay man on worke but for 14 dayes, and if he doe for any longar tyme without the leve of the serchars, he shall forfeyte and paye 3s 4d to be equally dyvided as is aforesaid.

Item, that the olde pageant maisters shall yerely make a dewe accompte of the money and of the playeng geare unto thoccupacion on Saynt Dunstane's even or ells the morowe after, apon payne of forfayture 12d a pece.

Item, that neither the corones nor gownes be lent to any under 8d a pece, and that it be paid or they be delyvered, except it be to some of thoccupacion, and the serchars to make accompte therof.

Item, that no maister of the said craft shall take any apprentyce for lesse terme than seven yeres, apon payne of forfaytur tenne marks to be payed and equally dyvided as is abovesaid. And at the comyng in of the said apprentyce within a moneth to paye 8d to the craft, and his name to be entred in the booke of the said gold-smythes. And at thende of his terme such apprentyce to be free of the craft, payeng his lawfull dewties to the said occupacione.

And over this it is ordeyned that if it shall chanse the maister of suche apprentice to die duryng his said apprentiship, than suche apprentice shall serve still with his maistresse if she have a iournay man sufficiently conyng to learne hym in the said craft, or ells the same apprentice to be sett over to some other maister of the said occupacione by discrecion of the serchars.

Item, that none that hath served his apprentiship within the said citie shall occupie as maister in the said craft before he be approved by the serchars of the same that he be an hable and conyng work-man in the said craft, apon peyne of forfayture of 14s to be paied in forme aforesaid.

Item, it is nowe further ordeyned and aggreed that noe stranger, ne other that hath not bene apprentice with this citie by the space of seven years or moare, shall sett up or occupie as maister of the payne of forfayture of tenne pounds, except suche stranger or said occupacion of goldsmythes within this citie or suburbs, apon others that hath not bene apprentice as is aforesaid be first allowed by my Lord Mayour (f. 222) and serchars of the said occupation for the tyme beyng, and doo alsoo paye before he occupieth as maister of the same occupation £10, thone half to the said chambre and thother half to thoccupation.

ORDINANCES OF THE MINSTRELS.[74]

Marginal note: These ordinances were reformed in the time of Hugh Graves, Mayor [1578].   [Latin]

Thordynancs of the musicians commonly called the mynstrells within the Citie of York, devised, ordeyned and stablished by the right honorable Parcyvall Craforth, Lord Mayour, his worshipfull bretherne thaldremen and Counsell of the said Citie of York, at the humble prayer and with wholle consent of the goodmen mynstrells and freemen of the citie aforesaid, the 25 day of Novembre in the fourth yere of the reigne of our most gracyouse soveraigne lady Queen Elizabeth [1561], to be frome thensforth for evermore dewly and firmely executed, fulfilled and kept in all poynts, aswell for the worship of the said citie as alsoo for the honestie, weale and good ordre of the science of thaforesaid mynstrells, in forme as foloweth, that is to saye:—

Forenars. First it is ordeyned, enacted and stablished that noo maner foreyner of what condicion he bee occupie any mynstrelsye, syngyng or playeng apon any instrument within any paroche within this citie or franches therof, apon any cherche holy dayes or dedicacion dayes halowed or kept within the same paroche, or any brotherhode's or freman's dynnar or dynnars made or kept within the same citie or franchise therof, upon peyne that every suche forayne mynstrell after monytion to hym gyven by the maister or serchars to paye for every tyme that he shalbe fonde doyng contrary to this acte 3s 4d, the one half therof to remayne to the use of the common chambre of this citie and thother half to the common boxe of the said arte.

Election. Item, that the felawship of the mynstrells, freemen of this citie nowe beyng and theyr successours forever, shall have power, authoritie and libertie every yere at the fest of Saynt (f. 222v) James thapostle to assemble theym selfs in Saynt Anthony Hall or

---

[74] It is recorded in House Book 23 f. 40 (*York Civic Records*, Vol VI, pp. 30-31) that the ordinances of the minstrels were to be observed as they were enrolled "in the old registr of parchment with the bosses".

other convenyent place within the said citie at a day certayne by theym to be lymyted, and soo assembled by their common voyces and assents or of the greater partie of theym, to choise three hable persones of the same felawship to be a maister and twoo serchars of the said sciens or craft for the yere folowyng. And if any persone soo chosen maister or serchar refuse or forsake the said office of maistership or serchar, every persone soo refusyng to paye 20s, thone half therof to the common chamber of this citie and thother half to the behof of the said craft.

Accompte. Item, that the common boxe of the said felawship shalbe and remayne from yere to yere in the custodie and kepyng of the maister and serchars of the said craft for the tyme beyng. And of all suche money as the same maister and serchars have at the ende of their yere or within twenty dayes next after, shall gyve and yelde up unto the said felawship or the greater part of theym a trewe and iust accompte in wrightyng, apon peyne every of theym makyng defalt to paye 10s to be equally dyvided to thuses aforesaid.

Quarterage. Item, that every brother of the said science shall paye yerely towards the supportacion and bryngyng forth of their pageant and other chardges of the said craft 8d by yere, that is to say 2d in every quarter. And that every suche freman beyng a brother of the said arte not payenge the said quarterage every quarter day, that is at thende of every quarter of the yere or within 15 dayes next and immediatly folowyng after any of the said quarter dayes, and refusyng to content the same, to paye for every default 3s 4d to be equally dyvided in forme aforesaid.

Presentacion. And that every freman or brother of the said craft present every of his apprentics to the maister and serchars of the said craft for the tyme beyng within one moneth immediatly after that any suche apprentice shalbe bonde, payeng at his presentacion to the comon boxe of the said craft 20d. And if any of theym be negligent and doo not present his apprentice within the said moneth nor pay the sayd fyne of 20d, every suche brother soo offendyng to forfayte for every default 10s, thone half therof to be to the chambre of the citie, and thother half to the common boxe of the said craft.

Assembles. Item, that yf any persone enfranchesed in the said craft or brother of the same, warned by any of the said serchars for the tyme beyng to come to the quarter dayes or to assemble of the maister and serchars of the said craft for the tyme beyng with others the bretherne of the same craft, and without reasonable cause absentyng hym self not willyng to come thether, to paye for every default 2s to be equally dyvided to the uses abovesaid.

Misdemeanour. Item, that no persone enfranchesed in the said craft or brother of the same presume to rebuke, revyle or gyve any slanderouse or vilaynouse word to the said maister or serchars or to any of theym for the tyme beyng or to any (f. 223) other persone beyng brother or freeman of the said felawship or craft, apon peyne to paye for every tyme that any of theym shalbe founde culpable of any suche approbriouse or unsittyng woordes to paye for every default 6s 8d, thone half therof to be to the said chambre and thother half to the common boxe of the said craft.

Teachyng. Item, that none of the said felawship beyng a mynstrell enfranchesed and brother of the said craft, teache or enforme any other persone other then his owne apprentyce in any poynt or feate of mynstrelsie, (except he be a freeman's sone of the same craft), nor goo with any stranger to any weddyng or any other feast onely to labour with hym within the said citie or liberties of the same, without the lycence of the maister of the said craft for the tyme beyng fyrst obteyned, apon payne to forfeyte for every default 6s 8d, to be devided and employed as is aforesaid. Provided that this acte doo not extende to any brother for teachyng any gentleman or freeman of this citie and their children disposed to learne any thyng for his pleasure.

Apprentiship. Item, that noo freeman of the said craft take any servant by covenant for a yere or otherwise, onelesse he be apprentice for the terme of seven yeres at the least accordyng to the laudable custome of this citie, apon payne to forfeyte for every offence 20s, thone half therof to be to the common chambre of the said citie, and thother half therof to the common boxe of the said craft. Provided that this acte doe not extende to the waytes of the Citie of York for the tyme beyng to hyre any man to helpe theym in their watche.

Secretts. Item, that no brother freman of the said craft at any tyme open or disclose any woords or sayeng towchyng their scyens, spoken at the common or privie meatyngs of the said craft or any of theym (except it be to any of the said bretherne or at the tyme of their said assemble), apon peyne to forfeyte for every suche default 6s 8d, thone half therof to the use of the said chambre, and thother half to the said craft.

Enhablyng. Alsoo that noo freeman brother of the said craft shall, at any tyme herafter, sett forth his or their apprentice or apprentices to labour in any compaynye as a mynstrell, within the said citie or liberties of the same, before the said apprentics and every of theym be examyned and admytted by the said maister or serchars for the tyme beyng, apon peyne to forfeyte for every defalt 3s. 4d, thone half to the chambre of the said citie, and thother half to the common boxe of the sayde craft.

Apprentics (void). Item, that noo freeman brother of the said craft shall frome hensforth have no moo apprentics but one att ones, except he have bene either maister or serchar of the said craft, or ells twoo at one tyme at the most, apon payne to forfeyte for every default 20s, the one half therof to the common chambre of the said citie and thother half therof to the common boxe of the said craft.

Pageant. Fynally, it is further ordeyned and by consent of all the good men of the said mystery or craft fully aggreed that (f. 223v) the said felawship of mynstrells of their proper chardges shall yerely from hensforth bryng forth and cause to be played the pageant of Corpus Christi viz. the Herold, his sone, twoo counselars and the messynger inquyryng the three kyngs of the childe Jesu, sometyme accustomed to be brought forth at chardges of the late masons of this citie on Corpus Christi day, in suche like semely wise and ordre as other occupacions of this citie doo their pageants.[75]

(ff. 224-225v) LEASE OF TANGHALL.

Robert Shorton, clerk, prebendary of the prebend of Frydaythorpe within the Metropolitan Church of St. Peter of York,
  to the Mayor and Commonalty of York,
the manor or capital *mease* called the Tanghall, part of the prebend of Frydaythorpe, two closes called the Greate Tanghall Felde and the Letle Tanghall Felde and another close called the Tonge Grene, with all lands and tenements, houses, orchards, gardens, meadows, *leasues,*[76] pastures, rents, reversions, services, free farms and hereditaments pertaining to Robert Shorton as in the right of the said prebend, and situated in the City of York or within one mile thereof.

---

[75] This last ordinance is printed as a footnote by Lucy Toulmin Smith, *York Plays* p. 125. In the text of the plays, the heading *Mynstrells* has been added after *Masonns* in a sixteenth century hand. *ibid* p. 123.

[76] *leasues, leasows*; pasture, meadow.

Term. 99 years from the feast of the Annunciation of St. Mary the Virgin last.

Rent. £23 p.a. to the lessor and his successors, to be paid in equal portions on the feasts of St. Peter ad Vincula and the Purification of St. Mary the Virgin, between the hours of eight and twelve before noon in the Metropolitan Church of York at the altar in St. Stephen's Chapel, in the *overende* and north side of the said church. If the rent was a quarter of a year in arrears, the lessor was to have the right of re-entry to the premises, together with the severalty of the same ground in summer and winter.

Three years before the end of the term of ninety-nine years, Robert Shorton's successors were to renew the lease, at the same rent, to the Mayor and Commonalty for a further term of ninety-nine years, and so from ninety-nine years to ninety-nine years *unto thende of the worlde*. If the Mayor and Commonalty should refuse such a lease, the prebendary and his successors should hold the premises without impediment. The lessor was to discharge the Mayor and Commonalty of all charges on the premises except tithes. They were to be allowed to dig clay, gravel and sand in the closes, but were to fill in the pits so made within the said term. They undertook to leave the closes in good condition and profitable pasture at the end of the lease, to repair the hedges and ditches and maintain the boundaries in their present condition or better. Robert Shorton covenanted that if he or any of his successors should recover, at the cost of the Mayor and Commonalty, or otherwise obtain in the right of the said prebend, any land, pasture, rent, or other hereditament pertaining to the premises leased, and situated within the city or one mile from it, the Mayor and Commonalty should occupy the same to the end of the said term without paying more than the sum aforesaid.

Proviso that whenever the prebend should be vacant by the death of the prebendary, the Mayor and Commonalty should pay to the Dean and Chapter all rent due within that period; and that the Mayor and Commonalty should not allow the common officers of the city, such as the sergeants and their yeoman, to exercise their authority within the said manor and closes.

The Mayor and Commonalty were to repair and maintain all barns, oxhouses and stables, and within the next three years and every following twenty years to make a rental and boundary of the lands and rents and deliver it to Robert Shorton or his successors, or to the clerk of the Chapter of York. They were to be allowed to maintain, repair, pull down or sell, or otherwise dispose of the manor or chief *mease* of Tanghall and the houses thereto belonging, except as aforesaid.

The bond of the Mayor and Commonalty of the same date in 100 marks, to ensure payment of the rent of £23, was to stand in full effect for every year in which the rent was a quarter of a year in arrears.

Ratified by the Dean and Chapter with the consent of Cardinal Thomas [Wolsey] legate *de latere*, primate, and Chancellor of England and Archbishop of York.

Sealed by the Archbishop, the Dean and Chapter and Robert Shorton, and by the Mayor and Commonalty respectively.

Given, 20 May 17 Henry VIII [1525].   [English]

Ratified and confirmed by Thomas [Wolsey], by divine mercy cardinal priest of the most holy Roman Church under the title of St. Cecilia, Archbishop of York and legate *de latere* of the apostolic see to England, primate of England and chancellor.

Given at his house near Westminster, 14 July 1525.   [Latin]

Also ratified and confirmed by Brian [Higden], Dean of the Metropolitan Church of York, and the Chapter thereof, in the Chapter House, 26 August 1525.   [Latin]

(f. 226) ORDINANCES OF THE CARPENTERS AND JOINERS.[77]

For the weale of this honorable Citie of York and honestie, quietnes and profyte of the carpentars, joynars and carvers inhabityng in the same, at the specyall instance and prayer of Christofer Willughby, William Walles, Edwarde Tarne and Raulf Meryman, serchars of the said science or craft, Richard Graves, William Robynson, William Johnson, Thomas Faull, Edward Dacres, John Tison, John Hill, Thomas Grethed, Robert Granger, Christofer Kichenman, Thomas Palazer, Rogere Walkar, Anthony Prest, Thomas Mason, William Hogeson, George Thomsone, John Ramsden, Petre Gill, Leonard Craven, John Todde, Leonard Wilson, Thomas Thorpe, Thomas Jakson, Robert Dikson, Nicolas Baynebrige, John Lovell, William Jakson, Symon Burdon, William Greggs, William Thomson, Richard Henlake, Petre Nelson, John

[77] Earlier ordinances are printed in *York Memorandum Book* 1, pp. 148-50; ibid., II, pp. 193-4, 277-83, and *York Civic Records*, Vol. V, p. 112.

Revell, Bartholomewe Hill, Henry Gyles, Thomas Plowghman, William Sibson, Mathewe Wilson and John Robynson, good men maisters of the aforesaid occupacion, the 21th day of July in the fyveth yere of the reigne of our most gracyouse soveraigne lady Queene Elizabeth [1563], in the secunde tyme of the mayoraltie of the right honourable Thomas Appleyard, Lord Mayour of the said citie, after diligent perusyng and examynacion had of and in the olde ordinauncs of the said occupacion of joynars and carpentars, the same ordynauncs apon good and iust consederacions ware by authoritie of the said Lord Mayour, his worshipfull bretherne thaldremen, Sheryffs and pryvay counsell of the said citie abridged, reformed, ordeyned and stablished to be from hensforth firmely observed and kept by every of the said occupacion and craft forever in maner and forme as foloweth: —

Unyon of the crafts. In primis, for good unitie, ordre and quyetnes forever hereafter to contynewe in the felawship of the said joynars, carpentars, carvers, whelewrights and sawiars, it is ordeyned and confirmed by the said presens that accordyng to the good meanyng of formar ordynauncs, the said carpentars, joynars, carvers, whelewrights and sawiars shall at all their assembles, rekonyngs, elections, busynesses, accompts and meetyngs concernyng their said occupacion goe and use theym selfs lovyngly togithers as one ocupacion, and none of theym by reason of any their science or craft to chalenge or clayme any superioritie or preemynence of thother, otherwise than as thordre and degree of their offyce or auncienty shall requyre. And alsoo that the head serchar beyng a carpentar shall from hensforth be at the election of their Mayour, Aldremen and Sheryffs of this citie one yere, and the head serchar beyng a joynar another yere, and soo forth yerely from hensforth *alterius vicies*. And that the good men of the said craft doe from tyme to tyme ordre (f. 226v) their elections of serchars for the quyet performyng herof accordyngly, apon peyne of every one of theym whatsoever he be offendyng in any poynt of the premysses to forfaite 6s 8d *toties quoties*, the one half of whiche forfayture to be levied to the use of the common chambre of this citie and thother half to the nedes of the said occupacion.

Assemblees. Item it is ordeyned that as oft as the said serchars of the said occupacion will their bretherne of the same for the weale of this citie and the said occupacion to come togider to gyve their advice and counsell in suche things as they shalbe demanded of, if any brother fayle and come not withoute reasonable cause of excuse, he shall paye 3s 4d as oft tymes as he so offendith, thone half to the chambre and thother half to the said occupacion.

Counsell disclosed. Item, it is ordeyned that if any of the said crafts discover or disclose the lawfull counsell of the said occupacion, or any thyng that ys sayed emongs theym, at the day or dayes of their assemblee for weale of this citie and of the said occupacion, that he or they that soo discloseth the said counsell shall forfayte as oft tymes as they are fonden defectyve 3s 4d, in forme abovesaid to be payed and dyvided.

Disordre in talke. Item, that none of the said occupacion at their meatyng shall disorderly speake or talke or take the tayle owte of an other man's mouth, but kepe sylence at the comandement of the said serchars, apon peyne of forfeytyng for every suche default 2d.

Disagreeng. Item, it is ordeyned that if any of the said occupacions or crafts above rehersed lie an other of his bretherne in malice or call hym false, or stryke hym or profer hym any stroke at any metyng for the weale of the said crafts, that he shall forfeite 6s 8d in maner and forme abovesaid to be payed and dyvided.

Terme of apprentice. Item, that no man of the said occupacion shall take any apprentice for lesse or fewar yeres than seven yeres, apon peyne to forfeite for every suche default 6s 8d, thone half to the chambre and the other half to the said occupacion.

Admyttans of apprentice. Item, that every apprentice of the said occupacions shall from henseforth paye for their entrie in the felawship of the said occupacions 2s 6d. And when the yeres of suche apprentyce is expired, then he to paye for his entrie and admyttance in the same felawship not above 3s 4d, accordyng to the statute therof made in the 22th yere of Kyng Henry the VIII [1530-31].[78]

Hyerlyngs. Item, it is ordeyned that if a yong man that is not connyng in worke of any the said occupacions come into this citie to learne his occupacion bettar, if he be hired in the said occupacion for meat, drynk and 20s by yere or above, then his said maister that so hireth hym within fouretene dayes than next after shall pay 20d in the forme aforesaid to be dyvyded, and if he hire hym under the some of 20s, the said maister that so hireth hym shall paye 3s 4d in the forme (f. 227) abovesaid to be payed and dyvided. Alsoo the said maister shall not take more apon hym of whois worke

[78] *Statutes of the Realm,* 22 Hen. VIII c.4.

he that is not conyng workith than he that so is not conyng in that occupacion can deserve, apon peyne of 3s 4d in the forme abovesaid to be payed and dyvided.

Reteynyng. Item, it is ordeyned that none of the said occupacion shall sett any of worke within this said citie over 14 dayes, except that he be bonden servant for the whole yere or bonden apprentice, apon the peyne of 3s 4d in forme abovesaid to be payed and dyvided.

Searche makyng. Item, it is ordeyned that if any worke within the said city, liberties and precyncts of the same any thing perteynyng to the said occupacions that is unsuffyciently, unhably and unworkmanly wrought, that the serchars of the said occupacions at the desyre of the ownar of the same work shall searche it, and if it be fonden unsuffyciently wrought by the sight of the said serchars, he or they that herin be fonden defectyve [shall] forfeite 6s 8d in forme abovesaid to be payed and dyvided. And over this, he that is so fonden defectyve shall make suffycient amends to the partie therby greved or hurt.

Admyttans of foryner. Item, that every foreyne or strange carpentar, joynar or carver that hath not bene apprentice within this said citie, shall paye to the said occupacion for his entrie [bef]or ever he begynne to worke 3s 4d, and at the tyme when he shalbe habled by the serchars a suffycient workman, then he of frendship to make an hablyng dynar accordyng to the auncyent custome used emongs the said occupacions of this city, soo that the chardges therof excede not above fyve shillyngs.

Contributaries. Item, that every citizen that engrosse or bye any bourds or latts to retayll or sell ageyne within this citie shalbe contributorie and paye towards the chardges of bryngyng forth of the pageant of the carpentars etc., soo that suche contribution shall not excede above foure penyes a pece in any one yere.

Forynars not to be set on worke within the citie. Item, it is ordeyned that there shall no franchesed man nor unfranchesed man within this said citie doe sett on worke any foreynar comyng to this citie, except that the said foreynar and the said persone or persones so settyng the said foreynar on worke come unto the said serchars of the said occupacions, and soo doe compounde with the Chambreleynes of the said citie and the said serchars for the tyme beyng for a fyne therefor not excedyng the some of 3s 4d, under peyne of 6s 8d to be payed undilayedly and devided as is abovesaid, as oft as the said foreynar is soo founden and presented with any man workyng within the said citye or liberties of the same.

Free of turnars' pageant. Item, it is ordeyned that none free of the said crafts within this citie, usyng throwyng or turnyng in their work, shalbe contributory nor pay any thyng to the occupacions of ropars and turnars of the same towards chardges of any pageant, but shalbe frome hensforth (f. 227v) therof quite ageinst the said ropars and turnars. Provided alwayes that if any of the said occupacions doe throwe or turne bolles, disshes, dublers[79] or wheeles or suche like stuff as perteyneth onely to the turnars' craft, every suche to paye pageant money to the said ropars and turnars accordyngly.

Searche of foreyne stuff. Item, that all strangers and foreynars that bryng any ioyned stuff, bourds or latts to this citie to sell shalbe serched and paye their pageant money unto theis said occupacions.

Who may sett up and occupie. Item, that no maner persone other than suche as nowe doe laufully use the said artes shall from hensforth sett up and occupie the craft or mysterie of joynar, carpentar or carver within this citie, except he hath bene brought up therin seven yeres at the least as apprentice, nor shall sett any persone on work in the said art or occupacions beyng not a workman at this daye, except he shall have bene apprentice as is aforesaid, or ells havyng served as apprentice will become a jornay man or be hyred by the yere, apon peyne and forfayture as is conteyned in the statute therfor provided in the fyveth yere of Queene Elizabeth [1562-63].[80]

Default of presentment by the serchars. Item, it is ordeyned that if the said serchars fynde a default in the said occupacion and present it not to the Mayour and the Chambreleynes for the tyme beyng, that the serchars for their concelement as oft tymes as they are therin fonde defectyve forfeite 3s 4d to be payed and dyvided as is aforesaid.

[81]At thassemble of the right honorable Richard Calome, Lord Mayor, his worshipfull bretheren Aldermen and Counsell in the Counsell Chamber upon Ousebridge, the first day of Septembre 1570, at the humble petytion of the good men of tharte or occupacion of joynors of this cytie, the article or proviso ensewinge was by consent of the said worshipfull added to ther ordinarie to be at all

---

[79] *doubler, dubler*: large plate or dish.

[80] *Statutes of the Realm*, 5 Eliz. c.4, XXIV. The penalty imposed was 40s. per month.

[81] Also entered in House Book 24 f. 212 and printed in *York Civic Records*, Vol. VII, pp. 14-15.

times hearafter observed for ever, viz.

Joynars' serch. Provyded allwayes that from hensforth yt shalbe lefull for twoe of the searchers aforesaid beynge joynars, to make searche of all manner of suche worke and stuff, onelie as anie of the said arte or occupacion of joynars or carvers shall worke of there owne stuff for anie manner of persone or persons, whether they be required or not, and yf in ther said searche they doe fynd anie the said stuff deceyptfull or the worke therof not workmanlye (f. 228) wrought, than the maister worker therof upon dewe presentment by the said twoe searchers to forfaite for everye suche default 6s 8d *toties quoties*, thone half therof to thuse of the chamber and thother of the occupacion, and that none of the said joynars soe offendinge shall lett or withstand them in ther sayd searche upon lyke paine to be devyded as ys aforesaid.

18 August 14 Elizabeth [1572], in the time of William Allyn, Mayor. [Latin]

Evell latts. Item, yt is ordeyned that yf anie citizen or strainger shall at anye time hereafter goe about to utter and put to sale within this cytie anie evell maid latts and not lawfull according to thassise they to forfaite the said latts.

At thassemble of the righte honorable William Allyn, Lord Mayoure, his worshipfull bretheren Aldermen and Counsell, in the Counsell Chamber upon Ouse brig the 12th day of December 1572, at the humble petycion of the good men of tharte or occupacion of joynars and carpentars of this cytie, the artycles ensewinge was by consent of the said worshipfull added to ther ordynarie, to be at all tymes hearafter observed for ever, viz.

Forinars' stuff. First yt ys ordeyned that no franchised man nor unfranchised man shall take into his howse anie forinar's stuff under couloure of deceipte, nor to aide the said forynar or to be factor to buye anie stuff for anie other man but for their owne uses, nor to buye and sell againe anie of the saide forinar's stuff, but that the said forinar or strainger may bringe ther stuff unto Thursday Markett to thentent that dewe searche therof may be ther maid at all times as other occupacions doe, upon paine of forfaytinge of 20s, thone half to the chamber and thother half to thoccupacion.

Number of apprentycs. Item, that no man within this cytie beyng joynar or carpentar shall have or take anie moo apprentyces than (f. 228v) one, untill suche time as that one shall have served his apprentyshippe thre yeares at the least, and after thois thre yeares to take an other apprentice and no moo, so that he have no moo apprentices at one time but twoe, in maner and forme aforesaid, upon paine of 20s, thone moytie to the chamber and thother moytie to the occupacion.

Departure before the worke bee fynished. Item, that no carpentar or joynar within this citie that taketh anie mane's worke by great or taske and will not fynishe the same, but goeth to others to worke, wherby the partie ys greved and doth compleyne to the serchers, and the serchours doe will them to goe to yt as they have done heretofore, that they that doe offend therin shall forfayte and pay suche fyne as ys apoynted by the lawes and statuts of this realme.

(f. 229) ORDINANCES OF THE PLASTERERS, TILERS AND BRICKLAYERS.[82]

The ancient ordynances of the mistery or occupacion of plaisterars, tylars and bricklayers of the Citie of York, diligently perused and examyned by the right worshipfull William Allyn, Mayour, the Aldermen and Privay Counsell of the said citie at their assemble in the Counsell Chambre apon Ousebrig, the 19th day of Decembre in the fyftenth yere of the reigne of our most gracyous sovereigne lady Queene Elizabeth [1572], and by the said Mayour, Aldermen and Counsell with the full consent of William Maxwell and John Lawrence, searchers and others the goodmen maisters of the said craft beyng alsoo present, were than and there dewely reformed, augmented, ordeyned and stablyshed to be frome thensforth firmely observed and kepte forever to the worship of the said citie, comon profite of the queene's people and honestie of the said occupacion as foloweth: —

First, it is ordeyned that what parsone soever he be of the said occupacion of plaisterars, tylars and bricklayers that is warned by the searchars to come to their assembles and cometh not at the howre appoyneted withoute a reasonable cause shall paye 12d, thone half to the common chambre of this citie, and thother half to the said occupacion.

Item, that no maister of the said occupacion shall put any apprentice or servant whatsoever, he for to work in plaistryng, theakyng or bricklayeng owte of this maister's company, unles that he be first sene by the searchars and knowne by theym to be a good work-

---

[82] Also entered in House Book 25, ff. 30-30v and printed in *York Civic Records*, Vol. VII, pp. 57-9. See also ordinances of 1475, ff. 142-142v above.

man, apon payne of 3s 4d, to the use of the chambre and occupacion aforesaid equally to be devyded.

Item, that every maister of the said occupacion havyng or that herafter shall have any apprentice, shall bryng his indentures of apprentiship before the searchars of the same craft for the tyme beyng within 14 dayes next after the makyng of theym, to thyntent the same may (f. 229v) be enrolled in the citie registre and to pay for enrollyng of every suche indenture 12d, that is to say 8d to the Common Clark and 4d to the chambre, apon payne of forfaityng of 3s 4d to be paied in forme aforesaid.

Item, that what man soever he be of the said occupacion that withdrawith any maner of good oute of any good man or woman's place or places within the said citie, suburbes and precyncts of the same, unto the valewe of 4d and that proved dewly, shall be reiecte and put oute of the said occupacion and never after that to work within the said cite.

Item, that foure searchars shalbe yerely frome he[n]sforth chosen indeferently, that is to say, good and honest men and good workmen of the said occupacion, in the feast day of Saynt James the Apostle, for to searche over and trewly to present to the Mayour of the citie for the tyme beyng, all suche defalts and forfaits as they shall fynde in the said occupacion, and that every one of the said serchers shalbe lovyng and honest to thother as becometh theym to do, upon payne of 6s 8d to the use of the chambre and the occupacion aforesaid equally to be devyded. Provyded allwayes that they shall not have any moo voyces at eleccions than they had whan theyr was but twoo searchers.

Item, that noo maister of the said occupacion shall take any apprentice for lesse terme then 7 yeres apon payne of 40s, thone half to the common chambre of the said citie and the other half to the occupacion aforesaid.

Item, if any work of the crafts aforesaid fortone to be searched by the searchers of the same craft and it be founde by theyme faltie and not hable wrought, that the offendar in the same work shall lease and pay at every tyme 3s 4d to the use of the chambre and occupacion aforesaid equally to be devided.

(f. 230) Item, that the artifecers of the said craft shall goo with their pageants throughe the citie as other occupacions and artificers doeth.

Item, that whatsoever he be of the said occupacion that doeth myseuse his searcher unreverently or any other of his brethene, either in worde or dede, and that proved, shall forfait every tyme 3s 4d to the use of the chambre and the occupacion aforesaid equally to be devided.

Item, whatsoever he be of the said occupacion that shall use hym self disordrely in talk at the common place or at any other of their assembles, after that he be warned by the searchers to hold his peace and doeth not, shall forfaite and pay 3s 4d, thone half to the chamber and thother half to the occupacion.

Item, that no man within this citie beyng plaisterer, tylar, or bricklayar shall have or take any moo apprentics than one untill suche tyme as that one shall have served his apprentyshipp foure yeres at the least, and after thois foure yeres be ended to take one other apprentice, soo that he have no mo apprentyces at one tyme but twoo in maner and forme aforesaid, apon payne of 40s, thone half to the common chambre and thother half to thoccupacion.

Item, that whatsoever he be that is a forreynar or a straynger that shall work within the said Citie of York or withoute in the suburbes, or within any other liberties of the said citie, or any other man within the citie that doeth set hym on work, unles he will compounde with the Lord Mayour and the searchers of the said occupacion for the tyme beyng or oft as the searchers shall take theym, shall both the maister and the said straynger forfaite and paye either of theym 6s (f. 230v) 8d in forme aforesaid.

Item, that whatsoever he be that shall buye any plaister to burne and sell ageyne and is noo tylor, shall pay yerely to the pageant maisters of the said occupacion 4d, apon payne of 12d to be payed in forme aforesaid.

Item, that whatsoever he be that maketh any tyle or brick to serve the citie withall shall paye yerely to the pageant maisters aforesaid every one of theym 4d, apon payne of 12d to be payed in forme aforesaid.

Item, what brother soever he be of the said occupacion that shall absent hym self away frome the searchers hows on thois 2 metyng dayes that they shall yerely frome hensforth make their dynnars apon, and have warnyng to be there, excepte he have a reasonable excuse shall paye for his dynnar apon payne of 12d, to be payed in forme aforesaid.

Item, whatsoever he be that doth not serve forth his tearme of his indentures with his maister, or with some other brother of the said occupacion within this citie, shall not be brothered amongest the occupacion, upon payne of 40s to be payed in forme aforesaid.

Item, that noo farreynar that hath not bene apprentice within this citie, shall be free or brothered with the said occupacion under the somme of 3s 4d, accordyng to the statute therof made, to be payed in forme aforesaid.

Item, that every lymeburnar beyng a forreynar (f. 231) shall paye 4d for his pageant money, apon payne of 12d to be payed in forme aforesaid.

Item, that every tylar, plaisterer and bricklayer within this citie shall paye their pageant money yerely before Saynt James daye whan the playe is played, whansoever they shalbe demanded by the pageant maisters, apon payne of 12d to be payed in forme aforesaid.

Item, that twoo maisters of the said occupacion shalbe yerely chosen equally to governe both pageants of the said occupacion aforesaid.

Item, that if any maister of the said occupacion shall at any tyme herafter discover or disclose any their counsell or secretts that shalbe talked emongs theym at any of their assembles or metyngs for the wele and profite of the same occupacion and not hurtfull to the common welth and it dewely proved, shall forfaite 12d to be payed in forme aforesaid.

Item, if the searchers of the said occupacion for the tyme beyng or any of theym do not make dewe presentment of the articles conteyned in this ordynall of any of theym, and knowyng any persone or persones to offende therin, or doo concele, withdrawe or kepe bake any money that ought to come to the common chambre by reasone of any offence or offences to be commytted contrary to the same articles, that than the said searchers and everey of theym so offendyng apon dewe prof made shall forfaite and pay 6s 8d to the common chambre of this citie.

Item, that whatsoever he be that shall burne any plaister and put lyme emongs the same, and do sell the same within this citie or suburbes therof, shall forfaite every tyme that he offendith herin 6s 8d to the use of the (f. 231v) chambre and occupacion aforesaid equally to be devyded.

(f. 232) On 24 October 24 Elizabeth [1582], William Plomer of York, tailor, and Katherine, his wife, came before Robert Brooke,

Mayor and Keeper of the Rolls in the county of the same city, and Leonard Belt, Clerk of the Peace, and sought the enrolment of the following deed. The said Katherine, on examination by the Mayor, acknowledged that it had been made by her without compulsion from her husband. It was therefore agreed by the Mayor that the deed should be enrolled in the common register in the Council Chamber on Ouse Bridge: —

(ff. 232-3) QUITCLAIM.

William Plomer of York, tailor, and Katherine, his wife,
    to John Jackson of York, maltster, and Margaret, his wife, and the heirs and assigns of the said John,
two cottages and two gardens in Middle Water Lane, now in the several occupations of Elizabeth Gibson, widow, and William Watson, fishmonger, situated between the tenement of the Mayor and Commonalty on the east and the tenement lately of John Hargill on the west, abutting on Middle Water Laine in front and the land of the Mayor and Commonalty behind, and containing in length 13¾ yards and in width 11 yards.

Sealed by William Plomer and Katherine, his wife, and by Robert Brooke, Mayor, with the official mayoral seal at William Plomer's request.

Given at York, 24 October 24 Elizabeth, 1582.   [Latin]

On 3 August 24 Elizabeth [1582], William Plomer came before Robert Brooke, Mayor and Keeper of the Rolls, and Leonard Belt, Clerk of the Peace, and sought the enrolment of a deed of sale according to the act of parliament for the enrolment of such deeds.
                                                       [Latin]

(ff. 233v-235) BARGAIN AND SALE.

William Plomer of York, tailor,
    to John Jackson of York, maltster, and Margaret, his wife,
two cottages and two little garths in the Middle Water Lane [as above]; and one cottage and a little garth in the Farr Water Lane, formerly in the occupation of Robert Sigeswicke, and now of Richard Westmerland, shipwright, containing in breadth 5¾ yards and in length from Far Watter Laine on the south to the land of the Mayor and Commonalty on the north 10¾ yards.

Consideration. £20.

William Plomer was to deliver all deeds relating to the premises to John Jackson before the next feast of St. Bartholomew the Apostle.

The property was to be held free of all previous grants or charges, excepting the rents and services due to the chief lord of the fee, a lease made to Richard Stephenson, maltster, of the two cottages and other premises in Middle Water Lane, of which fourteen years were yet unexpired from the feast of the Annunciation of Our Lady next, and the life estate of Margaret Walton, widow, in the said cottage in the Farre Water Lane.

William Plomer convenanted to make further assurances of title if requested within the next seven years, against the claims of himself and Katherine, his wife, of Nicholas Haxup of York, baker, and of the Mayor and Commonalty.

Given, 2 August 24 Elizabeth [1582]. [English]
Subscribed. Enrolled by me Leonard Belt, 1582.

(ff. 235v-236) FEOFFMENT.[83]

William Tewer of York, cook, and Alice, his wife,
to John Fell of York, cook,
a messuage or tenement and a garden in Overousegate, in the parish of All Saints', Pavement, now or lately in the occupation of Henry Palfreyman[84] or his assigns, and situated between the tenement in the occupation of John Metcalf, junior, on the west and the tenement in the occupation of Henry Rychardson[85] on the east, and extending in length from Overowsegate on the north as far as Copergate on the south.

Consideration. £15.
Given, 25 October 24 Elizabeth [1582]. [Latin]

On 23 January 25 Elizabeth [1583], Joan Turner of York, widow, came before Robert Brooke, Mayor and Keeper of the Rolls, and Leonard Belt, Clerk of the Peace, and sought the enrolment of the following deed, which she acknowledged to have been made by her.

(ff. 236v-237) FEOFFMENT.

Joan Turner of York, widow of the late Edward Turner of

---

[83] See also ff. 238v-240v.
[84] Henry Palfrayman, *cowper*, on f. 238.
[85] Henry Rychardson, *cordiner*, on f. 238.

York, gentleman, and formerly the wife of Thomas Fale of York, gentleman deceased,

to Robert Beckwith of York, goldsmith, and William Allin, draper, and their heirs, to the use of the said Joan Turner for life, without impeachment of waste, remainder to the use of Elizabeth Dicconson, one of the daughters of Thomas Dicconson of Kirkby Hall in the parish of Little Usburne, yeoman, kinsman of the said Joan Turner, and the heirs of the body of the said Elizabeth, remainder to the use of Edmund Fale of York, scrivener, and Anne Dicconson, the other daughter of Thomas Dicconson, and the heirs of the bodies of Edmund and Anne begotten, remainder to the right heirs of the body of Anne, remainder to the use of the aforesaid Thomas Dicconson, his heirs and assigns.

messuages, lands, tenements, meadows, pastures, woods, under-woods, rents, reversions, services and hereditaments in Tockwith in the County of the City of York, lately in the tenure of William Thaite or his assigns, and lately belonging to the Priory of Helaughe, now suppressed, and now in the tenure or occupation of Robert Huntar or his assigns.

Reciting that by a deed dated 16 December 37 Henry VIII [1545], John Broxoline of London and John Bellowe of Great Grimsbye in the County of Lincoln, esquires, gave and granted the said premises to Thomas Fale and Joan, his wife, and the heirs and assigns of Thomas. Thomas Fale had devised them in his will dated 1 March 13 Elizabeth [1571] to the said Joan, his wife, her heirs and assigns.

Appointment of Adam Simpson, innholder, and William Walker, scrivener, as attorneys to deliver seisin.

Given, 5 November 24 Elizabeth [1582].   [Latin]

(f. 237v) [Blank].

(f. 238) *Enrollement of Apprentics.*

Miles Nortton, sone of Robert Norton of Newton Ouse in the County of York, husbandman, by indenture bearyng date the 25 day of November in the tenth yere of the reigne of our soveraigne lady Queene Elizabeth [1567], did putt hym self apprentice with Stephen Morland of the Citye of York, tylar, frome the day of Saynt Katheryn the Virgyn next comyng after the date of the said indenture for terme of eight yeres fully to be complete, as by the said indenture more playnly appereth.

Raulf Hesyllwall, sone of Richard Hesilwall late of Westchester decessed, by indenture dated the 20th day of February in the thirtenth yere of the reigne of our soveraigne lady Queene Elizabeth [1571], did put hym self apprentice to—— [not completed].

On 24 October 24 Elizabeth [1582], William Tewer of York, cook, and Alice, his wife, came before Robert Brooke, Mayor and Keeper of the Rolls, and Leonard Belt, Clerk of the Peace, and sought the enrolment of a deed of sale according to the act of parliament.

(ff. 238v-240v) BARGAIN AND SALE.
William Tewer of York, cook, and Alice, his wife,
to John Fell of York, cook,
a messuage or tenement and a garth in Overousgate [as above, f. 235v].
Consideration. £15.
William Tewer and Alice, his wife, covenanted that they and the heirs of Alice would convey to the said John Fell, a legal estate in fee simple of the messuage and garth and acquit him of all charges and previous grants of the property, except the rents and services due to the chief lord of the fee and the lease to Henry Palfrayman of which eighteen years were still unexpired.
They would make further assurances of title within the next three years if required.
Given at York, 24 October 24 Elizabeth [1582].   [English]

On 5 February 25 Elizabeth [1583], Edmund Smith of York, carpenter, and Helen, his wife, came before Christopher Maltby, Mayor and Keeper of the Rolls, and Leonard Belt, Clerk of the Peace, and sought the enrolment of the following deed of quitclaim. The said Helen, when examined alone by the Mayor, acknowledged that she had made the deed of her own free will without fear of her husband.

(ff. 240v-241) QUITCLAIM.
Edmund Smyth of York, carpenter, and Helen, his wife,
to Matthew Daile of York, labourer,
a messuage or tenement, and all houses and buildings pertaining to it in Uglefurthe, formerly belonging to St. William's College of the Metropolitan Church of York now dissolved, and lately in

the tenure of Geoffrey Smyth, father of the said Edmund Smyth, and lately in the tenure or occupation of John Jaikes.

Sealed with the official mayoral seal by Christopher Maltbie, Mayor.

Given, 5 February 25 Elizabeth [1583].   [Latin]

On 22 June 25 Elizabeth [1583], Ralph Emondson of York, goldsmith, and Joan, his wife, came before Christopher Maltby, Mayor and Keeper of the Rolls, and Leonard Belt, Clerk of the Peace, and sought the enrolment of the following deed. When examined alone, the said Joan acknowledged that she had made the deed of her own free will and not in fear of her husband.

(ff. 241-242) FEOFFMENT.

Ralph Emondson of York, goldsmith, and Joan, his wife,
to John Fell of York, cook,

a burgage, messuage or tenement, formerly called the *Paycocke*, now called the *Maiden Head*, and two gardens, one called the *Garding* and the other the *Lowe Garth*, situated in Fossgate in *Crux parishe* and now in the occupation of the said Ralph Emondson and Joan. The messuage and the garden called the *Garding* lay in width between the land formerly of Nicholas Clarke, baker, deceased, now in the occupation of Henry Smythe, carrier, on the south, and the land of William Beckwith, Alderman, now in the occupation of William Gill, tailor, on the north, and extended in length from Fosgate in front on the west, as far as a *lane* being the land of the governor and society of merchants, now in the occupation of John Cripling, innholder, behind on the east. The other garden called the *Lowe Garth* lay in width between the land of the late Nicholas Clarke, now in the occupation of Henry Smyth, on the west, and the land of the governor and society of merchants, now in the occupation of John Cripling on the east, and extended in length from the said messuage and the *Garding* as far as the River Foss.

Made in accordance with certain agreements specified in an indenture made between the parties on 30 January 25 Elizabeth [1583].

Sealed, at the request of Ralph Emondson and Joan, his wife, with the official mayoral seal, by Christopher Maltby, Mayor.

Given at York, the last day of January 25 Elizabeth [1583].
                                                           [Latin]

On 22 June 25 Elizabeth [1583], the said Ralph Emondson and Joan his wife also sought the enrolment of the following deed of sale according to the act of parliament.

(ff. 242-243v) BARGAIN AND SALE.
Ralph Emondson, and Joan, his wife,
to John Fell,
the burgage, messuage, or tenement and two gardens in Fossgate [as above].
Consideration. £80.
Ralph Emondson and Joan, his wife, covenanted to deliver the deeds of the premises before Whit Sunday, if requested, to convey to John Fell a legal estate in fee simple before Easter next, to acquit him of all charges and claims, except the rents and services due to the chief lord of the fee, and to make further assurances if required within six years.
Given, 30 January 25 Elizabeth [1583].   [English]

(f. 244) On 22 June 25 Elizabeth [1583], the said Ralph Emondson and Joan, his wife, also sought the enrolment of the following deed.

(ff. 244-244v) QUITCLAIM.
Ralph Emondson and Joan, his wife,
to John Fell,
the burgage, messuage or tenement and two gardens in Fossgate [as above].
Sealed with the official mayoral seal by Christopher Maltby, Mayor.
Given at York, 20 April 25 Elizabeth [1583].
Subscribed. Enrolled by me, Leonard Belt, Clerk of the Peace.
[Latin]

(f. 245) On 15 August 26 Elizabeth [1584], John Massie of Westminster and Maud (*Matilda*) his wife, came before Thomas Appleyard, Mayor and Keeper of the Rolls, and Leonard Belt, Clerk of the Peace, and produced —— [incomplete].   [Latin]

(ff. 245-246v) BARGAIN AND SALE.
John Massye of Westmynster, in the County of Myddlesex, cook,

and Maud, his wife, one of the daughters of Geoffrey Fothergill, late of York, locksmith, deceased,

to Richard Pyrrye of York, innholder, and Jane, his wife,

two messuages or houses and a garth in Blackestreete [sic] in York, now in the tenure or occupation of Michael Wreakes.

Consideration. £10.

John Massye and Maud, his wife, covenanted to deliver the deeds of the premises before the feast of St. Michael the Archangel next, to acquit Richard Pirrye and Jane, his wife, of all charges and claims, except the rents and services due to the chief lord of the fee and the life estate of Janet Fothergill, widow of the late Geoffrey Fothergill, as devised in his last will and testament, and to make further assurances of title.

Given, 13 August 26 Elizabeth [1584].   [English]

(ff. 246v-247) QUITCLAIM.

John Massye and Maud (*Matilda*), his wife,

to Richard Pyrrye and Jane, his wife,

two messuages or houses and a garden in Blaikstreete [as above].

Sealed with the official mayoral seal by Thomas Appleyard, Mayor.

Given at York, 15 August 26 Elizabeth [1584].   [Latin]

(ff. 247-247v) BOND.

John Massye

to Richard Pyrrye

in £20, for performance of covenants made in an indenture of the same date.

Given, 13 August 26 Elizabeth [1584].   [Latin and English]

(f. 248) On 15 December 39 Elizabeth [1596], Alice Sandwith, widow of Anthony Sandwith, showed to the jurors of the Inquisition Post Mortem on the estate of the said Anthony Sandwith, held before James Birkbie, Mayor, in the *Guihalda*, the following deed, sealed with the common seal in green wax.

Marginal note: For rent to the Mayor and citizens, 26s 8d for 4 tenements in Thursdaye Market.

(ff. 248-248v) FEOFFMENT.

Nicholas le Fleminge, Mayor, and the Commonalty of York,

to John de Esebye, citizen,
a piece of waste land in Thursdaye Market, containing in length
63 feet between the land held by Master John de Woodhouse of
the Mayor and Commonalty on the one side and the market on the
other, and 3½ parcels of land in width.

Rent. 26s 8d p.a.

All John de Eseby's tenements in York were to be subject to
distraint to ensure payment of the rent.

He was to build on the land as seemed best to him.

Given at York, the Sunday after the feast of the Nativity of St.
John the Baptist, [1 July] 6 Edward son of Edward, 1313.

Subscribed. Examined by me Thomas Rogerson, Common
Clerk.[86] [Latin]

(f. 249) *A Remembrance of the ground at the west end of Alhallos
Churche Yerde in Northestrete belonginge to the Maior and
Commons of this Cittie.*

Which conteynith in breyd at the east end 15 yereds and a half
and at the west end 14 yereds and a half, and in length frome the
east to the west of the north syde 22 yereds and a half quarter, and
of the sowith syde 22 yereds and a quarter. Which said ground was
vewed, bounded and measurid in the presents of Mr. William
Allen, Lord Maior, Mr. Gregory Paycoke, Mr. John Dyneley, Mr.
Robert Maskewe and Mr. Hugh Graves, Aldermen, Mr. Lutton,
Mr. Fawks, James Wilkynson, Robert Shereshawe, Thomas Hum-
fray, William Drynkell, Thomas Thomson, officers, John Clercke,
William Halley, John Nicholson and others, the 30 day of December
anno domini 1572.

The same ground was also viewid and seyne by Mr. John Dyneley, Lord Maior, Mr. Maskewe, Alderman, dyvers of the Chamberleyns, the brigmaisters and other my Lorde Maiors officers, the
second day of Aprill anno domini 1577 and 19 Queen Elizabeth.

(ff. 249v-250v) [Blank.]

[86] Thomas Rogerson was Common Clerk, 1590-1603.

INDEX OF
PERSONS AND PLACES

Note: C=Cumberland; D=Durham; E.R.=East Riding; L=Lancashire; N=Northumberland; No=Nottinghamshire; N.R.=North Riding; W.R.=West Riding; Y=Yorkshire.

304 YORK MEMORANDUM BOOK

Frost, Isabel, 72-3; Thos., 34; Wm. (son of Thos.), 34; (jun.), 34; (Mayor, 1396, 1397, 1400-4, 1406), 30, 32, 33, 34, 35, 36, 39, 49, 72-3, 148
Frothyngham, Alice, 87; Pet., 87
Fryston, Pet., 163; Thos., 223; Wm. de, 87
Fulford [ER], 21. Fulford cross, 132, 231
Fulthorp — see Soureby; Margaret, 202; Thos., 202-4, 206; Wm. de, 31
Furbur, Ralph le, 84
Furness [L], abbot and convent of, 128-9
Fyn—see Finn
Fysher—see Fisher
Fyssh—see Fish

Galbeke, Wm., 119
Galby, Agnes, 128; Wm., 128
Gale, Gaile, Gayll, Geo., 245, 259, 266
Galtres, forest of, 132, 136, 175, 230
Gare, Robt. del, 2, 13, 74; Thos., 92, 158, 185; (sen., Mayor 1420), 27, 28, 32, 40, 41, 65, 70, 83-4, 88, 89; (jun., Mayor 1434), 83, 93, 108, 114
Garforth, West [WR], 234-5
Garforth Moorhouse [WR], 234-5
Garnar, Joh., 169
Garnett, Ric., 224, 228, 250; Robt., 5
Garston, Joh., 55, 83, 84, 101
Garth, Joh., 176; Thos. del, 19
Garton, Robt., 169; Thos. de, 18; Wm., 77
Gascoigne, Anne, 235; Hy., 198-200; Joan, 84; Joh. (Sheriff 1421), 47, 76, 102, 158; (merchant), 106-7; (gent), 234-5; (Esq.), 263; Thos., 235; Wm., 80, 84, 226, 228, 234-5
Gate Burton [Lincs], 5
Gateforth, Joh. de, 29
Gateshead, Wm., 47, 53, 70, 75

Gaunt, Gaunte, John of— see Lancaster, Duke of; Robt., 160-1; Wm., 205
Gaunter, Alexander le, 85
Gawke, Juliana, 159; Wm., 159
Gayregrafe, Agnes, 68
Gayte, Thos., 169; Walter, 174; Wm., 129
Geggs, Roger, 266
Gelderd, Robt., 249
Gerrard—see Jerrard
Gibson, Eliz., 288; Jas., 246
Gilbanke, Thos., 251
Gilbert, Joh. son of, 8
Gill, Hugh, 84; Pet., 278; Walter, 73; Wm., 292
Gilliot, Chris., 228; Joh., 169, 175-6, 179, 207, 216, 218, 222, 243, 247; Wm., 257-8
Gillour, Paul, 239
Gillygate, 65
Gilmyn, Robt., 270
Gilsland [C], lord of, 101
Girlington, Nich., 104, 130; Wm., 64, 92, 109, 125, 130, 139. See also Grillyngton
Giry, Wm., 4, 7
Gisburgh, Joh., 52, 78
Gisburn, Joh. de, 1, 2, 3, 4, 7, 9, 10, 11, 13, 15, 31, 72, 189n
Glasen, Joh., 190, 243
Gloucester, Joh. de, 85
Gloucester, Dukes of, Humphrey, 88-9, 118; Ric.—see Richard III; Thos. of Woodstock, 52-3, 165
Glover, Wm., 66
Goddard, Joh., 35; Ric., 234
Gokeman, Thos., 247, 251
Goldbeter, Hy. le, 38, 87
Goldesburgh, Ric. de, 15, 16; Ric., 237
Goldsborough [WR], rector of, 134
Goldsmyth, Wm., 48
Goldthorp, Golthrop, Ric., 259, 267
Goldthwayt, Thos., 244
Gollen, Joh., 120
Goodmanham, Goodmadame [ER], 249, 250, 265
Goodramgate, Gotheromgate, 200, 216, 253

Gook, Joh., 202
Gower, Roger, 80; Thos., 27, 80, 136; Walter, 79
Gowle [?], Wm., 134
Grafton, Joh. de, 37-8
Grape Lane, 81
Granger, Robt., 278
Graves, Hugh, 273, 295; Ric., 278
Gray, Gra, Graa, Grey, Hy., 174; Joh., 95, 99-100, 110, 170; Lawrence, 12; Margaret, 99-100; Ric., 95; Thos., 32, 148; (Mayor 1375, 1398), 6, 7, 8, 9, 10, 11, 12, 13, 15, 21, 25, 28, 31, 32, 33-4, 81; (Mayor 1497), 209, 210, 212, 216, 222, 248, 250; (of Barton in Ryedale), 127; Wm. (Bailiff 1346), 3, 7, 9, 10, 11, 12, 23, 33-4, 81, 87, 111; (Bp. of London, former Dean of York), 85. See also Grey
Grayngham, Robt. de, 86. See also Grengham
Grayson, Joh., 192
Graystoke, Graystok, Lord ——, 256; Joan, 106; Ralph, 106
Greatham [D], 203
Green, Grene, Greyn, Brian, 257-8; Joh., 126; Kath., 126; Ric., 246
Green Dykes, 132, 231
Greenbank, Miles, 216, 218, 222, 248; Robt., 214, 215
Greenfield, Wm. de, Archbp. of York, 110, 112
Greggs, Wm., 278
Grengham, Wm. de, 147. See also Grayngham
Gretham, Thos., 31
Grethed, Thos., 278
Grey, Reginald de, of Ruthin, 166. See also Gray
Greyn—see Green
Grillyngton, Wm., 158. See also Girlington
Grime, Gryme, Wm., 112
Grimsby, Gremmesby, Grymesby, Joh. de, 155; Wm. de, 8
Grimston, Wm., 52
Griselay, Joh., 113
Grondman, Jaspar, 122

SUBJECT INDEX